ARTISTS

AND

WRITERS

BY SANFORD SCHWARTZ

The Art Presence

ARTISTS

AND

WRITERS

SANFORD

SCHWARTZ

YARROW PRESS

NEW YORK

1990

Text copyright © 1990 by Sanford Schwartz

Acknowledgment with thanks is made to the following publications where the contents originally appeared: *The Atlantic* (chaps. 26, 29, 30, 31); *The New Republic* (chap. 14); *Dissent* (chap. 2); *The New Yorker* (chaps. 3, 8, 10, 11, 12, 13, 15, 16, 17, 21, 27); *Artforum* (chaps. 23, 25); *The New Criterion* (chaps. 5, 18); *The American Scholar* (chap. 22); and *The New York Review of Books* (chaps. 4, 6, 7, 9). Reprinted with permission from *The New York Review of Books*. Copyright © 1983 Nyrev, Inc.

Library of Congress Cataloging-in-Publication Data
Schwartz, Sanford.
Artists and writers/by Sanford Schwartz
p.   cm.
ISBN 1-878274-02-3: $24.95.—ISBN 1-878274-01-5 (pbk.): $14.95.
1. Arts, Modern—20 century.   2. Artists—Psychology. I. Title.
NX456.S4 1990
700—dc20   89-29036
CIP

Printed in the United States of America

Cover painting: Philip Guston. *Untitled (Two Hooded Figures in a Car)* (detail). 1971. Oil on board, 12 × 14″. Private collection

Design and composition by The Sarabande Press

Yarrow Press
225 Lafayette Street
New York, New York 10012

To Carole Obedin

CONTENTS

CONTENTS

CONTENTS

CONTENTS

PREFACE

THE BACKDROP FOR MANY of the following chapters was a vibrant and budding moment in the history of painting. In the early eighties artists began showing in New York who asked to be judged by a new set of terms. For the first time in a long while there were also strong new painters from Europe, and the even more unexpected part was that the Americans and Europeans complemented each other in their ambitions and tastes. Both had a feeling for images for their own sake and for creating pictures with weavelike, inner-and-outer space and alluring, palpable textures. Only a proportion of the articles and reviews here are actually about these painters (and I have hardly touched on all of them). There are as many other pieces on various Old Masters, twentieth-century classics, and artists who have been on the scene since the sixties. But for the past seven or eight years I have found myself thinking about all sorts of exhibitions—Fragonard, de Chirico, Watteau, and others—in relation to the tensions and goals of recent painting.

Is there a connection between the chapters on artists and those on writers? Is there even a connection between these "writers"? The list includes a dance critic and an art critic; a memoirist; a German Romantic and a contemporary American who write in so many forms that they're unclassifiable; a pianist; and an admiral. I think there is a certain overall unity. If the articles on art present one critic's evolving sense of beauty, the other articles are about the ways that different individuals create their own aesthetic. Horatio Nelson fits in, I was told, because he's presented as someone who made himself into a work of art.

The pieces on Eric Fischl, Fragonard, Philip Taaffe, and Julian Schnabel have not been published before. The others appeared in *Dissent, The American Scholar, The Atlantic, The New Yorker, The New*

Criterion, *Artforum*, *The New York Review of Books*, and a catalogue for a Marlborough Gallery exhibition. I'd like to thank the editors and checkers of these publications, especially Susan Moritz, for improving the articles. I've put the year each was published at the end, but they are presented in the order in which they were written. There are minor changes throughout, and a few of the pieces have new titles. I'm grateful to Ben Raeburn and to Anne Yarowsky and Michael Miller. It is a great pleasure to thank Pauline Kael for her encouragement.

ARTISTS
AND
WRITERS

ALEX KATZ'S DRAWINGS

MUCH RECENT NEW ART feels too knowledgeable and too innocent at the same time. Artists in their late twenties and thirties appear capable of immediately mastering many techniques, and producing work with an authoritative presence, yet the feelings they convey are often private and tentative, and frequently about childhood. Whether in work that is good, promising, or thin, there's a desire now to make art that says something about the way things looked and felt as a child, about the relationships between children and parents, between brothers and sisters. I think this is one reason why certain out-of-fashion artists have regained currency—Chagall for one, who showed how domestic life and the smallest, most personal memories could be the subject of serious art. This is one of the chief things that separates the emerging generation from the generation before it. Jasper Johns, Alex Katz, Dan Flavin, Roy Lichtenstein, and others who came to maturity in the nineteen-fifties and early sixties didn't have time for childhood, at least not in their art. Picking up the mantle of their fathers, the Abstract Expressionists, they felt the need to succeed immediately. They arrived with a great pressure on them, and it shows in the pressurized art they made—the ultra-refined, emotionally camouflaged, deliberately taunting styles of the many schools of one. If the attitudes and themes of these artists can be said to spring from any period in life it might be late adolescence or youth, a time of mingled independence, cocksureness and uncertainty. The most powerful members of this generation seem to have started off as so many Davids: they were a little nervous, but they were ready to go after Goliath, and proud that they were armed only with slingshots.

This modesty and not-always-certain but dauntless strength is one of the many veins in Alex Katz's paintings. It is seen even more clearly in his drawings. This Marlborough Gallery exhibition, the first to give the full range of them, spans nearly forty years. It goes from serious, full-dress, carefully realized studies done in the mid-forties, when he was a teenager, to sketches for paintings done this past year. Among the earliest are a very finished piece of a cast head, signed "Alec Katz," and another finished one of his younger brother Bernard, sitting in a chair, wearing a baseball cap, which is signed "Alexander Katz." "I didn't know who I was," he says as he looks at the two, delivering himself of a typically multilayered Katz remark. He is telling the truth, he's deprecating himself, and he is also leaving you with the impression that he liked the confusion — he knew somehow that it was good for him to be in the dark, as it has been good for him to take experimental risks, to look loony. He discarded natty British Alec and imperious Alexander almost immediately, sending the dapper and world-conquering sides of himself to the back of his mind, for the moment.

But the not knowing "who I was" stayed, and it gives this exhibition its frisky tone and mixed-nuts flavor. Among the loveliest and most surprising units is one of sketch-pad drawings, done in the middle to late forties, before and after Katz was in the Navy and while he was a student at Cooper Union. They may remind you of Reginald Marsh or Milton Avery — Marsh for the subject of anonymous, untroubled New Yorkers on the move, Avery for the unforced, almost unintended humor. But these sketch-pad drawings don't really suggest any artist. Except for the carefully noted clothes, which date the pictures, the sketches could have been done at any time. They're fragile, the line is often tentative, yet they are frequently more than on-the-spot records. When he draws slyly comic expressions, they feel novel: they are sweeter, kinder, more plastic than the expressions of people in cartoons, yet they aren't quite naturalistic. When he records profiles he can be classically exact, but he can also give these heads — one of a man in a fedora, for example — a starchy, clenched, faraway look, reminiscent of the faces of open-mouthed angels and soldiers in Italian Renaissance frescos.

Many of these drawings were made in cafeterias, luncheonettes, parks. Some of the best were done in subways. A few years before, Walker Evans had used this same turf, so to speak, for subject matter.

Sitting opposite his subjects, who were unaware of the camera, which was hidden in his coat and operated by a cable release held in his hand, he caught the way people's personalities, in subways, become limp and overcooked, how people can't help drifting off, even as they make an extra effort to hold on to their individuality. Katz's subway sketches are seemingly more photographic than Evans's photographs. Katz lops off heads, he cuts heads off at the nose, he shows the cubist jumble of the subway world. In one, he shows a young man amorphously pressed up against the forefront of the picture; a heavyset man and a woman wearing a hat and glasses are reading, in the background. There's a beautiful flow from one figure to another, back into space. The older man's profile is effortlessly right, naturalistic without fuss. But the young man is different—he is among the earliest Katz creations on record. He is someone we know and don't know.

This isn't the earliest Katz drawing of a handsome man whose handsomeness is a touch emphasized. In one of a number of very polished portraits he made in the Navy, and which is in this show, Katz gave a fellow sailor a movie-star glow. Yet we feel we could recognize that man on the street, whereas the face in the subway sketch is almost a type. His face (and overcoated body) are dreamy, a little feminine and soft, yet in a way that suggests something lean, sure, desirous, firm. The mood is of an adolescent who looks at himself in the mirror and savors what he sees; he hears the voices of the world murmur, "Yes, very fine, a beauty." Katz shows the floating-free moment of young self-love, the moment when everything feels perfect. He stops short, here and in all his work, of showing the next moment, when a young person may sense himself adrift. Yet that stage, when one's sense of oneself is suddenly drained away, seems to be part of the story Katz is telling, and it is frequently felt in his images. It is the melancholy undertone of his art.

His later drawings, mostly landscapes and figure studies, are more artful and experimental. There is a quietly audacious view of a stand of trees, seen from across a field, done in yellow ink, which radiates bright midday light. Other works suggest his affair with Pollock, whose drip paintings, Katz thought, were a way to see nature, specifically light coming through branches and leaves. But the big influence is Matisse, Katz's other main man of the moment, and his drawings of the time, many done in brush and black ink, are, taken together, a kind of Matisse idyll. Sometimes he approaches the French master analytically and gratefully, as in a wonderful 1950–51 series of trees, seen as arabesques of interconnecting thick borders, where he abbreviates and concentrates Matisse's ideas (particularly those, it seems, about floral patterning that Matisse brought back from his trip to Tahiti). In another drawing, *Camp Green*, of boys lying and sitting on the ground, the viewer feels as if Katz lived his daily existence so that he could make his own Matisses out of it.

Yet what Katz most wanted from Matisse wasn't his fluency or decorative line—it was his terseness. Sometime around 1954, when he was in his middle twenties, Katz began to develop his own flabless, unadorned style of drawing (and painting), and some of his most subtly original pieces are from that moment. These are drawings of people at the beach, of figures in fields walking toward us, of vast, nearly empty landscapes. Matisse is in these spare works, but barely. When he adapted Matisse's line to his purposes Katz removed the intellectual gracefulness of that line and gave it an element of Spartan honesty and a halting tenderness that aren't in his model. These pared-down drawings say, "This, only this, is what I see as I look out onto the landscape—no more." A big, uncategorizable personality gleams out of these delicate and compressed works. They issue from a hand that isn't comfortable making curves, that would rather make a firm straight mark, and yet, for some reason, wants to hold itself in check. Though the line is literally thin and sometimes stymied, the bearing of a whole body is registered in it.

Katz continues to make drawings somewhat like these. They are sketches for paintings, done to give him a set of possibilities to think about before going on. They're workaday objects, not intended to be admired aesthetically. His sketches for the paintings *Song, Laura Dean Dance Company* or *Rose Room*, for example, both of which show a number of people dancing or sitting, are virtually unconscious jottings, closer to the phrases about details for future stories that a novelist makes in his notebook. Yet these sketches grow on one.

There is no better place to see his intemperateness and impatience (which made him so responsive to Pollock and Matisse), or his workmanlike desire to set down the necessary facts of the scene before him. We may not be the proper audience to say if they measure up to Rembrandt's pen-and-ink sketches for paintings, but it is those hasty works, with their jabbing line and blotches, that Katz's sketches remind us of.

In the early seventies, Katz began making very finished graphite drawings. Large works with the completeness of paintings, they are most often of a single head or torso, seen in an expansive, sometimes ethereally soft light. They haven't been included in the present show because they're a different order of thing for him; they're sources of information about light and weight for use in paintings, and they are also what his public already thinks of as his "drawing." This exhibition doesn't put them in the shadow nor does it boost their importance, though it does move them to one side. There is an evenness of value to every aspect of Alex Katz's art. He does, of course, create masterworks, especially in his paintings and prints. But no one form—not his paintings, oil sketches, painted metal cutouts, cut-and-pasted paper collages, finished drawings, sketches, or prints—holds the essence of him. Each lets another part of him flower: his modesty, his bluntness, his awkward striving, his desire for suavity and seamlessness, his feeling for professional expertise.

The child of a mother who was a professional actress and a father who at one time had been part of an amateur acting group, Katz grew up feeling that performance—appearance—says everything, that the only meanings are in the surfaces of things. Perhaps if he had come to this belief through experience he would imbue the feeling with a cynic's sourness, or he'd find the world a comedy of gaseous platitudes. But his feel for the surfaces of life has a martial clearness and strength to it; he adheres to his faith in "show" and "style" with the same rectitude and firmness with which Blake insisted that transcendent beings came to him with poems and with images for prints and watercolors.

In surprising ways Katz is a very theoretical person, and his theories and notions about success and failure, particularly in painting, literature, and dance, which he shares freely with people, have quietly influenced many. For a wide variety of New York painters and writers about art, especially in the generation after his, Katz is a one-man testing ground for new ideas, and, with his historical interest in the styles of all periods, he has become, I think, as much of an influence as any other single painter or critic. One of his art's great themes is the beauty of youth, and he draws out young people (and all people open to new ways of seeing), partially because his ideas, for all the concision with which they're delivered, aren't neat, self-contained packages. His ideas are always a shade iconoclastic; they're delivered in a flat, no-contest way, yet they invite a response—as on the occasion, one night, when we were sitting around after dinner, flipping through the assortment of thick foreign and American fashion magazines our hostess had lying about. We were trading quips on the subject when she asked, "How much can you tell about a man from what he wears?" On the next beat Katz answered, in a voice and with a motion of his hand that said he was clearing the decks, "Everything."

Perhaps it is the theater in his blood that makes him go after the deliberately unexpected, that makes him, in his art, choose the empty expanse, the smiling small gesture, the pale tone, the sleek finish, or the minor chord when the sought-after effect is often the opposite. For European eyes his work may still appear to be about sociable encounters and the blemish-free faces of fashion models, but for Americans, or, at least, for those who have come to be familiar with him, his surface blandness is a taut skin stretched over feelings that are the complex opposite of bland. When he emphasizes the pretty—as in his subway sketch of the young man, or in some of his more finished graphite renderings of a tulip, a sofa, or a boy's lean chest—we know that he is really after the beautiful, but that he wants to get there indirectly. He wants to surprise us, to make us grasp for it.

Though we also sense that the pretty does represent the beautiful for him, and that to see the world through his eyes is to see everything in a transformed way. This is possibly why his paintings often have the haloed, becalmed quality of primitive and naive art. And possibly why his abrupt and seemingly plain drawings and sketches have such dignity and fullness. He is an ironical, indirect master. His passion-ateness is there but buried. He is a visionary of the shallow glossy surface of life, something that, before him, one might have thought it was impossible to be visionary about.

—1982

I WALKED WITH
INTELLECTUALS

WILLIAM BARRETT'S *The Truants: Adventures Among the Intellectuals* (Anchor/Doubleday) is a slippery and maddening book. It is an account of one man's intellectual coming of age, and it has the qualities of a backward glance at a busy, crisscrossed time. But it is also a subtle, unceasing—and, the reader may feel, not always conscious—attack on that time. Barrett recalls the days when, in the late nineteen-forties and early fifties, he worked for the formidable Philip Rahv and the somewhat more retiring William Phillips, the founders and editors of *Partisan Review*. Barrett had been a pal of Delmore Schwartz's before the war, when Schwartz, then in his early twenties, was achieving renown in New York literary circles for his stories and poetry. When Barrett returned from active duty overseas, he picked up his friendship with Schwartz, who had become a figure at *Partisan Review*. As Barrett tells it, Schwartz came to him one day, and, in a scene that might be an illustration of the title of Schwartz's best-known story, "In Dreams Begin Responsibilities," told him, without any prior word that this might happen, that he was now on the staff of the magazine. Barrett doesn't say much about this except that he was surprised, and that he accepted. He and Schwartz became associate editors, working under Rahv and Phillips, and for the next seven-odd years he was at or near the center of the quarterly that was left-wing in its politics, "modernist" in its literary values, and, by

7

general consent, the most influential intellectual magazine, certainly in those years, in the United States. He left in the beginning of 1952, at the age of thirty-nine, when differences with the editors, as friends and colleagues, made him feel it was time to move on.

A former professor of philosophy at New York University, William Barrett might, as a writer, be called a portraitist of ideas. In his best-known work, *Irrational Man*, a study of existentialism and its historical background, and in *Time of Need* and *The Illusion of Technique*, he presents ideas as they are embodied in biographical details and in works of literature and art as well as in formal studies of philosophy. *The Truants* moves back and forth in a fluid, unchronological way, weaving together recollections of moments in the life of the magazine with descriptions of the eminent European writers who came to New York after the war and of the Abstract Expressionist painters and their milieu. Embedded in the flow of recollections are studies of Rahv, Schwartz, Lionel Trilling, Mary McCarthy, Clement Greenberg, Hannah Arendt, James Burnham, and Sidney Hook as thinkers and writers. Barrett is a knowing judge of how the reputations of those he knew from his *Partisan Review* days have worn, and he has obviously enjoyed re-creating the sound of their voices, the way they moved, the lively cracks they made at each other's expense. Yet these people have a balsa-wood lightness. They seem defanged, too easily summarized. You wonder if they have become as musty as Barrett makes them, and you also wonder how much he wants to write about them. His tone is that of a TV talk-show host who looks over his guest's shoulder at his audience and winks, as if to say, "We'll just bother with this one a little longer."

The Truants leaves you with the grayed feeling that the immediate postwar era in New York was a time of fussing and bickering, mistakes and delusions, when everyone got it wrong somehow. What you take away, though, isn't a sense of loss or of a wasted period in Barrett's life; what you keep is a fishier feeling about why someone should smilingly dish his intellectual youth. Barrett sees the writers he came to maturity with as part of a grand design that encompasses American culture to this day. He believes they are somehow responsible for much of what he alludes to as the impoverishment and glibness of recent life.

Yet he never goes at them directly. When he points out the foibles, philosophic inconsistencies, and wrecked hopes of his influential friends, he does it in the spirit of a public-relations spokesman, someone who carefully presses his hands together and informs us that this is, unfortunately, an imperfect world and everything we do will mirror our flawed condition. But he presents himself as scarless and contented.

Barrett is aware that he has ambivalent feelings—especially about Philip Rahv, who struck him as a secretive, egocentric, truculent, but also somehow weak and vacillating man, full of angers and hatreds that followed him like a black cloud and kept Barrett at a distance. Barrett wants us to know that Rahv would have understood, respected, and wanted nothing less than Barrett's owning up to his ambivalence. Yet his ambivalence hasn't given him insights—it is simply the bind he is in. From the little he tells us of his own feelings at the time, the reader senses that Barrett, whether out of duty, respect, or fear, didn't say or do what he wanted when he was in the company of Rahv and the others. He presents himself as something of an invisible, frustrated, but obliging, gentlemanly outsider, and that is the vantage point he still has. You don't question the sincerity of the praise he offers Rahv and the others, but you don't feel that the praise goes deep, either. It's showy, flourishful. He has dedicated his memoir "For Delmore and Philip, restless shades," and his opening chapter, on Rahv, is entitled "Prologue: A Mass for the Dead." He tells "dear Philip" that *The Truants* is but a "poor wreath" placed on "your grave." The way he puts it, every time he lays a wreath he gets a go-ahead to dispense some more constructive criticism. But the inner check that makes him pay lip service also keeps him from being truly caustic, withering. If he were openly in conflict, he might seem more honest, and we might respect him more.

Attempting to justify his fault-finding tone, he says, "Our charity is needed more by the living, who are still struggling to cope with things, and who are easily upset by any disobliging remark. And when can one try to be candid about other people except when they are not listening?" But this waiting-for-later policy backfires on him. If someone gives the living "charity" instead of honest talk, and if someone waits for people to be gone before he can be "candid" about them, it's possible that he will always be thinking and feeling in a woozy, delayed, unspontaneous way. It's possible, too, that he will have a sense of anger inside him that will grow as time goes on and that will always come out muffled. That is the effect of *The Truants*, where you frequently don't know whose side Barrett is on, or whose interest he thinks he's serving.

There is the story of E. M. Forster's visit to New York. The English writer arrived with a person whose name Barrett has not thought worth looking up; this man is labeled Forster's "boyfriend, a London policeman." A meeting with Forster was arranged for Trilling, Forster's foremost critic in the United States and the author of an influential study of him. The meeting—Barrett got this story at the time from Rahv—took place at an "apartment-loft somewhere downtown in the East Village in the midst of a party of homosexuals," and Trilling, so the tale goes, was shocked and dismayed to see Forster in this company. The reader pulls back and is embarrassed, too, not only for Trilling and Forster but for Barrett, because there is something unseemly in his avid desire to recollect Trilling's embarrassment and in the way he mangles Forster in the process. "Trilling's beloved idol came on simply as an elderly queen camping all over the place," Barrett writes, unmindful of how he presents himself through his use of words. He goes on about how people at the time didn't have any knowledge of Forster's homosexuality and about how shocking, to him at least, were the reports of the novelist's behavior. He makes the requisite distinctions between the works Forster was then known for, which have no overt homosexual content, and the writings published later, where he tackled homosexual themes, and which are lesser works. But then, in the cold, tone-deaf language of a supermarket celebrity tabloid, he returns to the "great gulf" between Forster's well-known novels and "the spectacle of the aging queen turning on in public." Why was the moment re-created? To give us a taste of Philip Rahv's gossipiness? To show how people can humiliate one another? Barrett's unthinking enjoyment in recounting the gossip nullifies the story as we read it.

Barrett has a schoolteacher's instinct for spotting mistakes of fact and logic; he likes to correct, and you feel that he does this without being malicious, that he isn't fully aware of the effect he leaves. He is in Rome during the last days of the war, serving in the Army, and receives a call one day from Edmund Wilson, who is there picking up atmosphere and information for a series of articles for *The New Yorker* on conditions in Italy. Barrett describes how Wilson goes to Milan at one point and sees a sign in a bookshop window saying "Socialist books are not sold here," and takes that as evidence that the political right is gaining ground in the north. Barrett, who has couched this story in a series of impressions of Wilson that leave the reader feeling that Wilson was pompous and self-centered and that his famous flair for languages and facts could not always be trusted, happens to be sent to Milan a few days after Wilson returns. Curious, Barrett goes to the bookshop to see the sign, and it turns out that Wilson's Italian is faulty. The sign says "scholastic," not "socialist," books. "Months later," Barrett tells us, "when I was back in the United States, I looked up an old *New Yorker*, and, sure enough, Wilson was telling its readers that rightist sentiment was running so high in Milan that bookstores would not sell socialist books."

Barrett wants to set the historical record straight but he doesn't get the cleansed feeling he seeks. Why, we ask, didn't he alert Wilson at the time that the Italian was mistranslated? And if Barrett wasn't able to get to Wilson before the article appeared in the magazine, why didn't he tell Wilson of his mistake thereafter, so that it would not be repeated when Wilson included his article in a book? Barrett wants to put finishing touches on past history, but he himself is loose with facts. He tells us that during those days in Italy he drew Wilson's attention to the case of the Russian refugees in Rome. The refugees feared that the Allies would allow Soviet officials to come through the camps and send them back to the Soviet Union. Barrett thought the subject would be of interest to Wilson, but Wilson, whom he has been portraying as someone who only "saw what he wanted to see," didn't, Barrett says, pursue the subject. But Wilson did. He described the situation—and the fact that it was Barrett who drew his attention to it—in *Europe Without Baedeker* (1947).

Though Barrett sprinkles some diplomatic compliments in the

paths of the people he's writing about, he never gives them the true laurel. Of all his subjects, he has the most praise for Trilling as a writer. But he never pulls out the stops and says unequivocally that these men and women at one time or another wrote great criticism. He doesn't give the reader the remotest sense of how rich American criticism was then. He doesn't give an idea of how varied and packed almost every single issue of *Partisan Review* was, or even how the magazine, as an object, looked. It might be said that there was more energy in criticism at the time Barrett is writing about than in any art form except painting or perhaps poetry. Few novels of the time have the twisting, raw but precise declarations of feeling, the lively scorn and enthusiasm for daily life, and the lyrical appreciation for earlier American and European personalities and social conventions of the critical writing—contributed by full-time critics, philosophers, poets, novelists, and historians—that found its way into *Partisan Review* and other small magazines. Possibly this was because for many Americans who came of age in the forties there was no better, more immediate way to do justice to the new themes and awarenesses that presented themselves than through criticism. For writers who had grown up in the Depression, criticism was also the most apt place to insist that art be no more important than the most crucial issues of life. One of Philip Rahv's most famous essays is "The Heiress of All the Ages," which might be called an ode, in the form of literary analysis, to Henry James's heroines. Rahv wrote about James's vision, which grew grander over the years, of the American girl as the figure who would come to be the rightful inheritor of "all the ages" of European refinement. In many ways, Rahv was writing about himself and his contemporaries—not only among the critics. They felt themselves to be the heirs of Europe's fortune. At least as early as right after the First World War, Americans sensed that they would take on the mantle of Europe, and journalists wondered when New York would become the new Paris. But it was the generation of the forties that felt the weight of the new cultural and political adulthood sitting on its head.

It was a fragile, self-conscious, and belligerent generation—maybe because it felt it had lived through the death of Europe and knew that the time had come for it to prove itself. These qualities are perhaps most vivid in the Abstract Expressionist paintings, where tenuous and delicate feelings are spread over great expanses of canvas—where the painters seem to be saying that they want to be monumental and are willing to work in the grandest of European manners, and where they also show, in the marks they make on the canvases, their frightened and impatient awareness of what it means to take on so much. The combination of fragility and headstrong, argumentative strength is also there in the thrusting quality of the writing. Barrett speaks for many people when he presents the "New York Intellectual" of those days so skeptically. There is something forbidding and steely cold about many of these personalities and their work. Whether in Meyer Schapiro's art lectures and writing, Saul Bellow's novels, or Mary McCarthy's theater reviews, ideas were made to live, ideological enemies were knifed brilliantly, and we were left convinced that no aspect of the world's history was foreign to these buoyant warriors. What wasn't wonderful was the feeling that the warrior was showing off.

Barrett, though, never goes into whether these people, in their work, can irritate—or excite—us. He is too determined to present them to us as bulls led this way and that by the ideological rings in their noses. He keeps worrying the issue of how the figures he came to maturity with did or did not give themselves to their respective faiths—Rahv to Marx, Trilling to Freud, Greenberg to Kant and "historical inevitability" in the development of art styles. He faults Rahv for his "simple and comprehensive explanation of the world, above all *unquestioned*, so that it could have the redeeming stability of religious faith." But elsewhere he slaps Rahv because "his mind was not logical but intuitive—and sometimes intuitive according to his own devious patterns." (Barrett's preference is for predictable intuition.) What he doesn't get is that while many of the most brilliant historians, essayists, poets, and painters of the period may have been drawn to one ideology or another, or may even have been ideologues (as he calls Rahv), ideology does not sum up the work they produced. He wants us to see Rahv, Greenberg, and Trilling as fogged in by ideology, forced to forget the realities of life and to misconstrue the

13

novels, paintings, and poems they wrote about. But he never goes deeper, to see why this generation, in so many different guises, needed Marx—or Freud or the concept of "historical inevitability"— to set its hopes on, or how those overriding ideas were the catalytic agents for perceptions about art and literature that have their own life, and don't necessarily make us think, when we read them, of the ideas that fed them.

Trying to create a gap between the supposedly idea-bound writing of his intellectual companions and the art and literature they were drawn to, Barrett subtly belittles those subjects. His chapter entitled "The Painters' Club" is an intimate view of some of the Abstract Expressionists at the moment before their reputations were made. He tells us he called the Eighth Street hangout generally known as the Club the Painters' Club, because that made it easier for his "literary friends" when he was talking about his downtown visits. He still sees it as a relief from the *Partisan Review* world. "No doubt," he says, "my intellectual friends would have found many of the ideas of the painters crude or naive; but then the suspicion was beginning to dawn on me that the way that the intellectuals looked at things might not be the only or in all cases the best way of looking." He likes remembering the art scene and the Greenwich Village of those days as an American "Vie de Bohème." The artists "had yet to make their big splash before the world and they were not rich." As he presents it, it was a time of much jitterbugging and robust thoughts. Willem de Kooning looks at "the work of the old masters with the wonderful directness and energy of a child," and, more than once, Barrett has him responding to some supposedly profound formulation about the new American painting with "Gee!"

The reader believes that Barrett genuinely liked the Club and that he was especially fond of de Kooning and Franz Kline (Jackson Pollock, as Barrett saw him, tended to be either dead silent or on the verge of eruption or drunk and loutish); but he never says anything about the work of these artists. What he wants to remember is that in the good old days they were blissful, poor, unencumbered by dealers and reputations, and, perhaps best of all, living refutations, in their heartiness and simplicity, of the ideas that Clement Greenberg and,

14

later, Harold Rosenberg, foremost among others, would see embodied in their art. Barrett's reader is informed that after the artists began making money the blissful days ceased, and some of the figures, de Kooning in particular, began drinking heavily. The reader is not informed that it was at this time—in the late forties and early fifties— that almost all of the Abstract Expressionists were finding their most distinctive and original styles. It was the classic moment for Kline and Pollock and, possibly, for de Kooning, too, and also for artists Barrett does not mention: Mark Rothko, Clyfford Still, Barnett Newman. Each man's time of exploration and indecision was now over, and in these years they were making the first and still most fresh-looking examples of the paintings that would give American art its first international renown. Barrett's position is that these men—or, at least, de Kooning and Kline—were always warm and simple but fame somehow ruined everything. "The subsequent history of the New York School was to be, at least in part, an indecent traffic with ideas, in the course of which it is really remarkable that some good painting managed to get done," he announces, not making it clear if the "traffic with ideas" stood in the way of the later development of the Abstract Expressionists or if this traffic got in the way of the "New York School" art that came after them. He certainly isn't interested in anything that followed the A. E.'s; he dismisses each succeeding style as another empty trick.

If Barrett leaves us confused as to when artists began to be weighed down by ideas, it's possibly because he doesn't want to raise the question of what his Club friends did or did not achieve. Essentially, he thinks about them only as a foil to the gossipy, analytical-minded, cynical literary intellectuals. It never occurs to him that the painters shared any of the ideas or aspirations of Greenberg or Rosenberg or of writers who weren't interested in the visual arts—Rahv, for instance. He isn't prepared to see in de Kooning's work something more furious and frustrated than "Gee!" Nor does he want to imagine de Kooning's naivete and childlike directness as possibly the response of a very canny and learned man, though that has occurred to many who have known and written about the painter, and it is felt in his recorded remarks and sly, witty statements about painting.

15

Barrett talks about going with a friend to a young painter's studio in the mid-fifties and finding her disconsolate about her work (which Barrett thinks is "not without its merits"), because she feels it may not add anything to "*Painting.*" He takes the scene as an example of the deadly influence of critical thought, which had then already filtered down from the desks of writers such as Greenberg and Rosenberg, to destroy instincts in the studio. Greenberg's influence on new art was vast in the fifties and for much of the sixties; but, contrary to Barrett's feeling, most good artists, from any era, are aware of where their medium is, especially when they're on the verge of finding what's individual about themselves; like rising young writers, lawyers, and politicians, they think a lot about where they fit in, and how they can advance their enterprise. Greenberg didn't invent the idea of an ongoing tradition in art, he revitalized it for his time; his ideas developed at the same pace, and with the same backtrackings, as the most difficult new art of the forties, and his opinions and formulations may have given these artists an incentive to keep growing. His ideas about what qualities make for world-historical art did harden and become simplified, and a school of painters (accompanied by dealers, critics, and museum curators) did come into being in the wake of those ideas, because, in the beginning at least, the ideas were irresistible to many people, including people of great talent. But a greater number of later artists rejected Greenberg, and found themselves by going around his path—and the path of the Abstract Expressionists.

The Truants seems to lead up to the pages, toward the very end, where Barrett takes on Rahv's work as a critic. When Barrett writes about Rahv's essays you feel that there is finally a floor under Barrett, something his opinions can be judged against. He has been telling us that Rahv's political pieces are strident Marxist mouthings, and that, given the barest opportunity, Rahv, in conversation, would gleefully analyze people's motives to shreds. The "best part of him," we are told, is in his essays about literature; and then Barrett goes on to whittle away at those essays. He leaves the reader feeling that, while Rahv was important because many of his ideas have been picked up by teachers of literature, those ideas have the weight of very debatable notions. The most he can say for Rahv's piece on Franz Kafka, which appears as the introduction to the Modern Library edition of Kafka's stories and has for long been the essay most people know this author by, is that it is "fine." Handing down a B + on Rahv's "Tolstoy: The Green Twig and the Black Trunk," he declares that it is "one of the best short introductions" to Tolstoy "as a writer."

Reading Rahv now can be a little difficult, partly because his ideas about nineteenth-century and modern literature have become so widely accepted that they don't seem as if they were ever his own, partly because he doesn't spend time trying to re-create the texture of the writer he is presenting. He is invariably in the thick of the most important distinctions from the first paragraph. Barrett tells us that Rahv was obsessed with Edmund Wilson, and it is easy to see why— Rahv wanted to be an august critic. Yet he couldn't move with Wilson's limberness and command from one subject to another. You can tell that he didn't enjoy writing, and it rarely feels as if he discovered things about himself as he wrote. Yet his writing is personal. It has its own blend of tortuousness and velocity. He must be read slowly for his ideas to be absorbed, yet the effect of his sentences is of a great freight train hurtling by.

Rahv is often "judicial," as Barrett calls him, but he wasn't ever "judicious," which Barrett also says he was. ("Judicious" is the tone Barrett must believe he achieves.) There is a sense of crowding and nervousness and an awareness of what others may think behind Rahv's words; he fights hard, as a writer, for his big view. He was known for his devotion to Russian nineteenth-century literature, especially Dostoevsky and Tolstoy, who gave him his best opportunity to describe the profusion of social and psychological tensions that he felt the biggest characters in literature had to be visited by. The Russia of his articles and portraits is, in part, the fantasy Russia that many Americans have long carried in their minds. It is the country of undiluted soul feelings, the place where happiness is always mixed with a sense of the painfulness and emptiness of things. Wanting always to sum up the combative, beleaguered, and lonely position of the modern man, his pieces sometimes have the effect of being pressurized, miniaturized Russian novels—ones where all the action is conveyed in a rambling but relentless conversation between two men during the course of a stifling St. Petersburg night. When he is dismissive and curt, he is Russian, too. When he writes to sweep away the false views of other critics or to say how some novelist isn't truly modern, he seems to be facing the tundra as he puts the words down. There is a grinding anger to him then; he really feels that he is looking at a vast nothing, that the figure he is writing about is bad for culture and life and that we will be led astray by admiring or believing in him.

Rahv couldn't be Edmund Wilson because, for all that he may have wanted to speak with fluency and with the assurance, as he might have put it, of a landowner from one of the old families, he realized he had to be a writer of one thing, which was large and small: the endless trial of being modern. Barrett tells us that Rahv had no interest in or comprehension of the new American painting of the time, and the reader has no cause to doubt him. Yet Rahv was very close to the Abstract Expressionists in his feelings, especially Rothko and Newman — Rothko in the way he turns the great modern writers into mammoth far-reaching essences that hover before us, Newman in the way his determination to deal only with the largest issues often left his world stripped of texture, barren. These painters, too, wanted their work to stand for one magnified thing; they knew that their art might become severe and flat in the process, but they wanted to run the risk. The risk almost seemed to be the point.

When Rahv died he left his money to Israel, an act that Barrett says "puzzled many," presumably because Rahv hadn't been known for Zionist sympathies or for being pro-Israel. Barrett wasn't surprised, though, because years before, in a conversation in Washington Square, when Rahv had been talking about the "tepidness" of life in America, he impetuously said he wished he were in Israel. Barrett sees Rahv's will as a sign that, at the end, "something more human than literary . . . broke through," and that there was something "more youthful and yearning" underneath Rahv's "cynical postures of the ideologue." Barrett's is a legitimate way of interpreting what Rahv did. But from another point of view this interpretation makes mush out of Rahv's spirit. It takes the punch out of his gesture, which says "Screw you" to America, and "So you think you know everything about me?" to his friends and public.

Rahv's unexpected parting gift to Israel also has something in it of the flaunting and wrenched farewells by suicide of many of the writers and painters of the time. For the generation of the forties, everything led up to the grand, confounding gesture, whether in one's work or life. It expressed the trapped feeling so many had about their situation in history, and also their wanting to break loose from that entrapment. They wanted to be the new American creators, men without a past, and they also felt themselves to be the last true ambassadors from old Europe to America. They couldn't get the achievements of the great nineteenth- and early-twentieth-century Europeans out of their minds. Their desire for that greatness and their doubts over whether they would achieve it did not, taken together, make them any friendlier as individuals. In a way, William Barrett is a man of his time. He himself is more like the picture of the black-souled Rahv he has drawn than he knows. *The Truants* leaves a very bleak, dead message; it says that most of the achievements of the men Barrett came up with proved futile or delusory. The difference between him and his subjects is that, while he has a strong feeling for futility and impermanence, he is a comfortable man. He doesn't feel himself to be a stranger in the world, or, if he does, he doesn't write from such a view. Not feeling that estrangement has kept him a stranger to his own generation.

—1983

THE MYSTERY AND
MELANCHOLY OF A CAREER

THE GREAT SURPRISE OF the Museum of Modern Art's Giorgio de Chirico exhibition is how little de Chirico looks like a man of his time. His most famous pictures, the majority of which were done in Paris between 1911 and 1915, when he was between twenty-three and twenty-seven, are, in spirit, earlier and later than the period they come out of. Ingenious, fanciful, and ghoulish, they're a little like beautifully preserved Victorian Punch-and-Judy theater sets; but they have a hip, chic, self-possessed air, which is un-Victorian, and a theatrical, science-fiction light that will probably always make them appear to have been born yesterday. The show has been beautifully installed, in a lean, old-fashioned, strictly-the-pictures way (there are no explanatory wall labels to slow you down), and the Modern's timing is perfect. Like many painters and sculptors now, de Chirico wanted to tell his life story in his work and to ruffle the state of art by putting more sex in his pictures and by making them literary. And he moved with a freedom similar to the freedom people have now. Operating as if the entire history of art styles were at his disposal (as many artists have been feeling since the late seventies), he seems to have believed that the more he stylized the more personal he could become.

The Modern's show—which William Rubin, who directed it, describes in the catalogue as "the first in-depth, large-scale exhibition focusing on the great early work ever to be held"—was a revelation to me. I never imagined that there would be such a likable spirit of boys'-book ingenuity pervading de Chirico's art, or that his pictures, when seen in number, would form so complete a world. And yet when I thought about the work and went back, the pictures felt emptied; they didn't become weak or less brilliant or dated overnight, but they seemed too quickly used up. I kept thinking about Munch after seeing the de Chiricos—to some degree because of the similar shape of their careers. Theirs are perhaps the two most dramatic of the many stories of modern artists who withdrew from the arena. Both, after a relatively short, hectic stretch of innovative work in their youth, spent away from their homelands, in cosmopolitan centers, retired to their own countries and, in a mood of bitterness mingled with pride, passed the many decades of this second and final act of their lives making pictures that commented on—sometimes repeated, often repudiated—their renowned earlier ones. Munch died in Norway at eighty, much decorated by his countrymen but, one feels from looking at his late work, long a living ghost to himself. De Chirico lived to ninety, dying in Rome in 1978; he, too, was an honored figure on his

home ground, but, for most of his contemporaries and for the succeeding generations, he had stopped producing challenging and influential work around 1917. Munch and de Chirico came together in my
mind even more because they drew their material from a similar
terrain: the apprehensiveness that is felt during adolescence and
youth. And yet Munch, with his more painterly approach—his
harsher, more bullied but also more fondled surfaces—transcended
that material; he made his themes the basis of a more grown-up,
emotionally elastic art. There is a softness and a reverberation in
Munch that, after you have spent time with de Chirico, you begin to
crave.

Munch's images seem to come from a young man who has known
jealousy, frustration, impotence, and humiliation in love, and, no
longer having to live through it, wants now to proclaim—even to brag
about—how messy and lousy it was. De Chirico describes a moment
in life that precedes Munch's. De Chirico's is the time just before the
balloon of virginity is broken, when sexual adventure is longed for but
when the greater pleasure is in prolonging the fantasies of sex. His art
is all about sex but there is no sex in it. When, in his Paris pictures, he
shows men and women together, they're no more than wispy tooth-
pick figures in the far background; their shadows have as much
presence and character as they do. One of the very few paintings of
the human figure de Chirico made in those innovative years is *The
Child's Brain*, which is believed to be of his father, Evariste. But this
ominous and amusing figure, unclothed as we see him from the waist
up, and with his eyes shut, is slightly unreal (the picture has the look,
in a good way, of a circus poster); and the rest of de Chirico's people
are true stand-ins: statues, busts, mannequins, silhouettes, sometimes statues seen from the back. Women are in these paintings in the
form of the many images of a recumbent classical, full-breasted, yet
surprisingly unfluid and menacing, and never quite focused, statue of
Ariadne. Women are perhaps also there in the spirit of the many
wonderful shadowed arcades and porticoes, the enveloping railroad
stations, and the yellow circus-caravan-like trucks with open doors
that reveal nothing inside. We feel the male force everywhere: in the
awesomely large towers and brick factory chimneys, in the bananas

and the heads of stubby cannons that jut into the scenes from the side, in the shaftlike shadows, possibly from chimneys, that seem to sniff the bolts of light into which they are cast.

These elements overlap, they gently, precariously touch one another; but they don't blend together, and they have no more substance than the bolts of light. This is the realm, you feel, of someone who hasn't yet done anything but whose head buzzes with images and expectations of future actions, based on what he has read and on what he has watched others doing. De Chirico paints that realm, not out of impatience or with a gnawing nervousness but as if he were under a spell, as if he were the class valedictorian of that tense, trapped moment in life. I think this is partly why his pictures can have such an instant hold on people—why they can seem so immediately graspable and familiar, even if you don't quite get what is going on in them as pictures—and yet why they don't increase in mystery and beauty as you think back on them. They're glamorous and worldly paintings made about a relatively static, sliver-thin moment in the course of growing up.

There is a blind strength about de Chirico; you don't have to know the biographical details that underlie his paintings to sense that his technique and intellectual equipment are far in advance of his experience of life. He builds his pictures with the same spooky dominion that children have when they rearrange the contents of doll houses or when they position their toys for the night. Children feel so godlike and confident when they're on their knees looking down on their make-believe sites that they often re-create the relationships that frighten them most. They bring some dolls or pieces of furniture forward to act as guardians and shove others into the dark to punish them or to keep them protected. Left on their own, children may make what for them are thrilling and happy dramas out of feelings that, when they're with adults, keep them frozen or on guard. De Chirico's paintings have the same doubleness of feeling. They're images of forlornness and emptiness created in a mood of such power and freedom that it doesn't occur to you that there is anything wrong or off about them.

De Chirico seems to have invented his poetic house-of-cards language to make paintings about his adolescent feelings of autumnal sadness and of the unrelatedness of things—those melancholy feelings that sensitive young people, as they approach their twenties, hold on to more and more tenaciously, in the belief that their sadness makes them deeper than others. By the evidence of the work he did in his first couple of years in Paris, de Chirico had more than his share of such feelings. But when they evaporated, perhaps in the excitement of being there and being praised, he had the mental swiftness to move on. He didn't get rid of those early feelings, though. He shifted them, in the form of his deserted arcades and bittersweet light, to the literal background of the compositions. In the paintings he did in his mid-twenties, he doesn't appear to get rid of anything—that is one reason it's so great to see so many at once. Each painting seems to contain something of the one before. Perhaps inspired by the cut-and-pasted paper collages that Picasso and Braque were doing at the time, de Chirico invented a form of collage for himself—one where we feel space the way we do in photographs with distinctly separate, though equally focused, foregrounds and backgrounds.

As you move from picture to picture at the Modern, where they are hung in chronological order, you feel you are looking at scenes from the life of a budding conquistador. In his images of trains speeding in the distance, of pennants waving, of enveloping railroad stations, of a satiny dark green nighttime sky about to be irradiated by a blond dawn not far off, you almost get the sensation of movement and penetration. Writers have explained the frequent appearance of locomotives and railroad stations in de Chirico's pictures by noting that his father was a railroad engineer. James Thrall Soby, the painter's champion and the author of the standard account of his early work, doesn't say exactly what Evariste de Chirico did for the railroad company in Greece but implies that he helped plan the Thessalian track routes, then being mapped out. What might also be ascribed to de Chirico's feeling for his father's work is the way you absorb his images, which is the way you take in buildings and vistas from the perspective of a train window. His towers, walls, and plazas seem to flash by, and you are made to feel the power that comes from seeing things that way: you feel you know them more intimately than the people do who live with them day by day. I don't think any other artist has made so vivid and lasting a record of the confusing entry into, and eventual conquest of, a great city. Yet we only infer this subject. We're never given tangible proof that we are in Paris or in any particular modern city or specific site. If he was thinking of any place, Soby suggests it was probably Turin, where he and his mother had stopped for a few days on their way to Paris in 1911 (and where he promptly fell in love with the same aspects of the city that he had read that Nietzsche loved).

De Chirico may make us think of Turin, or at least of Italy. If he has always been a more beckoning artist for non-Italians than for Italians, it's probably because he thought of his true homeland, at least when he was in Paris in his twenties, the way a tourist does. De Chirico's parents were Italian, but he was born in Greece and spent his child-hood and youth there. His late teens were passed in Munich, where he went with his mother, Gemma, and his younger brother, Andrea. (Evariste died when the family was still in Greece and Giorgio was seventeen.) By the time he arrived in Paris, he had spent barely two years' time all told in various Italian cities.

And yet it feels as if Italy were what he wanted most. (You might say that it was his parents, the Italians in Greece, that he wanted to hold on to most.) It's amazing, at the retrospective, to see him single-handedly inventing a visual vocabulary that would nourish an entire generation of Surrealist artists. But he hits his deepest note at the very beginning of his Paris stay, in what now look to be the most conserva-tive of his breakthrough paintings: his street and empty-plaza scenes. It's in these works (which fed the Neo-Romantic artists, especially Eugene Berman) that he draws closest to Munch's emotional power; he can be compared with Seurat, too, who, in his few images of the near-empty squares, railroad tracks, and deserted working-class sub-urbs of Paris, made perhaps the first pictures that show the haunting, muted poetry of the modern city. De Chirico's purest urge, I believe, was to paint places—maybe not as an Impressionist but as a kind of literary, philosophical Impressionist, a Monet of dreams. At heart, his most full-blooded works—*The Nostalgia of the Infinite*, say, with its mythical tower such as Jack would find after climbing the beanstalk, or *The Mystery and Melancholy of a Street*, where a silhouette-flat girl with long, streaming hair runs with a hoop from shadowed streets into a bright, empty square—are postcard souvenirs raised to the level of great art. No matter how theatrical and complicated their formal structure, they are immediately legible from any distance, and they leave you with the impression of a place that you have been to.

De Chirico's images are unexpectedly perfect distillations of the austere, minimal but not parched surface coating of Italian life. He gets not only Italian earth, building, and sky colors but color combinations that show Italian taste. His paintings embody the feeling that Mediterraneans have for sun-bleached colors and for unpainterly, ornamental tutti-frutti spreads of color. And he gets the opposite of tutti-frutti—the Italian desire for (and desire to parody) French or English good-taste colors; he composes (as none of the Spanish masters of modern art would) with a feeling for the contrast of navy and white, and navy and tan—colors Italians give to cars and think of as the colors of adult business dress. His images bring back memories of travel in Italy and of scenes from Italian movies. His broad, empty squares, often with the suggestion of the sea beyond our immediate line of vision, remind us of the sites Monica Vitti lost herself in in Antonioni's movies. The last scenes in *L'Avventura*, with their sense of a beautiful predawn realm that belongs only to us—yet which we're too stony to feel—and the final image of a man sitting on a bench and a woman standing behind him, seemingly at the lip of the world, could have been made as an homage to the painter. Many of de Chirico's Paris pictures leave the impression of being nocturnes, and that, too, feels Italian. It's as if, with his eyes accustomed to a harder, brighter Mediterranean light, he saw the dimmer, softer French light as so many shades of a permanent evening. He uses twilight settings again and again, as a kind of new toy, the way Bertolucci, in *The Conformist* and *Last Tango in Paris*, sank into the possibilities of the blue light that comes in the late afternoon of a winter's day in Paris.

Why did de Chirico abandon his early art—his heady air, his erect shadows, his feeling for angles and thrusts and the jokes of bohemian life—for an insistence on the techniques of the Old Masters? Commentators hint that there was some buried psychological reason for it, but the reason seems to be right there in the work; you feel him running out of steam sometime after he left Paris for Italy, in 1915. He and his brother—who had changed his name to Alberto Savinio, and was known primarily as a composer of modern, difficult music, though he also painted and wrote—were drafted into the Italian Army that year. Because of Giorgio's always uncertain health (he suffered from digestive ailments and bouts of despondency), he was transferred—along with Alberto—to an office job at headquarters in Ferrara. Their mother set herself up in an apartment there, as she had done in most of the other cities her sons had traveled to. Though they worked for the Army during the day, Giorgio and Alberto took their meals with their mother and slept at her apartment, and they managed to continue with their painting and writing. (Giorgio, too, wrote throughout his life—essays, an autobiography, poetical sketches, historical studies about artists and theoretical papers on the state of art, and the novel *Hebdomeros*, which was published in Paris in 1929.) Giorgio continued to make accomplished paintings in Ferrara and also for a short time after he moved to Rome at the end of 1918 (again living with Gemma). Among the most memorable are *The Sacred Fish*, *The Dream of Tobias*, and *The Amusements of a Young Girl*, with its lovingly painted wood spools, glove, and glimpse in the background of the red Castello Estense, in Ferrara. But his pictures seem to shrink, literally and emotionally. There is still a spell about them, but it is a self-conscious spell. We're more aware of the thin black lines that contain the forms, and he seems to be showing off his admittedly great compositional skills, packing the pictures too tightly with things.

Distance and light, which he had made protagonists of his Paris paintings, now appear in the cramped form of pictures within pictures, as if that were the only way he could think to keep the real world in his art. One of the best from this time, *Great Metaphysical Interior*, shows window shades, pieces of painting stretchers, and boxes, all standing upright like sentinels. Among them is a complete miniature framed painting of a grand Victorian three-story structure, possibly a sanatorium or a hotel, set on a winding road, with immense mountains and a large lake in the distance. We could be at one of the small tourist towns in northern Italy at the base of the Italian Alps—at Gardone, say, on Lake Garda. We're looking at a banal vacation setting, but the image is magical. Not quite realistic and not quite cartoonish, it has the quality of a perfectly preserved memory. The picture has a dense, high-noon light and an almost primitive presence; our eyes settle on it and don't want to leave it. *Great Metaphysical Interior* and other works of the time that have a painting within the painting mark the beginning of the end for de Chirico, for they show that he was becoming uncertain of his allegiances. The little Gardone-like painting within the painting seems to have all of Italy in it; you feel that it contains the essence of travel, and, though it is a piece of realism, it is closer in spirit to the radical paintings he did in Paris than is the rest of the picture, with its unreal, Cubist air and its quality of being a collection of suggestively mismatched bric-a-brac. Back in Italy, though, he had no need to re-create an imaginary Italy. The chief thing he retained was the cool, ambiguous mood he had invented in Paris.

He must have been proud of that mood; in his work from 1911 to 1915 he had released his fantasies of power and speed and his pervasive feeling of emptiness; Apollinaire and Picasso, among many others, had let him know how high these works stood in their regard. Working in some obscurity in Ferrara, he no doubt felt that continuing to develop his Paris style was a way of preserving the excitement of those years. The problem was that he had less to paint. He had never been a painter of memories but, rather, a painter who sought to make memories for himself in paint. In the works of 1916 and 1917, in which he paints biscuits and rolls and wrapped candy surrounded by an excess of studio props and boxes and lines that refer to nothing, you feel him pushing his vision forward but strangling himself as he does so. If his Paris pictures are the work of a young man who strokes himself and readies his body for the moment when he will plunge into the hazardous, unfathomable, beckoning currents—who thinks as much about his own beauty as about the women who will come to appreciate it—the Ferrara paintings are the work of the same young man who is now overly fit but still waiting on the bank. The undercurrent of disorientation in the earlier de Chiricos is lyrical, but the sense of jumbledness and confusion in the later ones is mostly debilitating; it is the too tightly knit disorientation of a Hamlet who never gets a chance to stab somebody.

De Chirico's capitulation, around 1920, to a reactionary style—accompanied by his virulent, garrulous hatred of all "modern" art (Picasso was one of the very few of his friends from the prewar days whom he continued to respect)—is predicted in the work he did in Paris and Ferrara. Those works plainly say that he was looking for a past; he wanted a setting that would be his own and would also be a stage for the dramas of classical antiquity that he, not only an Italian but one born in Thessaly, felt were part of his birthright. Taken on a literal level, many of his most successful pictures are about strategies for achieving formal newness and keeping the classical Mediterranean past in there, too. *The Song of Love,* of 1914, which William Rubin calls the artist's masterpiece, might be described as an image of the meeting of the old and historical (the glamorous head of the Apollo Belvedere) with the new and blank (a red rubber glove and a green ball). But there are deeper reasons for de Chirico's abandonment of his advanced art. The underlying content of that art is the holding back from things; the pictures are about waiting, keeping oneself clean and untouched. The undercoating of nightmarish dread in them comes from someone who fears making a certain move. Possibly that move is growing up, feeling oneself an adult. An artist who takes boyish fears and a youthful sense of aloneness to their expressive limits probably does so because he sees adulthood as a compromise, a fraudulent state. The Dorian Gray of modern art, de Chirico lived out his worst expectations. He made compromised adult art. He spent his last sixty-odd years producing pastiches of Old Master, museum-bound styles—possibly because that was, from the beginning, what he thought growing up meant. His puckered, too juicy later paintings seem to be what his early, sublimely crisp works keep at bay.

The vituperative, self-righteous, almost buffoonish anger he radiated in the long latter part of his career—and which is just below the surface in his numerous self-portraits, where he often garbs himself as a knight of one order or another—must have come in part from his realization that he hadn't simply made a decision one day to abandon his modern style. What happened was that he lost the tension that had produced it. He came to a point where he couldn't put that tension in art. The jangled nerves and paranoid imaginings remained in him, though. They sputtered out of him in the form of cranky pronouncements. Having kept the feelings of youth fresh long after most men do, he suddenly became old. He was old in spirit long before his actual age warranted it; he was in his early thirties when he became a zealous defender of old, dead things.

De Chirico may have come to be so insistent on academy-taught skills and on the lessons of Raphael, Renoir, Delacroix, Courbet, Signorelli, and everyone else because somewhere inside him he doubted whether he himself was a pure painter, and he was right to doubt. For all the beautiful, deft passages in his early work, for all his youthful training in the academies in Athens and Munich and his studies, when he was in his thirties, in the galleries of older art in Florence and Rome, he was more a great image-maker than a great painter. Whenever his art came to life after 1920, it was most often because he invented a method of rendering something that had never been seen or done that way before—when, for example, he painted water as a herringbone pattern in his young-male-bather series of the twenties and thirties. There are a few paintings from this series in the small group of works that Rubin has assembled to give an idea of what de Chirico was doing at the time; the artist's liveliest—the most elegant and witty—versions of the theme are in his drawings, though, and none of the bather drawings are in the show. The bather pictures in whatever form are reminiscent of the magical—but also tricky, theatrical—effects in Cocteau's movies, and they have some of the spirit of those movies. In his images of superbly built, anonymous boy-men who disappear into isolated cabanas by the sea or immerse themselves in the flat, herringbone waves, de Chirico was making tableaux, in the Riviera Modern style of the period, about the desire to lose yourself in something that will allow you to remain youthful, unchanged forever. It is the desire that underlies his early art.

Paintings gushed from de Chirico in his last six decades; he was producing paintings and works on paper—and sculpture—at his customary great rate even in the mid-seventies, as a large exhibition at Wildenstein in 1976 showed. Most of his later works were taken from subjects in classical, Renaissance, and Baroque art—there are pictures on the Judgment of Paris theme, and of heroic mythological horses with streaming manes and luxuriantly thick tails. And there are still lifes, often of fish or fruit, that may be indebted to Courbet but don't have the spirit of any earlier artist in them; they are most like the work of someone who knows too much to continue to paint as if he were a student yet who won't, for some reason, break out of the approach suggested by his teachers. (They're a sensuous version of Walt Kuhn.) The Modern's selections of de Chirico's later work, drawn mostly from the twenties and the mid-thirties, give an idea of how he inched his way into his new, neoclassical self. Taken together, they make it seem as if, turning to small canvases and dry, powdery surfaces, he became musty and limp and that was the end of it. But that wasn't the whole story. After the thirties, while keeping the same mix of mythological and still-life subjects, de Chirico went into high gear. Then, as may be seen in the picture book of his work that Isabella Far, his wife, brought out in 1968, his palette became greasier and brighter, and the stroke of his brush became coarser. Occasionally, in those overripe years, he also produced drier, more cartoonish—and genuinely outlandish—paintings, full of images of the sun with blobby or spearlike rays, club chairs, battling gladiators, immensely long strings that wind their way through landscapes and in and out of stage-set-like rooms. Apparently done with slapdash speed, these pictures look as if they were throwaways to him. They don't work for us, either, yet they could have been the basis of something fresh. It's hard to imagine, though, how he himself could have built on them. There's something naughty about them; they might be products of a part of him that wanted to ridicule his role as the knowing-master-in-his-studio. It was up to others, principally Philip Guston, to take these cartoonish, unfelt but potent images and make of them something other than oddities. Guston approached these seemingly knocked-off later pictures with a fan's enthusiasm, and they supplied his own powerful late art with one take-off point after another. Painting a realm of decay—of worn-down but clownishly apprehensive battlers, of old shoes and cigarette butts and moldy leftover snacks and remnants from long-gone cultures— Guston was ready to see that de Chirico had barely tapped the possibilities in his images of deadness. Guston brought out the grotesqueness, the funny and also frightening fatuousness, that lay buried in de Chirico's cardboard world.

The catalogue for the show is less than invigorating. It includes so-so reproductions of the works, and essays by American, German, and Italian scholars. Rubin's piece, "De Chirico and Modernism," has the greatest sweep and fluency. He wants to dispel the idea that his subject is primarily a literary, symbolical painter, and this is legitimate, up to a point. Obviously, de Chirico was a master constructor of plastic forms. But Rubin's determination that we realize how formal de Chirico's thinking was—that we see his attempt, in this passage or that, to emphasize the flatness of the canvas—pulls us away from the spirit of the pictures. Rubin wants to save de Chirico by making him more of a member of the family of modern art. But, again, de Chirico escapes; despite the clear intellectual and aesthetic connections that Rubin makes between de Chirico and Picasso, Henri Rousseau, the Futurists, and others, you feel that the painter meshes with these men and movements in only the vaguest way. And that doesn't diminish him. He becomes a figure of more stature—maybe even a more "modern" one—when he's thought of as the young man who, coming to Paris from the Mediterranean via Munich, studied or got to know the most adventurous talents of the day in both cities, was buoyed by their company and ideas, and yet created a body of work that shows that when he was most original he barely thought about any of them.

The rest of the articles in the catalogue are about such subjects as de Chirico's influence on art in the twenties in Germany, on the Surrealists, and on Italian art theory; and how we can decipher the images and objects—the sunglasses, palm trees, railroad stations—in his early works. The more you read in these too glossy pages the further you feel you get from the paintings. De Chirico's pictures are endless in their meanings, in a hall-of-mirrors way, and his influence on twentieth-century art was tricky and continual: up to sometime in the forties, his images probably set the course for as many developing painters as those of any other single figure (though he has never, as have Picasso and Matisse, given painters, once under way, new thoughts about how to continue and enlarge their enterprise). But de

Chirico was only twenty-three when he began making his most famous works. He was a genius, probably a mama's boy, and no doubt on his way to being the monster he became later in his life—the self-proclaimed maestro devoted to his own dignity. He was also a young man full of bookish perceptions, and when, as in these essays, so much erudition is expended on something that was learned to begin with, the effect is a heightened hollowness.

He was a kind of scholar himself. He wanted to make connections between his readings and between what he read and his instincts. He said that when he read Nietzsche's *Thus Spake Zarathustra* he had many of the same feelings he had when he read *The Adventures of Pinocchio* as a child. His genius is that he brought Nietzsche and Pinocchio together in his paintings. He caught that time in some people's lives when they want to be a superman but feel they can do it only by going under the guise of a puppet, by deliberately woodenizing themselves. He will always make people, especially those who are on their way to being artists, stop in their tracks, because his paintings show the world being conquered through the application of pure style. He is the painter of the Italian moment in your life, when you want to walk through the streets with your collar up.

—1982

A TRAVELER IN THE REGIONS OF PURE FEELING

FOR OVER A HUNDRED AND FIFTY years, Heinrich von Kleist has been thought of not only as one of the most individual of the great Romantic writers, but as a force who will make you feel stronger and surer about yourself. His letters—now available in English for the first time, translated by Philip B. Miller, in *An Abyss Deep Enough* (Dutton)—have that awakening force. Written between 1793, when he was fifteen and still in the army, and November 21, 1811, the day of his death, they are about a boy's, and then a young man's, desire to see himself in relation to eternity. Well over half of them were written between 1800 and the spring of 1802, when Kleist was in his early twenties, to Wilhelmine von Zenge, his fiancée. He is proud to sign off many of the letters with "your lover," and he often talks about their upcoming marriage and the children they will have. But these aren't love letters. Heroic and uncertain in almost the same breath, he always wants to pose, and answer if he can, the biggest questions of life and experience.

Some of his pronouncements will make you stop and think about whether you agree with him—as when he tells Wilhelmine that "all ceremony stifles the emotions. It preoccupies the mind, while the heart remains dead." But most of his insights have a settled rightness to them. When you read his thoughts on, say, how people begin to have more charity toward others when they fall in love, you want to mark the passage, because he is clearly coming on this perception as he writes, and he makes you feel as if you are hearing it for the first time. You keep seeing yourself in him, the way you see yourself in Anne Frank when you read her *Diary*. Kleist may remind you of yourself at your best, as she does.

Yet while you don't lose your admiration for him, and you don't grow impatient with his determination to report continually on the state of his soul, you are left a little etherealized by his purity. Not that he writes only about his frustrations and expectations. Especially in the hundred-odd pages of his correspondence with Wilhelmine, there are lovely, snapshotlike glimpses of everyday life in the Napoleonic era. Within a few months of his engagement, he is off traveling through Germany and, later, France, in search of adventure and in the hopes of finding the right occupation for himself. He meets young German intellectuals, looks at art in the great galleries of Dresden and Paris, and wanders through Paris's muddy streets. He stands in the Louvre, admiring the works of classical and Italian Renaissance art, and is asked by a Frenchman, "Was all this painted here in Paris?" He reports home on the latest fashions ("Tie the ribbons of your bonnet from your ears along the edge of your cheeks so that the bow adorns the exact middle of your chin"). He tells about romantic coach rides in the moonlight, where he luxuriates in his lonesomeness. And he tosses off passages of unromanticized, journalistic travel writing at its best, as when, in talking about the sandy-soiled Baltic towns, he describes how they sit on "a stretch of ground originally intended rather for whales and herrings than for people." Visiting a hospital in Würzburg, he re-creates the living deaths he has seen with an unflinching firmness worthy of Géricault, who was making paintings in the morgue and insane asylum in Paris at almost the same time.

But he is unable to lose himself in the outside world for long. He can't get away from speculating about his fate and the worth of his character, and, because he is so trustworthy and compelling, his self-judging mood casts a grayed spell on the reader. The letters have the effect of a kind of therapy that lets the patient sink into an introspective war with himself, a battle where, in pouring over his every motive and feeling in isolation, he gets caught in an emotional gridlock.

Even after Kleist became a public figure, he continued to believe he might, as he says, make a "botch" of his "entire life" at any moment. In the correspondence that follows his break from Wilhelmine in 1802 (he never does marry), we follow him, on a less daily and intimate basis, on his whirlwind yet frequently interrupted career as a writer, editor, and publisher. In the nine years that remained to his life, he wrote eight plays and eight stories, struggled with a number of works, including a two-volume novel, that he was dissatisfied with and destroyed, and attempted to open a map, book, and art publishing house. Between 1807 and 1809, he published *Phöbus*, a magazine devoted to literature and the arts. Then in 1810 he founded the *Berliner Abendblätter*, the city's first daily newspaper, which was distributed free in its first months, and which he also edited and contributed to. Yet the letters that cover these years of tremendous accomplishment and Herculean labor bespeak very little self-satisfaction. He virtually never talks about his work. He is never at ease with himself. He never shakes for long the despair that is in his farewell to Wilhelmine, from May, 1802: "Dear girl, write me no more, I have no other wish than very soon to die. H.K." His letters end with him writing to his friends and family about his preparations to achieve this wish. On November 21, 1811, shortly after he turned thirty-four, he took his own life in a suicide pact with Henriette Vogel, a married woman then living with her husband and children, who was terminally ill with cancer, and whom Kleist had only recently met. The title "An Abyss Deep Enough" comes from one of his last letters, where he says he wants "to find an abyss deep enough to leap into" with Henriette.

Kleist's letters are revelatory. They make human, complete, and down-to-earth a figure who, for English-speaking readers anyway, has been one of literature's mystery genuises. They show an Everyman simplicity, and a fear of being crushed, that Kleist's plays and stories, in their intoxicating speed and charging, fearless assurance, only hint at. If you have read and loved Kleist, you will wolf down *An Abyss*, which includes, in addition to the letters, twenty-one of his short, lively essays—the best of which are about the psychological processes that make for liberated or hamstrung art—and twenty-four of his even shorter, often half-page-long, anecdotes.

A few of these pieces are familiar. "On the Puppet Theater" has been available. Probably his most influential single essay, it is, on the surface, a discussion between two men about the superior grace of inanimate things, and about the burden consciousness places on our acts. Ironic one moment and straightforward the next, the essay is like a fable that might be told by a wise man to a passing stranger in a Middle Eastern bazaar. Its points never settle in the mind, and that has contributed to its fame and appeal. It seems to say different things each time it is read. Parts of Kleist's review of the work of the painter Caspar David Friedrich, his contemporary, have appeared before, too, usually in studies of Friedrich or of Romanticism. This piece contains one of the startling moments in writing about art: Kleist's remark about the picture *Monk Before the Sea*, that, looking at it, "the viewer feels as though his eyelids had been cut off." The piece on Friedrich, which was originally published in Kleist's newspaper, is included here in its entirety.

But the majority of these essays, pieces of journalism, and anecdotes have never before been translated into English. Miller doesn't say what proportion of Kleist's nonfiction writing this "selection" represents. (Presumably he has included all of the letters.) Considering how little there is of Kleist altogether, one would like to know; it would have been helpful to have a list of the titles of the other pieces, to get a sense of how wide his range of subject matter was. This is the only detail that Miller hasn't attended to. His notes to the letters and articles are helpful and never intrusive; he has also supplied a handy chronology and an introduction which gives a good sense of Kleist's place in European literary and intellectual history, and of how layered his themes are. The book's design is pleasing, too. A large, classical typeface has been used for the many chapter headings, and that suits Kleist. The image of the imposing, blocky print, set at the top of these slightly smaller-than-average-size pages, is a continual reminder of his little-big-man strength.

Kleist wasn't a popular author during his life. He wrote less for a wide audience than for the literary powers of the time, and he made those powers nervous. They regarded him as an unstable writer and person, and took his suicide as a confirmation of their doubts. Not long after his death, though, he began to be thought of with a rare affection, and that hasn't changed to this day. He is a writer that few writers can feel superior to, but one most writers can feel parental toward, no matter what their age or sense of their own stature. It's possible his first audience will always be writers, or other artists, because, while he doesn't write about artists in his fiction (many of his characters are aristocrats and are generally of historical and mythological vintage), he takes to the limit the urges that almost all performers, in any field, have. He's a supreme showoff, yet he works with the intensity of someone who isn't a professional—someone who, you suspect, will never professionalize his feelings.

He often writes about shifts in power; he's a specialist on how people stretch and lunge for power, and yet how, once they have it in their hands, their immediate instinct is to whip it, like a Frisbee, off to their partner. In its precision and muscularity, his prose is a power tool, too. Even in translation, his writing has a self-conscious, but not fussy, beauty. It's easy to imagine him at work, sitting there, thinking of how impressed his reader will be with him. But you also sense that part of him is convinced that the art of writing is an indulgence. In his letters, he keeps fingering this thorn; he can't shake the belief that doing one good deed in the world is worth more than a lifetime spent in bringing to the surface and making presentable the stirrings and hunches that are within. And in much of his writing, he makes his readers conscious of his refusal to be artful. Yet he is so honest and rigid about not giving more than is necessary—he is so determined that each sentence be as clean and polished and count for as much as the ones surrounding it—that he ends up with the opposite of what he intends. Wanting to produce the most bare-walled Protestant prose ever, he comes out on the other side, with a style of compressed extravagance, an almost Catholic style.

To Americans, Kleist is less familiar for his plays than for his stories, all eight of which were brought out by Criterion Books in 1960 as *The Marquise of O—and Other Stories*, in translations by Martin Greenberg. Subsequently issued as a paperback, this volume has for long been the chief way most of us have known Kleist. It is an amazing book. (It is also graced by two introductory pieces, by Greenberg and Thomas Mann, that seem inspired by the chance to present the tangled themes and emotions in the works that follow.) Each of the stories is different in setting and flavor, and each has seemingly its own kind of deliberate, sought-after formal flatness; there are elements in them of fairy tales, tall tales, news reports, essays. Kleist rarely says what his characters look like or what they wear, let alone what the weather or light is like. He doesn't describe why his people do what they do, he doesn't get inside them. There is usually something artificial and operatic about his settings, too: Renaissance Germany, Chile in the seventeenth century, the West Indies. But we don't stop to wonder about any of this because we don't have the time. His people are too busy doing something or responding to what someone else has done, and we have to follow the chain of events closely or we're lost.

His stories are so unpredictable and rich, in part, because no one in them is the way he seems at first sight. Kleist introduces everyone to us as plywood flat, then begins revealing different, contradictory flat layers behind the first. And while he keeps everything on the level of a report filed in the *Police Gazette*, his rushing, anonymous-toned, adjective-less style leaves the impression that hairbreadth distinctions about feelings have been made. It's for this reason that *The Marquise of O—and Other Stories* becomes in memory a fatter book than it is, and why, after reading two or three stories in it, you are too full to go on for a while. He presents emotions in unfiltered, simon-pure states, yet his meanings don't announce themselves at once—they remain pleasurably cloaked—because those separate emotions have been carefully and quickly laid one on top of the next. You feel he has given you the world in a cameo. You feel like the Marquise of O—, who finds herself pregnant one day and doesn't know who the father is or how it happened.

Some of the liveliest moments in his letters are of him at his most commandeering and audacious. You hear the son of a battalion commander and the descendant of generations of Prussian military officers when he tells Wilhelmine that his half-sister Ulrike "will always know where I *am*, but you, my beloved girl, will always know where I *am going to be*. Well then, in short: tomorrow my direction is— *Pasewalk! Pasewalk?* Yes, Pasewalk, Pasewalk." The cocky young instructor in life's ways is almost visible when, at the end of the same letter, he directs his fiancée to "Always have a map of Germany at hand and find the place where I am." Kleist the supercompressor among writers is in these lines: "With what emotion I once again saw Mainz, which I had seen as a boy. How could it be described? Those were the richest seconds in the entire minute of my life!" The Kleist who hardly seems aware of how essentially witty his view of things is is capsulated in the sentence: "It was hell that gave me this half-talent of mine: heaven grants a whole one or none at all." And at least one passage recalls the ecstatically ambivalent, one-idea-laid-on-top-of-another rhythm of his stories:

> I myself, to be sure, have excited the expectations of others by certain uncommonly promising strides; and what should I now answer, when they ask how I have fulfilled them? And why *ought* I fulfill *their* expectations? O how burdensome it is—it may be true, I am some sort of failed genius, but failed not in their sense, but in my own. Knowledge, what is it? And if thousands excel me therein, do they excel what is in my heart?

A natural swaggerer, he also writes with a missionary's desire to make his evasive, inward-turning readers snap to. "Do not trust the feeling that tells you you cannot change," he writes to a friend in a letter of 1801, and his writings, from the full-dress plays in verse, through these carefully composed letters, to the generally short essays, form an encyclopedia of kinds of quickened feeling. Perhaps his most rounded formulation of this belief comes in a letter of 1806: "Every first motion, everything spontaneous is beautiful; but gnarled and crooked as soon as it comprehends itself." The Napoleonic Age was not a slothful moment, and it's likely that Kleist's dislike of introspection and his insistence, in his letters and essays, on why you must do what you feel (and think about it later) reflects the era. This attitude may also reflect his desire to escape his well-known shyness—he found it very difficult to speak fluently in public gatherings.

In his finished writings, though, he never says why it is crucial to follow your instincts. The impetuosity he describes seems to come out of nowhere. Even his characters are surprised by it. One of the reasons *The Prince of Homburg* and, to a lesser extent, his other plays are so airy and easy to read, and seem so unconnected to the literary conventions of the past, is the way that, as Kleist's major characters go into tailspins, the lesser characters stand back dubiously, with open mouths, and utter "What?"—usually at the same moments we are feeling "What?" The tailspins and abrupt turns in mood are more surprising and dreamlike in the stories, where there is often no dialogue, and the faintings and seductions are simply embedded in the this-is-what-happened-next flow. We're reading and suddenly his people bash each other's heads against the wall, they put pistols in their own mouths and do away with themselves.

But the undertow of his work isn't so optimistic. The story he wants to tell is about the impossibility of endeavors and the knightly beauty of failed things. His writings have been read as justifications of power and might over the individual, and it's not hard to see why. Though it is never his main point, he catches that moment when you feel patriotic for the first time—when you can be carried away by the idea of giving yourself to your country. Kleist blurs the distinctions between being a revolutionary and a reactionary. He writes as a junior, but one who understands the wavelengths of his seniors. His stories and plays say, in effect, "No, I will not be a general. But I will win the general's war for him." His longest story, and one of his most famous, "Michael Kohlhaas," set in the time of Martin Luther (who is a character in it), begins as a tale of a horse breeder, Kohlhaas, whose person and property are maltreated, with cavalier contempt and indifference, by the local nobility. Unable to have these wrongs redressed, even acknowledged, by following every available legal course open to him, and finally overwhelmed by the accidental yet brutal death of his wife, who has sought to deliver a petition in his behalf, he takes matters in his own hands and in a short time has become a rebel insurgent.

Kohlhaas is a good man, he has been manhandled, and we are on his side. His speed in becoming a warlord surprises us, though, and his ruthlessness and the arson and pillage his followers leave in their wake make us uncertain that he is doing the best thing. (Kohlhaas, though it does not literally mean coalhouse in German, was the model for Coalhouse Walker in *Ragtime*.) But then, in the last two-thirds of the story, which has the length of a short novel, he's moved to the side as we follow the wranglings of the many court chamberlains, princes, electors, and counts whose reputations, even lives, depend on the positions they take on what to do with Kohlhaas once he has been locked up. The reader feels at first that Kleist wants to show how independent, unrehearsed acts are crushed by the selfish schemes of the scared, deadwood juntas that keep things as they are. But it becomes clear that he has set up the story so he can also show how an old, entrenched, and sluggish power machine hauls itself into battle position, cleaning its house as it moves its troops to the front.

In an 1805 letter to a friend, Kleist says about a mutual friend, a writer, "It is strange, the powers that sometimes develop in a person while he strives to make use of quite other ones." The remark is prophetic, for he, too, in the shape of his career and in his vision, developed powers he hadn't set out to. He wanted to be a great lyric and tragic playwright, and his plays show how big his ambition was. But when his efforts as a playwright met with little success, he began to write stories, and he put the fleetest, most mysterious part of himself in them. He no doubt believed himself to be the poet of the individual, and he will always be best known for his confused, quicksilver, impetuous, and demanding young men and women. Yet he wrote about the families and court and state officials that cluster around his heroes and heroines with more sympathy than he himself may have been aware of.

Kleist became almost as great a poet of the family as he is of the child. Maybe this is why the themes of his stories and plays reveal themselves to us so slowly. Events in them move by with a Mercury-like dispatch, but, at the end, we feel we're not far from where we were at the beginning. I don't think this happens because Kleist is a chuckling ironist who wants to point out how no lasting changes can be made in the world. Nor does it happen because he has a tragic vision through and through. What he is after, I believe, is to get things back to where they once were. He is after the restoration of states which, on the chart of human development, come almost before childhood. He wants the parents of the world to tower over us as gods, to fill the roles of life-creators and protectors that they were given. There is an expendable, jerked-about, straw-man lightness to almost all Kleist's central characters, not only to Michael Kohlhaas but to the Prince of Homburg, to the Marquise of O—, to Toni, the fifteen-year-old mestizo heroine of "An Engagement in Santo Domingo," and to the weaselly Nicolo, the creep-hero of "The Foundling." But the figures of power and the older people in these and in his other works, who nurse and shout and banish and condemn, have an underlying stability and pleasing dignity. If Kleist had written *Hamlet,* he wouldn't have given the members of the court any more psychological depth than they have, nor would he have let them off the hook, but he probably would have made them more solid than they are. He might have made Polonius a charging monument to staleness rather than the windbag he is, and he might have given Claudius a conscience; you can imagine Kleist giving Claudius a disfiguring telltale skin disease and sending him off with it to a distant chamber in the castle, where he'd slowly scratch himself apart until, in the last act, he would be brought on to explain his deed.

And yet Kleist isn't an exonerator of authority. It's Kohlhaas, Toni, the Prince, the Marquise, and the others who are the true heroes and heroines, and who have the last word. Nervous, outgoing, generous, they are the ones who precipitate the action. They are the ones who shove their gone-to-sleep elders—generally the male figures—and leave them different, rejuvenated people. Kohlhaas brings out in his superiors a keen-wittedness and a sense of the precariousness of their positions and lives that, so it seems, are new for them. By her steadfastness, the Marquise eventually makes her rageful, rigid father a loving and humble man. Bringing the drowsed-down world back to its senses, Kleist's heroes and heroines, who are often virtuous and untested sons and daughters, even become the elders for the moment. Then, towering over all the other characters, yet suddenly purposeless and adrift, they surrender themselves to the newly roused authorities. They often go to their deaths, which in Kleist's scheme of things is even more desirable than having power in this world.

The jacket of *An Abyss Deep Enough* is a detail of Caspar David Friedrich's painting *Wanderer on the Fog-sea*, which shows a man in a dark suit, his back to us, his hair tousled, looking out over mountain peaks shrouded in fog. It is an apt choice for a Kleist collection, because his life and writing leave the image of a lone figure advancing into a frightening but enticing next world. Kleist rarely talks about death at length, but the subject is frequently at the edges of his thoughts, from the letters he wrote as a teenager on through. Miller has emphasized this aspect of Kleist with his title, and in placing the words ". . . not to be," from Hamlet's soliloquy, under the book's dedication (which is to Heinrich Blücher). A good majority of the two dozen anecdotes Miller has included in *An Abyss* are about death, too. These miniature tales, which first appeared in Kleist's newspaper, are often about how people meet with gruesome ends. They have come down to us because, says Miller, the complete run of the paper was carefully saved and stored by the Brothers Grimm, who lived two hundred miles from Berlin and subscribed to the *Abendblätter* mostly for what they called Kleist's "truly priceless anecdotes."

Told in a deliberately artless way, the anecdotes are a bit like the Brothers at their most concise and far-out—as in their "Mrs. Gertrude," where, in the course of its one paragraph, a headstrong little girl wanders into the wrong house and is transformed by the lady of the title into a log and thrown into the fire. Kleist's blackout tales don't have the same snap or cozy-and-scary atmosphere, but they are more contemporary in spirit. They're a little like the supposedly tasteless jokes about dying that some people can't help making—that they themselves are surprised they keep coming out with—at funerals. Though the anecdotes represent only an index finger's worth of his talent, they are worth reading, if only because they show what Kleist the man, not the literary artist, was like when he let it rip. There is a contemptuousness and cruelty in his tone that is unusual for him; he's giving death, and people who treat it with kid gloves, a good kick.

But in his letters, he lets death kick him. He is absorbed by death; he sees it as the ultimate awfulness, but he also keeps referring to it because, it seems, he likes the pressure. He carries the fact of his mortality with him the way kids sometimes take an object with them from their house—often an object they don't cherish, maybe even one they hardly look at—when they go away for a night or for a weekend. But then—it is hard to pinpoint where in the letters this happens—we sense him becoming too familiar with death; he talks about death as if it were the point, instead of the antithesis, of life; he turns it into a refuge from troubles, a place he wants to go to.

He makes you feel—or takes you back to a time when you felt—death in its purest, most physical form. Possibly that was at night, when you were in bed, and imagined what it would be like if one of your parents were to die. At the time, you don't tell yourself that you will have to die if your mother or father dies—you don't go that far; you are belted with the fuzzier, more enveloping idea that life, somehow, would have to stop; you feel you couldn't go on with your parents dead. The image may be so overwhelmingly awful that you banish it; it may be the first thought that you remember pushing out of your mind. It's possible that you will return to these feelings, though, if only because you don't understand why they weigh you down so. And when you're older you may look back and remember when you were troubled by them as a time when you really were walking on thin ice. You're glad you have replaced those fears with ones that are easier to handle; but you may wonder at the processes that keep you from finding death as awesomely terrible as you did as a child. You may even miss those early awarenesses, for their intensity. You may feel that life has grown over you, like moss, and that you have lost your capacity to feel the unknown, and how frightening the unknown is.

Kleist seems never to have lost those early awarenesses. That is part of his allure, especially if you come to him at a time when you are absorbed by the subject of suicide, and think of it as your secret weapon—when suicide seems to be the best way to tell the oblivious world how resolute, and how wronged, you have been. In his stories and in his person, Kleist epitomizes the daredevil, and also chivalrous, belief that life means something only when you can, as he says in a letter of 1802, "throw it away with a noble gesture." (It is a belief that men, possibly, are more drawn to than women.) But the reader of his correspondence is made to feel that this belief is less invigorating than wearying. It is an unintended gift of the letters that they show how a courtly, self-sacrificing spirit can corrode a man.

In the letters from his last year, and especially in those from his last days, which the editor has entitled "The Suicide Letters," Kleist is still traveling through the regions of pure feeling for us, and now he is in the land where the sky is always arctic blue. These few letters have a different cast from the others, though. He writes about his last feelings with the lidless extra vision he saw in Friedrich's art. Kleist's words say that he is happy to be leaving this world, but what is heard isn't happiness, it's the voice of someone on a rhapsodic spree. He speaks as if he himself has finally become one of his Machiavellian, knife-carrying heroes when, in a letter to Marie von Kleist, his cousin through marriage, he bids her "Good-bye! You are the one, the only one on earth whom I wish to see again in the beyond. Ulrike too?— Yes and no; yes, and no; no, and yes: I leave it to her own feelings." In this letter, or when, say, he writes to Henriette Vogel about how she means everything to him—and sounds as if he wants, with his river of short sentences, to hypnotize both of them in the process—he seems to be no more than his originality; he is spirit stripped of matter and ready to take off.

These letters do not stir you, they don't make you feel that you have lost a friend, as Vincent van Gogh's last letters to his brother Theo do. But then we rarely feel that Kleist seeks to clasp hands with anybody—we are drawn to him despite the fact that we never quite feel he's addressing us. There is a skipped moment in his conception of people. Though not all his works literally take place at night, many leave the impression of being set in a sexual pitch-dark, a milieu where you might not know—you might not even be able to see fully—your partner, and where you might not wake from the encounter. The image left by one of his best stories, "An Engagement in Santo Domingo," is of a long Caribbean night, when it is too dangerous to go to sleep, everyone carries a lantern, and no one knows if the next face they raise their light to see will be a white man's or a black man's or, regardless of its color, the last face they will ever see.

Kleist breaks through his period—he draws right up to where we are now—because sex in his world is a detonation, a boom that makes you forget who you are. Yet you want him to take his world further, out beyond the enclosure where, when people come together, there can only be rape, instant seduction, or, as in his engrossing and awkward play *Penthesilea*, a colossal infatuation that feeds on itself until the sexually bloated but still untouched heroine staggers away to her death. Few of the characters who mean most to him live beyond sex. He presents the courtly devotion a man pays to a woman as a powerful and all-encompassing bond, and his long-married couples have the same trust in, and believable affection for, each other as the wise and benevolent kings and queens of fairy tales. But when men and women come together for him it is a thunderclap without rain, a fuzzied shock moment that sends both parties away still thirsty.

There was a knot at the center of Kleist's feelings, and it wouldn't come undone—it got only tighter. He seems to have felt himself so alone in the world that he never quite believed fame, during his life or posthumously, would be possible. But he couldn't stop thinking about whether and how he would be remembered; any romance, with any person or thing, in the here and now, was pale in comparison with the affair history might have with his name. He was turning the no-win situation over in his mind from his earliest days. In a letter of 1800 to Wilhelmine, when he was still uncertain of how he would make his mark, and had not yet seriously entertained the idea of being a writer, he wrote that he didn't know how Christ would have been able to be crucified if he hadn't been able to see his mother and disciples, with their "moist glances of rapture," down there beneath him. In a letter to Ulrike from the year before, he wondered how Socrates, too, faced the problem. How can a man be a hero if there is nobody there to appreciate it? His instincts told him that nobody would be there for him, that his message would go unrecognized.

His instincts were right. Miller says that even in Germany Kleist is still a hazy name for most people. But the instincts that made him wonder about Christ and Socrates were right, too, because he is an author whose readers feel unusually close to him; they are a following, almost. It's likely Kleist's importance will never be taken for granted. He may always be a personal discovery for each reader. On the day of his death, he wanted to make it clear that he had no illusions that even his friends would remember him fondly; he wrote Marie, "There was a moment when I decided to have a portrait painted; but then it seemed to me again that I have done you too much wrong ever to be able to expect that my picture would give you much pleasure."

He left a portrait, though, in *The Prince of Homburg*. All of his writings comprise a portrait of his feelings, of course, but this play, the last work he left in complete form, is the grandest, most ample single presentation of him. (It was given its American premiere in New York in 1976 by Robert Kalfin, at the Chelsea Theater Center, with Frank Langella as the Prince, and broadcast on TV the following year.) The play can make you feel physically lighter, as Kleist's letters do. Almost everything Kleist wrote makes you feel as if all your bodily sensations have rushed to your head, leaving the rest of you airy, tingling, sucked-out. But this play also leaves you feeling as if a heavenly softness has come into you. It follows the fortunes of Prince Friedrich Arthur of Homburg, an impetuous young warrior-nobleman. In his letters, Kleist is fond of saying that he would be satisfied if he could achieve roughly three things in life (he keeps changing his mind about what they are). Then, he says, he would be ready to die. His Prince wants essentially three things, too: to serve his country, to be swooningly in love, and, most of all, to keep a jutting, actorish profile on his actions at all times.

The Prince is a wonderful character; he has the dimension of Hamlet or Heathcliff. Though he is in great straits for nearly all of the play, he has an underlying sunny enthusiasm. He gives you an idea of what Hamlet or Heathcliff might have been like if they didn't have cause to be angry or to feel insulted. Guilty of not following orders at a crucial juncture during a battle, he is sentenced to die, even though his last-minute storming of the enemy's fortifications and demolition of their troops have secured the victory. We're at the Battle of Fehrbellin, it's 1675, and codes of honor and duty say he must be punished; but the codes can be brushed aside, and his superior, the Elector, who has long watched over him as if he were his own son, is willing to play a power game with him. He will let the Prince go if he says he has been treated unfairly—if he, in effect, begs for his freedom.

There are many tracks in the play. At least two subsidiary characters, out of their affection and growing love for the Prince, pull strings to have a stay of execution; and the Prince, meanwhile, has been going through a personal revolution. First, he believes his imprisonment is a joke and a formality. Then he learns that the Elector means to stand by the codes of military behavior, and this erases every moonstruck and chivalrous thought he ever had. He acts the way heroes aren't supposed to act, but the way you suspect you might act at such a moment: he goes straight to the Electress, whom he calls his aunt and who raised him after the death of his mother, and begs her to intercede. He's frightened, crying, and on his knees so quickly we laugh at him before we understand that he's in a cold sweat.

He announces that he will give up every bit of self-respect, including his claims on the Princess Natalia, his fair lady. He conjures up an image of total surrender for himself: he will go off to his estates in the Rhineland and work on them, as the most dutiful and obscure of private citizens, until his death; he will go through a living death so as not to have to suffer a real one. But later, when he's given the terms of his release, he realizes that he can't allow himself to go so limp; he can't bring himself to defend and explain what he has done. Deciding that he doesn't want a pardon, he's filled with a new command of himself and the situation. He entirely forgets that he will have to face the firing squad the next day. He feels himself a true prince, and he feels aligned with the Elector, too, as one member of the nobility to another. He sees an aristocratic generosity in the Elector's offer that the Elector hadn't intended.

Constructed with an elegant symmetry and the teacup-and-saucer lightness of a drawing-room comedy, *The Prince of Homburg* streams to its conclusion; it moves so fast, and ties together its dramatic elements so neatly, that it is only after you have seen or read it that you are aware of how many solid, big shifts have been made. The Prince has touched his own depths, and, without knowing it—though we are aware of it—he has made the Elector, who tears up the order of execution at the last minute, a bigger man. Kleist doesn't tell us enough about the Princess to enable us to know if her shrewd and courageous behavior is new for her, but we are led to believe that, in making one quick-witted deal after another with the Prince, the Elector, and the army, in behalf of the two men she loves and her country, she, too, has become emotionally ennobled.

And what may be the play's true climax occurs when we're hardly aware of it. At one moment toward the end, when the Prince is expected by the assembled court to arrive and plead his case, we're told that he will be a little late—he has stopped by the cemetery gates, and is looking in at the grave being dug for him. The image is reminiscent of many paintings by Friedrich, the master painter of mortality-gazers. When this seeming nonevent is reported, we feel only that the play has paused, to take a breath of air. Later, Kleist's reason for inserting it becomes apparent. For it is only when the Prince lingers by the cemetery, and we imagine a smile beginning to spread on his face as he's engaged by his new role, that it sinks in that he has diffused death's power. He has fallen in love with it, the way he earlier fell in love with the Princess and his charge into battle. The point isn't that he looks forward to his execution—it's that death is no longer the terrifying unknown. There are no more unknowns for him. He is ready now, as never before, to live his life.

Kleist wrote *The Prince of Homburg* with few expectations of seeing it put on stage. During his lifetime, not one of his plays was performed as he wrote it. The closest he got was when Goethe, without informing him, mounted a production of *The Broken Jug* that had no resemblance to the play and was a fiasco, and when parts of *Penthesilea*, chosen and arranged by someone other than Kleist, were read at what he calls a "rehearsal." In light of this, it's all the more remarkable that there is such an expressive ease to *The Prince of Homburg*. Built like a drawing-room comedy, it has the breadth of Shakespearean tragedy; yet it's too flashy and fast to be one or the other—it is too touching one moment, and too frightening the next, to take a proper place in the ranks of great literature. Only an imposing author could have brought it off, yet Kleist wrote it with the desire, which is in so many of his letters, to stare down the life-and-death dilemmas. In a more direct way than many plays that are earlier and later than it in date, *The Prince of Homburg* makes you feel as if it is all happening to you. Kleist takes you back, to relive your worst childhood fears, and then pulls you through them and out to the other side, where those fears can be smiled at.

Kleist's own death was a cold and forlorn scene, yet he must have died knowing that, in the small but bursting collection of stories, plays, essays, and pieces of journalism he had produced with such speed, he had expressed the longings and doubts he had been turning over in his mind since he was a teenager. He may have been aware, too, that, whether he wanted them or not, new themes were bubbling up in him, and that, to treat them, he might have to alter the tone of his work. Maybe the awareness that he would have to face another, and more devilish, period of groping was one of the things that drove him to take his life—that, along with the censorship difficulties with French and Prussian officials that forced him to cease publication of his newspaper, and the crucial loss of patronage he suffered with the death of Queen Louise, one of the few people he is known to have revered. His career was dedicated to the beauty of first feelings. But in fashioning the life and near-death of the Prince of Homburg, he wrote in praise, too, of second thoughts. He found himself saying good things about the philosophical reflectiveness that had always been very much a part of his nature. The deepest message of the play is that it is possible to be loyal to both spirits at the same time—you can be less pure than you expected to be and still be strong. Perhaps Kleist believed that his changing sense of things would have sapped him, as a man and a writer. On the basis of *The Prince of Homburg*, though, it's likely that he wasn't about to lose his core subject. Few writers have shown how swift a sword the fervor of youth can be. At the end of his life, Kleist may have been on the verge of showing the different power and freedom you gain by growing up.

—1983

ANSELM KIEFER, JOSEPH BEUYS, AND THE GHOSTS OF THE FATHERLAND

THE PAINTINGS ANSELM KIEFER showed in November at the Mary Boone Gallery in New York are huge by any standards, but you feel so much easy, flowing energy in his arm, and it takes so little time to adjust to their scope, that you wish they were bigger. The pictures, most of which are landscapes, are all at least nine feet high and ten or twelve feet across; *Landschaft mit Flügel*—or *Landscape with Wing*—the largest painting in the show, is a bit more than ten feet high and a little over eighteen feet wide. The sizes themselves aren't record-breaking; American artists have been working with roughly similar dimensions since the forties. But Kiefer's paintings of orangy-yellow fields are big in a new and different way. They aren't wall-like, they don't resemble vast, friezelike Oriental screens, and they don't convey a sense of unruffled, intimidating power. If anything, they're close to the paintings from the Romantic era in the Louvre, the ranks of Géricaults, Delacroixs, and Courbets that make you gulp and then laugh the first time you see them because you never imagined paintings this big. Kiefer's landscapes have the same combination of earnestness and theatricality. They're the work of someone who has an almost hollow, yet engaging way of announcing that he must work big because he has great material in him.

Now thirty-seven, Anselm Kiefer has been talked of for the past few years as possibly the most distinctive and original of the many new German painters. In a report in the September-October 1982 *Portfolio* on the summer's Documenta 7 show in Kassel, Gerald Marzorati wrote that Kiefer's new landscapes stole the mammoth international exhibition and that the painter's "name was repeated around the tables like a mantra." The seven paintings he showed in New York, all of which were made in 1981, bear out Marzorati's report in more ways than he intended. Because there is something you want to be drawn into, and, later, pulled out from, about Kiefer's paintings. Enthralling and bleak at the same time, they're like a visit to a great cathedral on a winter's afternoon, when the light is sunless and white, snow is in the air, and you have the place to yourself. As you go away, you may believe that you have taken the sacred and sad drama into yourself, and that it has ennobled and elevated you; later, though, you may be left with a feeling that your experience can't be made part of the rest of your life, and that it sucks out from you more than it gives.

Kiefer has exhibited in New York twice before, most recently in April 1982 when he also showed good-sized landscapes with high horizons, where the broken soil seemed to be rising up and about to topple down on us. In their presentation of a gashed and violated earth, those primarily black and rust-brown pictures had a poetic and psychological depth that no recent American landscape painting could match. (They made you wonder why American landscapists have been meek and blandly lyrical and impersonal for so long.) Kiefer's paintings kept some viewers at a coolly admiring distance, though; a bit too pointedly grim and dark-toned, they were original but less moving than they had it in them to be. The paintings he showed in November were made around the same time as those he showed in April, yet, consistently larger and brighter in color, and containing more references to German life—such as a title from a

Wagner opera or the name of a German city, which he paints right onto the canvases—they felt as if they were from a less cooped up, more liberated time in his life.

These are pictures you want to linger with, in part because Kiefer is a big and still relatively unknown personality. They hold you mostly, though, because the moods of the individual pictures keep shifting, from something enraptured to something trampled. The images themselves keep going in and out of focus, too, no matter what distance they're viewed from. Kiefer often works with straw and sand and bits of string, which he paints over or lays on top of the paint (and, on occasion, on top of blown-up, indistinct black and white photographs, which are stapled to the canvas). In some paintings, the straw is meant to be itself, straw in a field, while in others it seems to be used primarily for its flamelike color and crinkly texture. But whether there are bale-sized chunks of it or merely strands of it here and there, Kiefer doesn't seem to be doing anything more than sloshing around the straw, paint, and bits of string as if in a shallow bowl, like a prospector tipping and tilting his pan, looking for gold.

Never attempting to be realistic, he yet always creates the illusion of a furrowed, wet, believable earth. He rarely spells out that these pictures are about war, either, yet he suggests nearly every aspect of it. Looking at his landscapes, we feel that we're simultaneously foot soldiers and pilots. We feel that our faces are about two inches from the mucky ground and that we're also soaring high above it. In *Landschaft mit Flügel*, he has hung an enormous bird's wing, made out of lead, from the top of the canvas. Hanging down on two narrow cords, like a medal on a pilot's chest, the matte, hammered-out, pale gray wing makes the splotchy tan and black landscape of ploughed fields and distant marshland look sparkling and seem miles and miles beneath us. We believe that there is a whole bird there, guiding our path as we fly across the vast landscape. We're reminded of the magpie, with wings outstretched, that glides across the cold winter sky in Bruegel's *Hunters in the Snow*, leading the hunters and their dogs back into the village. And yet Kiefer's picture has an intimate quality, too; it's like a large version of a display that might be found in a glass case in a war museum. It's like a browning old photograph of an obscure battlefield that a museum curator has thought to decorate with a shredded object found on that field.

The one time Kiefer goes at the war directly, though, in *Innenraum*, he falters. The only work that isn't a landscape and doesn't suggest the outdoors, this essentially black, white, and brown painting shows an immense room that has dark, imageless panels on the walls, a gridded floor, and a gridded ceiling. We believe we are in a once grand stateroom that was always forbidding and is seen here in the moment before it will collapse or go up in flames. The trouble is that we register this too quickly. We're too immediately reminded of the chilling and ugly grandeur of fascist architecture; Albert Speer's *Inside the Third Reich* has a photograph of the reception hall of Hitler's Chancellery (which he designed), taken after the hall was destroyed—it was clearly the basis of Kiefer's painting. Maybe it's because Kiefer worked so closely from a photograph that *Innenraum*, though it is roughly as large as the other paintings in the show, is so puny and tight in scale and proportions. And maybe because the image is so photographic in feeling, his approach seems illustrational. He isn't doing more than dolling up an existing image by spreading viscous and bedraggled materials over it. He isn't telling us anything about Nazi wreckage that we don't already know. But in his landscapes, he reveals the Second World War, as a subject, in a pleasurably slow and indirect way, and he blends it in with other events and themes in German history. Loamy and ravaged, his images of straw-bestrewn earth feel as if they have in them mixed together the bequests of Hitler and Wagner and everyone else going back in time to the elves and trolls of the Teutonic forest primeval.

Kiefer appears to be flaunting his Germanness, and he has been criticized for this in his homeland. According to the catalogue for his retrospective held at the Folkwang Museum in Essen in 1981 (which traveled, though with some changes in the selection of pictures, to the Whitechapel Art Gallery in London in the spring of 1982), his countrymen have objected to his art over the years because, in their eyes, he's flirting with the ghosts of the Fatherland. Certainly he doesn't keep his material at an oblique or satirical distance. He doesn't want to tell us about the stunted, garbled lives that crawled out of the war, as does, say, Georg Baselitz, whose upside-down heads and figures are painted with a chicken-claw hand in squawking colors. And he doesn't show the tensions in his divided country, as does, say, Jörg Immendorff, whose cartoonlike epics are often set in a sweatier version of the same glittering and disillusioning cabaret that Christopher Isherwood's and George Grosz's characters met at.

Kiefer wants to work from the vantage point of an innocent, a troubadour-knight who composes elegies for the tragedy of all German history and, maybe too, of all European history. *Balders Traum*, of an immense, black and tan field, flecked with red, from which hangs a large, yellowed branch of what is probably mistletoe (it is attached from behind the canvas), has a benedictory, moment-of-silence breadth that makes us feel that the image has as much to do with the futile waste of the First World War—or any war—as the victories or defeats of the Second. The picture seems to be less about a specific site than a re-creation of a moment when everything was lost, to no purpose.

Kiefer's wounded-soil romanticism is unsettling to his fellow Germans and it leaves us up in the air, too. He is a tricky artist to judge. You believe that, even before he has thought through his individual works, he knows the effect he's after: he wants the members of his audience to bury their differences in the presence of his pictures, to be hushed, to walk out of the gallery with their heads bowed. He seems to be a liberal by temperament who is turning to his like-minded friends and saying, with the quiet, calm voice of someone who knows he has the final word, "There are emotions, you know, that go deeper than our political ideals, and unite us with all men." He is giving us the same stultifyingly fatalistic message, which is supposed to make us feel anonymous but also good, and which puts us in the position of a little boy, looking up at and honoring his father, that Michael Cimino wanted to leave us with in his movie *The Deer Hunter.*

Yet Kiefer does something positive and breezy in telling us that we don't have to tiptoe around the German past. You like the way he lumbers along at his own backwoodsman's pace, unfazed by the fact that so many painters, writers, and movie directors have treated everything that has happened in Germany between the twenties and today as if it were a gruesome dream or a self-consciously tacky, melodramatic farce. He is pious, but his piety doesn't sum him up. The viewer feels that, on some level, Kiefer's lofty resignation is no deeper than a decal to him. It is a jazzy idea that makes him hot and provides him with the spur to do what he most wants—which is to bowl us over with pictures of overarching immensity.

When he writes "Nürnberg-Festspiel-Wiese" across the sky in *Nürnberg,* he may be supplying the work with the key to its meaning. Even if we have a literal translation and gather that he's referring to a festival and the fields connected with the medieval city, we assume that the words are loaded with outside references, especially since Nuremberg was the site of Hitler's most famous rally and also of the war crimes trials. But there is something so appealing about the awkward formality with which Kiefer has written these words that we bypass their connotations and take them in as lovely elements in the composition. The script has the simplicity of the letters you would see on a blackboard in kindergarten; the lettering seems to emanate from the child's-toy, wood-block houses and village church with a steeple, drawn in a mock-crude, Fauvish style, on the horizon line of the painting.

When he writes "Die Meistersinger" in the clouds that are above the field in *Die Meistersinger,* he may be saying that it's time for Germany to stretch its Wagnerian muscles and take pride in its past once again. Or he may be saying, "Look what Wagner and his lofty conceptions have brought us to—a rank field, a moldy legacy." Yet when you see the words Die Meistersinger up in the pale blue and cloudy white sky, your immediate response, unless you come equipped with thoughts about this opera, is that the title has an audaciously grandiloquent ring, and that it fits this mightily proportioned, straw-embowered, orange-black European landscape in the same corny and stirring way that Ile de France fits a transatlantic luxury liner, or that Man O'War fits a racehorse. Putting the words Die Meistersinger up in the narrow strip of sky of a landscape that has clumps of brushy straw all over it, Kiefer emphasizes how much of an object—almost a living, breathing object—rather than a painting, this is. We feel the distant trees, the fields, and the sky together as one noble, immense, silent creature, one that might raise itself on its haunches and slowly move away.

Kiefer's paintings have a special power for many people of his generation, and not only his fellow Germans, because they put in an unexpectedly stately form some of that generation's most potent—and least precise—early memories. Especially if you were born during the Second World War or in its wake (as Kiefer, born in 1945, was), his landscapes prod you with the idea that there are feelings stored up in you about the war and about your own past that may be more rhapsodic than, and are certainly different from, those that have been presented over the years, and that your generation alone possesses. For many kids growing up in the late forties and early fifties, in this country and in Europe, countless daydreams, and sometimes bad dreams, were set in a Second World War milieu that we knew from TV documentaries, picture books, photo spreads in magazines, and movies. I pored over the pages on Hitler and the Third Reich in my World Book encyclopedia when I was, I suppose, in the early years of grade school, and one of the first books that I knew was for grown-ups but that I remember feeling was as much—or even more—for me was a picture history of the Second World War, published by *Life*. It was a large, heavy volume with thick, glossy paper and a red, leatherlike cover.

The images that held me most were Hitler's face, the enormous, narrow banners with swastikas in the center, and the Nazi helmets. The helmets, which made those of the American soldiers seem clean-cut, and those of the British soldiers quaint, were most frightening and mesmerizing in the pictures of the Nuremberg rally, where the helmeted troops, lined up in rows, seemed to go off into infinity. The rally pictures never became stale or dull; I always imagined that I was actually at the rally, caught in the ranks, and then I would be faced with the same dilemmas: How will I manage not to be seen? How do I get out?

Even more trance-inducing was Hitler's face. Whenever I looked at him in the World Book, I sensed I was doing something that should be kept secret; I had a hunch that people would wonder and worry about me if it were known that I spent so much time reading about and scrutinizing him. He was one of the first people, living or dead, who made me feel embarrassed about something in myself. What made me keep returning to him had to do with a test I gave myself. I think I wanted to see how I would stand up, facing such badness and ugliness. Would I give in? Could I fall under his power? Did I really like him? That was the one impossible thing—that I would develop some feeling for him. Whenever I opened to his page in the World Book, the same tension sprang out. He must have represented the cockeyed, crazy essence of the foreign, adult, outside world.

Germany was the country of some of our most frightened childhood feelings—it was a kind of negative Narnia or Oz, because its villains, the Nazis, were so purely evil. But it wasn't only scary. Identifying yourself, if only for a flicker of a barely conscious moment, with sleek and impassive Nazis allowed you to mentally mow down all of the people in your life who always did the right thing and won every point. Vanquished in history's two biggest wars, Germany also stood, perhaps especially for boys who weren't yet adolescent, and who were more interested in the fact of winning or losing than in the ideals that lie behind opposing sides, as a noble wreck. For a kid, whose life is full of monumental and permanent-seeming obstacles, it sometimes made you feel bigger and clearer about yourself to look out on things from the vantage point of the defeated. You didn't think you were a loser; you felt you were a winner, but in a way that wasn't so clear to others at the moment.

Based on what has been shown in the galleries in the past few years, there are no American—or Italian—artists Kiefer's age who have as powerful a connection with the war (or with landscape) as he does. The war isn't felt in the paintings of Julian Schnabel, who holds the same preeminent place among newer American painters that Kiefer does among German ones, and who works with the same vast, Homeric sizes. But Kiefer, with his images of tank-ridden and fertile fields, presented in ashy and golden colors, is only making more explicit the despair-loving, heroically hopeless mood that is in the work of many of his contemporaries. Many artists now seem to want to convey some version of the saddened romance that the German past and the Second World War have given Kiefer. It is as if artists want to re-create experiences that they themselves didn't have directly but whose aftereffects are swimming around inside them.

The man who has possibly more of those heroically hopeless experiences in him—or has preserved them best—is Joseph Beuys. Kiefer studied with Beuys between 1970 and 1972, and Kiefer's landscapes are, in part, a salute to his teacher. Kiefer's paintings don't resemble specific works by Beuys, and there aren't details in them that can be called borrowings from him. But Beuys's spirit hovers over these landscapes, and, if you are acquainted with his art, it's hard not to think of him as a kind of invisible, ghostly character in them. Beuys is no doubt the most significant artist Germany has produced since Max Beckmann, and, in a way, he has become influential for doing exactly the opposite of what Beckmann did. Beckmann became the foremost German painter of the first half of the century because he assiduously internationalized his art; his work stands as a model of how an Expressionist was able to recharge and replenish his viewpoint over many decades by absorbing the un-Expressionist lessons of classic French painting. Beuys has gone in the other direction. He has become more and more of an influence for Europeans and, in the past five or so years, for Americans, too, because he has slipped his own sensuous and oblique brand of German soulfulness back into the mainstream.

Much of his career is based on a single event that happened during the Second World War. In 1943, his combat plane crashed in the snow in a part of the Crimea that was aligned with neither the Soviet Union nor Germany. As the story goes, his buried, unconscious body, given up for lost by a German search party, was found by Tartars, who took him to their camp and revived him by swaddling him in fat and then wrapping him in felt. He returned home, to Cleves, which is near the German-Dutch border, after the war, and for a number of years gave himself to a time of nervous, listless self-absorption, much of it spent doing manual labor—cleaning stables, working in fields.

He emerged in the fifties, purified, apparently, of his lingering fright, and ready for action. He has gone on to re-create, in one form or another in much of his art, what happened to him in the Crimea when he was twenty-two. Many of his sculptural pieces, works on paper, and performances tell a story of death and rebirth, of being lost and cold and then saved and warmed. Going about the world for the past twenty or so years, lecturing at universities and public halls, staging his "actions," attempting to link arms with youth and to change its consciousness, he has been, despite his witch-doctor manner, as much a living example of Germany's return to life from the rubble as any of its politicians, industrial designers and engineers, or business executives.

And yet Beuys's idealistic politics, whether described by him in statements or interviews, or presented in straightforward seminars or group-therapy-like happenings, never seem to be truly what he stands for. His utopian, free-spirit belief that each of us is an artist has always seemed to be an ephemeral afterthought for him; his ardent, mystically positive social, aesthetic, and medical theories, which are linked together in his mind and which he diagrams on blackboards, like a football coach or a philosophy professor, have almost come across as a pose, and have helped to keep him a slightly unbelievable figure to Americans and even, possibly, to Europeans. What is real and tangible about him is his stricken yet dangerous presence. Beuys isn't someone you suspect you could, or would want to, have as a friend, but there is a blend of vanity, vulnerability, and deadness in him that makes you want to gaze at him and, if only for a while, float into his sphere.

He once did a number of collages which incorporated the image of Greta Garbo, taken from photographs. As artworks, these pieces are stillborn and silly—an artist with a regular-size ego would have filed them away in a cabinet in the studio. But it's clear why he was drawn to her, and why he was trying to bring her into his domain. Because Beuys must realize that he himself is equal to, or perhaps more important than, the sum of his individual works, and that, like the stars of silent movies, his greatest piece of poetical equipment is his face. The most extraordinary photographs of him are those taken in his youth, in the years after the war, just as he was getting underway as an artist. There is a wonderful snapshot of him from this time in

Caroline Tisdall's catalogue for his 1979 Guggenheim retrospective and another, more posed picture in the suavely produced, book-length catalogue, published last year, of works belonging to the German collector Erich Marx.

With his hair cropped close and his shirt buttoned all the way to the top, in the photo from the Guggenheim catalogue, he could pass as the creep at school who was always off on his own and yet who also made you feel as if he could be listening in for the teachers. He might also be taken as a former member of Hitler Youth, still at the ready, his body tense and Doberman-like, and yet now glazed-over in his eyes, lost within himself. Scared and sad, and seemingly in love with his haunted beauty, he appears, for American audiences anyway, as a European Montgomery Clift—a Clift, that is, who could also be wily and devilish, and who could easily spend a night or two off by himself in a forest, with nothing around him but his leather jacket, sustained by the nuts he might crack open and eat indifferently.

Beuys probably believes that the core of his work is in what he calls his "actions"—his generally slow-paced, often frightening performance pieces, where his stiff movements suggest a wind-up doll that forever seems to be creaking out its few final steps. There is another Beuys, though, a less arresting but equally mysterious and poetic man found in his pencil drawings, watercolors, and oils on paper. And it is in these pieces, though they don't represent his most formidable efforts, and are among his earliest mature works, that he presents the same moody, penetrating, and transfixed side of himself that is in those early photographs. It is the side of him that most haunts Kiefer's work, I think, and that of some American painters now, too, particularly Julian Schnabel.

A number of Beuys's whisper-soft, sketchy graphites were at his retrospective at the Guggenheim. The most memorable were those that looked to be abstractions at first glance, but which included, buried in the scumbled lines, images of, among other things, women and noble yet bony and wilted stags. The sketches appeared to be as frail and precious, as objects, as the few drawings which remain by some of the early Renaissance masters—Pisanello, in particular. Beuys's drawings were surprisingly similar to the northern Italian painter's drawings in spirit, too. Beuys's images seemed to be so many fragmentary, twisted, shell-shocked versions of Pisanello's world of leggy princesses, nomadic horsemen, and pensive stags—that heraldic world where the satiny, carved, and gilded beauty of the medieval castles is a stone's throw from the uncivilized beauty of the mountainous pine forests that surround the walled castles. Seeing Beuys's exquisite drawings, many of which were delicately touched with color, sometimes pale purple, you had a glimmer of how much his work is about a yearning to create a modern version of that heraldic world, a kind of outpost realm that is lawless and fierce and calls to us, too.

The best place to see that realm is in three superbly produced, large-format, hard-to-find volumes devoted to his work on paper that have been brought out in Germany over a period of years by different publishers, under the direction of Heiner Bastian. The first volume, of pencil drawings, is in German only; the second and third, of watercolors and oil pastels respectively, are in English and German. The writing is by Franz Joseph and Hans van der Grinten, brothers who have collected these works. The van der Grintens are close friends of Beuys's and also come from Cleves. Their lengthy descriptions of the individual pieces, at least as translated into English, amount to elevated gobbledygook, but that doesn't matter. The viewer doesn't especially want the images, the majority of which are from the fifties, to be explained. It's more pleasurable to go back to these books each time as if to a hoard of illustrations to nursery rhymes or tales of chivalry made by an artist whose mind was set to wandering, and who came up with pictures that, in their own unhinged way, are so many new versions of the rhymes and tales.

Beuys's drawings and paintings create a setting where abstraction and representation slide in and out of each other so easily that you forget that they were ever thought to be different. He moves from barely decipherable images of, say, a sled or a bee seen in magnified close-up or a boat tossing in a harbor or a nude woman at rest to pages that appear to be no more than studies of vapor or of fiery, phosphorescent textures. And while these disparate images don't relate to each other in any clear way, and don't, taken one by one, quite stand up on their own, they seem to connect and tell a story. Even the purely abstract pieces feel as if they contain messages. With their novel and delicious combinations of copper tans and waxy earth browns, surprisingly sensuous grays and metallic yellows, blushing strawberry reds and assorted blues, ivories, and smoky purples, these works, many of which are on pieces of scrap paper, suggest off-the-cuff distillations of remembered events or transformations of theories and thoughts into color. The viewer senses that there is a code underlying the images, and that if the code were broken we might see, among other things, what happened to Beuys in the Crimea, what it was like for him to return to Cleves, and how he turned his memories into one man's private mythology.

It isn't necessary to know anything about Beuys's biography, though, to believe that these pictures are about an unhappy period for him. With their sweeping, curtainlike washes, and the emphatically fragile and weirdly tiny figures that sometimes appear in the washes, the images leave the impression of someone whose life was cloaked and hidden. The variety and spontaneity of the pieces imply that Beuys was reluctant to give up his hiddenness; he may even have wanted to perpetuate it. Though it's apparent, from his not making something full-fledged out of any of them, that he was impatient, too, and that he was working to release himself. If the underlying confusion and fear expressed in these paintings and drawings seep into you, you know why Beuys has wanted to bring more of the real, outside world into his art. The smothered and scarred quality of these works also hints at why he is a torn personality: a man who has the greatest artistic energies and is determined to leave art works behind him, and yet who, out of a belief that art itself is a paltry thing, is inclined to stomp on and leave in a decaying and rubbled state many of the things he produces.

Anselm Kiefer isn't struggling to relieve himself of unhappy and somber memories—he's searching them out. There is a father-and-son rightness—and edgy wrongness—about the way Kiefer complements and alters Beuys's themes. Beuys has always wanted to enchant people, and he has been successful at it in a variety of mediums. Yet,

whether because of the grueling and chaotic conditions of his youth
and early manhood or other reasons, Beuys himself seems unenchant-
able. Without being cynical, he is a very professional shaman; his
professionalism is there in his face, which is lost in its own spheres and
is simultaneously appraising the degree of our lostness. Kiefer, at least
in his work, doesn't have that wary eye. He makes art about his own
enchanted absorption with his sorrowful material, and he hopes his
audience will be carried aloft, as he is.

Yet Kiefer seems to be holding back some part of himself. His
pictures make us hungry for something we can't quite name. It's not
that they are formally incomplete, or that we wish he had included
figures in his images. An actual figure in any of the landscapes, or in
Innenraum, the interior, would be ruinous. It's that there is a starved
and yearning quality about these works. (This may be why, though
they're monumental in size, our eyes take them in so quickly, and we
wish that they could be even larger.) It's as if he has made so many
great settings that now await the man or woman who will measure up
to them and, emotionally, complete them. It's almost as though he has
made sets for Joseph Beuys to finally let himself go in, to lope through
as the hero that Kiefer—and, possibly, his generation in Europe—
may have been longing for, and would love to have in their midst.

Looking at Beuys's work and at the numerous photographs of him
that have been published, you understand why Kiefer would want to
lay down some part of his spirit for this man. Like the ashen-faced,
enfeebled King Arthur, Beuys says to us, his knights, "Find the
Grail. Relieve me. Bring life back to this winter-bound kingdom."
More than he himself is probably aware of, Beuys implores us to help
him lift the damper from his zombied soul. On the rare times when he
has been photographed in a jubilant (or even pleased) moment, his
pent-up sexual glamour pours forth, and, whether you admire his
work or not, you feel that a weight has been lifted from your shoulders,
too. There is a photograph of such a moment in his Guggenheim
catalogue. It was taken in 1976, after his students rowed him across
the Rhine in what was presumably one of his "action" pieces. Striding
along the rocky beach in Düsseldorf, swirling into his arms the
hooded cloak that he wore when he stood at the prow of the boat

during the crossing (there's a photograph of him in the boat, too), he has a big, beautiful, gleaming smile. Though there is no one else in the picture, you sense that he is moving toward other people, just outside the frame of the picture, who are as buoyed up as he is.

If German artists have few peers at portraying unhappiness, they have also given world art some of its most memorable images of happiness. It is not an everyday or a passionate kind. Best seen in the paintings of the Romantic landscapist Caspar David Friedrich, it comes at certain softened, early-morning moments, when the world appears newly washed and the sun is felt rather than seen. This happiness doesn't exist in Beuys's sculptural pieces or in his works on paper, which seem to absorb rather than radiate light. But it's felt in Kiefer's art, especially when he includes skies and clouds in some of his high-horizoned landscapes. In Kiefer's scheme of things, these details are probably no more than finishing touches, and he hardly draws them in a clear-cut way—he merely lathers on his blues and whites. Yet each time I saw his show, it was these clumps and globs of fleecy white and of a pale royal blue, a steely Prussian blue, and a serene slate blue that my eyes settled on, and that I didn't want to stop lapping up. No recent artist has made me want to stare so long and appreciatively at sky and clouds.

When Kiefer paints skies and clouds, he seems to be attempting to bring the beautiful into his art. Evidently this is a difficult thing for him. It probably doesn't square with his desire to encompass the past or to be honest about being a German today. Yet you sense that part of him wants to paint more of the natural world's warmth, and you wish he would. It is a big achievement to make us live through the old German painfulness in a new way, as he has. His bigger accomplishment, though, may be in painting a new version of German beauty.

—1983

DAVID HOCKNEY

WHEN DAVID HOCKNEY showed his photographs for the first time, at the Sonnabend Gallery in New York in 1976, the striking thing was that they had what his paintings, drawings, and prints lacked—the light and texture of the real world. His subjects were the same as those in his canvases and graphic work: a nude boy with a beautiful body, seen from the rear, in a bathroom; a couple of good-looking Panama hats, placed, along with an afternoon tea service, on wicker chairs; the entrance to a Mediterranean beach, caught at a hazy and fragrant moment, probably after the day's activities are over. The surprise and pleasure of the show came from seeing the actual bodies, objects, and places that, in so much of his other work, led such a juiceless, tepidly stylized existence.

The photographs left a mellow memory on their own, too. By the standards of other photographers (and of most other painters whose photographs are known to the public), Hockney's photos, all of which were in color, were old-fashioned and unexperimental. It was clear that he didn't like to play with light—he wanted only sufficient light for his immediate needs—and so his pictures had a toasted, golden tonality, a kind of Kodak glow, and a lack of crisp, stark definitions. In appearance, his elegantly composed photos weren't so different from those an advertising firm would use to make us want to run off to some corner of Europe (or, in the case of the nudes, to buy a cologne). Yet these mild, even commercial factors combined to make the pictures refreshing. Hockney's seeming lack of interest in the art of photography, combined with the fact that his subjects clearly absorbed him regardless of whether or not he caught them with a camera, gave his photos a distinct place in the field of recent photography. His smooth and friendly snaps, it seemed, might even be able to hold their own next to the work of photojournalists and art photographers; in that company, his photos might stand up in the same way that paintings by some naive artists hold their own alongside the canvases of trained painters.

In 1982 Hockney showed his more recent photographs, which were Polaroids, at the André Emmerich Gallery in New York, and while this show didn't make as vivid an impression as the first, it led some people, especially those who find his worldwide fame a livelier topic than his art, to believe that his photographs were his most solid work. I thought so, too, and looked forward to seeing more. Yet the experience of seeing *David Hockney Photographs* (Petersburg Press), the first formal, book-length collection of this work, based on an exhibition organized by Alain Sayag at the Musée National d'Art Moderne in Paris in the summer of 1982, was like that of being flattened out by feathers. It's not that inconsequential pictures have been chosen; while nothing from the 1976 or 1982 exhibitions has been reprinted, the pictures that are here are of similar subjects and have the same soft light and elegant appearance. It's that close looking at a good number of Hockney's photos (or, I believe, at a good number of his pieces in any medium) takes the viewer outside the realm of anything imaginative.

Hockney himself seems to know this. "I may be one of those people," he remarks in the introduction,

> who in the end will say, "the only good things I ever did were all those photos, all the other stuff is junk, or pointless." This has occurred to me once or twice. For instance, Cecil Beaton thought of himself as a photographer and as a stage designer but I think that in the end the best work he did was his diary . . . it is more unique, more original, and I think he will be remembered more often because of it.

Spending time with Hockney's photographs, I was taken down to this resigned state; I was left with the belief that his photos are his "best work" because they make the man a shade more real.

David Hockney Photographs reflects the painter's uncertainty about the worth of his photos. This book has the heft of an overproduced souvenir rather than that of a full-scale presentation. It reproduces enough work, though, in almost a hundred plates, some of which are made up of many separate photographs, to give a sense of his range in this medium. And it includes a long introduction by him which picks up where *David Hockney by David Hockney,* his profusely illustrated autobiography, left off. (The autobiography, made up of over twenty-five hours of taped conversations with Nikos Stangos, who edited them for book form, has the length of a novel and reads like one. Published in 1976 in a run of over fifty thousand copies and reprinted in 1980, it is becoming scarce in its second printing, an accomplishment for an expensive art book.) As a conversationalist, Hockney is almost in the same league as Andy Warhol and Alex Katz. He isn't as funny (or as theatrically and relentlessly naive) as Warhol, and he doesn't come out with the show-stopping opinions about talent and success and failure that make interviews with Katz so startling and enjoyable. Hockney isn't as taunting as either of the Americans, but he has something of their humorous frankness, and, like them, he wants to reach the widest possible audience. He enjoys sharing the details of his life and work habits, and while he doesn't draw many conclusions from those details, he gives them a taut simplicity—a slight twist. He always has the shape of his entire career on tap.

In the text for *David Hockney Photographs,* which was put together from taped conversations with Sayag—and edited by Raymond Foye and David Robbins—he tells about what he was feeling when he made the shots and about the business of photography in general. And most of the pictures, the majority of which are in color, have an instant, picturesque appeal. Two of the most attractive, *Gregory asleep in the train from Glyndebourne* and *Dover England,* a view out to the Channel through the door of a dimly lit, empty ferry station, aren't the work of a sensibility that can be pinned down—a mind you believe you can enter—but the images create a pleased, anticipatory mood, the way travelogue shots in movies can. There's an ingenious image-within-an-image-within-an-image picture called *Tourists, China,* where Hockney and five other people, most of whom are grinning, are seen peering into a mirror that is part of a beautiful yellow and blue sign, which also happens to be a billboard for snapshots taken by other tourists.

And there is a witty unit of twenty-four SX-70 Polaroids called *Ian + me watching a Fred Astaire movie on television, Los Angeles.* In a jumpy but easily read sequence, Hockney places, in no clear-cut order, shots of Ian's smiling and engaged face; a pack of Marlboros on a table; scenes from the movie; shots of the TV itself; tight chinos; a fireplace; the dark room; Ian's white socks; an ashtray; a bulging crotch; and flames, seen through a metal fire screen. Hockney casually creates a picture short story that neatly sums up the cozy excitement of a stay-at-home date.

Hockney says of the picture of Gregory, where he is asleep on the train, that "I thought he looked very handsome and suddenly saw him in a slightly different way . . . he is more *there*, he is more the person," and we agree. That's what draws us to the picture. Though it isn't a sloppily composed photograph, there is a rumpled quality about the lighting and about Gregory's body and face that makes us feel we know him a little more than we know the people in most of Hockney's other photographs and in practically all of his paintings and drawings.

In the handful of photos he has included of his parents, especially of his father, Hockney goes further. There are only three pictures of Kenneth Hockney, and his face is seen in only one of them, but he is the sole person in this collection, other than the artist himself, we have distinct feelings about. In the photograph where his face is visible, he's smiling and happy, looking away from the camera. Dressed in a tie and jacket, his arms folded into each other, he sits before the packed, neatly messy shelves of his workshop at home. In a photo that is only of his effects, we see his bedside table at St. Luke's Hospital in Bradford, England (where the family is from). This is the only still life I have ever seen by Hockney, in any medium, where the objects are arresting in themselves and pull the viewer into their own world. We see, placed on top of a laminated pale-blond table with heavy-duty plastic edging, a watch, a glass of water, and a white denture case marked BEST DENTURES. Standing along with these things, keeping guard over them almost, is an illustrated announcement card from one of David Hockney's exhibitions. (Hockney says that what the "best dentures" case implies is so: his father had other cases marked "next best dentures," "good dentures," "not very good dentures," and "not bad dentures.")

The strongest image of the three is *My Father photographing a sign, Paris 1974*, where we see a man with his back to us, facing the Musée des Arts Décoratifs, which happens to be having a David Hockney exhibition. If the photo weren't titled at the bottom—Hockney titles and dates all his photographs at the bottom—this would be a moderately striking and mysterious picture of a man in a slight crouch, wearing a hat, standing beside a parking meter whose silhouette somewhat echoes his own. With the title, though, the picture takes on a spooky charm. It has the quality of a dream you might have where you're the lead in a school play, your parents are in the audience, and, while you stay on stage, part of you magically gets to go and sit next to your parents and watch them looking at you. It's a dream that leaves you depleted, perhaps because it catches that snapped-apart moment when you become emotionally bigger and older than your parents, but it's one you are glad you had, because it marks a moment in your education of yourself, a more real moment than most that come through formal education.

My Father photographing a sign held me because it seems to contain the emotional basis of Hockney's approach to everything. On some level, he always plays the omniscient but vacuous role he has here: that of a mild, impassive master of ceremonies, a watcher of people from the rear. It is as if his chief awareness of things is the freeing yet forlorn one of always having been above and beyond his parents, or at least his father. There is something almost embarrassing about Hockney's father in these few images; he seems exposed, juvenile, weak. It is a perverse measure of how strongly Hockney creates his own bland and impersonal mood that when someone with a bit of enthusiasm appears in his pictures we draw back, and feel that person's spiritedness as a kind of weakness. Once you see Kenneth Hockney and feel his wizened, satisfied, and bustling presence, you become aware of how pacified and characterless all of Hockney's other subjects have been made, though most of them are his close friends and work associates. In the suite of photographs he showed at the

Sonnabend Gallery, his father steals the show, too. In a picture of his parents standing on the steps of a house in Bradford, Laura Hockney, the possessor of a face of great firmness and dignity, looks off and away. His father, though, planted on the steps and facing the camera head-on, is grinning, playing for his son, pointing what looks like a Brownie at him. Hockney says that his father liked to make paintings of Laurel and Hardy, and there is something of Stan Laurel in Kenneth Hockney here; he is a physically bulkier and more pre-possessing version of the movie comedian.

There is a gap between what Hockney gives us and what he feels about it. Whether in his comments about his life or his work, he presents a land of childlike prettinesses, but he himself doesn't see as a child—though perhaps it might be said that he sees as a very neat, careful child, a child on permanent good behavior. Looking at the stiff, doll-like figures of his paintings and prints (which might be taken as a parody of a child's point of view), you may feel that he uses a childlike way of seeing because he never experienced being a child, and that he has continually sought to make an art of childlike sim-plicities to make up for what he feels he missed. Hockney himself, as an artist, seems quite old, even aged—as a draftsman and painter, he has the touch of someone whose hand shakes ever so slightly. Ex-pressively, he has the stinginess of an aged person, too, someone who gives us only so much and no more.

One of the reasons people are drawn to him is his honesty. He doesn't mince around about his homosexuality, in his art or in his various autobiographical writings, and he doesn't camouflage his desire to be situated in sunny, foreign climes. He takes material that has a chichi, exclusive edge to it and lets us like it in the way he does. His readers and the viewers of his photos, paintings, and graphics know exactly the pleasures he is after, and travel with him, jumping in this little car or getting on that old train, going from one site to another. We feel comfortable with him, as if he were our Mum and our Dad in one guy.

We drive with him into a little town somewhere in France and see a small building that has lovely proportions and stands off by itself, almost waiting for our eyes. We sit for hours at the Café de Flore in

Paris, watching everybody go by. We spend an afternoon in the amusingly ornate lobby of a nineteenth-century German spa, writing letters and absorbing the pleasantly frayed atmosphere. We check into a hotel in Marrakech, and, as we walk out on our terrace, encounter the fading light and faraway noises of the early evening. We work all day in a studio in a sleepy part of Los Angeles and then, when our friend comes home, go to a neighborhood bar before dinner, and then, after dinner, return home and read and watch TV. There is such a nugget-clear moment in this text, when he talks about a trip he made with Peter Schlesinger, who is the subject of many of the photographs: "In the winter of 1968 Peter and I took the Orient Express to Munich, to see a show of mine. I remember one morning when we were both on the bottom bed, we opened the curtains, and it was snowing. It was fantastic to lie in a little couch with a nice warm body next to you, gazing out the window at the cute little Bavarian villages half hidden under the snow. It's a wonderful way to travel."

Hockney's world isn't exotically different—it comprises very graspable, pleasant moments all of us have had or can easily imagine having. This is why, I think, even if you're certain you have had your fill of him, you still keep a tiny desire to go to his exhibitions of new paintings, or to see his new sets for an opera, or to flip through this book of photographs. The colors of his palette are always mixed to give us the sensation we have when, say, we walk on a plane bound for somewhere and, for an instant, we're hit with the thought that brand-new, tasty pleasures lie in our path. Hockney is our foremost painter of that instant of holiday freedom.

And yet he never makes that holiday freedom into anything more than a little artificial flash in the mind. For someone whose material is so often the pleasure of bodies and the charge of foreign places, and who thrives on many kinds of older art, his own art ought to be sensuous, but it isn't. Formally, it has a chalky dryness. (His pictures spell out his freedom about his own homosexuality, but if, in his use of materials, he conveyed anything of the rounded firmness or wetness or hairiness of any sexuality, neither the homosexual nor the heterosexual side of his large audience might be so comfortable with him.) There is a matte quality to Hockney's vision. It's there when he talks and it is in his art. Whether he paints in acrylics or in oils, he gives surfaces the unglistening, unluminous finish of gouache or of the bright water-based paint kids use in school. His pen-and-ink line drawings are inert in another way: they appear to be careful tracings of existing images. Nor are there patches in his paintings, photographs, or graphics where the viewer wonders, "What is he thinking of?"

Reading Hockney's autobiography and his text for this photography book, you're struck and surprised by his devotion to the craft of picture making. He doesn't show off his learning, he doesn't make craft into a mystery that we will never understand. He does the opposite: he informally and invitingly draws his reader into the sometimes purely technical, sometimes only logistical, processes whereby his paintings, photographs, and prints are made. He presents those processes as things that he finds himself having to learn but that he will never be a true master at. When he says, "I don't really know too much about exposures," the reader believes him and likes Hockney's combination of modesty, flippancy, and indifference because the reader knows it's accompanied by a willingness on Hockney's part to learn about exposures if and when it becomes important for a specific problem. But he sees his paintings, prints, and work for the stage too much in terms of the different skills needed for the various jobs. Some vital impulse gets snuffed out in his keeping himself in a state of constant apprenticeship.

In the photography book, Hockney relates an exchange that inadvertently comments on his perception of art as a series of tasks. It's 1973 and he has gone to see the portraits of himself and Henry Geldzahler that Andy Warhol has done. Hockney doesn't say what he thought about his portrait, but tells us that "Henry didn't like his—he told Andy that he'd left something out. And Andy said, What? Henry said, You left the art out. And Andy replied, Oh, I knew I forgot something." Hockney never leaves out the art. That is, he never forgets to be artful—but the real stuff is missing.

In the past few years, his itch to find, and then surmount, obstacles has spread to photography. Using an SX-70 Polaroid camera, he has been producing large composite works, sometimes made up of over a hundred separate shots, that show the subject, be it a person or a fountain, from many slightly different distances and angles. These were the type of pictures exhibited at the André Emmerich Gallery in 1982, and a handful have been included in *David Hockney Photographs*. Hockney has Cubism in mind, and the pictures do have the buzzing busyness of a Cubist image, where each little facet seems to angle in on the still life or the model in its own independent way. Hockney's fascination with the Cubist period and with Picasso in particular was one of the underlying strands of his autobiography, and it has grown since 1976. It has almost become a sub-theme of his art (as a romance with Picasso, Braque, Gertrude Stein, and the last golden era of Parisian life was once a continuing inspiration for Red Grooms). Hockney's wish to pay homage to things French—and to Picasso especially—was the strongest emotion left by *Parade*, the Metropolitan Opera's three-part "Evening of French Music Theatre," for which Hockney provided the sets and costumes and, apparently, along with Manuel Rosenthal and John Dexter, the overriding conception.

For some people, Hockney's recent multiple-viewpoint Polaroids are his most satisfyingly complete works, and he says that he has been greatly stimulated by them. They have made him think about photography as something more than a way to record the details of his daily life, and given him new ideas for his painting. Yet they don't deliver more than his straight, one-shot photographs. Once you have put yourself through the endless number of subtly different positions that Hockney must put himself through to get these cubified reworkings of reality, the idea loses its novelty, and it isn't replaced by anything. The technique is no more than that, a technique.

In some way, this head-with-a-hundred-eyes view is less related to Cubism than to a certain distinctly English kind of scrappy, helter-skelter lyricism. The composite photos have the amusingly complicated appearance and rhythms—and less complicated underlying content—of Joan Littlewood's movie *Sparrows Can't Sing*, the Beatles' movies, or John Lennon's books. The difference, though, is that Hockney's spirit doesn't mesh with such a larky approach. Unlike Littlewood or Lennon, he doesn't have the satirical energy of a passionately larky creator. These very handsome photo arrangements don't leave us with the feeling that Hockney (or anybody) sees reality this way. We're left only with another, if more polished and novel, aspect of Hockney's artfulness.

For me, the most commanding and vibrant picture in *David Hockney Photographs* is a black and white shot that the painter made of himself in a photo booth in Berlin in 1962, when he was twenty-five. He isn't wearing eyeglasses, which, especially when he dons his oversize, goggle ones, make him appear forbidding and a little ineffectual. Hockney's specs negate the flamboyant message of his bleached-blond hair. They lend a note of the hesitant schoolboy—of the asthmatic Piggy, say, in *Lord of the Flies*—to his makeup. Without them, he hardly resembles David Hockney. Clothed in a striped blazer and a striped shirt, and with a cigarette sticking out of his mouth, straight at the camera, he exudes a bullying confidence that is different, too. With the photo-booth flash making his thrusting, square-jawed face look bleached out, and with that face topped by a crudely but stylishly close-cropped blond-white thatch of hair he has the menacing giddiness of a Soviet sailor revving up for a weekend's leave in a foreign port.

The photo-booth picture isn't a Hockney, of course. Yet this document has been subtly Hocknified. Entitled *Machine photograph rephotographed*, it has no doubt been enlarged from the original, and the date and "Berlin" have been written on the top in pen and ink. Hockney has also added his name in pen and ink, in large, slightly wobbly and baggy capital letters that walk up one shoulder and down the other, like a string of elephants from a *Babar* book. Taken together, his additions and the photo itself form a work of art; closer to being a densely packed novel than a picture, it tells a story whose protagonist is David Hockney and whose overriding emotion is bravado blunted.

There is a sturdiness in Hockney. It isn't felt in his individual pieces, many of which are airy to the point of barely being there at all. Yet the mass of his work leaves the impression of a willed industriousness—one that, however, bestows on each piece, be it a photograph, a design for a set, a painting, or a lithograph, only the lightest bit of itself. In the photo-booth picture, Hockney's strength is evident as it never is in his own art. It's a relief to be hit by the icebreaker force of this image; its lurching power is the antithesis of the too nicely removed, compositionally well-adjusted distance from which he makes us see the figures in so many of his pictures (and which makes those figures maddeningly unreachable).

The photo-booth picture shows the renegade and the powerhouse that are missing from his art. And it catches him in the act, as it were, of undermining his brutishness with the charmingly animated and docile lettering. Hockney, it seems, can't help dressing up the image with his name, and when he thinks of us looking at his name his chief desire is that we will love him immediately. His lettering says, in effect, "Take me home." If he hadn't drawn his name on the picture this way, the photo might pass as an actual mug shot. Adorned with the lettering, the image shows someone who has made himself a prisoner of his own desire to please.

—1983

THE LOVERS

MAN RAY, THE WEIMARANER who is the star of William Wegman's *Man's Best Friend* (Abrams), has one of the most intelligent, alert, and handsome faces in the history of photography. If he were a man, he might be a leader, a hero; the mixture of gravity and self-possession in his face would make men willing to follow him anywhere. What he does, in these large color Polaroids, is, at least at first sight, simply a still-photography version of what the dogs in the dog acts did on "The Ed Sullivan Show." In these staged portraits, which occasionally include another dog or a person in the shot, Man Ray is an image of such self-contained attentiveness that he doesn't quite seem to be a dog. The difference between this Weimaraner and the seemingly boneless spaniel that slipped and slid over the glassy floor on the Sullivan show, all the while keeping a patient and droopy countenance, is that Man Ray isn't embarrassing. Like Buster Keaton, he may be permanently unarousable, but he never ceases to be potent. His virility, like the actor's, is always felt; it is right there under the surface.

Man's Best Friend may be the most original book of photographs since Robert Frank's *The Americans* (1959). Like *The Americans*, it is a rarity in photography, a true book—an arrangement of individual shots that, taken together, enrich each other and leave a distinct, large impression. Frank's realist photos, the product of a road trip through the country, have everything—every mood and time of day and type of person—all seen through disgruntled and sorrowful eyes. Wegman's pictures have a more inward kind of everything. Simultaneously lush and surrealistic, silly and fairy-tale-like, they contain as many different moods and textures as a good variety show on a night when it surpasses itself. The images go from being brilliantly weird (with an undertone of something serene) to being unexpectedly romantic (with an undertone of something insane). They range from *The Kennebago*, where Man Ray, wearing an Indian feather headdress, is seen drifting by in a bright blue canoe on a lake, to *Double Profile*, where Ray holds his head over the shoulder of a striking big blonde, and together they gaze into the distance, a dark knight and his Rhine princess.

Practically each of the images in this beautifully printed and designed book seems to turn upside down, or poke fun at—or at least remind us of—something we have seen before. Essentially a series of impersonations by one dog (with wigs and makeup and costume changes and props), Wegman's pictures come across as a collective takeoff on the most influential body of photographs of the seventies: Lucas Samaras's numerous Polaroids, in which from shot to shot he struck theatrical poses, mimicked various primal moments, danced as if he were Salome, and turned himself into a werewolf. In the pristine sparseness of most of Wegman's setups and in his subtly having left traces of the fact that many of the pictures were made in a studio, his images also parody many kinds of magazine photography, from dog food ads to high-fashion shots.

Perhaps the most spectacular parody is *Brooke*, where Man Ray has been outfitted with designer blue jeans, which barely stay on his rump. Trailing his hopelessly unsnug Ralph Laurens behind him on the floor, he glances back to beckon us on, the way Brooke Shields and every other female and male model of jeans has for the past few years. Wegman's pictures seem to rib, too, the solemn masterworks that some fashion photographers take when they're doing their own, noncommissioned work, such as Irving Penn's glacially pretty portraits of tribesmen in mud masks, which were taken in an old-time, traveling photographer's portable studio.

But what a viewer feels most strongly in these pictures is the relationships between a photographer and a sitter that have been conducted before a camera. Wegman and his Weimaraner began working together, on staged photographs and videotaped performances, in 1970, the year the dog was born. In his introduction, Laurance Wieder says that Wegman initially had no intention of using his pet in his art. The puppy—Wegman bought him for $35 in Long Beach, California, and at first wanted to call him Bauhaus—simply barged into the setups. He howled and sulked when he couldn't get before the camera. The color photographs in *Man's Best Friend*, which were made between 1979 and 1982, with a large-format Polaroid camera, mostly at Polaroid's studio in Cambridge, Massachusetts, are the last phase of that partnership. (Man Ray died in 1982; *Man's Best Friend* is dedicated to him and to the American Surrealist painter and photographer he was named after.) The pictures may make you think of some of photography's most celebrated collaborations, especially Alfred Stieglitz's many portraits of his wife, Georgia O'Keeffe, and Richard Avedon's portraits of his father, Jacob Israel Avedon, seen in the few years before and then right up to his death. Wegman's pictures suggest a little of both of these partnerships. The portraits of Man Ray seem to be a record of a courtship and also of a less charged—but possibly closer—relation between members of the same family.

Yet the odd thing about these photographs is that, after I spent time with them, it was Man Ray whom I continued to think about and who was real for me, not Wegman. I felt I could describe Wegman's humor and his artistry, but he himself never became someone I thought I knew, and that put a damper on the pictures. The tension of an artist's mind at work can't be sensed in these images, and so it's possible to love them, and to find that they set off more associations in your mind than many photographs (or paintings) do, and yet also find them only the beautiful shell of someone's feelings.

Wegman is in his Polaroids, of course, but in a very submerged way. Wegman likes puns and he enjoys making words and images play off each other. The titles of his individual pictures often add a mysteriously necessary concluding note, and he may have intended his book's title to read as a concealed, inside-out message, too. "Man's best friend" is dog, but Man Ray's "best friend" is Wegman. It's as if the book were indirectly a portrait of William Wegman, and as if he were the dog—the steadfast, mute one.

Wegman's earlier work with Man Ray wasn't deeper than these Polaroids, but, partly because Wegman himself was often in the photographs and videotapes, his relationship with his dog was clearer and his art was less muffled. There are a few of his earlier photographs, which are in black and white, in *Man's Best Friend* and a larger selection in *Wegman's World*, the handsome catalogue for a traveling retrospective that Lisa Lyons organized for the Walker Art Center in Minneapolis. Many of Wegman's videotapes were also on view at the show.

Seen now, Wegman's work of the early and mid-seventies (the work by which he first became known) brings back, almost intact, the moment when Minimalism, Conceptual Art, and the latecomer in that time of elegant severity—Process Art—were all on the scene at once. Part of what made his videos and earlier photographs absorbing was that it was hard to tell what he thought about those movements. Whether starring Man Ray or himself alone, or both together, his pieces appeared, at first sight, to make a mockery of the self-conscious restraint and the underlying presumption of the time. He caught the early seventies' way of announcing that the truly advanced artwork was no more than a document of an act or a gesture. His videos, without being sluggish themselves, had a perfect molasses-slow, instructive pace, and his photographs had a perfect Spartan bareness. If you didn't see that their content was often a subtle jumble, you might have thought them excellent illustrations for a how-to manual.

Wegman was more than a humorist in these pieces, though; his art had more emotional levels than most parodies do. In his mid-twenties when he began making them, he was a young artist who unquestioningly wanted to work in the traditions of the most challenging art of the moment, and, seemingly overnight, without having to go through any period of awkward maturing, he mastered the look and style of that moment. There were times when he seemed almost chained to the Minimalist and Conceptual ideas he was working with. The viewer didn't have to know much about those ideas, though, to feel that there was something held down about Wegman.

In some of the tapes, he faced the camera head-on and addressed us directly, as if in character. He spoke spontaneously and haltingly, the way someone would talk to you at a party, and yet, in retrospect, his chats had the completeness of formal soliloquies. With his straggly, shoulder-length, red-blond hair, which often resembled Little Lord Fauntleroy's and usually appeared to be a bit oily, Wegman played a vaguely anxious hippie who did what he assumed society and his parents thought he should do, and, in the process, kept getting himself twisted and skewered. In *Deodorant*, he demonstrated a new deodorant that he believed was an excellent product, except that you had to spray it on for a while — like for a couple of minutes. He goes on talking calmly about how effective it is, meanwhile turning his armpit into a frothy swamp. In *Rage & Depression*, he was a guy who had to undergo shock therapy because he was so angry at everybody. The problem was, when the doctors put the electrodes on his chest he started to giggle and the giggly expression became frozen on his face. He says he's still depressed, but now, with his permanent smile, everyone thinks he's happy—which makes everything weirder and worse.

Wegman wasn't only a counterculture nice guy; there was something likably sneaky and withheld about him, too. He was often seen wearing a jeweled ring on his index finger; it was surprising, because he hardly seemed to have anything of a pasha (or a biker) in him. The ring suggested that there was a budding sensualist in him, waiting to come out and take over, and that there were reserves of power in Wegman that he wasn't fully aware of.

Not exactly a dropout or a rebel, a mouse or an impresario, but a little of all of these, Wegman was a beautifully blurry foil to the razor-sharp presence of his costar. In those works, Man Ray was a piece of undiluted sinewy muscle, a generally silent animal who occasionally let out startling, loud barks. He was keener, leaner, and sexier than his owner. The young Ray's almost frightening eagerness to participate comes across most clearly in the videos, where he is in action, but it is there in the still photographs, too, where his face is rarely seen close up—just his flabless body effortlessly perched in uncomfortable and preposterous positions, sometimes on wood boxes that are too small to hold all of him.

In a video entitled *Duet*, we watch him and another, less avid Weimaraner intently looking at something that, in the course of the piece's few masterfully prolonged minutes, slowly goes up and down before them, then to their left and to their right, then suddenly around them, then up and down again, over and over. (What the dogs are watching, and what we in the audience don't see until the very end, is a tennis ball. Seeing the ball is actually an unnecessary and deflating touch.) In *Duet* and, less spectacularly, in almost every other piece, Ray acts as if he were in a trance of obedient behavior. He's like a model for ads for a dog obedience course taught by a madman. Ray's powers of concentration are so developed they're funny; they're as scary as a cobra's, too—they hold out a promise of something unknown and deadly.

In the color photographs in *Man's Best Friend*, the tables are turned. It's Wegman, the unseen author of these spotlessly clean shots, who is felt as the lean, sinewy, precise one, and Man Ray who is sloppy, fallible, and human. By the time Wegman began photographing his pet with Polaroid's large-format camera, Ray had lost his taut, naked-seeming good looks. By dog years, he was almost in his seventies. His coat had gone from being silvery-tan to silvery-brown, and his eyes—once spectral and amber-gray—had become dark and absorbent. They no longer appeared to bore right through what they were trained on; they now seemed to be appreciating what they saw.

In the process of aging, Man Ray had become something less—and more special—than a Weimaraner. The star of these photographs is slightly muttlike, more of a basic dog. And Ray's being such a basic dog is better. These pictures are so elegantly lighted and composed and so witty in conception that if their star had been a fine example of an unusual breed they might have seemed tricky or coy. They might have been too similar to the chic fashion stills they often kid. Ray's rounded, monumentally ordinary presence, though, gives them a weighted and gentle center.

Looking at *Man's Best Friend* with Wegman's earlier work in mind, a viewer may feel that, over the course of years, Wegman gave up a part of himself to Man Ray. It is as though Wegman couldn't stand being the experimental, uncertain, vulnerable fellow he was in his earlier work, and so he merged himself with his commandingly thoughtless, always assured partner. Wegman isn't a naive or a folk or a primitive artist, but when he was working with his dog in these Polaroids he operated with the same freedom that self-taught artists often have. It is a freedom that comes from being oblivious of the world—of what other people might think. In some way, Wegman's Polaroids are contemporary equivalents of primitive and naive paintings. The photos have the same becalmed, somnambulistic mood that Henri Rousseau's work does, and Wegman's color recalls Rousseau's, too. Enamel-dense and satiny, Wegman's generally dark blues, reds, and greens have a once hot, now cooled-off lustrousness; they're like the colors of cars at night in the tropics.

Wegman's freedom lets him get right into his dog's mind, and look out from it. Probably no one has gone to the lengths he has to poke fun at and to appreciate the thing that distinguishes dogs and isolates them from all other animals (and which we tend to forget, especially if we don't own one). That is, their affecting, dopey, baffling, and constant—and, because of that, sometimes infuriating—friendliness. People who have been irritated by these pictures probably haven't had dogs, or are basing their protective feelings on memories of having had them when young, and can't enjoy the satisfying way that Man Ray isn't—and is—being used in these photos. Far from having to submit to something, Ray is being given the chance to fulfill one of his biggest needs. Sitting for Wegman's camera, he gets to keep his master under constant surveillance. For him, the photo sessions may have been a bit like a stretched-out version of the crazed and blissful moment in a dog's life when his master picks up his lead, the metal clasp clinks, and he realizes that he's going to be taken for a walk.

Wegman is getting even with Ray, too, of course. That's why these photographs have more layers than Wegman's earlier work. Then, he surrendered himself to a brilliant pet, a puppy genius who took over the show and needed the scantiest material to build up an act. Wegman and Ray were more purely collaborators in their early pieces. In *Man's Best Friend*, though, Wegman is the director. He is more consciously in awe of his dog's acting capacities, and he has more reason now to push Ray around. Anyone who has allowed himself to become seriously involved with a canny and demanding dog, especially a large-sized and quick-witted purebred, one with a more human tempo than small dogs have, knows he has fallen into a trap. He has learned to read the signals in the animal's eyes, and, in the process, has made an emotional contract with the animal. The contract can be broken in a second, in a way that a relationship with a person or a child usually cannot; yet a relationship between a dog and a person who gives himself to a dog's soft eyes generally has a stifling closeness, because there is no room for argument or change or growth. Turning Ray into a tart (in *Louis XIV* and *Royal Hawaiian*) or a housewifely char (in *Tall Dog*), Wegman, on some level he himself may not be aware of, is slapping his dog for having sucked so much time and energy out of his, Wegman's, life. On a still deeper level, Wegman seems to be slapping himself, too, for having fallen for Ray.

The strongest images in *Man's Best Friend* seem to be pulled from this underground terrain, where dogs, the most domestic and tractable of all animals, have a psychological power that no other animal can match. In the pictures where the camera gets to within inches of Man Ray's face, and his eyes look up into ours and appraise us with a stare worthy of Iago, Wegman suggests the insidious side of a dog's ceaseless desire for closeness. These images feel as if they come from Ray's depths, and as if Ray, speaking for all dogs, says, "We know you—we always have." In these close-ups, and in the pictures of his bowed head and especially in *Dusted*, Man Ray is as much of an individual, a presence we feel we know, as any animal in the history of art.

Dusted is the single most powerful image in *Man's Best Friend*. It encompasses the silliness and sadness in the many different kinds of Man Ray portraits, and goes off on its own orbit. Ray sits at a medium distance from the camera, and, looking off to the right, seen almost in profile yet presenting a full, clear view of his overall body, he is being rained on by flour. Coming down from some source outside the camera's range, the flour has covered almost all of him and is sprinkled, in starlike puddles, over the floor in the foreground.

Ray is once more being made a fool of, but this time it isn't so funny. Absorbing the image, we become angry at Wegman. We feel that he has gone too far—that Ray isn't participating in the joke, that he doesn't understand what's going on. Yet these responses fade away after a while; being dusted comes to seem an ennobling act.

Dusted is the picture that loses least when it's reproduced in black and white; yet, in its color, it is one of the most subtle of the photographs. There is an ethereality to the powdery, bubbly flour and to Ray's chalky tan coat; the very dark background, which may be black, has a penetrable, night-sky quality to it. *Dusted* seems to be composed of living black and white, and that matches the picture's spirit, which is of parting and farewell. (It is the last plate in the book.) The photograph might almost be showing the end of one life and the beginning of the next—the moment that Man Ray has died and is being taken up into the light. Working with his dog for so many years, Wegman may have felt he was under a spell. He may even have wanted all along to create an image that would express that spell—the attachment he and Ray had for each other, which continually prompted Wegman, in one cycle of work after another, to release more of his talent. Whether or not he wanted to create such an image, no other picture shows how much his dog meant to him as *Dusted*, where Man Ray has turned away and gone on to something else with the same abrupt simplicity with which he usually wanted to participate. The picture makes it seem as if Wegman's many thoughts about Ray had always been leading up to the moment when Ray would finally leave him.

—1983

THE ROOKIE

ONE OF THE MANY DECEPTIVE things about John F. Peto's trompe-l'oeil paintings is that, at first sight, they look as if the artist weren't exactly sure how to make a trompe-l'oeil painting. Peto's images are practically the same as those of the numerous other American fool-the-eye painters of his time—the late nineteenth and early twentieth century. He gives us primarily head-on views of envelopes, tickets, snapshots, clippings from newspapers, and other generally flat things (and sometimes sculpturally rounded objects, such as musical instruments) that are seemingly pasted, tacked, nailed to, or hanging from a wood wall or a door. At his recent retrospective at the National Gallery, though, a viewer could initially feel that Peto was, at heart, a lyric poet who wandered into the tricky trompe-l'oeil world by mistake, and obediently stayed. Unlike William Michael Harnett, his contemporary and America's best-known trompe-l'oeil painter, he isn't a maker of brilliantly crafted and gleaming, expensive-looking objects. Peto's surfaces are among the most delicate in American art; without being dry or pasty, they look as if they had yet to develop a protective outer shell. And he isn't, in temperament, a practical joker—or a raconteur or an inventor—as many of Harnett's followers were.

Yet Peto takes us in, visually and emotionally, as much as any trompe-l'oeil painter ever did. He makes us get very close to his pictures, because we want to see if, inches away, his beautifully fuzzy images will cither become more sharply focused or turn into total blurs. Examining, say, his weathered wood boards, which often have initials and dates carved into them, you find yourself mentally running your hand over the surfaces. Re-creating what it would be like to actually touch that wood—answering Peto's call, as it were, to help him make his images crisper—you feel that you have been in a kind of limbo, because, for a moment, you have forgotten that you have been looking at a painting. And he leaves us feeling tripped up this way—as if somehow we'd seen a ghost—in picture after picture.

Except for a portrait, a landscape, a coastal scene, and an unfinished self-portrait, every painting in the National Gallery's handsomely installed show, whose curator was John Wilmerding—he also wrote its accompanying book, *Important Information Inside: The Art of John F. Peto and the Idea of Still-Life Painting in Nineteenth-Century America*—was a trompe-l'oeil image or a still life. Peto worked in a narrow range of subject matter. He even had a single color that he used repeatedly for his backgrounds—a dark pine green. Yet the exhibition, which included over sixty pictures, was unusually absorbing; more than most retrospectives, it had the effect of a tour of a man's mind, where all his disparate thoughts were laid out, waiting to be sorted. Part of the show's freshness, of course, came from the fact that the painter is so little known. Peto—his family was of English descent—was essentially discovered by the art critic Alfred Frankenstein in the late forties, when Frankenstein was researching Harnett's career and the flowering of trompe-l'oeil painting that lasted from the Gilded Age through the turn of the century (or what he called "the saloon era in American painting"). Frankenstein found that the paintings that had been thought to be by Harnett working in a painterly, brushier style—even paintings that had Harnett's monogram on the front—were actually by Peto.

Thirty-five years ago, Peto was virtually unknown. Records showed that he sent a few pictures to the Pennsylvania Academy of the Fine Arts when his work was getting under way, and that when he was in his mid-thirties he moved from Philadelphia to Island Heights, New Jersey, a small riverfront town. He married, and lived there with his wife and daughter in almost complete obscurity for the next two decades, dying in 1907, at the age of fifty-three. He never had a formal exhibition, he seems to have kept no records and made no statements about his pictures, and there were only a handful of accounts of him or of his work in newspapers of the time. Since Frankenstein unveiled him, a small number of Peto's paintings have turned up in museums and at auctions, and he has become something of a name. But very few of his pictures have been reproduced in color, and the National Gallery's show was only the second he has had. (The first was at the Brooklyn Museum in 1950.)

Even if Peto were better known, though, he would still be one of the more fascinating American painters—and not only of his period. His pictures have the quality of entries, in a coded language, in a lifelong journal; taken together, they form a puzzle that asks to be solved. Peto's work has been called melancholy, even tragic, and Wilmerding's disclosure that the painter suffered from Bright's disease in his last years may help explain why. "The kidney stones which gave him constant pain," Wilmerding writes, "were presumed in his day to be fatal, and he lived with forebodings of premature death." But Peto's pictures had a commemorative note from the beginning, and he was always drawn to the frayed, the worn-down, and the erased. The corners of his pamphlets and sheets of music are chewed and crunched, the spines of his leather-bound books are on the verge of becoming powdery, the surfaces of his tin lanterns, copper pots, and candlesticks are rusty and tarnished, and the paint on his wood beams has faded, leaving exposed—and softened, caressable—edges. Paintings from any period of his life would look brotherly hanging next to works by later American appreciators of cloaked and discarded things: Robert Rauschenberg and Walker Evans, Joseph Cornell, Jasper Johns, and Elie Nadelman.

But if Peto's paintings produce in the viewer more of a trapped— and less of a released or a revelatory (or even a resigned)—feeling than tragic art generally does, it may be because the dispirited mood of his work doesn't seem to go deep. You believe that if these paintings could be shaken and juggled a little their muffled surfaces might fall away, revealing underneath something cheerful and untouched and ready to go. Peto's cautiously made yet sensuous pictures, and the facts of his isolated yet industrious life presented in Wilmerding's book, leave the impression that the painter was a peppery and cocky—and also a dignified—man who stopped short of expressing the forceful side of himself in his work, or expressed it indirectly. It's even possible to sense that the melancholy spirit of his art was a badge to him—a way he wanted to be seen.

Among the show's surprises was the formal strength and assurance of Peto's still lifes. He may be the only American still-life painter whose touch and feeling for light are comparable to the European masters'. Especially in his small pictures—some are less than ten inches high—of food or utensils, which are usually seen close up, at the edge of a table, his powdery yet dense and slightly viscous surfaces recall Chardin's. And his light, which falls on the tips of objects and makes them glow softly but seems to come from a blindingly powerful source, recalls Vermeer's.

In his often very dark backgrounds and in the way he simply lines up his objects in a row, many of Peto's pictures are as eerie and solemn—and have the same surprising glamorousness—as classic Spanish still lifes. In *Market Basket, Hat and Umbrella*, he takes objects that we associate with a rural summer's-afternoon moment in American life—the moment of Mark Twain's and Winslow Homer's boys and girls—and, placing them on a plain wood tabletop, with a glistening black background, gives them an almost embarrassing elegance. It's like the first time you saw your mother and father in evening clothes, coming to say good night before going out. In *Banana and Orange*, the banana lies on its side like a lover turned in on himself in bed, while the half-peeled orange seems to push up from its rind like a hot morning sun rising out of bright yellow clouds.

Peto's still lifes make us feel so protective of the painter himself, though, that it is hard to think of them only as refined works of art. Not that he's sentimental. Even in *Help Yourself*, which ought to be sentimental—it shows candy canes and pieces of nougat and caramel spilling out of a paper bag, and transports the viewer to a turn-of-the-century American Christmas—he straightforwardly paints only what is before him. It's that, more than most still-life painters, he gives his subjects the quality of being substitutes for people or things no longer there. His small still lifes are like objects in the attic you didn't know you had lost or were looking for until you unexpectedly come upon them. They have the same pacifying power that the glass ball with the snowstorm in it had in *Citizen Kane*. Kane wasn't looking for the ball (he was tearing apart his wife's bedroom after she left him); but when he found it he was relieved, and didn't want to let it go. He made it seem as if finding the object from childhood wiped out in a flash all the messy mistakes and complications of his adult life.

Going back and forth from Peto's still lifes to his trompe-l'oeil paintings, you understand how he needed both approaches, and how each fed the other. It is as though he always wanted to produce a sense of unattainability, and kept changing his mind about how to do it. He went from showing lovely things in a glowing light, seemingly there for the grasping, to showing in his trompe-l'oeil paintings a kind of dead-letter realm that has very little light and where our belief that we can lift out something from it is made into an ironic—but never quite sour—joke.

He brings these approaches together in *The Poor Man's Store*, a view through an open window to shelves laid out with fruit, a gingerbread animal, a plate of doughnuts, a box of peanuts, and peppermint sticks and other candies in glass jars. The morning sun seems to be shining on these ordinary but wonderful things, and we want to linger with them and with the dark room behind them; yet the painting has the effect of many Surrealist pictures, where we're often unsettled or rebuffed by what we're drawn to. One of the peaks of his career, *The Poor Man's Store* is subtler and richer than most Surrealist images, because Peto isn't overtly psychological and he isn't trying to bait us. He invites us to drift back into a time when we were small and would have craved these plain and simple things, and leaves it up to the viewer to come to his own conclusions about the experience.

What makes the picture itself seem almost like a toy is that it doesn't have a proper frame; its frame, which is made of wood, is a witty and seamless continuation of the canvas, and shows the window's open shutter, a ledge, and a bit of the wall surrounding the window. Peto wasn't the only trompe-l'oeil artist to blend a painting with its frame; it was done because almost any kind of frame looks too dressy on—and cuts against the intended flatness of—a trompe-l'oeil image. But probably no trompe-l'oeil master made his built-on frames so crucial an aspect of his pictures as Peto did in *The Poor Man's Store* and in *Toms River, The Cup We All Race 4*, and *Portrait of the Artist's Daughter*. These pictures all appear to float on the wall; they're as prepossessing as altarpieces, and Peto's colors stand out more sharply and seem brighter in them than anywhere else. It's logical that he went to the limit in them: he was turning the painting into a leftover in itself.

If Peto's best trompe-l'oeil and still-life paintings have a shifting, miragelike beauty and tension, it might be because he led a kind of trompe-l'oeil life. His art was as much an attempt to redo Harnett's as his painted nails and wood boards are like the real things. Peto's relationship to Harnett (who worked in Philadelphia around the same time Peto did) is only a shade better known than his relationship to other painters of his time and to earlier painters. What is known is that Peto, who was six years younger, took many of his still-life and trompe-l'ocil arrangements—of inkwells, musical instruments, mugs, pipes, horseshoes, heaps of books—from paintings that Harnett had already done. Peto made those compositions his own; and he probably created the "letter rack" picture, which is a type of trompe-l'oeil image—Peto finished his first letter-rack painting a few months before Harnett finished his first. But Peto never deviated from the enterprise that Harnett began: that of shifting back and forth from tabletop still lifes to trompe-l'oeil images of objects on a wall. In some cases, he was reworking pictures Harnett had made ten years before. That Peto's images seem to be continually solidifying and decomposing as we look at them may come in part from the fact that he was often channeling his feelings through another man's forms.

Peto was possibly drawn to Harnett, and Harnett was possibly encouraged by the younger man's attentiveness, because they were both no-nonsense professionals. Most of the other trompe-l'oeil artists made their pictures for a while, then switched to completely different kinds of painting, or were methodical eccentrics who could put away their brushes for twenty years if they didn't have a particular visual joke they wanted to paint. Peto and Harnett, though, wanted to make a splash both at Academy exhibitions and with people and businesses that had little interest in art. Peto was probably even more of a go-getter. In his late twenties, when he was first hitting his stride, he seems to have thought of himself as a smart businessman-artist. The earliest examples of his letter-rack pictures are charming glorifications of the idea of men working among other men. Commissioned by professional men Peto knew in Philadelphia, the paintings are veiled portraits of individuals and their occupations, made up of calling cards, advertisements, and mementos stuck in and out of crossed tapes tacked to a wall.

Peto's eagerness shows in the photographs of him in the book, too. They are almost as mesmerizing as his paintings. He has the look in many of them of a man whose belief in himself as a success or a failure changes daily. One of the best is of Peto and Harnett in Peto's studio in Philadelphia. The time is the eighteen-seventies, when they must have been keeping tabs on each other's development. Handsome, dark-haired, and conservatively dressed, a faint smile visible beneath his bushy mustache, Harnett looks bemusedly off to one side of the photographer. Nattier and more bohemian in appearance, Peto holds his violin under his chin and lurches forward, his bow thrust out before him on the floor. He's smiling, too, and he is clearly excited about being photographed with the older man. Peto appears to have been of a little less than medium height, and he, too, wore a mustache. He kept his hair close-cropped, and that is partly why he seems our contemporary in the photos (a number of which he probably took himself). He also looks quite modern because, whether he's happy or displeased, he almost always seems to be giving everything in him to the camera, the way an actor does. Even in a picture where we see him from some distance and can barely make out his features—he's alone, sitting by the side of a country road, wearing a derby—the tenseness in his body makes it seem as if he were playing a part.

Peto and Harnett apparently saw no more of each other after 1880. It has been said that they feuded; certainly they went very different ways. After spending many years in Europe, Harnett settled permanently in New York. By the time he died, in 1892, at the age of forty-four, his work had become increasingly polished and grand in scope. By that time, Peto had been living for three years in Island Heights. Tucked in between the fairly populous community of Toms River and the busier oceanfront places a few miles away, Island Heights is a dry town, as it was in Peto's day, and, with many of its modestly ornate Victorian two- and three-story houses still standing, it has something of the same pretty and sleepy air it had ninety years ago. It was a resort for families, usually from Philadelphia, and for yachtsmen; it had been developed, though, as a Methodist camp-meeting site, and that seems to be the reason Peto went there initially. He was a sometime professional cornet player; he played to supplement the income he had from his parents, and the revivalist meetings gave him regular work.

On a little hill overlooking the Toms River, he built a house with a porch and with a turret rising up in the center. In its lack of frills and its blunt, almost squat proportions, the house—there are photographs of it in Wilmerding's book—is like Peto's work. It's a secretive structure that makes a passerby stop and want to know what it might be like inside. Peto called it The Studio, and made his actual studio in its central and largest room. He seems to have been especially close to his daughter, Helen. He photographed her often and included her image (in the form of carte-de-visite photos) in a few of his paintings. He stuck rings in the overhead beams in his studio–living room and made a swing there for her so she could play while he worked. After he moved to Island Heights, he seems to have gone back to Philadelphia only for art supplies, and he rarely went anywhere else. He apparently gave away or sold many of his paintings to neighbors or to the summer boarders he and his wife took in, and he occasionally exhibited a picture at a druggist's in the town.

Peto's life story isn't crammed with incidents, but, like some folktales, it is simultaneously sad and odd and comic, and it teases us into finding an underlying thread. Thinking about his work and trying to relate it to his self-created isolation, I kept coming back to the theme of competition. I don't think he was ever free from the thought of competition. It is as though he had a sense of who he was only when he was measuring himself against Harnett (or against men in general)—and yet he thought he was a nobody, and would automatically lose, whenever he was in competition. Maybe it was this feisty but no-win attitude that kept him in the position of forever developing but never breaking loose from Harnett's ideas. Like a rookie, Peto seems to have believed that he had to prove himself each time he took up a canvas. And his work never lost a rookie's special kind of grace, either. There were very few routine pictures in the show. To the end of his life, he kept his surfaces raw and vibrant. He didn't need gallery exhibitions and reviews for his art to stay limber—his judging audience was in his head.

He may have believed that Island Heights was a prison he created for himself, and he also may have wanted to dethrone the absent Mr. Harnett. Even if a viewer knows nothing about Peto's life, he can sense the artist, in effect, hitting his head against the wall in some pictures. Peto often shows carte-de-visite photos of Abraham Lincoln tacked to wood walls or stuck in letter racks, and frequently flanks Lincoln's image with the dates of his birth and death, torn notices, and ripped and empty envelopes. These images ought to be moving; they ought to cap the show, to be Peto's grandest expression of the elegiac mood he wanted to convey. The paintings with Lincoln's image in them are oddly unemotional, though—they were among the few pictures that I didn't want to linger with. Possibly, it's that in the format of a trompe-l'oeil painting he couldn't convey everything he felt about the slain President, the Civil War, and its aftermath, which was the era of his youth. Then, too, he worked from an engraving of Lincoln—Wilmerding reproduces it in his book—that is distant to begin with. (It is very similar to the one used for the five-dollar bill.) Lincoln's image has an obligatory presence and puts a deadening lid on every picture it is in except *Old Time Letter Rack*, where the photo has been turned upside down and Lincoln's head has been cut off by an envelope. If there are other paintings nearby with that photo of Lincoln right side up in them, a viewer can tell, from the clothing, that the flipped and headless image is Lincoln's. If there is no way for the viewer to know, Peto has his little joke to himself. You feel, though, that Peto wanted us to know. *Old Time Letter Rack* is like an expertly handled murder that the murderer is quietly proud of and half hopes we will find out about.

Peto is even icier in *For a Sunday Dinner*, a picture of a plucked chicken hanging head down on a door, which was taken, with very few changes in its outward appearance, from a painting Harnett had made some ten years before. Harnett's *Plucked Clean* (which Wilmerding reproduces) is primarily a study of form in which the chicken happens to be a pathetic creature. (The painting reworks a motif that had been in European art for two centuries.) Peto's bird, though, is an individual animal whose neck has just been wrung—the blood dripping down the wall is dark red and looks fresh, and parts of the body are still clenched. And Peto appears to have painted it with an unseemly ease and enjoyment. There's a satiny luster to the picture's surface which he rarely gets elsewhere, and the bird's few remaining feathers have been flicked on with a devilish hand.

And yet Island Heights must have been a haven for him. Possibly, he felt he was making the right business move in going there—he had a steady market all to himself in the town. A specialist in fakery, though, did he ever suspect (as we do) that his life there was a bit of a charade? His existence as a husband, father, and householder—and as a proper neighbor of the vacationing families, the yachtsmen, and the Methodists he performed for—is imaginable as a piece of fool-the-eye theater, in which he was the leading character. Might he also have realized that, because he handled his art as if it were a cottage industry, his productions would eventually come to light in the same dawning, spooky, and unpredictable way that a viewer perceives what is happening in one of his trompe-l'oeil paintings? You believe that there was a sardonic puppetmaster in him who would have savored the joke of so many of his pictures winding up in the hands of forgers and then, bearing false monograms, being passed off to dealers as "Harnett"'s for years. This Machiavellian part of him might have been amused, too, by the fact that since so many of his paintings went to people who happened to be passing through Island Heights—people who presumably had no special interest in art and thought of their Petos as souvenirs (and whose descendants no doubt thought of the pictures as souvenirs)—it is still impossible to say what proportion of his work is known. One of the finest pictures in the show, *Toms River,* was discovered only recently. (It is now in the collection of Baron Thyssen-Bornemisza, of Lugano.) It's possible that other Petos, even works as good as *Toms River,* may still turn up.

His carefully lidded anger, his frustration, and his ambition are all packed into *The Cup We All Race 4,* which was made a few years before his death. The painting shows a little tin cup hanging on a hook on a cracked old green wood wall. Gouged in the wood, in capital letters that slant this way and that and are themselves a feat of realist painting, are the words and the numeral that give the picture its title. Along with *The Poor Man's Store*, which was made about twenty years earlier, before he moved to Island Heights, *The Cup We All Race 4* presided over the exhibition. The two pictures may be the most original and resonant images of, respectively, the desires of childhood and the realizations of adulthood in American art. It is as if Peto had reached into the inviting window of his store and pulled out one of the rigid and bright and new things in it—and then, years later, made a portrait of the now much-handled thing. From one painting to the other, he seems to be getting older right before our eyes. And yet, though the cup is a humble and dented object, and he may be saying, "We knock ourselves out—for this trinket," the later painting hardly seems a confession of failure. It's another case of Peto fooling us—and possibly himself—with surface despair. *The Cup We All Race 4*, which must be one of the earliest paintings, American or European, to make use of a graffito, has the presence, and something of the funny belligerence, of a heraldic shield.

Wilmerding says the picture's title "evokes nostalgia for a lost frontier past," and that makes sense, since Peto, and not only in his ambivalent Lincoln pictures, was very much a member of a generation that nervously watched as America, in the Civil War and the subsequent boom period, suddenly lost its youth. Wilmerding adds that the cup "may also represent the drink Peto's neighbors sought despite local Methodist prohibitions," and that seems right, too—the painter had to be the sliest citizen of Island Heights. The phrase and the cup also might be an ironic reference to the sailing meets along the Toms River, which Peto could see from his house, and in nearby Barnegat Bay. In the face of a great number of his pictures, though, these aren't the first interpretations that come to mind. At the exhibition, which was an echo chamber of the history of art, and showed one man's single-minded pursuit of the laurels of his profession, there was little doubt about who was racing and what he was racing for.

—1983

THE KID WHO GOT
STRAIGHT A'S

JOHN UPDIKE HARDLY seems able to write a sentence, for any occasion, that doesn't have a shapely, rhythmical balance to it, yet there is something shapeless and directionless about *Hugging the Shore* (Knopf). Many collections of reviews seem scattered until the author's aims become apparent, and in reading these literary reviews we do learn what Updike's tastes and prejudices are. But I put the book down with a frustrated and almost angry feeling that I had been in the company of a brilliant person who is running on automatic.

Hugging the Shore is dissatisfying, but it is phenomenal, too. It has the heft of a Bible, and it has a Biblical diversity of subjects and insights. It is packed with phrases, sentences, or paragraphs that give us a handle on books and authors we haven't read or heard of, or that bring back well-known books and authors in refreshed, new ways. "Goldilocks and the Three Bears" is described as "an Oedipal triangle passingly invaded by a golden-haired loser." Randall Jarrell's children's books "have a sinister stir about them, the breath of true forlornness felt by children." John Cheever's "instinctive belief in the purity and glory of Creation brings with it an inevitable sensitivity to corruption; like Hawthorne, he is a poet of the poisoned." About Maurice Blanchot's novel *Death Sentence:* "It is as if Jesus Christ, years later, were writing, in the affectless voice of the hero of Camus's *Stranger,* His own troubled, 'indeterminate' Gospel."

Hugging the Shore includes humor pieces, sports and travel reporting, essays on such subjects as a small-town police force and New England churches, and, in an appendix, a sort of patchwork autobiography, composed of interviews, testimonies before panels, and introductions to books of his that have been reissued. The bulk of the collection, though, is a section, made up of nearly a hundred reviews, introductions, and essays prepared from talks, that Updike calls "Other People's Books." In these pieces, written over the past eight years, primarily for *The New Yorker,* he covers—to give a rough idea— classic nineteenth-century figures (Flaubert, Hawthorne), and twentieth-century authors, some established (Joyce, Auden, Hemingway, Edmund Wilson, Nabokov, Isak Dinesen), some only beginning to be better known (Henry Green, Bruno Schulz, Flann O'Brien). There are sections on Japanese, Indian, and African fiction writers and on travel writers and historians of Asia and Africa. He reviews experimental French novelists (Raymond Queneau, Robert Pinget), new German and Eastern European fiction (Peter Handke, Milan Kundera), and contemporary British and American novelists (Kingsley Amis, Don DeLillo, Christina Stead, Ann Beattie). And there are pieces here on European and American essayists, sociologists, memoirists, historians, scientists, theologians, and anthologists of folk and fairy tales—reviews of James Boswell, Isaiah Berlin, M. F. K. Fisher, Carl Sagan, E. B. White, and Claude Lévi-Strauss.

Doris Day is here, too. Updike, who says that the singer and actress is one of his idols, reviews her autobiography, and talks with admiration about her hardy professionalism. There's a spooky blandness to his voice in this review, as if he were speaking while hypnotized. His tone is rosy and smiling, but his words describe a dogged person who didn't let the many batterings that she sustained in her private life interfere with a rigidly craftsmanlike approach to her work. Though Updike points out that many of her costars think she's sexy, he never says, or even implies, if and how she's sexy to him. His attitude recalls that of a boy who proudly and willfully aligns himself with someone he senses needs defending. He seems drawn to her because she gives him a chance to be her protector.

Updike's image of Doris Day as a spunky workhorse is very similar to the one he gives us of himself as a critic. Making one astute distinction after another about the work of so many novelists, poets, and nonfiction writers seems to quench a perfectionist's desire on his part to get it right, but he himself rarely seems to be fazed by the activity, and that may be why his criticism produces in the reader an airy, irritating sense of unlimited mental energy that is still waiting to be used on something. Updike seems to stand before us, at the end of each review, a smiling, likable man, his chores over for the day, ready for the next activity.

Updike apparently wants this breezy, effortless effect. He calls book reviewing his "improvised sub-career," and he has always worked to have us see how unimportant it is to him. He gave his first collection of reviews, parodies, magazine columns, and odd essays the defiantly bland title "Assorted Prose" (1965). Entitling his second "Picked-Up Pieces" (1975)—it is composed primarily of reviews—he implied that his criticism was an ironic joke, and the book's jacket cover, which he designed, was part of the joke. It is a black and white photo of the author standing before a street of good-sized clapboard houses. With a trace of a smile on his lips, and wearing a casual outfit of a crewneck sweater on top of a turtleneck, he holds what appear to be leaves, or maybe candy wrappers, in his cupped hand. The title and the jacket say that he's not doing anything serious—he's just a fellow out for a walk, picking up stuff, cleaning the neighborhood. The idea is mildly witty, but odd; in Updike's determination that we see his reviewing as only an inconsequential chore he makes his book seem to be more about himself, though not in a way that's clear, than about the subjects of his articles.

With the title "Hugging the Shore," Updike says more emphatically that his criticism means little to him; and, again, in an effort to make light of it, he turns himself into the star of the proceedings. This jacket cover is also an informal black and white photograph of the author—this time he's wearing Bermuda shorts and sitting in a rowboat, with sea grasses, a shoreline, and a house behind him. In a contorted foreword, he tells us that he, too, finds the idea of hugging the shore tame and unappetizing. "Writing criticism is to writing fiction and poetry as hugging the shore is to sailing the open sea," he says, and goes on,

> One misses, hugging the shore, the halting mimetic prose of fiction, which seeks to sink itself in the mind of a character or the texture of a moment. What we love about fiction writers is their

willingness to dare this submergence, to give up, in behalf of brute reality, the voice of a wise and presentable man. The critic comes to us in suit and tie. He is a gentleman. He is *right*. A pox on him, as Goethe said.

If the message isn't clear that criticism is a waste of time for a real guy, he adds that, "as it happened . . . the payment for a monthly review roughly balanced a monthly alimony payment that was mine to make."

Updike flashes so many masks before his face that we barely know what he stands for. It's hard to take what he says about criticism literally; surely he believes that a critic can make as big and daring a leap in his work as a novelist can, and that, while some critics do speak as "wise and presentable" minds, some novelists and poets do, too. Updike's real point, I think, has less to do with criticism versus fiction than with the way he wants to be seen. He'd like to make himself look weak, and us feel sorry for him, since he has lost so much time toiling in the supposedly unchallenging and thankless role of a reviewer. There's a suggestion that we are to feel guilty, too, since presumably he has been toiling for our benefit. But then, not wanting us to be discomforted, or to think that he actually might be a timid man in a suit and tie, he tells us that he was only passing as a critic—he did it for the money.

This disembodied, playacting note appears in virtually everything Updike does. He always seems to want to get inside the skin of failure, and write from there; but he also wants us to know that the voice we're hearing isn't that of the real John Updike—he has shouldered this role only for the moment, for his and our good. He floats above his images of defeat, whether his tone is comic, as in his stories about the blocked writer Henry Bech, or whether his approach is more realistic, as in his attempts to see things from the angle of a small-city, ordinary American lug in his novels about Harry "Rabbit" Angstrom, and of a frustrated and impassive Third-World leader in his novel *The Coup*. There is something ungrounded even in Updike's novels and stories about suburban married life and child rearing; though the narrator speaks as a man who has weathered every domestic responsibility, he often seems to be, at heart, a passing observer taking notes. Yet, except in the Bech stories, Updike's tone isn't crisp and ironic—his underlying mood is too forlorn. Nor does he touch the tragic—his characters are too lightweight for that. What he gets is a hazy mixture of the two. The assumption behind Updike's dismissive words about criticism is that he lets loose in his own fiction—but he doesn't. His fictional characters don't venture into deep waters. Though they're seemingly free, they act, out of a blend of pride and resignation, as if they were imprisoned.

Updike's reviews produce the same tethered effect. He shows how criticism can be the record of our most instinctive responses, and yet, whether he knows it or not, he leaves us with the feeling that our choices don't matter much. Updike's only real criterion as a reviewer is that a work be true to a kind of inner human realism, or what he calls the "home base of all humanism—the single, simple human life that we all more or less lead, with its crude elementals of nurture and appetite, love and competition, the sunshine of well-being and the inevitable night of death." It's hard to argue with this point of view, and he uses it in a flexible way. He can show how a naturalist novel is emotionally phony and unrealistic, and how a seemingly impenetrable work of pure literary experimentation—a novel by, say, Robert Pinget—is, when examined, surprisingly down-to-earth. And at first it's exciting to read a reviewer who doesn't treat some writers as sacrosanct, or imply that others are beneath his attention.

Updike's approach takes us back to some of our earliest, and perhaps most spontaneous, feelings about books. The title, author, number of pages, publisher, and date of publication of each book he reviews are put in small type at the head of the piece; the format recalls book reports done in grade school, and these reviews might be called grade-school book reports taken to the heights. They're also extended and polished versions of the carefree, impulsive, on-the-spot verdicts many of us write in our minds when we browse in a bookstore. No critic passes finer, more specific judgments on so many aspects of a book, right down to its merits as a piece of craftsmanship. Yet Updike can't bring himself to simply dismiss, let alone damn—or lose himself in love of—another writer, and that leaves a neutralized, almost inert, vision of literature.

Updike's range is encyclopedic, but he has a terrain all his own: the overlapping generations of writers, primarily novelists, who became internationally prominent either in the late thirties or, more often, after the Second World War—Céline, Borges, Günter Grass, Nabokov, Muriel Spark, Beckett, Raymond Queneau, Lévi-Strauss, Iris Murdoch, Henry Green, Saul Bellow, Italo Calvino, and others. Updike admires some of these writers a lot, and, in many cases, even in the cases of those he is skeptical of, his running descriptions of the range of their talent and their impact are probably as lively and shrewd as any American critic has produced. But he makes so many delicately shaded, overlapping positive and negative remarks in his analyses of them, and of the older and more recent authors he covers, that virtually everyone comes out with the same weight and consistency. Writing in praise of, say, Calvino's *Invisible Cities*, or Nabokov's career, or the letters of Franz Kafka, he wants us to be amazed, or reverent. There is something so glazed and preordained about these pieces, though—they sound so much as if they're official wrap-ups—that, shortly after having read them, you find it difficult to remember what, exactly, he said.

There is more grit to his writing when he is ambivalent, and he often reviews books that demand a mixed notice: novels by novelists who, in his opinion and by general consent, have done their freshest writing long before; belated translations of, or posthumous collections of previously unpublished work by, esteemed writers. And he's peerless when, say, reevaluating Colette or Andrei Bely's *Petersburg*, or when, analyzing recent Bellow, Grass, Margaret Drabble, Anne Tyler, or Kurt Vonnegut, he makes it clear that the work is the product of a distinguished mind, or has powerful moments, and yet doesn't tie together as a whole (or when the situation is reversed). His separate reviews of Bellow's *Humboldt's Gift* and *The Dean's December* and of each of four Anne Tyler novels are amazing. Though he is dissatisfied somehow with what they've done, he sinks into their novels, recasting and improving them as he goes along. Some of their material is set in the past, but they both write, to a degree, as social historians of the present, and Updike's reviews, which tie together in the reader's mind, form a kind of composite three-author portrait of life in America from the mid-seventies to the early eighties. The portrait isn't really adventurous. Updike shows Bellow's material as being too sour and inactive, too much about the loneliness of genius, and Tyler's as being a shade musty and evanescent. Updike seems to see himself in their books, though.

Yet even when he is ambivalent, Updike often doesn't dig deeply into what bothers him, and his reluctance can be infuriating, because he isn't timid. And his mind seems more pliant, more able to see into the telltale crevices of things, than, say, Edmund Wilson's or Alfred Kazin's. He always wants to convey what the texture of someone's prose is like, and he isn't afraid of saying that an aspect of a prominent sociologist's or historian's thought is vapid. He's aware of shortcomings in, say, Bruno Bettelheim's psychoanalytic interpretation of fairy tales, *The Uses of Enchantment;* he tells us that Bettelheim's "enchanting presumption of life as a potentially successful adventure may be itself something of a fairy tale." But he doesn't go beyond that perception, which would seem the opening gun of a real analysis of the issues. Wanting primarily to congratulate Bettelheim on his own terms, Updike turns him into a benevolent friend of the family.

Updike's analyses of Roland Barthes are congratulatory, too, and they also shortchange the subject. Updike is skeptical of the French essayist's work at first, and he goes furthest into his mixed emotions when he says, of *The Pleasure of the Text,* "One cannot help but feel that the authors so whimsically cherished are being condescended to and impudently pillaged." In other reviews over the years, Updike becomes increasingly an admirer, but less concrete; especially in his most recent, 1980, piece, he isn't evaluating Barthes for us so much as showing us that he can talk Barthes's language. The effect is of two mandarins overheard at court. In these and other reviews, as in many of his nonliterary essays, grouped in a section called "Persons and Places," a reader may feel that Updike has put away his dissatisfied self, and that he wants to talk with the voice of an insider, or of a genial, wry, community-minded appreciator, a voice from beyond the fray.

One of the most striking lines in *Hugging the Shore* comes from a review of *The Dean's December:* "Bellow believes in the soul; this is one of his links with the ancients, with the great books." The line makes sense about Bellow and about Updike, too. There is an extra, intangible dimension in all his work, though it may be seen most purely in his short stories. Talking about R. K. Narayan, he says, "a short story, like the flare of a match, brings human faces out of darkness, and reveals depths beyond statistics." Updike's stories, both the naturalistic ones and the sermonlike monologues, have that flare. Where they take us, though, is into the darkness. In Updike's finest moments, we feel the way we do when, in the country, especially in the fall and winter, after being indoors all evening, we go outside and the night sky is unexpectedly clear, starry, and endless—and we see both the beauty of the moment and, in a good way, the smallness of our concerns.

Reading a good amount of Updike's fiction produces the feeling that he is less a storyteller by temperament than a journal keeper. It is a person's illuminating or dispiriting moments that he most wants to re-create, and many of his best stories have the confessional, blurting-out drive of a powerful journal entry. He resembles some journal keepers, too, in that he seems to continually describe and analyze those moments because, doing it, he can put off settling some other, larger issue—an issue he knows he will never settle. Updike always asks the right questions, in his reviews as much as in his fiction; yet, perhaps because he feels he cannot bring certain problems to a head, or doesn't want to, he comes up with answers too quickly.

If readers feel personally close to him, it may be because he seems to be addressing us directly, asking us to witness something for him and thereby give him, for the moment, some relief. In his novels especially, his details are photographically precise, but they're see-through details—they seem worked up, like evidence. The real point is almost always one man's psychic and spiritual dilemma, and we invariably feel that Updike himself is that man. That his stories seem fuller than his novels may be due to the fact that he puts fewer documentary details in his stories—he goes straight for the dilemma.

His preoccupation with himself, though—his keeping himself the biggest figure in his work—has come at a cost: Updike, in his person, has a glamour and an expansiveness that his writing does not. As he has grown older—he is fifty-one—his face has become weathered and massive, and his big frame has filled out. In a documentary shown on TV in July, "What Makes Rabbit Run?," his eyes have the animation, and he moves with the slightly awkward assurance, of a boyish national hero, and, in a way, he is one. He is the spruce young conqueror of our literary life even more now than he was, say, fifteen years ago. Seemingly more prolific than ever, as a novelist, critic, short-story writer, and poet, he personifies artistic energy. Yet his work has become grayer. He has always wanted to describe the muffled and unstated connections between people—how people unconsciously hurt, or draw strength from, each other. In his earlier work, though, particularly in the stories about his parents and grandparents and his hometown, the remembered details seemed to come to him faster than he had time to organize them, and his scenes were crowded and brimming. His themes have not changed, but, increasingly now, the details seem arbitrary, and there's something schematic in the way he shows those muffled connections.

And, preoccupied with his own continually unfinished business, he doesn't give himself, in his work, to other people. His writing lacks a hero—or a heroine. There is a near-hero: a character whom we take to be the author's father. (He appears, with a different name each time, in many of the early stories and in the novel *The Centaur*, where he's a high-school math teacher.) He's harried, and often maddeningly gullible and self-deprecatory, but, tall and big-boned, he is kind, and a fighter, too. He isn't someone, though, that the reader fantasizes becoming. Nor do we dream of Updike's narrator and/or central character, the man who, whether he's called Orson, or Rob, or John, or Stanley—or Henry Bech, or Richard Maple, the husband in *Too Far to Go,* or Félix Ellelloû, the central figure in *The Coup*—we feel is Updike himself. Seen as a boy, an adolescent, a college kid, a young married man, a father, an adulterer, a lover, or a divorced man, he casts a now appreciating, now apprehensive eye at the world; he's omniscient. At the end, though, he slips out from making a decision about what he has seen and felt. Sometimes a decision has been made for him: Bech finds himself divorced, and is last seen wandering at a fashionable but wearisome New York party; Ellelloû is forced out of the presidency of Kush by a bloodless palace coup, and retires, with his family, to the French Riviera. Yet these, and Updike's other, men are never really damaged. They are superior, expectant, worried, a little cynical, and a little lost at the beginning, and they haven't changed much by the end.

They ought to be big; they're vain, and they preside, uneasily, over their worlds—what happens to the other characters never truly matters. Yet they think of themselves as nothings, and so do we. Women fall for them and there is always a sexual note in the air, but the reader remembers them less as sexy than as men who always have sex on their minds. And while they have jobs, or work at something, they appear to be jobless; they're waiting for some big thing to happen. We feel we're supposed to embrace them, because they present themselves to us as sheepish and stricken; but we aren't given anything to embrace them for.

Updike's women often seem stronger than his men, yet their strength is seen only in relation to weak men. What's rocklike about his women is negative things—their misplaced heavy enthusiasm, their obliviousness—that the protagonist thinks about with more anger than he admits to himself. Though Updike's women are more than cutouts, it's hard to imagine what they think about when they are offstage; they rarely seem to have independent minds. The one who does—she appears, under different names, in *The Centaur,* the novel *Of the Farm*, and in many stories—is always recognizably his mother. With her wary, potentially volatile, yet always lidded power, this character has a real presence. But maybe because we're never made to like her, we believe that she is a bigger—a more frightening and wracked—person than Updike shows. And Updike's small children and adolescents, though they say charming and authentically kidlike things, and are alive on the page, are faceless in memory.

There are, of course, vivid individuals in his fiction. His cranks and creeps, who generally dog the central character's path or embarrass him, are often wonderful. Among the best are the butlerish and manic fuddy-duddy from Oxford in the story "A Madman," the belligerently profane Gregg in the novel *The Poorhouse Fair,* the blandly annoying yogi in the story "The Christian Roommates," and the dank Marvin Federbusch in "Three Illuminations in the Life of an

American Author," one of the Bech stories. Updike is clearly drawn to these impulsive, blithely selfish, untormented souls—he gives them the best lines. Unconcerned about looking foolish, they're the antithesis of his central characters. But he doesn't linger with them. He seems to see them as unchanging forces, not people who might grow in dimension.

Unwilling to push his central male characters over the edge, Updike is too forgiving toward his other characters—as he is too benign toward the authors he reviews. He'd rather leave everyone shuffling along; maybe they'll be stronger when they reappear in his next novel or story, or in the next book of theirs he will review. That may be why his endings are more like postponements, and can be abrupt, inconclusive, pat—too sour or too ethereal. His narratives and reviews often have the quality of being visited, at the end, by an angelic outsider or by a wise old King Solomon—a spirit, as it were, who descends for this moment to gently draw the curtains on the stage we've been watching or to lift the proceedings to a loftier realm. And possibly because Updike won't let his fictional subjects fulfill their destinies, his black moods appear in choked-off, harping, and indirect ways. His manner of pointing out the flaws of his characters and of the subjects of his reviews is, in tone, often lordly and unengaged—more condescending than he may realize. It's as if he felt he was being kind to them by being unengaged.

Certainly no one thing explains the fuzziness at the core of Updike's work, but in his early stories, especially those set in a small Pennsylvania town, we feel we're seeing the dilemmas in his own life that first pulled him in opposite directions and left him with his sense of the unresolvableness of things. Some of the most intense, packed stories—"The Alligators," "A Sense of Shelter," "Flight," "The Happiest I've Been"—involve the courtship rites of teenagers. The stories aren't about sex, though. They're about a character (his name is always different) who courts because he feels he ought to, and who is often most at peace when circumstances let him off the hook. Updike's young man knows he's superior to virtually everyone; he's the kid who gets straight A's, and he is more perceptive about everything outside school. But, except for his parents, there isn't anyone in his town, maybe anyone in the whole county, who can appreciate what that means. No, he has to win in the eyes of his classmates, and yet to be average is, in a way, to slum, and the tension in the stories comes from the way the young man keeps being caught by his more popular peers—and by himself—in the act of trying to pass. There is even a moment when, at a luncheonette one snowy day, in "A Sense of Shelter," he looks around at the kids who are with him in his booth and realizes that, somehow squeezed out of the tables with his fellow seniors, he has settled for being a leader of a band of brainy but childish juniors—kids who are at a loss at parties and would never know what to do after a prom.

There's a European, nineteenth-century note to Updike's early Pennsylvania stories. They form one long tale of a provincial teacher's son, a gifted, questioning, and kind young man, a prince by nature, who grows up knowing that he will never be a true prince and that, no matter how much he accomplishes when he goes away, he will always be the teacher's son when he comes back to his town. The stories are moving but they aren't cathartic, because the young man never consciously decides to risk isolation and face the fact of his superiority. We're never sure which role he most wants. What he settles for is a priestly, in-between role. Though he doesn't put his future course of action in words, it's clear that he will leave, and live up to his brilliant promise, but he won't let himself fly. He'll be like a man who, ashamed of his inherited riches, develops a limp, when there is actually nothing wrong with his legs, so the world will realize that, in some way, he has paid his dues.

The character's moment of settling is best seen in "The Happiest I've Been." After a long night of hectic and wearying Christmas-season partying, from house to house, the nineteen-year-old John Nordholm and his friend Neil Hovey finally get going, in the early morning hours, on their long drive to Chicago, where John is going to join his girlfriend. In the very last sentences, John, who's at the wheel, thinks about the beautiful prospects of his girl waiting for him in Chicago, and of the pleasingly long and empty winter journey stretching out before him. And he realizes how good he has felt when, earlier in that night, two of his peers, in different times and places, have fallen asleep right next to him. He feels honored because, essentially, they have taken him for granted.

The Pennsylvania stories present a picture of an only child who continually watches, and tries to account for, two mighty figures—his mother and father. They are the only people in his numbingly ordinary world who are as sensitive and perceptive as he is. Though he finds his guileless father an embarrassment, and there is always a gulf between him and his mother, he wants to keep them, and their past, on a pedestal, and the reader understands why: if not for his parents, there would be nothing for Updike's young protagonist to believe in. He seems to make a religion out of being an average kid, even of being a proud son and celebrator of his state of Pennsylvania, because it keeps him, in his mind, from outgrowing his parents; if he outgrew them he'd be truly alone.

Updike's aesthetic—his belief in the "home base of all humanism"—seems to stem from that awareness: the facts of the world have to be honored because otherwise there is nothing. It is as though realism preserves him from a nihilism that he suspects is his truest response. And if he can become edgy and taskmasterish when he's talking about the "home base of all humanism," it may be because the idea is possibly something of a myth to him. He sometimes seems to be saying, "I've stayed loyal to my belief in the average, I've paid my dues to the everyday—so should you." Updike is at his sharpest when he straightforwardly describes his ambivalent responses. But just as his fiction is often most alive in those moments when one of his embarrassing or babyish individuals takes center stage, so he reveals more of himself when he writes about authors—Herman Melville, Knut Hamsun, William S. Burroughs, in particular—who feel hampered by, or are oblivious of, the "home base" of anything. It's not that these pieces are his best. Updike doesn't fight these writers directly; his relationship to them is not as clear as it might be. But, for the reader, there is a welcome friction in Updike's attempt to make some writers presentable, or to put others in their place. Writing as a defender of the faith, Updike also seems to be looking at men he might have been.

107

In "Melville's Withdrawal," the longest and oddest piece in the book, he tries to make Melville a kind of clubman. Updike wants to tell us that *Moby-Dick* wasn't, as a legend has it, a critical or financial failure, and that, contrary to some other myth, Melville didn't stop writing after it. Analyzing what Melville did write in the remaining thirty-nine years of his life, though, Updike believes that he was "right to withdraw, when he did, from a battle that had become a losing battle." There is little in Updike's densely detailed piece that is factually new. What is new is his attempt to pull out the passion and tension from Melville's life and work. Updike creates a Melville who, though he had little taste for the small change of literary life, was, right through the publication of *Moby-Dick*, a regular working author, selling his wares in the marketplace like any other. To prove that his subject was hardly an unappreciated genius, Updike shows how well *Moby-Dick* was received by reviewers and how reasonably Melville fared through the sale of his books. (Updike even tells us how Melville's advances and royalties translate into dollars today.) He'd also like us to see that Melville, no longer having anything to say after *Moby-Dick*, made the right professional move in gradually leaving the literary scene. To illustrate this, Updike makes mincemeat out of most of the good-sized books Melville wrote in the drawn-out final act of his life. Updike pounces on the opportunity of describing what he perceives as the bloated, stagnant, or dry qualities of *Pierre* and *The Confidence-Man;* but even "Benito Cereno," "Bartleby the Scrivener," and *Billy Budd*, which also followed *Moby-Dick*, are unexciting to him. He tosses bits of textbook praise in their direction.

It's debatable if Updike finds any of Melville exciting, especially when we learn that Melville's "favorite pastime," in his writing, is "woolgathering upon absolute matters in an atmosphere of male companionship." But Updike's chief concern isn't Melville's writing—it's Melville's wounded and groping behavior, which seems to grate on him and which he wants us to see in a new light. He tells us that Melville, when still in his thirties, became obsessed with "greatness, in the sense that Shakespeare and Dante possessed it," and that he was right to withdraw to his "public silence and private poetry" when his juices presumably ran dry after *Moby-Dick*, because then, at least, he "preserved his communion with greatness." By these words, Updike may believe that he has reburied Melville as a pro. But the words are blurry; mightn't he also be saying that Melville was overly ambitious and that he spent his last thirty-nine years in a sulk?

Knut Hamsun is another undomesticated individualist Updike wants to straighten out. Updike has written more extensively about this novelist (in reviews here and in *Picked-Up Pieces*) than probably any other American critic. For Updike, as for many of us, Hamsun is as fresh and urgent now as he is known to have been to his original audience. When we read him, nearly all sense of historical time and place disappears; we forget that the setting is Norway in the late nineteenth and early twentieth century—we experience his characters' every wavering impulse, whether cruel or tender, in a magnified way. Yet Updike, who describes this writer so well, always sees a hitch; he invariably shows how Hamsun's vision is centered too exclusively on fevered, isolated, and unpredictable hobo geniuses. Updike's point is: can we trust the insights, however liberating, of such adrift and unconnected minds?

In *Hugging the Shore*, he reviews two of the writer's later, and not so successful, works, *The Wanderer* and *The Women at the Pump*. The review of *The Women at the Pump* is called "Saddled with the World"; the title comes from a line of Hamsun's and Updike uses it to describe what he believes was the novelist's predicament as he aged: to keep writing, he was forced to bring more of the facts of the everyday world into his work, and he wasn't suited to the task. As Updike presents it, Hamsun couldn't settle down and tell a sustained story about his "characters and their interwoven lives"—his spirit was too anarchic, footloose, Olympian.

Updike's feeling about Hamsun is very similar to his feeling about Melville. He isn't simply saying that their later work is poor. He's implying that these solitary wanderers received their comeuppance: they became "saddled with the world," or had to "withdraw," when they ran out of the egocentric artistic capital of their youth. He may be looking at them with a mixture of wariness and longing, too, because, in their work, and by the example of their lives, they represent a freedom that Updike, in his work, rejects. It is almost as though the three of them were brothers, and he were the proper one, and he felt genuinely sorry for them, and genuinely superior, and he knew, too, that they were getting away with something he couldn't. Demonstrating how Melville had to withdraw from a "losing battle," he seems to be reassuring himself that any writer would become a loser if he believed that he was superior to his public—or if he was presumptuous enough to think that if he couldn't be in Shakespeare's company he wouldn't want to be in anyone's company.

And if Updike appears a bit unsettled by Hamsun it may be because Hamsun's characters do what Updike's characters think about doing. Updike's world is more like Hamsun's than he may realize. Rabbit Angstrom, at least as he appears in Updike's first novel about him, *Rabbit, Run*, has the makings of one of Hamsun's solitary, cussed, dissatisfied, and tragic rovers. And all of Updike's men, though they are generally married, are unattached bachelors at heart. Except that, never set free, always self-saddled to the world, they somehow are never as happy, or able to sink as deeply into their loves, as Hamsun's men.

Updike makes you want to shake him, because he always seems to be denying a part of himself. You feel that he has it in him to be the romantic monster he disapproves of in others, and that, by a flick of a switch, powerful emotions might pour forth. He says he's hugging the shore as a critic, and he shows his fictional characters doing the same thing. But whenever his criticism or his fiction has a special bristling energy, his underlying question often seems to be: How do I weigh anchor and get out of here? How does a man break loose? Perhaps it's because he hasn't found an answer for this question that his writing has a bottled, untouched quality. Updike found his assured voice, as a critic and fiction writer, when he was fairly young, and that voice hasn't changed. Nor has it ever seemed quite his own creation. Writing with an eerily developed authority and fluency when he was still in his twenties, Updike could almost have been mimicking the tone of a professional author. In some way, he still mimics. Whether his subject is Roland Barthes or Rabbit Angstrom, he wants to show us that he has mastered the appropriate lingo for the occasion.

Updike has always been celebrated for his language, yet his twining rhythms and shifting textures often seem to be a cover for him. He frequently seems to mean something different from—even the opposite of—what he says. He tells us, in his fiction and reviews, that he has volunteered to be saddled with the world, or to be a kind of lifeguard, patrolling the shore, for us. He wants to be our Lancelot. Yet if we sometimes aren't sure if we have heard him right, it is possibly because he means what he says only as a gesture—he has given us only half of his thought. A reader may sense that it is up to him to supply the concluding half, and to say, "Please, you don't have to sacrifice yourself." Updike's own story is a stonier, and also a bigger and more anxious, one than any he has yet told. He has shaped a language for himself that doesn't do justice to his emotions. They are able to come out only between the lines. When John Nordholm drives out of Pennsylvania that morning, in "The Happiest I've Been," he wants to list the reasons why, at that moment, he's happy. The story's title, though, and what we hear in his words, suggest that what he is actually talking about, in a kind of code, is his unhappiness.

—1983

HEATHCLIFF WITHOUT CATHY

AT THE BALTHUS RETROSPECTIVE at the Metropolitan Museum, I saw a young man walking around with a kind of secret, inner smile on his face. He wasn't looking at the pictures carefully; he was walking slowly through the middle of the rooms, letting the atmosphere swirl around him. For me, there was almost as much life in his face as in the exhibition, which felt wan—there were few paintings that had life as paintings. The young man may have been entranced by the range of virtuoso technique on display, or by the painter's many images of girls shown daydreaming and in moments of sexual reverie. My hunch, though, was that he was responding to the spirit that underlies the

111

work but isn't made compelling or fresh: its sense of proud, romantic isolation.

Balthus—his real name is Balthasar Klossowski—is a painter that many of us have been drawn to and, at other times, have felt very uncertain about. Now seventy-six, he is popularly known for bringing risky sexual subject matter into high art. His renown is also based, especially in art circles, on the image he has conveyed of a lofty, removed painter-poet who rejected the art of his time to pursue the ageless problems of his métier. He wasn't the only young painter in Europe between the wars to go back to traditional figure and landscape motifs; yet few others did it in such a grand manner, or presented in their work such a self-contained world. Balthus rejected not only abstraction but the breakthroughs of, say, Matisse; and while his images of people in streets or in darkened rooms had the dreamy oddness of the art of the Surrealists, who were his near-contemporaries, he didn't treat his images ironically, as they did. He planted references from Italian Renaissance painting up through Courbet in his work, implying that significant art stopped with this French realist—the last giant before the Impressionists brought everyday light into art. And Balthus set his pictures in a world Courbet might have recognized. His interiors, his few portraits and Parisian scenes, and his more numerous moody landscapes and views through the windows of his château at Chassy convey an ideal of rude aristocratic elegance. His interiors often include a few pieces of uncomfortable-looking provincial wood furniture, and the practically bare rooms appear drafty and damp—as if a person accustomed to a cushioned existence would find it a challenge to live there. He takes us to a realm where every object and vista is purer and starker than it is in real life, and where even the way someone sits in a chair asks to be appreciated as art.

Balthus's work can be stimulating in a group show. Encountering one or two of his pictures, which don't seem old-fashioned, exactly, or modern, either, sharpens your sensibilities. You may want to look at Courbet, for example, to see this painter as Balthus might; and you may develop a hunger for the modern art he rejects—you can turn to Matisse and believe you see his liberating color for the first time. But at the Met's retrospective—the show opened at the Centre Pompidou, and is his first major exhibition here since 1956—Balthus's paintings have very little cumulative impact. He is clearly a man on a quest, but the quest may have less to do with painting than with a desire for a stoical, aesthetic existence. He seems to have the "look" of a picture in mind before he gets to work on the canvas—then to sweat it out with his materials to produce that "look." He appears to be more in love with the idea of being a great artist than with the making of pictures. And his quest has little urgency to it. He seems, and he can make a viewer, a bit numb.

The best paintings are almost all from the thirties, and at the start of the show. Two early pictures, *Garrison in Morocco*, a crazy scene of soldiers in outlandishly high fezzes attempting to capture a white horse in a yard, and *The King of Cats*, a self-portrait of a very trim and imperious young Balthus—he's being butted by a huge cat with staring eyes—are charming and beautiful as objects. The Moroccan painting has the bright, unmixed colors—and both pictures have the glossy smooth finish and the awkward stiffness—of naive art at its best. Far more distinctive are the 1936 portrait of André Derain and the 1937–38 portrait of Joan Miró and his daughter Dolores. They are probably his finest paintings. Though they are the least outwardly Balthus-like works in the show, these portraits of fellow-painters—both are in the Museum of Modern Art's collection—give us our most tangible sense of what it might be like to look at the world the way Balthus does. The Derain is the more comic and anecdotal. With his left hand hammily placed on his chest and his body encased in a monumental striped robe, he walks toward us, his eyes raised above ours, a mafioso thinking his thoughts. Behind him is a girl slumped in a chair, her eyes shut. Her face seems enclosed in a filmy vagueness. Is she the big man's recent conquest? Is she a daydream he's having as he fingers his shirt? Is she the reason he strides toward us with a look of disgruntled greatness? Balthus makes Derain fatuous, but he clearly admires, even adores, him.

The Miró has less of a story buried in it, and that, plus its slightly larger size—it's a bit over four feet high—makes it the stronger picture. In the exhibition catalogue, Sabine Rewald notes that the "slightly bored" expression on Miró's and his daughter's faces possibly derives from the fact that Balthus worked on the painting for months. The wide-eyed Dolores, who stands between her father's legs, does seem a little stir-crazy—or is she hypnotized? And while Miró, in his tightly buttoned-up suit, does look pinched and haggard, we sense that he also may be acting the part of a harried clerk.

The Derain and the Miró are two of the peaks of European portraiture, and paintings you fall in love with, for subtle reasons: for the amazing harmonies of tans and oranges, ecru whites and oatmeal whites, soft pinks and metallic blues; the effortlessly graceful way the figures are placed in relation to the four sides of the pictures; the way the background of the Miró is neatly divided between a charcoal-gray bottom half and a tan-gray top, to form an elegant abstraction on its own; the way Balthus balances tiny, hallucinatory distortions in scale with a seemingly simple descriptive realism; the way he makes you feel the suede of Miró's shoes. They're the most memorable shoes in modern art. Historically, the portraits derive from a revived interest in romantic, storytelling painting in the thirties; but the pictures seem unrelated to any particular moment in the past. They suggest possibilities for a kind of satirical, psychological—but nonliterary— realism that, it seems, is still barely tapped.

Right around the time of the Miró portrait, though, a veil comes down on Balthus's art. His color begins to be dissatisfyingly dark, and everything seems to be happening behind the surface, not on it. Works from the late thirties and early forties such as *The Children, The Game of Patience, The Golden Days,* and a number of pictures of a girl named Thérèse have long been his signature pieces. In reproduction, these images of girls alone in rooms, dreaming away the long afternoons, or playing with cats, or looking at themselves in mirrors— sometimes sprawled, legs apart, on chaise longues—resemble Old Master paintings. They appear to have the same powerful contrasts of light and dark. In actuality, though, they have surprisingly little inner light, and their dingy gunmetal-green tonalities and the airless impersonality of their surfaces keep you at a distance. These works ought to be poetic, suggestive, even disturbing—and perhaps for many, on a first viewing, they are. But they don't take on a second, longer life, in your mind, as paintings. They amount to remnants of a modern artist's too carefully balanced attempt to re-create the look of nineteenth-century art.

A landscape from this time, though, the 1939 *Larchant,* uses that nineteenth-century look in a quietly impressive way. The focal point is a twelfth-century church—half its belfry is gone—that is set in the center of a small town. Surrounding the town are low hills and a vast, empty, flat plain, which stretches far off into the darkened distance. *Larchant* presents a mood rarely seen in painting. We're not sure if we're looking through the eyes of an embittered, or simply a disillusioned, man, but clearly something is keeping the blue of this late-afternoon sky, and the earth colors of the fields and town, from being as sizzling as they might be. This is a landscape seen after a moment of ecstasy has died down and a note of asperity has set in. It's a view of the boredom and clamminess of rural life by a man who says, "This life is fine for me."

Beginning in the late forties, Balthus animates his surfaces more, and makes sharper the contrast of light and dark; but his color becomes increasingly filtered and woozy. His surfaces begin to appear to be something other than paint—velvet, tile, plaster. Initially, these encrusted surfaces seem exotic—they ask to be inspected closely. On repeated viewings, though, they primarily communicate a lot of layering and relayering and an underlying indecision. Balthus finds it increasingly hard to make oil paint look like oil paint. Hues are invariably mixed, to create nacreous, in-between shades. When bright color is applied, it's for effect, to highlight the masses of inert, indecipherable colors—as when, for instance, he weaves, as a finishing touch, an orange-red, a violet, or a bright green onto a sea of coagulated iridescent tan.

Crunching and mushing his medium into submission in picture after picture, he becomes an artist of such greeting-card prettiness in some of his later paintings that it is impossible to know what is on his mind. In the 1957 *Girl at the Window,* for instance, where the girl, seen from the rear, looks out on a morning landscape in which all color seems about to dissolve into a fluffy white-lavender, he isn't an ironist of bad taste—there is too much care visible. Is it that, having spent so many years determined to assert the right taste (in clothes, furniture, and art), he worked his way inside out, to a static condition where everything has to be pretty and nice? In terms of technique, he has gradually become an artist of the sweet and the cottony—exactly what he appeared to scorn at an earlier point in his life, when he presented himself as that puritanical dandy the King of Cats.

Not all his later work is overcooked. The 1955 *Nude in Front of a Mantel*, which is in the Met's collection, has a novel combination of monumentality and tenderness. The picture shows a young girl—she may be eleven—standing before a white mantel in an empty corner of a room. On the mantel is a mirror and a blue pitcher. The painting is effective for almost musical reasons; it's lovely because a number of very small, formal elements shift against each other, to create a mood of pleasure and happiness. The picture is like a piece of chamber music for blues and whites. Your eyes go back and forth between the pitcher's soft sky blue—it's tinged with violet—and the wallpaper's duller, robin's-egg blue; then you play these blues off against the glowing alabaster white of the girl's body and the mute, chalky white of the mantel. These blues and whites, in turn, are threaded together with a soft tan and a dull gold—the colors of the mirror's frame and of a line that runs around the wainscoting.

That this painting is relatively more successful than Balthus's other later work may be because there's more air between the colors. It also helps that we barely see the girl's face. Standing before us in strict profile, she holds up her long hair with her arms, which largely cover her head. The bit of shadowed face that is visible is like a sliver of the moon—the moon with a girl's profile. We feel we know her, and we like her. But we don't know, and it's hard to like, the people in the rest of Balthus's later work. He's in trouble when, from the late forties on, he includes faces. He's thought of as a master of subtle, ambiguous states of feeling, but there's something tacked-on about that ambiguity. His drawing of facial features, and the razor-sharp edges he gives to bodily forms, are often graphic and unpainterly. You believe that the faces on his figures could be entirely different if the thin lines that demarcate the eyes and mouths were subtly changed. His people might grin at one another as easily as they glare. And the feeling that they are only "making faces" undercuts the sense of immovable weight and dignity that he strives for in his color and composition.

In some ways, Balthus's work is more satisfying when seen in Jean Leymarie's album-size 1979 *Balthus* than in the exhibition. This happens in part because the large, superior reproductions give some of the pictures, especially those from the early forties, a radiance they do not possess. Balthus seems more substantial in Leymarie's pages because, too, without being an illustrational artist, he is a kind of book artist. Many of his values as a painter, and, it would seem, as a person, come from books: from reproductions of pictures, from literary and historical accounts of the past. His most vibrant and intense work—the set of illustrations he did between 1932 and 1935 for Emily Brontë's *Wuthering Heights*—comes directly from a book. Each roughly ten inches square, these pen-and-ink drawings (most are in the first section of the show) have a bluntness lacking in his later drawings and in most of his paintings.

The drawings remind you that Balthus, the epitome of French taste, is a Central European by heritage and in spirit. He was born in Paris, but his parents, both of whom were painters—his father also wrote a study of Daumier—were from Silesia, then part of East Prussia. His father's family was from Warsaw, his mother's family was originally Russian, and Balthus spent much of his boyhood and youth in Berlin and Geneva. Like the people in Oskar Schlemmer's Bauhaus paintings and set designs, Balthus's *Wuthering Heights* characters have a bobbing weightlessness, no matter how firmly they're planted on the ground. Balthus's figures have even more in common with those in the drawings by the Polish writer Bruno Schulz, who supported himself as a drawing instructor. (A selection of his drawings accompanies his *Sanatorium Under the Sign of the Hourglass*.) Schulz's people, like those of Balthus, have heads that are a touch too big for their bodies, confront each other with balletic poses, and loom out from nearly bare, cramped, stagelike backgrounds.

Done when he was in his mid-twenties, Balthus's illustrations of Brontë's novel are based on a pitch-perfect sense of her whiplash rhythms, her exclamation-point style. He does exactly what she does: he makes each character fervent in his or her own way. He seems to see himself in the sometimes secretive and blank heroine Catherine Earnshaw, in her thickheaded brother Hindley, and in the omnipresent nursemaid Nelly. Mostly, though, he's Heathcliff. He gives Heathcliff his own features, and Sabine Rewald notes that, at the time he did them, he had reason to see himself in this character. Balthus was in love with a young Swiss woman, Antoinette de Watteville, and, like the Heathcliff who comes to Wuthering Heights as a boy and virtually becomes a member of the Earnshaw family, Balthus—a "poor and unknown painter"—lived with Antoinette and her brother at their "mansion" when he was in Bern.

There are some other reasons for his identifying himself with Heathcliff that Rewald doesn't mention. In his youth, Balthus had, as Heathcliff does, a thatch of hair, "like a colt's mane"; and, like Brontë's foundling-hero, he is a man with a single name. Long before he did these illustrations, he had adopted Rainer Maria Rilke's suggestion—Rilke was a friend of his mother's—that he use the nickname he had in his family, originally spelled Baltusz, as his only name. The biggest cause for his seeing himself in Heathcliff, though, is that he had already lived, and told, Heathcliff's story. When he was eleven, Balthus created a booklet of forty pen-and-ink drawings about his adventures with a cat, named Mitsou, whom he loses, searches for—and never finds. (Two impressive plates from the booklet are reproduced in the exhibition catalogue.) Published in 1921, with an introduction by Rilke (whose enthusiasm for the pictures led to their publication), *Mitsou* is a child's version of *Wuthering Heights.* They're both about lone, somewhat untamed boys who lose a loved playmate and devote their days to finding her.

Balthus's illustrations go through the first half of Brontë's novel—when Heathcliff and Cathy spar with each other and run off to the moors and dream together, then go in fatefully separate directions, and Cathy dies. Balthus may have stopped there simply because he wasn't engaged by the second part, which might be called "Heathcliff Without Cathy." Maybe, though, he felt that his own art began at that point. This, anyway, is what a viewer senses.

Balthus's subsequent work presents a view of the world that the grown-up Heathcliff might have. The Heathcliff of the second half of the novel, after Cathy's death, is a threatening and morose country squire. He lives surrounded by dimwits and oblivious of the damp, unkempt conditions of his household. Since he feels that little matters in this world any longer, he may even be pleased by those boorish conditions. Taking title to Wuthering Heights and Thrushcross Grange, through marriages he arranges, he wins his boyhood vendetta against Hindley. He becomes the master of all the land he can see. But he is essentially only repairing past wrongs; he's given no pleasure by anything he does. He is one of the most sensual brutes in literature, but emotionally he's a virgin. Though he marries and fathers a son, he feels he is really keeping himself for Cathy. He believes he can achieve consummation of his passion only in death, when his body will mix with her body, under the soil.

The overcultivated, stagnant, and unreal quality of Balthus's art, especially from the late thirties on, may derive from the way he, too, seems to continually pay homage to, and keep himself in readiness for, a person or a thing he never quite had and knows he will never truly possess. We miss a male presence in his work after the time of the Derain and Miró portraits. The few male figures who appear are merely watchers; in the landscapes we sometimes see, from the rear, an emaciated and irritatingly stylized elongated man, and in the interiors there's an occasional gnomelike boy, who has the lasciviousness, and sexlessness, of a court dwarf.

Balthus perhaps, like Heathcliff, became too deeply immersed in his fantasy of the past. It's also possible to feel that he didn't go deeply enough into his fantasy. He wanted to fashion a great museum style out of his themes, and you know why he would want to do so. Yet, enlarging his pictures, eliminating most of the flavorful but bizarre little details (or pushing them to the corners), and simplifying his conceptions, he went from being an unpredictable provincial to being a resigned grand seigneur. That he has always wanted to work with large sizes is to his credit; but he brings the same inch-by-inch intensity to his big pictures that he brings to his easel-sized ones, and there's a strain. In such large works as *The Room* and *The Passage du Commerce Saint-André*—they're both from 1952–54—and in the paintings of the sixties and seventies, many of which were made in Rome, where he was the director of the French Academy, he seems to labor as much over the backgrounds as over the figures. The result is a neutralizing standoff between the two.

The single large painting in the exhibition which has a genuine spaciousness is *The Mountain*, of 1937—a panoramic tableau, about eight feet high and twelve feet wide, that shows seven people placed in different spots in an Alpine setting. *The Mountain*, which is in the Met's collection, is Balthus's crossroads picture: it pinpoints how colossal his ambition is and, too, the stumbling block at the heart of his approach. At the lower left of the painting is an exaggeratedly sardonic-looking fellow with a pipe jutting out of the side of his mouth. Bent on one knee, he looks in on the scene, squints, and seems to say, like a prematurely old bachelor in a small town who is obsessed with the lewd doings of the local kids, "What's this non-sense, now!" Next to him is a young blonde hiker who holds her hands together straight up over her head. Catching the full rays of the late-afternoon sun on her face and the top part of her body, she seems to be stretching after a deep sleep. Next to her, in the lower center of the scene, enveloped in shadow, is a sleeping young woman (who may be dreaming the entire tableau). Seen progressively farther away are a little boy wearing an old-fashioned red vest, a couple out for an afternoon walk—they're looking down into a gorge—and, in the far distance, a lone man walking away from us.

The Mountain can strike a viewer, on some days, as one of the great twentieth-century pictures. It is perhaps the most ardent of all mod-ern dream paintings; neither Magritte nor de Chirico was ever as romantic or as muscular. It says to a young painter, "Go all the way with whatever is in your head." On other days, the painting can appear whimsical and arch, because the disparate, puppetlike charac-ters, the magnificent setting, and the ominous mood don't form an emotional whole. (It doesn't help to learn that the picture was in-tended to represent Summer in a projected cycle of paintings of the seasons.) Unlike Magritte and de Chirico, who paint enigmas, Bal-thus seems to say, "There's a secret here, and you're not going to find out what it is." He's tantalizing us, and he does it, to one degree or another, in virtually all his work. This may be his idea of the true poetry of painting. His desire to be private in public, though, is experienced as a limitation. We feel that on a deeper level he's covering up something he senses about his own character.

Thinking about *The Mountain* after looking at the *Wuthering Heights* illustrations, you may wonder if the painting was Balthus's attempt to create his own Brontë novel in paint. The craggy setting, which is the Bernese Oberland—though he made up much of the topography— suggests a Continental version of Brontë's treeless moors. And the model for the stretching blonde is Antoinette de Watteville, who was his model for Cathy (and who became his first wife the year the painting was made). Along with the cold blue sky and the sunny, pale green and tan landscape, she is the most solid element in the painting. With her Buddha's smile and stiff-armed gesture, she's a weird and slightly cartoonish creature; yet she is far warmer, and more real, than the girls he later paints in conventionally realistic, or Old Masterish, ways. Seen in the light of his later work, she seems to be his salute to the Swiss, German, Alpine—or, at least, non-French—side of himself. She also might be his farewell to the part of him that felt he was the young Heathcliff. She might be called the last living Cathy in his art.

—1984

DAVID SALLE

THE ELEVEN PAINTINGS David Salle recently showed at the Leo Castelli gallery are very large—a number of them are in the range of eight feet high by twelve feet wide—but they wear their monumentality lightly. These collagelike pictures, which frequently include objects affixed to their surfaces, are so beautifully composed and yet seem to have been assembled with such nonchalant speed that they're elating. Looking at one of them, you feel that you have stepped into the artist's mind, you're with him as he makes his moves, and the whole operation is as simple as casually rearranging the objects on a desk. Salle (pronounced "Sally") has generally been grouped with a number of American and European painters who have come to the fore in the past few years and who use the figure in their work. Labeled "Neo-Expressionists," they have attempted to bring a romantic and often impassioned note into contemporary art, and to make paintings that encompass references to history, to comic strips, to old and new art. Salle has a lot in common with these artists, but his new pictures, which were made within the last year and are larger in size and weightier in appearance than any he has done before, make clear what his previous work suggested: that the "Expressionist" label doesn't really fit him. No label does. His work is as emotionally full as that of any current American or European painter, yet in spirit he is, at thirty-one, closer to being a new kind of classical master.

Salle seems to think about a painting the way a formalist might. That is, as a flat plane on which the artist arranges different elements—some of which recede, some of which push forward—to create a whole that is balanced but pulses. In a way, Salle redoes formalist art with an apparently autobiographical array of images— sexy, satirical, ironic ones. The backgrounds of his pictures are often softly brushed-in monochromatic drawings of figures. He places over these backgrounds, among other things, deft line sketches; figures from cartoons; clusters of geometric shapes (which recall the art and design of the thirties); and patches of smeary, expressionistic brushwork (which recall the fifties). He places words over images, draws in a figure sideways over one that is upside down, and joins in the same picture a panel painted on canvas with one painted on, say, upholstery fabric. Salle makes us keenly aware of how one texture or color plays off another, and he has a sure instinct for how much variety a picture can take, so when we spot something that seems to be a slip or a miscalculation—a stain on a canvas, for instance—we can't help seeing it as another element in the composition.

B.A.M.F.V. is probably his most elegantly poised picture. It brings together, to list a few elements, shimmery gray-on-gray pastiches of fifties line drawings of a matador swirling his cape; an unsettling portrait of a ravenous and goonish cartoon duck; a melancholy little picture of a nude woman smoking; a bushlike wire-mesh object painted a pale olive green; voluptuous yellow-orange line drawings of the female nude; and a squarish slab of dense pink oil paint, casually laid on a smear of thinly applied pink. Painted, in part, on an apricot-colored sheet of satin, *B.A.M.F.V.* has the all-over composition—and presence—of Renaissance tapestries. These tapestries often presented to their audiences an overview of contemporary life in its most up-to-the-minute appearance. Salle's painting doesn't give us the appearance of contemporary life; but, shuffling vaguely risqué scenes and objects with not-so-charming cartoon characters, and suffusing both of them with boudoir and candy colors that we know were once considered tasteful and stylish and now seem amusingly exotic, he seems to capture the early eighties. He shows how the most up-to-the-minute thing about contemporary life can often be its enthusiasm for the recent past.

Salle's pictures don't have the public nature of most tapestries, though. He creates an immediate tension with his audience, because he makes us want to decipher these puzzlelike paintings, and we also sense that he may have a take-it-or-leave-it attitude toward those puzzles. If you are familiar with twentieth-century—and especially contemporary—art, you put a lot of mental energy into these pictures almost involuntarily. Registering the components, you're first a skeptic, then a passive enumerator, then a warmed-up partner. You say to yourself, "Oh, that carving of an ear affixed to the corner, that's Jasper Johns. . . . The lit light bulbs, they're just early Jim Dine. . . . I know that face, isn't it from an Oskar Kokoschka? . . . The way he uses words on top of images, Bruce Nauman did that. . . . Those legs from tables and chairs sticking off the side of the canvas, surely he's parodying Louise Nevelson. . . . That duck isn't Donald Duck—which duck is it? A duck from an actual cartoon? . . . Isn't the way he draws with one color over a single-color ground reminiscent of Raoul Dufy? . . . Why do some of his little line drawings make me think of 'Leave It to Beaver'? . . . Doesn't his sense of glamour owe something to Alex Katz, and isn't he also showing the tensions that underlie that glamour? . . . Isn't that drawing of a man doubling up in pain taken from the image of Lee Harvey Oswald being shot by Jack Ruby? Doesn't Salle look like that? Is he saying he's an Oswald?"

Salle's method of layering one image on top of another isn't new to art. The Cubists did a version of this seventy years ago, and there are no doubt earlier examples. But Salle makes it feel new. Perhaps only in movies have we seen something like the gentle and diaphanous effect he gets, of different images simultaneously drifting back into and rising up from other images. It's television, though, far more than movies, that his work seems to be saturated with. His method of constructing a picture recalls the way on TV in any given fifteen-minute period images flash by that are different from one another in texture and importance and yet come to seem equal in weight and value. The relationship between his often pale and ghostly large background drawings and the brighter, juicier, more densely painted images and objects that float over—and literally pop out from—them is comparable to the relationship between a TV show and a commercial break.

When, in *Tennyson*, he puts the poet's name in italic capital letters across an image of a nude woman lying with her back to us, Salle might be signaling that it's time for a cultural commercial. Some members of his audience may believe, though, that the reference is to Jasper Johns, who put the name Tennyson across the bottom of a 1958 abstract gray painting. Johns's picture is probably, in part, an ironic joke on Tennyson's being a kind of "good gray poet," but his image is solemn. With its stately lettering, the painting resembles a grave marker with the deceased's name at the bottom instead of at the top. When Salle writes the poet's name across the center of his picture, he appears to say that he himself wants to be linked with Johns and that he believes his painting-assemblages are part of an influential tradition in contemporary American art. Here he's announcing that he has joined the club. Spelling out Tennyson in enormous letters, and in a sans-serif type that would be perfect for a sneaker ad, he may be kidding Johns, too; he might be saying to the painter, "Must everything be veiled and portentous?" Or perhaps Salle's point is merely "The Victorian poet and a nude on a beach don't go together, right? So here they are."

David Salle is such a masterly mimic, and he can make his audience so suspicious of his motives, that you feel you are on thin ice in seeing themes in his work—even in talking about him as a painter. In

124

a sense, he's more aptly described as the inventor of a great picture-making device. Though some of his figures and faces are drawn freehand, many are taken from magazines and books. He projects the images onto a canvas (or whatever he's working on), and fills in, in shades of gray, with a fairly dry brush—or sometimes stipples on, in a single color—the enlarged picture. His cartoon "spots" and delicate line drawings are also often taken from printed sources, mechanically projected, and traced. He has the touch and eye of a born painter-decorator, though, and that's why his pictures work. He has a genie's intuition for knowing which color to place over another color so both will jump. And he stays in the mind as a figurative artist, too.

Brother Animal is one of Salle's most powerful "figure" paintings. It is made up of two adjoining panels (which together are about eight feet high and fourteen feet wide). The picture on the left is of two large, amorphous shapes. Painted in red and yellow, they may be lungs, or pieces of shad roe, or ornate bedroom slippers—or just shapes. Whatever they are, they seem both pliant and firm, and cast dense shadows. The painting on the right shows, on a dark blue background, a brushed-in drawing of a girl who is either buttoning up or taking off her shirt. In the distance is a dark-haired fellow with his arm outstretched, looking back at her. He's a bit crestfallen, and she's pensive; she might be looking at herself in a mirror, thinking about the encounter they have had or will be having.

Attached to this canvas (from behind) are two blond Charles Eames plywood chairs, which are placed high up and to the sides, like candelabra flanking a fireplace. (The legs have been removed.) The picture is so large that from almost any distance the curvy chairs appear surprisingly small and delicate; from ten feet or so they become flashes of light on the shadowy blue-black ground. A third element is an image of a building, placed on the right of the canvas. Drawn on top of the dark blue, in a glistening pink, and with a squirmy line that one might see used to decorate a cake, it suggests a grand and glamorous place at night—perhaps a hotel.

What is the image of the couple doing with the ambiguous shapes, the chairs, and the bubbly pink sketch? What do they add up to? It's hard to say, yet these elements feel right together. The image of the couple looks as if it were taken from a still from a tacky summer-romance movie or a TV soap opera, and it ought to be banal. But, treated as if it meant no more than the shapes or the chairs, it is unexpectedly imposing. We feel that a moment everyone has lived through and not thought about much—that moment on a date when one partner retreats—has been presented in an ultimately simplified way. And the chairs, which cast shadows on the canvas, suggest the room this scene takes place in. They're oddly protective; they're a bit like the trees in a romantic forest scene, which surround and darken the faces of the unhappy lovers.

Brother Animal doesn't have the snap or the formal unity of, say, *B.A.M.F.V.* Yet *Brother Animal* holds us longer, not only because a longer look is needed to make the parts cohere but because the image of the people who are clearly tied together—yet are placed with a gulf between them—dramatizes the sense of dependency and unconnectedness which pervades Salle's art. In his work, images take on life because they're seen in relation to other images. Yet no image, no matter how pale, ever loses its individual color and texture.

Salle has been thought of as one of the more cerebral of the new American and European painters, and his pictures do seem dispassionate at first. There is a somberness, even a bleakness, in his art, though—it comes out indirectly. Telling us that, say, a strip of decorative fabric or a cartoon vignette can count for as much as a realistic drawing of a nude, he's saying that everything is equally absorbing to him—and he implies that nothing commands his total allegiance. His work has such an overriding sense of formal grace that you can miss the fact that in his pictures faces are often drained, bodies don't have any pep and are turned in on themselves. His nudes, whose legs are sometimes spread, are sexy, sometimes even coarse, and he no doubt wants to challenge his audience with these elegant parodies of girlie-magazine photographs. These drowsily accommodating dishes, though—and the tough number in heels in *Midday*—are only some of the ways he shows women. In paintings here and in previous exhibitions, his women also appear in quiet domestic moments and in battered and indrawn states. (Men generally have a secondary role; they're seen in the distance, or they take the form of wizened or pathetic or donkeyish cartoon characters.) Salle has made some of the most sensual pictures in recent American art, yet his women are literally seen in the background and are dry, washy, colorless. The combination of desire and affection—and intangibility—is his special note. His pictures present a world where ideas and objects are bright and solid and people are mirages.

In *Portrait of Michael Hurson* Salle seems to make a joke out of this, and also indicates that his view may be changing. The painted image, which takes up most of the picture's space, is a still life of food—done in browns, a copper-tan, bright yellow, and green—over and through which are drawn, in a dark blue, three stark, primitive, open-mouthed faces (none of which resemble the artist Michael Hurson). Above the still life, sticking out through the fabric on which the picture is painted, are actual red and blue light bulbs, which are lit. They beam out "Idea! Idea!" The light bulbs are funny, but they seem a little incidental. This is the only picture in the show where Salle doesn't play off a cool, removed kind of painting with painting that is brighter and hotter; virtually every mark is emphatic and hot. It's possible, of course, that he is merely parodying painterly verve. Yet this picture is also different in structure from the others. He doesn't make every part of it, even the distant corners, equally balanced; there is a real velocity—a centeredness—to the composition. We take in the utensils and pieces of food, and the faces that are laced in and out of them, the way we'd watch a roller coaster racing through the loops of a pretzel-shaped track.

The Hurson painting is thrilling—you're unprepared for the energy it radiates. Complete with a lemon, a chop, a round of cheese, and butter biscuits, this large picture has the mixture of confidence and belligerence that ten years ago an American artist would have brought to an earthwork. Salle's chosen theme, so far, seems to be modern eroticism, but he appears to want to redo everything with his picture-making devices—or, at least, you want him to. A viewer can leave this show almost as excited about Salle's future work as about the work he has just seen. After that chop and those biscuits, you may think, God, what will he do with a tree?

—1984

A STRANGER IN PARIS

GILLES, THE HERO of Jean-Antoine Watteau's painting of that name, is such a known and loved presence that it was a small shock to find, at the Watteau exhibition at the National Gallery of Art last season, that the painting had been retitled *Pierrot*. Gilles and Pierrot were similar stock characters in the old comedies; they were simpleton-buffoons who dressed all in white. Some scholars now believe that Watteau specifically had Pierrot in mind. The new name takes some adjusting to, but it doesn't change the way we think about the painting. Watteau's actor, with his arms hanging down placidly before him, remains one of the most sheepish, isolated, and superior figures in art. He stands directly before us in this six-foot-high painting—it was made around 1720—unaware of the other characters, in the lower part of the scene. His pants are too short and his white shoes are tied with red bows; a ruff collar encircles his neck, and he wears both a skullcap and a straw hat. His face is as secretive as any by Leonardo, and there is a gravity to him that recalls Rembrandt. His blankness, though, is what is fascinating. At times, he's suggestively blank, like one of Manet's women; at other times, he's as defiantly impassive as an Alex Katz. He appears to know how awkward and uncomfortable he is— and, too, how his power comes from his willingness to be awkward and foolish. He is the first figure in art who, it seems, is one of us.

The Watteau exhibition—it opened at the National Gallery, went on to the Grand Palais, in Paris, and closed this summer at the Schloss Charlottenburg, in Berlin—had the same indirect and quietly magnetic power, and so did the artist himself. Shortly after his death, six of his friends wrote biographies of him, and there was a seventh by someone who hadn't known him. (Quotes from these accounts appear in the show's huge catalogue, written principally by Margaret Morgan Grasselli and Pierre Rosenberg.) Watteau's friends, who were artists, dealers, and collectors, clearly wanted to pay their respects to his talent and his memory; he was not quite thirty-seven when he died, in 1721, of tuberculosis. Yet they seem to have been equally desirous of describing his baffling and not so lovable character. We hear that he was shy, naive—also sharp-tongued, "difficult," and "impossible." Though he was severely critical of his own work, and he had a schoolboy's adoration for many artists, especially Rubens, he was surprisingly willing to hustle his pictures. He was a drifter, too: he didn't marry, and he never had an address of his own. He moved from one friend's house to another, sometimes staying a year or more. He doesn't seem to have ever been alone—or "with" any one person or family, either.

Watteau was also a bit of an outsider in Paris. He was born in Valenciennes, which France had annexed a few years before his birth but which had long been a part of Flanders, and he struck some Parisians as a rube. Yet as an artist he became recognized for his sophistication and urbanity. Although he wasn't prolific and his career lasted little more than a decade, he is given credit for introducing a new sensual and ambiguous tone into European painting—a tone that influenced artists through much of the eighteenth century. *Pierrot*, which is owned by the Louvre, may be his best-known single work, but he is most often associated with images of courtiers and women in softly lit woodland scenes. His very name has long been synonymous with a courtierlike approach to life, a kind of grace under sadness.

The exhibition, which included some forty paintings and twice that number of drawings, and was the largest gathering of works by Watteau ever, revealed him to be the same tricky character his friends described. He isn't exactly a master—he is more like an ambitious and sometimes mixed-up young artist in the process of becoming a master. And he isn't the wistful and romantic painter he is said to be, either. Few of his paintings are humorous, but temperamentally he's comic: he looks at people from a distance. The show was wonderful and absorbing, but not conventionally satisfying. I was genuinely drawn to only a handful of small oils, his drawings, and two of his last, and least typical, paintings—*Pierrot* and *Gersaint's Shopsign*. Yet I was left keyed up, not only because each of these late works is a one-of-

129

a-kind masterpiece but because everything he did comes together in them. You can be sympathetic to him even when his individual pictures are "off," because you see the direction he's heading in, and that gives him the immediacy of a contemporary artist: we want to figure out the relationship between the pictures that click and those that don't.

Watteau's fame is based on a type of picture called a *fête galante*, which he, in effect, invented. The *fêtes*, which make up the bulk of his work, show men and women (and occasionally children) in luxuriant parks; they stroll, lounge, read, glance at and reach toward one another. A girl may be on a swing, a courtier may play a guitar, and sometimes a dance is under way. Many people believe that Watteau, in these idylls, is a subtle poet of bittersweet love, of the small shifts in the relations between men and women. The actual paintings, though, feel empty and abstract. They're not dull, but they make us restless for some action to begin. Watteau doesn't seem to care about what is going on in these scenes—the expressions seem fake. Perhaps his *fêtes galantes* couldn't be properly judged in the Washington show. The large *Pilgrimage to the Island of Cythera*, in the Louvre's collection, for many his grandest picture, and a number of his most admired *fêtes*, including those in the Wallace Collection, in London, and one in the National Gallery of Scotland, couldn't be borrowed. Yet these works, seen in reproduction, appear to be as synthetic as the many in the show; you believe you're looking at "costume" pictures, which could have been made at any time, of people dressed in eighteenth-century satins.

The Two Cousins, which was in the exhibition, is striking because it isn't a "pretend" drama. In this picture of three people beside a pond in a park, the main character is a woman with her back to us. She shows no interest in the couple next to her, and looks off into the big, pale green sky. We do, too; we sense that something will happen, and she will be released from her trance. Watteau's placement of the isolated woman is elegant and daring, and the picture's unusual silvery-green tone transports us to a specific moment: this might be a late afternoon on a humid day in early autumn. In *The Faux-Pas*, another successful picture, we're also given the sensation of a specific

1. Alex Katz. *Subway I*. 1948.
Ink on paper, 7⅞ × 4⅞".
Courtesy Marlborough Gallery

2. Alex Katz. *Camp Green*. c. 1951–53. Ink on paper, 12⅞ × 19½".
Private collection. Courtesy Marlborough Gallery

3. Giorgio de Chirico. *The Nostalgia of the Infinite.*
1913–14(?) (dated on the painting 1911). Oil on
canvas, 43¼ × 25½". The Museum of Modern
Art, New York. Purchase

4. Giorgio de Chirico. *The Mystery and Melancholy of a Street*. 1914. Oil on canvas, 34¼ × 28⅛″. Private collection

5. Giorgio de Chirico. *Great Metaphysical Interior*. 1917. Oil on canvas, 37¾ × 27¾″. The Museum of Modern Art, New York. James Thrall Soby Bequest

6. Anselm Kiefer. *Nürnberg.* 1981. Oil and straw on canvas, 110 × 150″. Collection Eli and Edythe L. Broad. Courtesy Mary Boone Gallery

7. Joseph Beuys. *La Rivoluzione Siamo Noi*.
1972. Silkscreen print, 75⅛ × 40⅛″.
Courtesy Hirschl and Adler Modern

8. David Hockney. *Machine Photograph
Rephotographed*. 1962. Photograph, 10×8″.
Courtesy David Hockney

9. William Wegman. *Ayatollah #2*. 1980. Photograph, 24 × 20″. Collection Laura-Lee Woods. Courtesy Holly Solomon Gallery

10. William Wegman. *Dusted*. 1982. Photograph, 24 × 20″. Collection Gifford Myers. Courtesy Holly Solomon Gallery

11. John F. Peto. *Still Life with Cake, Lemon, Strawberries and Glass.* 1890. Oil on canvas, 10⅛ × 13¹⁵⁄₁₆″. Collection Mr. and Mrs. Paul Mellon, Upperville, Virginia

12. John F. Peto. *The Poor Man's Store.* 1885. Oil on canvas on wood, 35½ × 25½″. Museum of Fine Arts, Boston. M. and M. Karolik Collection

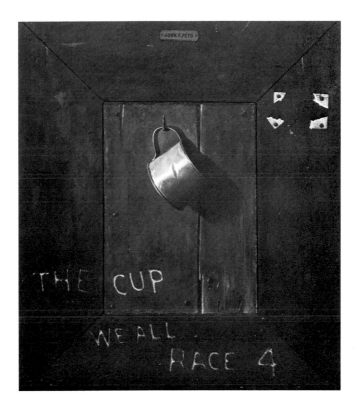

13. John F. Peto. *The Cup We All Race 4*. c. 1905. Oil on
canvas on wood, 25½ × 21½″. The Fine Arts Museums of San
Francisco. Gift of Mr. and Mrs. John D. Rockefeller 3rd

14. Balthus. *"Cathy and I escaped from the wash house to have a ramble at liberty."* (*Wuthering Heights*, chapter 6). c. 1933. Ink on paper, 10 × 9½". Private collection

15. Balthus. *Joan Miró and His Daughter Dolores.* 1937–38. Oil on canvas, 51¼ × 35". The Museum of Modern Art, New York. Abby Aldrich Rockefeller Fund

16. Balthus. *The Mountain*. 1937. Oil on canvas, 98 × 144″. The Metropolitan Museum of Art, New York. Purchase, Gifts of Mr. and Mrs. Nate B. Spingold and Nathan Cummings, Rogers Fund and The Alfred N. Punnett Endowment Fund, by exchange, and Harris Brisbane Dick Fund

17. David Salle. *B. A. M. F. V.* 1983. Oil on canvas and satin, 101 × 145″. Collection
Barbara and Eugene Schwartz. Courtesy Mary Boone Gallery

18. Jean-Antoine Watteau. *Four Studies of a Woman's Head and Two of a Seated Lady.* c. 1718–19. Graphite and chalk on paper, 9 × 13⅞″. Rijksprentenkabinet, Rijksmuseum, Amsterdam

19. Jean-Antoine Watteau. *Pierrot* (called *Gilles*). c. 1718–19. Oil on canvas, 72⅝ × 58⅞″.
Musée du Louvre, Paris

20. Jean-Antoine Watteau. *The Happy Age,
The Golden Age.* c. 1719–20. Oil on panel,
8¼ × 9⅝". Kimbell Art Museum, Fort
Worth, Texas

21. Jean-Antoine Watteau. *The Shopsign* (or *Gersaint's Shopsign*). 1720. Oil on canvas,
65¼ × 120". Schloss Charlottenburg, Staatliche Schlösser und Gärten, Berlin

22. Michaelangelo da Caravaggio. *Still Life with a Basket of Fruit*. c. 1596. Oil on canvas, 12³⁄₁₆ × 18½″. Pinacoteca Ambrosiana, Milan

moment. This time, it is a hot, dry autumn day. The picture shows a man grappling with a woman, who is seen from the back and appears to be pushing him away. They're toppling, and everything is flushed, charged with an orange-red light—even the leaves and the earth.

It was hard to linger with most of the *fêtes*, though, because there isn't enough of Watteau himself—his touch, his hand—in them. *The Embarkation for Cythera*, for example—it is a more profusely detailed, near-replica of the Louvre's *Cythera*—was off-puttingly bright, almost garish. It seemed to have been overcleaned in restoration, while other pictures, which were gummy and dark, seemed to need restoration (they may, however, be too fragile for it). The poor physical state of Watteau's paintings isn't merely due to age, though. His contemporaries talked about how the surfaces became parched, or cakey, not long after they were made, and it isn't necessary to know that he emulated many artists to sense that he was forcing himself to do things in these works which he didn't instinctively want to do.

Watteau had a more spontaneous approach to picture making than any other artist of his period (and many artists long after him). He didn't prepare for each painting with studies—he composed directly on canvas, as many modern painters do. Yet his overall method was indirect. In his earliest mature work, his subjects were characters from the theater—Harlequin, Columbine, Pierrot, Mezzetin. He painted them in his own invented scenes, which he set in stagelike forests. He didn't paint actors and actresses, though—he apparently didn't know any at the time. He had a collection of theatrical costumes, which he had friends, servants, or strangers dress up in. He sketched their faces, hands, bodies, and clothes, and kept the drawings in portfolios. When he wanted to make a painting, he turned to his portfolios and took, say, the image of a woman seen from the rear, or of a man peering at something, or of a fiddler, and copied it onto the canvas. He arranged these figures, faces, and gestures the way a twentieth-century collagist would arrange scraps of this and that, to get a good composition.

As Watteau grew older, his subjects changed from theatrical characters to beautifully dressed men and women, and the forest settings became fairy-tale glades, but his approach remained the same. Some

131

of his contemporaries said that his pictures were ruined because, wanting immediate results, he used his materials carelessly; other observers complained that he took forever. He probably did both. You can see how he wanted to make conventional paintings of this or that "scene," and also how he refused to part with the clothes, gestures, and faces from the drawings (which, by the time he was painting, were no longer fresh for him). The result is that the landscape settings, while often lovely in themselves, are essentially backdrops, and the clothes, gestures, and faces are so painstakingly delineated they're almost wizened.

Watteau's deeper dilemma, though, is that he wanted to base a romantic, courtly, and sensual art on his drawings, but they weren't made in that spirit. His drawings are the work of a brilliant cub reporter. Watteau might be called the greatest "sketch artist" who ever lived. In these studies, often done in a pale red chalk, with touches of white and black, he goes right for the person before him — what he wears, his gestures, the spirit of his hands, the way he looks at something. There are almost no background details in these drawings, and we're not aware that they are missing. Nor does Watteau impart a particular message about his different sitters; he doesn't isolate a dignity, a robustness, a vulnerability, an elegance, or a rawness. It's as though he worked too quickly for there to be time for style or psychology to set in.

The most impressive drawings are portraits of individual Persians and Savoyards — people Watteau might have been attracted to because, like him, they were strangers in Paris. The Persians (they were part of a retinue that accompanied the Persian Ambassador to Paris in 1715) and the Savoyard men, women, and boys were also people he didn't have to find costumes for; they wore unusual outfits as a matter of course. In his studies of a young Persian in a fur cap, who is slouched in a chair and seems to be daydreaming, and of a corpulent, prepossessing, older Persian, who looks off to the left, Watteau gives us everything we could want: precise descriptions of the appearance of these individuals and, it seems, of their thoughts. Yet he does it with such a modest and economical touch that we're moved — we believe that in some way he was unaware of his own power.

Watteau's drawings are so engaging, and each is so different from the next, that you wanted more than the ninety-odd in the exhibition. (They represent about a tenth of his output.) The show could also have done without so many of his copies of older art; they're animated, but, as can be the case with copies, they're dead at the core. (The deadness is felt in the eyes—they have a mechanical sparkle.) It's unfortunate, too, that some of his finest drawings couldn't be sent to Washington (they are reproduced in the catalogue): *Portraits of the Two Daughters of Pierre Sirois*, one of his most memorable images of women; *Portrait of Antoine de La Roque*, a drawing of a pale-eyed man with a direct gaze, who stands facing us, on crutches; *Head of a Man*, an unusual image of a face, turned to one side, that seems to nestle into the blank sheet of paper it is drawn on; and the awesome *Three Studies of the Head of a Young Black Boy*.

The exhibition's awesome work was *Pierrot*. He stands stock-still, on a little rise or wall. Below and behind him, passing by in a sort of chorus-line formation, are four people, whom we see down to mid-chest level, dressed in theatrical costumes, and a donkey, who is part of the troupe—he has faded red ribbons tied to a rope around his neck. At first, you think the scene takes place outdoors and the people in the background are standing in a trench or ravine. But they're jammed so close to Pierrot, and the sky is so flat and shallow, you wonder if this isn't a theater, with Pierrot standing on a set and the people and animal behind him standing on the floor of the stage.

What do they think of Pierrot? That's the question we keep coming back to. You read these faces from right to left. The man on the right in a red satin suit and hat pulls the donkey along—his energies are concentrated on the rope. Next to him is a woman, who, though she looks at the donkey, seems preoccupied—she seems to stare through the animal. Next to her is a man with a straw hat, the brim of which has been cut and resembles flames or waves. There's something flamelike about his raised brows and open mouth, too; he's clearly excited by something, but we don't know what.

The last two figures, seen on the left of Pierrot's legs, are the donkey and a man in a black outfit, who rides the donkey. This man—his outfit identifies him as a comic character called the Doctor—is the spookiest figure of them all. We know his grin and the upturned motion of his eyes from real life (and probably can't remember if anyone other than Watteau has put this expression in a painting). The Doctor has a face that you might encounter in a café when you sense that someone is looking at you—you turn and, sure enough, someone who seems to be engaged with his friends at his own table glances at you at that instant. You may be a little unnerved, and think his face implies "I've been watching you all along." Yet perhaps he means nothing by his look; maybe he has turned involuntarily, because he senses you're about to look at him. Watteau's Doctor, his face in shadows, seems to glance out at us conspiratorially and say, with his too wet lips, "So, how do you like our Mr. Nothing up there?"

The painting isn't about self-pity, though it may seem so if you have never really looked at Pierrot's face. (There is a full-page color detail of it in the catalogue.) Sleepy, hot, moist around the eyes, developing a double chin, with the impacted look of someone whose nasal passages are permanently clogged, he's the ultimate adenoidal schlemiel. We can almost hear him breathing through that open mouth. The subtle little snarl on his upper lip, though, makes you believe he's quite capable of taking care of himself, and when you look at his eyes you suddenly feel, This is a very levelheaded man appraising me. *Pierrot* raises countless questions as to its meanings— questions that you don't want definite answers for. Though he's a comic actor, this man could symbolize all artists; he could be a dancer, a mime, a painter in his smock, a poet about to recite. Is he dreaming about himself? Are the people at the bottom of the picture his conception of his audience? They are literally "beneath" him, "at his feet." Yet they seem to deliberately ignore him. What actually happens is that they don't see him, and that gives the picture its tension. You can't help feeling that you are Pierrot and that the people at the bottom ought, in some way, to acknowledge your presence. Does Pierrot think of himself as the donkey, the stubborn creature that these people (his friends? his colleagues?) yank along—and also "ride"? The donkey, after all, is the only one of the five who we are sure is looking at us. And he complements Pierrot. He possesses what

Pierrot lacks, or keeps hidden: a sexiness, a hairiness, a romantic beauty.

Watteau is one of the leading mystery men of French painting. His contemporaries were as uncertain about the meanings of his pictures as we are—he left no statements—and since almost none of his pictures were signed or dated (and individual ones have been re-painted over the years) his actual development can never be pinned down. The liveliest mystery concerning him, though, is whether he even painted *Pierrot*. After his death, his paintings and drawings were engraved and published, each in a two-volume set, by one of his closer friends, Jean de Jullienne. (It was through these books that Watteau's themes and compositions became influential in the first two-thirds of the eighteenth century.) But *Pierrot* wasn't among these engravings, and none of his friends mentioned it in their biographies. In fact, there is no record of the work's existence until, in 1826—over a hundred years after it was made—it turned up in a sale. It's also strange that *Pierrot* is the only life-size painting Watteau is thought to have made. He produced a couple of good-sized allegorical pictures, and a half-length portrait is attributed to him—it was in the show—but the majority of his paintings are surprisingly small. They're usually between ten and twenty inches high. And even when, as in the *Cythera* pictures, their dimensions are large, he worked on a miniaturist's scale. The paint handling, light, and color in *Pierrot* are different from anything else of his, too. In most of his paintings we're conscious of his brushwork and a soft light suffuses each color, but *Pierrot* isn't lustrous—it's evenly painted. Pierrot's outfit, with its folds and buttons and pockets and shadows, is one of the knockout passages of white in art, but it is far less shimmery than it appears in reproductions (including the one in this catalogue). And the sky, which can become a velvety gray-blue in color photographs, is a pale, dry turquoise. The painting has the muted, chalky tones of Venetian frescoes, pictures by Veronese and Tiepolo.

The underlying drama of the show was whether Watteau could have made *Pierrot*. Could he have leaped from being a painter of somewhat tremulous miniatures to this muscular, public work? Pierre Rosen-berg, in his catalogue notes on the painting, says that most scholars believe that he did. The same comic characters appear in his early pictures, a sketch exists for the Doctor, and the image of Pierrot standing stiffly before us is found in a few of his sketchier drawings and in the painting *Italian Comedians*. A viewer can feel, though, that the proof that Watteau painted *Pierrot* is right in his work. His drawings show that he instinctively saw people in a big, simple way. (It was only when he transposed those drawings into paintings that everything shrank.) More than that, I think there is a direct relation between the theme of *Pierrot* (and the uncharacteristically bold way it is painted, and the fact that none of Watteau's contemporaries seem to have known about it) and the theme of the *fêtes galantes* (and the precious way they're painted—and Watteau's evident difficulty in bringing them off).

The story Watteau instinctively wanted to tell, you believe, was about how people are detached from one another. When he painted the relations between men and women in his *fêtes*, though, he toyed with that story. He teases us (and himself)—he makes it seem as if these might be scenes of budding romance, and so we get nothing: neither romance nor disillusionment. But when he painted Pierrot, Watteau seems to say, "You want to know what detachment looks and feels like? This is it." *Pierrot* isn't literally a self-portrait. Scholars are fairly certain that the subject is a Greek-born actor named Belloni, who had left the theater to open a café; he probably commissioned the painting and used it as a sign for his coffeehouse. (The idea that *Pierrot* is a portrait of Belloni is strengthened by the fact that he and the painter had a few important things in common, and Watteau might have felt close to this man. As Donald Posner recounts it in his recent study, *Antoine Watteau*, both were in their mid- to late thirties when the picture was made, and Belloni stopped acting because of an illness around the same time that Watteau's own illness became grave—that is, probably just before *Pierrot* was painted. And the actor, like the painter, died a short while later, in 1721.)

Yet Watteau must have seen himself in Pierrot. As he was traditionally performed, this character represented the opposite of what Watteau was attempting in his *fêtes*. Pierrot was the antithesis of urbane, smiling gracefulness. Onstage, he was a sweet innocent; he was also an ignoramus, a boor, the butt of jokes, and a lech. He never got the girl, but he always kept trying. Watteau painted Pierrot a few times when his work was first getting under way (when his subjects were mostly theater characters), and then again about eight years later, toward the end of his life, when, probably, he made the Louvre's picture. Following him as he uses Pierrot in his early painting, lays the image aside during the years when he is engaged by the *fête galante* theme, and then returns to Pierrot, we might be reading an old tale. It is a story of someone who asserts himself tentatively at the start of his climb to fame, then puts a crucial part of himself on hold as he moves into deeper waters in his art (and, possibly, as he moves in a society he wants to conquer). Finally, he returns to his initial sense of himself, but with a power he probably wouldn't have possessed if he hadn't tried to pass as something he wasn't.

A handful of his Pierrot paintings were in the exhibition, and, going from one of these small works to the next, you felt as if you were getting scenes from the life—and facets of the character—of the Pierrot in the Louvre's work. The figures in these Pierrot pictures are more graspable and firmly planted than Watteau's figures generally are, and the paintings have what the *fêtes galantes* lack: a sense of mystery and sexual conquest, of real people sizing up each other.

In *Party of Four*, Pierrot, his back to us, stands before a man and two women who are seated on a bench in a park. The women seem to be taking Pierrot's measure in this tense nighttime scene; but the real drama is between Pierrot and the seated fellow, in a Mezzetin's outfit—he hardly seems to be more than seventeen. Considering that *Party of Four* is less than twenty inches high, and this figure is about eight inches from cap to toe, it is amazing how much Watteau conveys about him: we are sure that he is sweet and kind by nature, and nervous and sweaty at this moment. He is seemingly shown at the split second when he's altering his expression, from being startled by Pierrot to wanting to appear friendly to him. The viewer, anyway, finds Pierrot unnerving. Swaddled in white, his shoulders slightly hunched, and with his guitar slung over his back like a weapon, he is an ominous figure.

In *Pierrot Content*, our hero is no longer a mysterious stranger—he's just a creep. This is probably an earlier work than *Party of Four*, but it seems to present the next stage in the story. Pierrot is "content" because he has joined the group sitting on the bench. Smiling, his hands placed on his exaggeratedly out-turned thighs (he looks like a frog in a white jumpsuit), he sits in the center of the bench and stares straight ahead, while his companions turn to him and to us. He makes no attempt to be part of the group. He's happy just to have grabbed the center place. He's a simpleminded little bully.

Watteau's most complex small Pierrot picture is *Happy Age, Golden Age*, a roughly eight-by-nine-inch panel that might be called a child's version of the Louvre's painting (so it seems likely that they were done around the same time). The boy Pierrot in *Happy Age*—he's about four years old—faces us with a mixture of condescension and vacuity, and is oblivious of his four playmates, who surround him.

There's a crystalline beauty to the surface and colors of this painting. The predominant oranges, blues, and whites are icy and fiery at the same time, and the wet gray sky—and the smoke rising from a sketched-in castle in the distance—gives the picture a vivid wintry mood. The image itself is chilly, almost freakish; it seems at first to be a picture of dwarfs pretending to be children. We feel we're looking at the primal Watteau, the image that underlies all his pictures. We immediately see that his subject is dressing up, playacting— something we tell ourselves is the point when we look at most of his pictures of adults. (These kids express so many more emotions than the adults do in Watteau's paintings it's as if, as a person—and perhaps without being aware of it—he took children more seriously than adults, cared more about how they would judge him.) The girl on the right plays a housewife on a slow boil; she holds a slapstick under her left arm, her right fist is set angrily on her right hip, and she glares at Pierrot, her little man. He sits on a huge rock in the center, his hands on his thighs, his legs too short to touch the ground; ignoring her, he sends us a look that says, "She'll go away soon." Behind the rock is a child who, in an oddly affecting gesture, holds his hand to his head and looks off to the side; there's a red glow on his face, and he seems weighed down by his thoughts. Completing the picture are two girls on the left, who sit one in front of the other; the girl in the foreground holds her hands together and her mouth is slightly open, and the girl behind her cranes her neck. They're so intent on Pierrot and his woman they're barely able to hold themselves together politely.

Happy Age makes a viewer believe that, for Watteau, Pierrot personified indifference—being part of a company of people and yet unconcerned with them. Seeing the Louvre's painting as a kind of monument to indifference may explain why it didn't appear in Jullienne's catalogues and why Watteau's other friends seem not to have known about it. Surely they would have mentioned it even if they didn't like it—it is different in scope from everything else he did. Could Watteau have kept *Pierrot* a secret from them? Perhaps he felt that they would be uncomfortable with, even dislike, its lack of painterly surface refinement—the very quality, presumably, he had conditioned them to look for in his work. Or perhaps he felt that they would see something confessional in it: a picture of an artist-clown who is plainly unconcerned with his friends and colleagues. Mightn't Watteau, in these Pierrot pictures, and most of all in the Louvre's picture, be portraying his own itinerant existence—his way of being with, and yet not with, his friends?

And is it possible that in *Pierrot* he knew he had taken the motif of the spotlighted individual as far as he could, and felt free to go back to the motif of a group of people and show it as he truly saw it—as a gathering of total strangers? That is what a viewer believes when he turns from *Pierrot* to Watteau's second great work—and last picture—*Gersaint's Shopsign*. Not that the process was a simple or immediate one for him. It's probable that he spent a year in London in between. His friends thought it perverse of him to have gone there in the first place; he seemed to want to hasten his death by spending so long in such a damp climate, and he came back in a deteriorated condition. But we know that when he returned, whether because he had *Pierrot* under his belt or because he knew that time was running out, he acted with a dictatorial assurance he had never shown before. It was he who insisted on making a sign for his friend Gersaint's art gallery, on the Pont Notre-Dame, and on having it hung there. (Gersaint agreed reluctantly; he thought Watteau was wasting his time with a shop sign.) And though his health allowed him to paint only in the mornings, he finished this large picture—it is about five feet high by ten feet wide—in eight days.

The result was a breakthrough work: the most physically sumptuous painting he had ever made, his first picture with a city setting and a setting that feels as if it were a real place. It's also the first picture where, so his friends believed, he didn't go through the rigmarole of creating a composition from existing drawings. He painted directly from the model, and made the first figures about whom we feel, Oh, his contemporaries. Where the women in his *fêtes* tended to be so many shy, bemused, or self-possessed belles—prizes for men rather than persons in their own right—here they are formidable individuals. And where the men in his *fêtes* were often squirts or aging greasers, here they are, from one fellow to the next, angelic, handsome, and heroic—but always with an underlying comic twist. The men's faces, rendered with a dot-and-dash speed, make us smile, and yet each man is a separate personality.

The Shopsign might be called a day in the life of an art firm, compressed into one moment. Starting from the left, there is a young porter standing outside the shop—he looks on as one helper packs a portrait of the late Louis XIV in a crate and another moves a mirror off the wall. In the center, a woman with her back to us steps up from the curb and a man, already in the shop, offers her a gentlemanly hand. Next to them, a woman and a man, who also have their backs to us, scrunch over to appraise an oval painting, and, finally, at the right, three customers muse over a mirror being shown to them by, perhaps, Mme. Gersaint. *The Shopsign* is the flip side of *Pierrot*. *Pierrot* is an endlessly fascinating image, but a viewer may wish it had a bit more of Watteau's hand, his satiny touch. *The Shopsign* is not an immediately compelling image; there is no one figure or action we're drawn to at first, and the setting—a shallow yet grandiose room, its walls hung with paintings—is hard to keep clear in your mind. It was a convention of the time, when making a portrait of an establishment, to leave out the fourth wall, so the viewer could look right in. But Watteau doesn't make his backdrop straightforwardly fake; he is a touch too realistic, and leaves us wondering where the doors might be, how this shop actually functions.

The Shopsign makes up for this uncenteredness, though, in its paint quality. It is one of the very few paintings where Watteau was able to get the breathing life of his drawings into paint. *The Shopsign* is, in effect, an enormous version of one of his three-color chalk drawings on light brown paper. The painting's pervasive background color is a baked red-tan—a kind of aged burlap. On this background, the colors—lavender and pink, white and gray, rust red and pale green—appear to have settled, like a mist, and then been nudged into place by flecks of black. My favorite passage is the white sleeves of the shirt on the young man on the right; they might be described as two clouds that, blown about by different currents of air, happen to resemble the sleeves of a shirt. To appreciate these sleeves—or the equally amazing gray jacket of the man who bends, or the silvery-violet dress of the lady who enters, or the rippling white shirt of the packer—you need to get very close. And with your nose inches away from this large painting you find yourself doing exactly what the silly-looking man and woman who scrutinize the oval picture are doing. It's one of Watteau's jokes that he makes each of us into another prospective customer for M. Gersaint.

And the longer you stand before *The Shopsign* the more radical and right its lack of a center becomes. Watteau is so modest about the stories he's telling that it takes a while to realize that the painting is a vision of the unrelatedness of people and the simultaneousness of unrelated events. The picture is closer to Oriental screens in its structure than to anything in Western art, and it's exciting to realize that he evolved this scroll-like idea from the way he saw people. He showed separate incidents taking place at the same time in some of his *fêtes*, but, except for a rare work such as *The Two Cousins*, he dissipated the effect by presenting the various individuals in the form of undulating, too graceful roundelays—he didn't keep them separate enough. He showed the unrelatedness of people in *Pierrot*, too, where the figures beneath Pierrot might as well be in another painting. But we can't help seeing a connection between these figures, even if it takes the form of emotional unconnectedness. It is in many of his drawings, though, that he presents the idea of simultaneity most clearly. He no doubt worked spontaneously, and with pleasure, when he placed two, or eight—or twelve or more—separate faces (or faces, bodies, and gestures) on the same page, and kept them all floating side by side in perfect balance with each other.

With its clock and mirrors and its vignette of Louis XIV being packed away, and with our knowledge that Watteau died shortly after making it, *Gersaint's Shopsign* has been described as a painting about vanity and mortality. In his *Rococo to Revolution*, Michael Levey has also said that the picture is about "the shop of the human heart"—a place where people themselves are the true pbjects of contemplation and desire. Watteau's literal subject, though, is the art world of his time, and seeing the picture that way ties it to *Pierrot*. Between these paintings, he encompasses the two poles of every artist's thoughts. We go from an inside view of the artist himself—the isolated, edgy, swollen ego—to an inside view of the marketplace, that necessary second act of his life.

Probably no other painter has brought together so neatly both the pretentiousness and the genuine glamour of the art business. Watteau the satirist and reporter catches that sense of snobbish, knowing absorption with which people cloak themselves when they enter a gallery. He shows how everyone falls for it: the browsers, the professional collector-connoisseurs, the dealers, even the guys who move around and crate the stuff. And Watteau the poet shows how the marketplace is for the artist heaven and hell on earth—his chance to see what strangers and the future will do with his product. This room, where toilet articles and furnishings are sold alongside serious paintings in gilt frames, keeps changing its character as we look at it. It could pass as a great hall in a museum, a junk shop, a chamber fit for a palace, an auction house, or a stall. A viewer acquainted with Watteau's life may believe that the painter, a perennial guest, was also presenting his true idea of a home.

—1985

NOT HAPPY TO BE HERE

PERHAPS THE HIGHEST COMPLIMENT I can pay Caravaggio's work is to say that three hundred and seventy-five years have not dimmed its power to be showy, pushy, and hollow. The Italian painter—thirty-nine of whose pictures were recently the centerpiece of the Metropolitan's "The Age of Caravaggio" exhibition—is considered one of the revolutionary figures in European art. The reputation of Michelangelo da Caravaggio (1571–1610) is based on his having brought a new, everyday realism to painting and his making oil painting itself a more vital, true-to-life art. It is said that in emphasizing the contrasts of sharp, bright light and darkened, near-black settings he gave painting a theatrical immediacy. At the Met's show, the first major Caravaggio exhibition ever held outside Italy, it was obvious why he was a showstopper in his time, but his pictures are tacky, and you don't believe in them. What's historic about him is that he seems to be one of the first artists who are calculating about their material. He seems to use it brazenly one moment, sentimentally the next.

The Caravaggios were accompanied by five rooms (which you had to go through first) of pictures by painters of the generation before him in northern Italy, where he was from, and by his contemporaries in Rome and Naples, where he worked. The point was to show that he didn't spring from nowhere—and, more important, how different he was. That came across clearly. In the long prelude, there were moderately interesting pictures by Rubens, the Carracci, Gentileschi, Elsheimer, and others, but it was easier to look at the Caravaggios. They're less stuffy, religious, mothbally. Caravaggio's scenes—of Judith and Holofernes, David and Goliath, the Stigmatization of St. Francis, the Sacrifice of Isaac, the Supper at Emmaus—and his portraits of individual saints, such as St. Catherine, are starker, more elegant and monumental. You get everything immediately. The problem is that you don't get much, and there is little to come back to; there is no resonance, or mystery. Having so many pictures by artists other than Caravaggio may have seemed like filler at first, but they were necessary; without them he loses his punch.

According to the Met catalogue, more has been written about Caravaggio since 1951—when, in Milan, he was given his first comprehensive show—than in the preceding three hundred and fifty years. Though he was famous and influential during and right after his roughly fifteen-year-long career (he died at thirty-eight), his work was ignored or scorned thereafter. He is a true twentieth-century rediscovery (Roger Fry was among the first to champion him), and there is a modern sensibility poking out from his paintings. When you look at, for instance, his *Saint Catherine of Alexandria*, your first response isn't, as it might be with a Renaissance painter, There's St. Catherine. Your first response is, This is some woman dressed as St. Catherine. Caravaggio must be one of the first artists to make us wonder how much they believe in the mythical and Biblical personalities and tales they paint. And he was clearly drawn to certain ones because they gave him a chance to present his own obsessions. Taken together, his pictures tell a surprisingly complete and explicit story of homosexual love. We see the beautiful boys and young men—who seem to float, even the ones who aren't literally angels—and the weighed-down older men; the rituals of power and weakness (that is one way, at least, to interpret his various flagellation, crucifixion, and David-and-Goliath paintings); the eventual confusion as to which partner is the powerful or the weak one; and the degeneration of the story, in his last works, into violence for the sake of violence.

Caravaggio presents his themes so baldly, though, that when you think about them you're left juggling abstractions. His people are real individuals—they look and feel more like us than, say, Rembrandt's people do—but it's hard to warm up to, or be in awe of, or even remember them. You have little idea of what he feels about them as persons in their own right. He obviously had a great gift for reproducing every kind of animate and inanimate texture—skin, leaves, stuffs, shells—and he impudently introduced naturalistic details, such as dirty fingernails. But he stops with the appearance of people and things. And the glossy surfaces of his pictures don't help. They only keep us at a distance.

There are beautiful passages of painting, especially in his early work. They're primarily odd and quirky moments—when, in *Boy with a Basket of Fruit*, a very realistically painted leaf appears to press flat up against the picture plane. Or when, in *Bacchus*, he gets carried away painting a flask and a goblet of wine. At first, it's not clear that it is a goblet—it seems to be some purple oval shape with swirling black lines in it that the model holds in his hand. Caravaggio is thought to have invented still-life painting in Italy, and the most engaging works in the show were the three still lifes (and the still-life parts of his various pictures of boys). Not that they are top drawer. They're early work, and their authenticity has been questioned; and they're reminiscent of those overcrowded still lifes of assortments of fruit and flowers, with an additional butterfly or lizard, that are in every museum. But Caravaggio's, being among the very first, are awkward and airier, and their surfaces don't have quite the expensive-object gleam that most of his other paintings do.

In these large, horizontal works, Caravaggio lays out his subjects—birds or fruit and vegetables—in a random, all-over way that feels modern. The bird still life, which is the best, shows fifty-odd (lovingly painted) dead birds, who either hang on strings or have been set around a shelf. The subject and the composition recall Miró, and there's a Miró-like vignette in it: a plate of little birds, whose tail feathers have been plucked. Their heads face downward, their ends are up in the air, and a little black and white feather sticks out of each one's end. In much of his work Caravaggio seems to play with ghoulishness; he wants to see how far he can go with shocking people. He's doing that in this still life, but the effect isn't cardboardy, as it is in his paintings of people. Here it's funny and, in a way, more human. Our hero is an owl, the only bird who, his eyes wide open, is alive. Though he looks straight out, he seems quite aware that he is sitting in what might be called a bird morgue on a busy day, and he is not happy to be here. He is the only figure in the Caravaggio show whose apprehensiveness I really felt.

The greatest Caravaggio I have seen is, in fact, a still life (and an early work). It is *Still Life with a Basket of Fruit*, a roughly twelve-by-eighteen-inch oil that was supposed to be in the show but at the last moment (according to a wall label) was "disallowed" to come by its owner, the Pinacoteca Ambrosiana, in Milan. In its place was a black and white photograph set in a period frame. (Caravaggio might have liked this touch.) The picture shows a basket of fruit and leaves that sits on, and juts slightly over, a ledge; behind it is an ivory-colored wall. Because of the way the basket juts out, we feel we're looking up at it, and it can resemble a crown. Everything about the picture is surprising. The leaves and stems seem to itch to get out of the basket; they're like a bunch of cooped-up snakes. They're so real you want to touch them, yet the ones on the right especially are paper-thin—they appear as if they had gone too close to the wall and been sucked fast to it. The basket is also a lustrous and graspable object that, on one side, becomes a knife-edge-thin silhouette that joins with the wall. The wall itself is a character in the picture. It's of a yellow-gray ivory that, even in reproduction, feels warm one instant and cool the next. In this little patch of wall Caravaggio gives us the essence of all the flat, bare, dry—yet beckoning—walls that one sees on buildings throughout Italy. Even more than his figure paintings, this regal picture jumps out of its historical time frame. Without an accompanying label, it would be hard to say when the picture was painted. It seems kin to Oriental screens, Byzantine mosaics, folk-art paintings.

Thinking about this and his other, less dynamic still lifes in relation to the rest of his work, you can feel that in spirit and substance Caravaggio was always a still-life painter. His wizardry at painting fruit and leaves may explain why the faces of his people are so waxy and plump and pluckable, and why his settings are so shallow and boxlike. He paints light the way a still-life painter might, too. His light isn't mysterious; it's as if it were the product of spotlights that he had precisely arranged.

The most gripping aspect of the exhibition wasn't about art—it was about how an artist of high ambition goes off in a direction where he may not be doing what comes to him instinctively. You feel that Caravaggio continued to paint religious and mythical scenes and portraits because that was what a first-class painter had to do. He couldn't be a still-life painter, not because that was a second-class territory but because it wasn't a territory. At least in the Italian art of his time, he was the first man on the scene—so he had no one to measure himself against. And he seems to have wanted to measure himself continually. His very personality is about confrontation. His life story is punctuated with descriptions of run-ins with friends, strangers, and the law. He was arrested for illegal possession of arms, he was imprisoned for insulting an officer, he threw a plate of artichokes in a waiter's face—and on and on—and finally he had to skip town when, after a fight over a tennis match, he went all the way and killed a guy. He seems to have always desired to have someone or something to hit—perhaps in order to refresh his sense of who he himself was. Having painted his few still lifes, he may have felt (understandably) that there was nothing more to say. There were no traditions there to play off. He was the tradition.

Caravaggio is really less a painter-poet than a painter-engineer. His chief concern seems to be to make a picture look smart and solid from any distance. He seems to most want to arrange objects in a shallow space in such a way that they look as if they could tumble out onto the viewer. The little still life in Milan is his most successful picture in part because he states his aims with a primitive directness. He works as a trompe-l'oeil painter; he makes it look as though the basket might literally fall out of the picture.

As he got older, Caravaggio took his ideas to the limit. He drains away specific colors and reduces everything to blackish browns and whitish ivories. His space becomes so shallow it's an unreal dream space. The last room at the show included the work he did in the last four years of his life, when, after that tennis match, he was on the lam. After leaving Rome, he was in Naples, then Malta, then Sicily. On his return to Naples, his enemies caught up with him and disfigured his face with a knife. He fled north, landing in Port'Ercole, where he was mistakenly thrown in prison for a couple of days. He was released, but, heading south along the coast toward Rome, he caught a fever, and died of it a short while later. During these traveling years, he made large portraits of a named and of an unnamed Knight of Malta—

they may be of the same man. The one where the knight is accompanied by a blond-haired page, who shyly yet knowingly looks out at us (and has what resembles an eighties version of a fifties short haircut), is especially strong.

But this last room was stifling and hellish. Most of the scenes were gruesome. There was a *David with the Head of Goliath* where a pained David holds at arm's length the dripping head of the giant—Goliath's powerful face is said to be the artist's self-portrait. Bloody as they were, these were, in effect, showy pictures. They aren't more substantial than his earlier ones. He seems to paint more honestly, though. His figures are no longer so many preserved, waxy goods. His light is less glaring. Everything feels washy and far away. He could be making the art of an old man.

Though it's not the classiest picture, *The Toothpuller* (which is attributed to him) held me the longest. We see eight people seated or standing around a table. One fellow is having a tooth pulled while the rest look on. The picture is a bit like works that show Christ being gaped at and taunted and jeered. Except in this case there is no Christ, no one we identify with. You look at the people and you're pulled toward the clenched and sweaty faces of the man having his tooth pulled and the man who yanks, and it's like being sucked into a hole, into faces without souls—faces that are nothing more than the giving and the getting of physical pain. In this picture Caravaggio suggests Goya, though without Goya's irony or gusto. I found *The Toothpuller* nauseating, but it feels truer to Caravaggio than most of his other pictures. This time, he shows his horror straight; he doesn't filter it through the screen of a Biblical or mythological story.

Caravaggio is thought of as a raw and youthful artist, perhaps because his art has a melodramatic rashness. Certainly he helped get under way a new kind of monumental figure painting. Georges de La Tour, Rembrandt, and other seventeenth-century painters apparently borrowed from his lighting and composition (and you think of them when you see him). But Caravaggio is an end-of-the-line, rather than a pioneering, personality. And, in historical terms, he is one of the last distinctive individuals of the great age of Italian painting. He often painted martyrdom and ritual sacrifices, and, in a sense, he became what he painted. His body of work has the quality of an offering. His ideas were given life by later, less tradition-bound artists. When you turn from his dark backgrounds to Rembrandt's dark backgrounds, it's like going from an artificially darkened nowhere out into a real night.

—1985

THE CANADIAN

AS A WRITER, Glenn Gould cloaks his thoughts with a chipper, jokey superiority, and it's upsetting and disheartening. *The Glenn Gould Reader,* which has been edited by Tim Page, is a hefty collection of twenty-five years of record-liner articles, interviews, book reviews, humor pieces, autobiographical sketches, and essays on concertgoing and on listening to recordings. It is impressive in many ways. Gould, the Canadian pianist, who died in 1982, at fifty, turns out to have been a first-rate humorist and a polished (though sometimes wordy and highfalutin) essayist. But as a thinker and writer he pulls back from delivering exactly the qualities he delivered as a performer: his gravity and heat, his tension and sense of yearning—and his bite.

In the late fifties and sixties, when he was becoming world-renowned, Glenn Gould made people excited about classical music who normally might not have been—young people especially—because, like certain actors, he was all bite. He took the tinkling, antiquarian sound (and the lush, soupy sound) away from Bach and brought out the big, clean, mesmerizing rhythms. His many Bach albums—the *Goldberg Variations,* the *Well-Tempered Clavier,* and the *Partitas* especially—had real vroom and a barreling beat. When he took off on the fast passages, there were pennants flying in the wind. He seemed to play fast for the sake of speed itself. His Bach was good background music for driving.

Emphasizing the clarity and the firmness of each note—one didn't think of him as especially graceful—Gould was a kind of musical minimalist. He made piano notes sound like church bells pealing with a taut, rapid-fire action, like bells without reverberations. Gould didn't play as a custodian of the past, as it seemed other musicians did; he questioned it. A listener felt that Gould was in a conversation with the composer—Gould didn't take the man's genius for granted.

When he played composers later in date than Bach—Mozart, Haydn, Beethoven—he could be too questioning, and the results weren't so satisfying. If you came to these records out of your love for Gould's Bach (and if, like me, you found Baroque music in general more exciting), your response wasn't "Boy, he's mangling Mozart," it was "This music won't let him fly—or be pageantlike or sonorous enough; it has too much of its own set story to tell." It wasn't necessary to know the more conventional ways of playing Mozart or Beethoven solo piano music to sense a thwartedness in some of these performances.

Gould gave classical music a new intensity, and he himself was a more contemporary figure than most classical music performers. (There's a lot of vivid biographical material on him in two recent books: *Glenn Gould Variations*, which is made up mostly of memoirs and tributes by friends, including Bernstein and Menuhin, and Jonathan Cott's *Conversations with Glenn Gould*.) When Gould became internationally prominent (he was in his early twenties) he was an awkward, gangling kid, and he was also extraordinarily handsome. Part of the incredible success of his 1955 debut album, the *Goldberg Variations*—it is one of the industry's best-selling classical music discs—was due to Dan Weiner's album jacket photos, which showed Gould in different stages of recording. With his high cheekbones and long brown hair, he was a budding matinee idol. He was simultaneously imperious and hounded. Everything about his onstage and offstage manner said that he was oblivious of the public, or wanted to be. His conceptions were polished and resolved, but his performing was raw, skinless. Rapt, humming or singing as he played (he wished he could stop this, but it was impossible), conducting whenever a hand was free, he made his audiences feel as if they were intruding on someone living out a story created by the rhythms.

Gould's widely reported eccentricities were essentially by-products of that desire to be privately connected with the music. He had a well-known fear of catching cold, and dressed in layers of clothes in all seasons. He'd appear with a sweater poking out under his dress shirt, he'd take off mittens to reveal gloves underneath, and sometimes he played wearing mittens with cut-off ends. On occasion he'd take off his shoes when he played and, to guard against the cold, lay out a piece of Oriental carpet under him. He was notoriously finicky about the pianos he played; on the road, his (never quite fulfilled) quest was to find ones that matched the light, twanglike sound of his piano at home. He preferred to play from an unusually low vantage point—from about fourteen inches off the ground (most pianists play from twenty). As a kid he played sitting on a folding chair, and when he was older his father sawed off the legs of the chair and fixed them with adjustable ends so Gould could take the chair with him wherever he performed and get the right relationship to every piano he played. (He used this chair all his life.) Gould added to the living-room effect he created onstage by sometimes bringing along a jug of water and a bunch of pills, which he set out where they'd be handy, and occasionally a magazine, too, so that, during the performance of a concerto, say, when he wasn't playing, he'd have something to do.

Though he received rave reviews from the beginning, and most of his colleagues were fascinated by his approaches and awed by his technique, Gould was clearly a disruptive character—as an interpreter and as a personality. During his concert career (which ended in 1964—he concentrated after that on recording), stories proliferated about his not getting along with conductors. The feuds were often exaggerated, but Gould's public couldn't help seeing him as a rebel. (In pictures of him in *Variations*, where he waits during a pause in a recording session, or reads at the piano, he's reminiscent of the surly young Brando.)

The *Reader* shows that Gould consciously worked at not being a rebel. There is a backbone to this collection. Gould hated egoism and confrontations of all kinds—in music, the music world, and the larger world—and no one can take issue with that. But if you know his coiled, passionate playing, you may find his thinking willful, unreal; you hear a man who is determined to deny the most urgent part of himself. The volume, which adds up to a great artist's saying that he doesn't want to be an artist, unintentionally leaves a tragic note.

The *Reader*, of course, is more than a document of a self-deluding man. For funny one-liners alone, it's on a par with *Debussy on Music* (though Debussy's quips are invariably barbed). There are brilliant moments, when Gould proposes some delicious farfetched nonsense, or speaks in ziss or zatt axzent. Two of his humor pieces—a parody of Arthur Rubinstein's autobiography and an account of an imaginary conference of music critics held in the Alaskan wilds—are in a class with Thurber, Woody Allen, Veronica Geng. (Two of the critics are named Alain Pauvre and H. B. Haggle.) And in his occasional book reviews or pieces on pop music, Gould is a wonderful critic. His reviews of Joan Peyser's Boulez biography and Streisand's *Classical Barbra* album are especially good. Analyzing Peyser's very words, he shows how she may be more influenced by Boulez and more ambivalent about him than she knows. Gould's piece on Streisand, though chatty and informal—he adores her—is a full guide to her talent. Actually, Gould's unequivocal endorsements of all kinds of performances make you want to hear them. And whether he talks about classical music or pop, he never fudges his opinions. He has a firm set of heroes (Schoenberg, Stokowski, Bach, Streisand, and Richard Strauss are some); also-rans for whom he yet has sympathy (Mendelssohn, Scarlatti); figures he clearly has mixed feelings about (Mozart, Beethoven); and men to whom he wouldn't give the time of day (Chopin, Stravinsky, Bartók, the Beatles).

The first half of the book, which is about individual classical music composers and works, is more tantalizing than solid. There is one fine passage in which he says that Mussorgsky's "lack of formal concentration tends to absent the rhetorical instinct from his music and to give us a curious and almost unique sense of honesty. He is like a person who ceases to talk the moment he has nothing further to say." In most of these pieces, though, Gould becomes analytical at the clinching moment. If you are a musicologist, you may find it interesting. If you are not, you may feel abandoned because, with his cracks and asides on literature, TV, and politics, Gould seems to write with the man in the street in mind. On Richard Strauss, for example, he says exactly what he thinks, but he leaves the airiest sense of Strauss himself. Gould quotes a piece by Paul Rosenfeld on the composer, written in 1920, and it's like coming into a warm room after being out in the cold for hours. Rosenfeld doesn't like Strauss, but in a few sentences he makes the man and his work more vivid than Gould has in pages.

Gould is more concrete when he writes about a person or an issue in a theoretical way, and, as a theorist, he is a combination of mystic, futurist, and the take-charge leader of a boys' adventure story. He's like a hip Mountie, and you may find yourself drawn to him even while being uncertain about his ideas. His articles send out a call to individuality. He wants people to do what they want regardless of what "everyone out there" says to do or think. Yet he also believes that we overrate the artist who challenges his audience and changes the course of his art form. We overvalue, he says, innovation and newness for themselves. He calls Richard Strauss the greatest figure in twentieth-century music in part because the composer had the courage to turn his back on the challenging music of his time. Strauss, he says, produced his finest work when, in his old age, he wrote in a style that was more than fifty years out of date and was considered irrelevant to the "evolution" of music. Gould praises Petula Clark in a 1967 article partly because, while teenage girls identify with her, she makes the worthiest citizens of the community feel comfortable, too. He likes the way her lyrics are "self-indulgent" and "aggressive," and yet her scores, which he calls "hymnal, upright, and relentlessly diatonic," neutralize the words.

Gould was the foremost pianist to leave the concert stage, to work only in recording studios, and he's an astute critic when he writes about live music versus recordings. He believes that concerts are imprisoning for everybody concerned: they dry up performers, they rouse in audiences a sadistic desire to see "who can do it best," and— this is his sharpest point—they automatically make concertgoers feel that they ought to appreciate whatever they're given. He believes that we hear and judge music more freely when it comes in the impersonal, anonymous form of recordings. He happily foresees a future when concerts will die out, when technology will be such that the listener at home, at his control panel, will have the ability to splice together a section of a symphony interpreted by, say, Bruno Walter with another section of the same symphony interpreted by, say, Klemperer—and get an "ideal" performance. The implication is that eventually music won't be filtered through the egos of performers. Even composers will somehow become anonymous. It will just be a flow of recorded music, with no values, theories, dates, or personalities attached. The listener at his control panel, he says, will be the real artist.

What held me about Gould's belief in this faceless future was less the belief itself than the way it seems to grow out of his taste for music (such as Bach's) that, in a sense, has no "heroes." This taste, in turn, appears to have developed from a very physical response to sound. Gould knew how to read music at three (at five he was making up his own tunes—his mother was an amateur pianist), and his precociousness may explain why his theories can make you heady and, at the same time, can have a childlike simplicity. You believe that he had a sense of the right and the wrong way to do things long before most kids do and that his convictions were based purely on the relationships between sounds. This is an oversimplification, but I think that when he heard highly structured music, such as Bach's, in which a self-contained pattern is spun out, in which one "voice" holds the next in check, and in which both hands have equally important parts to play, he was given a sense of comfort and closeness. But when, say, he heard Beethoven and, to a greater degree, the Romantic composers (whom he couldn't abide) and any music that doesn't have a weblike unity, he felt that the piano was needlessly put in exposed, precarious positions. It was made to fight battles, to brood majestically, and, finally, to come to a state of noble resignation—and the whole drama, as Gould saw it, was phony.

Gould's ideas make you hear his performances and other pianists' work—and music in general—more keenly. You understand why he sweated out Mozart—why he, in effect, keeps saying to Mozart, in a mixture of anger, frustration, indifference, and concern, "Look, a lot of your prettiness is window dressing. There's no inherent structural need for much of this stuff.'' You see why Gould played Bach and the Elizabethans William Byrd and Orlando Gibbons (his favorite composer) with such enthusiasm and tenderness; it is as though, knowing that their music was structurally undramatic, he felt free to play it dramatically. It makes sense that, in his performances of piano concertos, he tended to minimize the piano's traditional sound—that of a suave baron, a tormented loner, or an embattled hero—and instead made the instrument into a frisky friend, or the guiding partner, of the orchestra. It's understandable why in his few recordings of chamber music (such as the Bach albums he made with Leonard Rose and Jaime Laredo), or when he played as accompanist for a singer, he produced such an unusually delicate and courteous sound—he was determined not to overwhelm.

Gould believed that music in which voices overlap was a symbol of the right way to live, and this belief took over his life. He turned his interviews into duets for voices by making his interviewers feel at ease and at their best with him, and, logically, he wrote interviews with himself. Hearing himself speak in the voices, and with the attitudes, of different stock types, he sometimes wrote, or spoke on the radio (or, as friends describe it in memoirs, called on the phone) as himself and, say, a nattering old Brit, or a zealous Teutonic pedant, or a fifties Beat pianist who's like, hip to the scene but, like, uh, you know, a slob. Gould made a number of radio documentaries for the CBC—they are portraits of musicians or about living in rural outposts—and most are really fugues for voices and sounds.

But there is another story in the *Reader,* one that is inferred. I heard someone concocting an elaborate myth for himself. I had the image of a child who is born with a great gift—an unthinking command of the keyboard, an effortless ability to read and feel music—and who is as mystified and troubled by this gift as he is proud of it. Looked at in one way, Gould's story is about the burdens that a prodigy may feel and the way he comes to live with his genius. It is a story about a person who, never believing that he has earned his universally admired power, first begins to deny that it means much, then to sabotage the system that supports it, and finally to envision a world in which such a superstar can be erased.

155

It wasn't only being a prodigy that seemed to weigh on Gould, though—it was being a prodigy in Canada. When he graduated from the Royal Conservatory of Music in Toronto, at thirteen, he was the youngest graduate in the school's history. Before he was twenty he had toured throughout the country and made radio broadcasts with the CBC, and at twenty-four he was the first Canadian musician to perform in Russia. He clearly felt he had an obligation to his country. He hints at it continually. He admires Petula Clark and Menuhin because, as he sees them, they're reassuring to the widest audience. And in his Menuhin profile (not a high point—it's sanctimonious) Gould suggests how much the spirit of public service meant to him as a pianist. In a (nongooey) preamble, he presents his grandmother, who was an amateur musician. She lived in rural Canada, where, in the early part of the century, "it was considered no asset at all to be an artist." She found a way to justify her feeling for music, though. When she played "those indefatigable anthem composers of the English Victorian tradition" on her reed organ, she was "convinced that with each scrupulous avoidance of parallel fifths the devil was given his comeuppance." She boasted about having to travel miles to hear Paderewski because he used his art as "an instrument of salvation"—he was a "missionary advocate." Gould says that his grandmother surely would have admired Menuhin, but he makes it seem as if any musician would want to use his art as "an instrument of salvation."

There's no question that Gould wanted to be a "missionary advocate" himself. You can feel, though, that in wanting it he was also making amends for his talent. He seems to be playing the part of a good boy when he talks about serving the community, and despite the cheeky assurance in his writing, there's a good boy's damper on it.

That mixture of cockiness and restraint is in his repertoire and his playing, too. He frequently recorded works that shift quickly back and forth between the high-flying and the sorrowful, and though it doesn't sum up his range, he often conveys the state of a man who is alternately elated and under some kind of gun. In a photo of him, taken when he was fifteen (it's in *Variations* and *Conversations*), you believe you can actually see Gould's desire both to undermine himself and to be proper. In a suit and tie, he's seated before a piano with his pet English setter, Nicky, beside him on the bench. Nicky's paws and Gould's fingers are on the keys. Nicky looks toward the piano with, it appears, real interest, while Gould, his head turned to the side, seems perturbed and a touch superior. The picture is merely a teenager's jokey stunt (which Gould himself may have cooked up). Taken literally, though, it is a picture of a kid who's making a fool of himself and nobly sticking with this silly performance, too, and who, in the determined and faraway look in his eyes, seems to be thinking about the course laid out before him.

Gould must have believed that his missionary work began when, in 1964—he was thirty-one—he left the concert stage for good. His decision was based, of course, on real needs, and was no doubt the right one for him. He hated the concert-circuit routine, and dreaded the necessary flying. (After 1964, he left Canada only when he went to New York for recording sessions and, after 1970, when he began recording in Toronto, he no longer had to leave the country.) And working out of a studio enabled him to keep his interpretations spontaneous. Even as a teenager, he was known for a phenomenal ability to learn compositions, but not from practicing. He rarely practiced; he generally absorbed music by reading scores. Ideally, he wanted to encounter a piece in the first few times he played it, and then not have to play it again. Performing only in a studio, he was able to come on a piece cold, try out different approaches, redo passages that were flat, splice together the passages that rhythmically fit together best—and leave it at that.

Yet Gould's decision to leave the concert stage was as self-imprisoning as freeing. He was right to say that the live concert is an artificial leftover of the days when musicians were part of the retinue at court and that the concert circuit, which generally makes a performer repeat "concert favorites," drains him of his freshness. He hoped that his departure would say to his colleagues, in effect, "We don't have to be court lackeys any longer." Yet the allegiance to a higher calling that made him leave the stage also made him record music that he had no powerful interest in, or actually disliked. Talking to Tim Page about his project of recording all of Mozart's piano sonatas and the fact that, in doing so, he played many with which he had no rapport, he said, "The honest thing to do would have been to skip those works entirely, but the cycle had to be completed." So which performer is in more of a bind: the concert hall virtuoso who plays his or her signature piece for the twentieth time, as an encore, or Gould, who plays, for the only time, and in a spirit of "well, this must be done," a compostion that he barely respects?

But what's truly contradictory about Gould's quest for an anonymous, egoless performer's art is that the man was obsessed with himself. His many interviews and self-interviews (and his review of a biography of himself!) say so. He left the concert stage out of an honest desire not to be a star. Did he see how much more of a star—and a confrontational figure—he became as a non-concert performer? He remained unusually accessible, especially to Canadians. He recorded music, wrote articles, and gave interviews at a steady clip. He wrote and starred in a movie documentary, *Glenn Gould's Toronto*, and gave occasional performances on radio and TV. He wrote and produced his own radio documentaries, and hosted radio shows—in which he talked to people about everything: sports, politics, music, religion, the stock market. Yet his giving himself to the public full-time, through mechanical means, only emphasized that he was depriving the public of the real thing. Certainly his own existence was priestlike and deprived. He was known to live, apparently alone, as a recluse. He slept by day and worked by night, and remained in contact with people through phone calls (and developed friendships, over the phone, with people he never met).

Gould became what he consciously rejected: a Napoleonic creator, a man with little connection with his fellows. So it makes perfect upside-down sense that he would write so well about Arthur Rubinstein. Rubinstein is associated with everything Gould rejected: the romantic composers (particularly Chopin), the piano concerto form, encores. Rubinstein embodied the spirit of the concert; he was about giving pleasure to a live audience. Yet Gould, in his parody of the pianist's autobiography, re-created Rubinstein's temperament with a flowing ease. "Memories of Maude Harbour, or Variations on a Theme of Arthur Rubinstein" is the finest piece of writing Gould did. It's a self-contained story; it isn't necessary to know a thing about music to enjoy it.

Gould's Rubinstein is a blissful egomaniac who is as superb at Monopoly as he is at Scarlatti and with his patronesses (and believes it his duty to say so). He is at his height in those moments when, just before a concert begins, he can spot an angelic creature somewhere in the hall and, with a devastating wisp of a glance, dedicate his performance—his life—to her. Gould finds one funny and fresh way after another to describe self-infatuation and, too, the trials of performing in the sticks. (One trial is a well-meaning toe-tapper in the front row.)

"Maude Harbour" is preceded by an interview Gould did with Rubinstein years earlier, and it is the most satisfying of all of Gould's interviews and of the pieces he did about himself and an older musician. Gould's interviews are always lively, but Gould himself is generally the subject, and he steers the interviews so everything stays amiable. And in his lengthy piece on Stokowski, which culminates in Gould's interviewing the conductor for a documentary, we never know what Stokowski thinks about Gould. Gould pours out his admiration for a man who seems oblivious of the pianist. But Rubinstein talks back. He is as much of a manipulator as Gould, and, in a gentle and courtly way, he draws Gould out of his shell. Gould becomes less a smooth, self-contained eccentric-genius than a man with a firm faith in his theories.

Rubinstein recalls the time when, in Toronto, playing despite a fever, he thought he got the better of Gould. "You would have canceled the concert, wouldn't you?" Rubinstein asks. "Ah, well, Maestro," Gould replies, "I'm not sure, actually. I suppose that I . . ." And Rubinstein breaks in: "Of course you would have . . . I see it in your eyes." Rubinstein also sees how much they have in common. He talks about the power a soloist can feel when he walks out on stage, how thrilling it can be to take hundreds of people, many of whom are thinking about anything but music, and then "play one note and hold it out for a minute—they will listen like they are in your hand . . . and this emanation cannot be done by a record." Gould, in turn, describes how the only thing that counts in the end is the record, and Rubinstein says, "You begin to persuade me." Though he wonders whether, regardless of their theories, they aren't both after the same desire to transform people.

Perhaps Gould and Rubinstein are so wonderful together because they brought a similar emotion to their playing. If Rubinstein's "voice" as a pianist is that of a worldly-wise, yet never jaded, lover, Gould's is that of an equally ardent, yet always would-be, lover. This spirit is in everything he did, but it is there most strongly when he plays certain late nineteenth- and early twentieth-century music, which he called "postromantic." Though they have been admired, these discs have been treated as a sidelight to his career, perhaps because his interpretations aren't controversial and many of the works are little known. My favorites are Gould's performances of Brahms Intermezzi, Scriabin's Third Piano Sonata, Sibelius sonatines, Gould's own transcriptions of Wagner—from *Die Meistersinger* and *Götterdämmerung*—and Alban Berg's Opus 1. These pieces are quite different from each other, but as Gould plays them they have in common a hovering, swirling, trancelike movement. In a way, they're extensions of his Bach performances. With Bach, many distinct voices, or themes, keep each other in check. With this postromantic music, we keep hearing the suspended state of one voice.

Listening to these recordings, you understand why Gould was nuts about Streisand. He wrote that she makes the "torchiest lyric an intimate memoir" and that she is "consumed by nostalgia," and, especially in the Scriabin and in the "Dawn and Siegfried's Rhine Journey" section of the Wagner, he moves in and out of these same emotions. He creates the same kind of lean, driving sensuality, where the music is undulant and wanders into byways and yet never loses a taut, crystal clear outline. He fashions his performances the same way Streisand does many of hers: as if every note were a buildup to, and a leave-taking from, a single moment of crescendo and release.

The 1977 Sibelius album may be Gould's most personal. He frequently experimented with odd and shifting placements of the mikes, and in this disc his experiments give the sound an atmospheric texture. In quick succession, occasionally even in the same piece, the music can sound as if it's coming from far away or extremely close up, and the piano's sometimes gurgling, echoing sound, plus the songlike and informal music itself, with its repeated phrases, its moments of dribbling off, and its surging returns, can make you feel as if you were in a summer house and hearing someone practicing from across a lake, or eavesdropping on someone playing for himself in a vast barnlike room.

The Sibelius pieces are more than background music, but part of what's memorable about this disc is the way it summons up so much of Scandinavian life, movies, art, and literature. In its suggestion that fond moments are being remembered and then abruptly turned away from, the music re-creates the tension associated with the too-short Nordic summer. The music recalls the mood of certain Bergman movies, particularly *Summer Interlude,* the story of a ballerina who thinks back on a love affair she had on an island when she was young. The music can make a listener think of the emotionally frozen heroes of Ibsen's late plays and of Munch's late self-portraits, where he presents his isolated old self; the music suggests the inner state of those men who, their life's work accomplished, sit looking out at water and distant islands.

By the time Gould died, a part of him had become, I think, such an emotionally frozen man. He seems to have wanted to live out his belief that the world would be a better place if art, as he says, were "phased out." Beginning in the mid-sixties, he sometimes appeared distant and disapproving on album jacket photos, as if to announce that he didn't want us to buy his records because he was his own glamorous selling point. In his last jacket photos, he seems impatient, angry at himself and at us, and his face and eyes look worn out. For a number of years, too, he had said that he would probably stop playing when he reached fifty. He even said that he thought he wouldn't live beyond fifty. And the mystically spooky thing is that he died, of a stroke, days after that birthday.

Gould must have entertained the idea that after he stopped playing he would go on to other things. Shortly before his death, he conducted (though not before a live audience) a string ensemble in Wagner's "Siegfried Idyll." He apparently had no plans to give up radio work, and the 1980 "Maude Harbour" indicates that he was becoming a

warmer writer. This is the first piece in which, prompted by Rubinstein, Gould brings some girls into his prose. That he may have felt
his real work was done, though, comes out in the fact that he chose to
rerecord the *Goldberg Variations*. (The 1981 recording was the last
released in his lifetime and the third to the last he made.) This is the
work with which he is most associated; it was his first album. Playing
it a second time—it is one of a handful he recorded twice—he appears
to say that his career has come full circle. He also seems to say that he
remained true to the "nonheroic" philosophy of the piece, which had
been his philosophy. Bach's series of thirty variations begins and ends
with the same Aria; the work is a classic example of music that doesn't
tell a story, that doesn't advance, that forms one big circle.

It's sad to think of Gould returning to the piece, and in a movie
Bruno Monsaingeon made of him playing the work, we are taken
aback by his appearance. He had aged in an unsettling way. When we
see his face close up—especially when he's smiling and taking pleasure in presenting a thought—he is still a male beauty. Over the years,
though, he had become rather heavy; not fat, exactly, so much as
bloated. In the movie, as he sways and bobs at the keyboard, he
seems to have become, in his person, an image of his ideas. His
clothes are gray, neutralized, nondescript. He's shapeless. The most
defined part of him is his dark, heavy-rimmed glasses, and they make
no sense, not only because he generally didn't wear glasses but
because he isn't, after all, reading music; he usually played with his
eyes closed. The glasses don't seem to be there to help him see out;
they're more like the lid on a bottle that seals off what's in the bottle.
Sitting on the chair that had been made for him in his boyhood, he
appears to have become all torso and head. He has gone so far into a
rhythm and a timing all his own that he is no longer of this world.

And he plays the Aria and the other slow passages of the *Variations*
so slowly that on a first hearing it seems as though he has given the
work a funereal cast. But what you take away is how physical, expansive, and witty this performance is. It isn't "better" than his earlier
one; it is such a rethinking of the material that it is virtually another
piece. The 1955 album is the work of a fearless twenty-two-year-old
giving a hot—and unshaded—performance. He presents each varia-

tion separately, with a pause before and after—they're so many gems—yet one crisp beat governs all of them, the fast and the slow. The 1981 performance doesn't have a unifying pulse. Gould's tone is unexpectedly silky, almost sumptuous, and he characterizes the variations (which he didn't do before). He emphasizes the special trait of each; he turns the piece into a gallery of cantering, prancing, elbowing personalities. He also edits many of the variations back to back, and plays them (I think) so the rhythms of one will mesh with the rhythms of the next. Much of the wit and beauty of the performance is in the wavelike and unpredictable way he moves along. There can be a tense little pause between two, or one will step up to—or plop down onto, or stream into—another.

It's debatable whether Gould became prematurely aged by his ideas. It is clear, though, at least in his second *Goldberg Variations* disc, that he became more pliant as a performer. He plays some of the variations faster than he played them in the earlier recording, but he never races. He always seems to have energy to spare. There's a softness and roundedness to his touch that he achieved in few other albums. He seems contented. Maybe Rubinstein was thinking of this Gould when he said, at the end of their interview, "We are going to meet with our ideas, you know. I can't say how that will happen, exactly, but remember my words: somewhere we will meet."

—1986

STUBBS

GEORGE STUBBS IS AMONG the handful of first-rate painters England has produced. A Stubbs, which is often of a person and an animal set in a landscape, is a subtle thing. At first, it seems like a very skillful version of the kind of picture that can't be taken seriously: a sporting scene, usually of a handsome, sleek horse accompanied by some stately folk. But Stubbs, whose dates are 1724 to 1806—and who was, this past spring, the subject of a retrospective at the Yale Center for British Art, in New Haven—had a supremely confident, if unflashy, hand. As you look at his paintings (and think about them later), you are filled with a sense of serenity and clarity. He makes everything—grasses, trees, people, leather saddles, horses, clothes, brick houses, empty fields, carriages, dogs, rainy skies, green meadows—look perfect, right, quintessential. And there is such a gentle breathing life to his color and touch that he cheats himself a little. We forget about him, the artist, and pass right into the world he has painted.

Stubbs's reputation has developed only in the past thirty years. He wasn't considered a high, fine artist in his time. He was just a horse painter—he was one of the pioneers of the sporting-scene genre—and the English, I think, are still cautious in their praise of him. The Yale show was the first he has had in the United States—it was a much abridged version of a show that was at the Tate last year (and that was, in turn, the largest show he has had in England). The Yale show was short on masterpieces. Stubbs's most amazing pictures—including two paintings of horses done life-size (one is of a rearing horse)— couldn't come, probably because of the difficulty of shipping such fragile monsters. Toned down as it was, the show left a feeling that Stubbs ought to be considered a giant, and there were seven or so paintings in it that are sublime—in a class with Vermeer, Piero della Francesca, and Chardin (at his best).

Stubbs's best work has a spooky freshness. From the clothes his people wear, we know that these are eighteenth-century paintings, but otherwise we might not know when they were made. His people look out at us (or look into the space of the pictures) with an open, penetrating quality that hardly any other artist achieves. Stubbs generally places his figures at a distance, in large surrounding land-scapes, so their faces are literally small—yet we feel we're looking at portraits of distinct individuals. And we love these people! Around the beginning of the show, there were some equestrian portraits and paintings of jockeys, trainers, and grooms with horses, and it was one great face after another. John Larkin, John Pratt, Simon Cobb, John Singleton, the Countess of Coningsby, and Joseph Smyth are the names given. I mention the names because, in some primitive way, a viewer believes that the pictures are as much about these individuals as they are about the art of painting. It's a kind of séance. You feel you are really with that person.

The jockey on Turf, in the superb painting of that name, has a pained, lined, superior, rather Spanish face. John Larkin, who's on Otho, seems sweet but weak. It's hard to tear yourself away from Stubbs's people. It's not that they're vibrant characters (à la Copley) or fascinating combinations of contrary qualities (à la Goya). They're just totally fresh individuals. Stubbs hasn't already understood them for us.

There's a formal, optical aspect to Stubbs's realism, too. There's an odd tension between the figures and the backgrounds. He usually painted his animals (or people and animals) first, then gave them a suitable background. In reproductions, the backgrounds can look like cardboard sets. It turns out, though, that he was a wonderful—but understated—landscapist. His landscapes don't have the jittery wetness of most English landscapes. His are drier, more monumental; his clouds are often massive, puffy banks of white. His backgrounds are filled with real, freshly observed details, but the interesting thing is that he plays them down, he makes a viewer have to peer to see them. You look at the people and animals, then at the quietly busy backgrounds, then you return to the figures, who now appear much softer, and it's like focusing with a camera.

It's this foreground-background split that makes many of his images startlingly alive. Looking at the second painting in the series *Two Gentlemen Going a Shooting* is like entering the Twilight Zone. This four-part series shows an outing of hunters and their two pointers. They go out one morning, shoot some birds, and, in the final painting, look at the day's kill in a darkened forest. The second picture is the special one. It's a very plain image. There's a house off to one side, an empty road, some trees, a pale empty sky, the men, and their dogs. The men and dogs are, of course, painted more sharply than the background. One man looks straight out at us; he seems to say, "Oh, hello there," and it's unnerving. Perhaps because his face and black hat, seen against the pale, dusty-green background, are so real, so touchable. Or because, while the setting is stagelike, we're given an immediate sense of a hot, muggy summer morning. Whatever the reason, you feel you have walked into the eighteenth century.

There is very little known about Stubbs. He apparently came on the scene—and was thought of as strictly a horse painter, with a sideline in other animals—when he was nearing middle age, and the few pictures of him show a heavyset, white-haired, not exactly handsome man. He must have been physically strong. He was the son of a currier and worked for his father in his youth, and one of his earliest projects, which was self-commissioned, was a book of large pencil drawings showing the anatomy of a horse. To accomplish this, he had to rig up one dead horse after another. It had to be backbreaking and stomach-turning work. He was helped by Mary Spencer, his common-law wife of fifty years.

He wasn't always inspired. About half (or more) of the paintings in the New Haven show struck me as merely all right. Most of Stubbs's work came from commissions. People commissioned him to paint their grooms and horses, or jockeys, or stableboys, or carriages, or the wild animals—or dogs—they employed or possessed. When his pictures don't succeed, it's usually because he doesn't aim high enough—the commission itself isn't challenging. Or because he's too imaginative, "artistic" (which happens rarely). The retrospective dispelled some notions about him. He's probably best known as the author of a number of paintings on the theme of a lion attacking a horse. He made seventeen over a thirty-year period—a half dozen or so were in the show—and he's generally represented in surveys and textbooks with one of these pictures. That ought to be changed, because they're about his most shallow works. A case could be made that they represent the ferocious and nerve-racked other side of his art—the reverse of his calm scenes of people and their horses. But the lion-and-horse paintings, which include pictures of a frightened horse being stalked by a lion and a lion digging his fangs into the back of a screaming horse, do not have the formal interest or the emotional depth of his "actionless" pictures. The lion-and-horse paintings are forcedly romantic. The lions are invariably wide-eyed, tawny creatures who charm more than they are meant to, and the horses, whose

166

necks arch in perfect curves and whose veins bulge, are like fatuous rock stars flaunting their profiles.

Stubbs's fame in his lifetime rested (and rests today) on his paintings of horses, but the surprise of the show was that while his paintings of horses (and of other animals) on their own have a solidity and beauty that no other animal paintings have, they aren't exciting. There is, of course, a lot to admire in Stubbs's paintings of animals on their own. His *Zebra* is particularly good. This handsome and sad creature stands alone in an inviting, softly lit forest setting. Stubbs alters his touch to match the hide or hair of the animal he paints. He puts the oil on so that when you look at his zebra—or his monkey, his poodle, his spaniel, or his many horses—you feel the flaxen softness, the oily smoothness, the damp ringlets. His touch is spectacular in *Cheetah and Stag with Two Indians*, a huge and fascinating painting— which doesn't quite jell—that shows Indians in beautifully painted white native outfits. They're the cheetah's keepers. In the nearby distance is a stag, who will presumably become the cheetah's victim as soon as he is released. The Indians (who actually came to London with this big cat in 1764) are painted with sympathy and are handsome, interesting-looking men—they put to shame Delacroix's various dark-skinned exotics—but the picture is fancy. We're not sure what's going on and we don't care. The life-size cheetah, though, is awesome. The animal's fur is freakishly alive and touchable. It's a cliché to say that a passage in a painting gives off its own light, but this cheetah really seems to.

Stubbs is most commanding and original when he paints people and animals together—preferably English people and their animals. Then there is a chemistry. You are given a sense of a nation's wealth and power, physical strength and happiness, all held in perfect, unconscious poise. You believe that you are looking at a country that shyly knows that it is great, that hasn't yet begun to congratulate itself. It's England—as a powerful yet still green nation—that you come away dreaming about.

It should be noted that while the show's catalogue is handsome the color isn't good enough. The reproductions don't compare with the paintings, and Judy Egerton, who wrote the catalogue (and organized the show), could probe a bit more. She repeatedly refers to herself as "the compiler"—annoying modesty, since she produced a lot of copy. The compiler tells about the lineages of the various horses and describes the people who commissioned the pictures. She says little about the paintings as paintings, or where they fit into the larger scheme of things. To some extent, this is understandable. Stubbs, like Vermeer, makes you tongue-tied. (And there is an unintentional poetry to Egerton's commentaries, as when she says of a dog in a portrait of Thomas Smith that "The hound is Wonder, bred in 1770, by Tatler out of Trickster.")

Yet Stubbs clearly had personal themes in his work, and they developed over the course of his career. A social history of eighteenth-century England—and an account of one man's moral values—could be deduced from his pictures. As an anatomist, Stubbs was more than an amateur and less than a professional; but it would be wrong to call him an artist-scientist, and he wasn't a naïf. He grew as a man and a painter. He started on a high note, went through a long middle period when he was on a kind of plateau, and then, in his last years, transcended himself. His earliest paintings have sparkling surfaces and, often, an audacious sense of space. His finest early works couldn't come to New Haven. They're long, horizontal hunt scenes and the magnificent, screenlike *Gimcrack on Newmarket Heath, with a Trainer, Jockey, and a Stable-lad*. In the far right distance of this six-foot-long painting (which was at the Tate), Gimcrack is handily winning a race. In the center, the jockey walks to the rubbing-down house, and on the far left there's Gimcrack again. The race is over and he's being attended to. One of the amazing things about Stubbs is his feeling for composition. Most of his pictures are built like that brick rubbing-down house; they're structured with an unshakable classical balance. Yet in *Gimcrack*—and there are other pictures like it—his design is totally modern and uncentered. He knows exactly how empty and wide-open you can leave a picture space and have it stay dramatic.

In his last fifteen or so years, he returned to the bright colors and the unexpected compositions of his early work. But now, instead of the figures being a touch spindly and toylike, they have a filled-out perfection. The last room at the show, which included five paintings and a print, and primarily represented work he did between roughly 1785 and 1800, was almost too much. Each picture was stunning, and each went off in a different direction. (The print was of one of the paintings.)

Phaeton with a Pair of Cream Ponies in Charge of a Stable-lad, which was one of them, is among the most blissful pictures in the world. Left to right, there is the phaeton—it's a small carriage, comparable to a sports car—then the ponies, the lad, and a yappy dog at his feet (who looks up at the ponies in an at-the-ready, shall-we-play? position). The scene is a little clearing, just outside a forest. The ponies wear exquisite robin's-egg-blue brow bands. They back up just a touch— they're not sure about the dog. Their forelegs form two triangle shapes. It is as though they had been choreographed. The stable lad rests his arm on the shaft and smiles at the ponies. The picture is mysteriously beautiful in part because of the way the phaeton sits there on the clean earth floor. Stubbs paints the base and wheels of this blue carriage with such a godlike clarity that you feel air circulating in and around the whole vehicle.

Stubbs received a number of commissions from the Prince of Wales at the end of his career, and he rose to the occasion. They're sumptuous. He painted the Prince's phaeton. That picture couldn't come— it looks fantastic in the catalogue—but another of these royal commissions, *Soldiers of the 10th Light Dragoons*, did. (The 10th Light Dragoons was the outfit that his father, the King, appointed the Prince head of.) Stubbs's picture of four enlisted men placed in a row, facing out, in a meadow landscape on a summer's day was probably the single most brilliant image and the most lusciously painted work in the show. As a composition, it is as startlingly direct and silly as any Rousseau. It is painted, though, with a wallop and a sensuousness that Rousseau never achieves. If Toulouse-Lautrec (who didn't have this muscle, either) had made it, you'd know to smile. But Stubbs is serious, so this is somehow great poetry and a great joke. On the left is a sergeant on a horse, his sword unsheathed. To the right are— standing—a trumpeter, a sergeant with a rifle, and a private with a rifle. The sky is one big enveloping pink cloud, with a patch of vivid turquoise showing through. The uniforms and the various pieces of equipment are painted so that you can see small details from a few feet away, yet up close the oil pigment is fresh and creamy and bright.

Stubbs does what Vermeer does (and what photographs sometimes do): he catches so transitory a moment that the faces and expressions seem to move as we look at the work. The mounted sergeant is haughtily full of himself, but the men on foot squint, fidget, suppress smiles. They look from the sides of their eyes; the private wants to see if he's doing it right.

Stubbs is a painter of an egalitarian paradise, a realm where grooms and jockeys and stable lads are as compelling to us as countesses and wealthy landowners, where everyone, no matter what his station, looks at life without irony. But there is an increasing sense of majesty in his art. He seems to trace, in his work, England's growing mood of self-importance. Stubbs's values as a person don't change. He doesn't become puffed up (from the *Dragoons* it's clear that he could go just so far with pomp). But his work expands. Did his contemporaries know that Mr. Stubbs the horse painter was becoming a great master? It's not likely. His subject matter was too colloquial. Though he had professional connections with fellow-painters, he may have always been considered a first-class artisan in a special line who carefully obeyed the rules of picture making. Now that craftsman was simply becoming more polished. Maybe he, too, saw it this way.

He reaches his height in two of his very last works, which were made in 1800, when he was seventy-six: *Hambletonian, Rubbing Down* and *Freeman, the Earl of Clarendon's Gamekeeper, with a Dying Doe and a Hound*. It is unfortunate that *Hambletonian* could not make it to New Haven. There is nothing else like it in English art. There is nothing quite like it anywhere. This approximately seven-foot-high-by-twelve-foot-long painting shows a famous race horse of the time being rubbed down after a race. The horse, his trainer, and his stableboy are the only figures in the picture, and they're life-size. Hambletonian has clearly had a rough race—he crouches somewhat and appears strung out. The stableboy comes forward to look at us from behind and under Hambletonian's neck. The trainer, standing at the far right, with the reins in his hands, stares directly out at us. He's a short, solid man in a black top hat, a dark tan greatcoat, and boots. A painting of a life-size horse is extraordinary to begin with, but it is the trainer who gives this picture its real strangeness. The strangeness has to do with his squat body, his powerful hat, his gaze, the way his body compactly fits into the far right side of the picture. He seems to judge, and to be impatient with, us (and to lewdly size up the viewer).

Hambletonian is still virtually unknown. It was commissioned by the horse's owner and has stayed in the family ever since. It is in a house in Northern Ireland—Mount Stewart—that is open to the public only for part of the year, and it has been lent only to three exhibitions. (It was cleaned for the first time for the Tate show.) There is something nightmarish and unpleasant about it. It's different from other big pictures, whether Picasso's *Guernica* or works by the Venetian masters or Pollock. They have a decorative airiness that makes us feel we're not being swallowed by sheer size. *Hambletonian* is not airy. It has the intensity of an easel painting, and an easel painting this size radiates so much energy that you want to take a step back. It takes a while to surrender to it. It seems less a painting than a thing. One wants to place it as a curiosity from a traveling circus, or a billboard painted a hundred and fifty years before its time. But it is really an incomparable painting.

Freeman, the Earl of Clarendon's Gamekeeper, which was in the Yale show, isn't awesome on a first viewing, but it is Stubbs's most complex work. Freeman has come upon his staghound and a doe in a dark forest, and he stands over them, crouching a little, facing us. The dog has done his job. The doe is dying. She is extremely gentle, beautiful, and graceful. She looks out at us. The dog is a fine creature, too. He looks up at his master; his tongue is out a little, he seems to smile. He is ready for his reward. Freeman's rifle is balanced on his top hat, which is in the darkened background. Freeman has a small knife in his hand, though. He's going to put the doe out of her misery. The composition is very unusual and takes a little time to figure out. The animals connect like dancers stepping toward one another—their crossed legs are balletic—but then we see that the dog stands upright on the ground and that the deer is lying back against Freeman's legs. The painter, you believe, wants this confusion. He wants us to slowly realize what has happened only a moment before and what Freeman (whose knife is quite small and not immediately apparent) is about to do. We are to see that the dog is no villain and that the dog, the gamekeeper, and the doe—this linking triangular shape—are one. All of life and death are tied together in this image, which expands as we think about it and which is worthy of Tolstoy.

Stubbs seems to be showing his own end in *Hambletonian* and *Freeman*. In all his work (and he was prolific), there aren't any other images of dead or dying animals. The various lion-and-horse paintings show fear and combat, but nothing of the emotion of these two pictures. Hambletonian is in some distress, and the deer is genuinely stricken. Their bowed and collapsed bodies, the helpless, calling-out look in their eyes affect us deeply. It is as though Stubbs had always thought of himself as one of his beautiful animals—one of his horses especially—and when he felt that he no longer had the goods as a painter he pictured his end in the terms that he knew best. He created two works of visual poetry that are as dense and fresh as anything in the history of art. He apparently made a few more paintings and then simply retired his brushes. He set himself out to pasture, so to speak. His last years were devoted to work with pencil and paper. He had been working on a study in comparative anatomy for some time before he stopped painting, and he continued with it right up until the end. It is said that his one regret when he died, which was on July 10, 1806, was that he hadn't finished it.

—1985

WE ARE ONE

THE WORK of the English artists Gilbert and George is oppressive, but it is also fascinating and original. At their recent Guggenheim show, I was struck by how many different feelings are encompassed in their work. The artists, who call themselves "living sculpture," do everything together so as to make a work of art out of their partnership. Their work consists of a stream of documents of that partnership—most done with photographs, which they call "photo-pieces." Do I love their art? No, there is a cold, thin, wacky, stilted quality to it; you feel you are witnessing a bloodless and bizarre self-parody of English manners. Yet Gilbert and George cast a spell. Here are two men who have, in a way, turned themselves into windup toys, and it is simultaneously sad and amusing, repellent, frightening, and moving to see how they have done it. And it isn't only as a life story that they are engaging. Their often large photo-pieces, which are a cross between political posters, enormous movie stills, and stained glass, have a formal presence all their own. In a satisfying way, the photo-pieces are tinny, inartistic, inexpensive-looking objects; they are like artworks made for people in a workers' colony—artworks meant to remind the drones about what is "good" and what is "bad." But Gilbert and George are more naive and more complex than real propagandists, and that is what makes their pictures so creepy. Think of Big Brother as his own Minister of Propaganda—a thwarted, would-be painter-poet who designed all the art in his empire—and you will have a sense of what Gilbert and George create.

Gilbert and George are like characters Alice might have encountered in Wonderland. They dress in the same style of worsted suit—they generally button all three buttons—and always wear ties (but not the same pattern). According to Brenda Richardson, the curator of the show—it began in Baltimore—and the author of its catalogue, they wear worn versions of the same clothes when they work in the studio. Their last names aren't in the biography they have included in the catalogue. This biography—it is as stylized as everything they do—is merely a listing of the art schools they went to. It stops in 1967, when, in their mid-twenties, they met and formed the team Gilbert and George. Since then, there has been only a single biography. Gilbert, who was born in the Italian Dolomites, has straight dark hair and has become stocky over the years; he is softly, shyly handsome, a bit reminiscent of Michael Palin. George, who is taller, has straight fair hair and wears glasses; he has become bald down the middle, and sometimes has a stern, disapproving, Philip Larkinish look. From accounts of their talk—and from the tone of their short writings, which they used to mail out to people associated with the arts—they have unusually courteous, old-fashioned manners. They sound and appear a bit like butlers. They aim, they say, to be "well-behaved." They live together and create every aspect of their artwork together, without any outside help.

Originally, they gave performances. In 1971, they performed at the Sonnabend Gallery in New York. Wearing matching suits, and with their heads and hands painted bronze, they stood on a platform for hours at a stretch, moving back and forth like robots on slow speed, mouthing the words to an old vaudeville song, "Underneath the Arches," which was played on a tape recorder beneath the platform. Five years later, they performed for the second and last time in New York. In that work, called "The Red Sculpture," their hands and heads (including their hair and necks) were painted a startling red. In the early years of their collaboration, they also made large drawings of themselves in different places—such as parks—and booklets, too, which described, sometimes in verse, what "they" (the boys, our friends) were up to now. Gradually, they began to use photographs. They took photos of themselves, the rooms they were in, and the sites in London that they moved through, then assembled the photos in units of four, say, or sixteen, to form multipaneled pictures. Every work they do has, usually placed in the lower right-hand corner of the image, a title, a date, and their signed names. In their early work, this information appears along with the royal arms—which makes it seem as if their products came from Harrods, or from a tasteful, reliable old firm. Usually, the pieces are signed "Gilbert" first, then "George"; the handwriting is almost identical. Occasionally, a work is signed "George" first. They create such a controlled, Tweedledum-and-Tweedledee sense of things that when George's name comes first a viewer becomes a touch nervous.

They live at 12 Fournier Street, in a working-class part of London. Originally, their studio was in the street-level floor of the house; eventually they bought the house. At first, it was empty, and they used the emptiness in some of their early photo-pieces. In works called *Dead Boards* and *Dusty Corners*, we see them standing in the

bare rooms, looking this way or that. Alongside the photographs of
them there might be photographs of the walls or corners of the place.
Gradually, they filled it with antiques, primarily English furniture
and pottery of the late nineteenth century. They have stocked the
house as methodically and industriously as they do everything; their
house, now bursting with stuff, is a piece in itself. (There is a
documentary photo of one of the rooms in the catalogue.)

Gilbert and George raise an immediate question in the viewer's
mind. Are they for real, or is their act an elaborate joke? Are they, as
they say they are, artists-moralists who want to document the conditions of modern life? The Guggenheim show made me believe that
they are contemporary versions of preacher-painters of long ago—men
who regularly had visions, then illustrated them. Brenda Richardson
believes that Gilbert and George's work forms a "scripture," and, in a
surprising and believable way, they make their viewers into pa-
rishioners; they say to us, "Look at what is happening to our world!
This is what it is really like out there." They have what one thinks of
as a pastor's way of being concerned with life's ugliness for a congrega-
tion's benefit—not for his own.

There is a very English quality to their intendedly simple sermons.
They are like modern incarnations of Ruskin or William Morris.
Gilbert and George's works are like modern Hogarths, too—like his
series of paintings for *Marriage à la Mode* or *The Rake's Progress*, where
we see the stages of a dissolute life or a virtuous life. In photo-pieces
from the seventies, Gilbert and George show themselves drinking,
surrounded by bottles and glasses, sprawled on the floor in a stupor.
Are they documenting their own actual bouts with alcohol—or pretending to have been drunks? Somehow it doesn't matter. We don't
really want to know. We like not knowing for sure. And it is charming
to see them grow and change their ways, in other works from the
period. We see them in martial-arts positions; they learn from the
Orient. They become tough, fierce; their faces and bodies imply that
they have the reckless, willing-to-be-puppets-for-truth quality of
members of the Red Guard.

They show themselves, in other seventies pieces, in conjunction
with bums, alcoholics passed out on the pavement, graffiti. Some of

the graffiti are "Queer," "Communism," "Poof," "Are you angry or are you boring?" And we see them standing there, or see their faces, placed alongside shots of graffiti, of smashed windows, of the dreary, anonymous new buildings on the London skyline. Gilbert and George seem to be taking it all in. Their seventies photo-pieces, which are in black and white, with some images dyed dark red, resemble the photo assemblages you'd see in the lobby of a hotel playing host to a meeting of the World Council of this or that concerned group. But with Gilbert and George in these pieces there is a tingle. Looking at these serious chaps absorbing the modern world's coldness and ugliness, we slip into a naive, wide-eyed spirit ourselves.

Beginning in 1980, their work becomes literally colorful, technically more complex—and weirder, more daring, less likable. Their pictures are more and more about sex, and we are increasingly aware of Gilbert and George as individuals. They aren't good boys anymore; they have become, in effect, dirty old men. Their images are smirky, crazy, unbelievable. They make large areas bright yellow, green, blue, red, or orange, and mix the colored areas in with blown-up black and white photos of people and things. They also make Calder-like images of masks, primitive animals, insignia. There's an uninhibited, childish, voodoo spirit inhabiting this work. You look at the photographed or drawn penises, the tongues, the bound boys, the faces that become sunflowers, the homoerotic military statues, the calla lilies that nuzzle together, the titles—*Rose Hole, Naked Love, Lickers, Youth Faith, Living with Madness*—and Gilbert and George floating through it all, and you aren't sure what's going on. Are Gilbert and George happy, liberated, spontaneous at last—or are they still living through the troubles of modern life for our benefit? Is their moment with boys similar to their moment with alcohol? Will they pass through it? Is it merely an abstract problem they have set up for the sake of their art? One feels that they are part of this homosexual world—that there is no choice in the matter for them. And this makes us think differently about their earlier work—makes us think that they have always been less conscious, more driven. It is as though, joined in a relationship that is closer than most marriages, they are freer to act on their impulses than most artists. Having each other, they don't have to think about what the real audience out there will think of them. They can experience anything and turn it into art. Living in a world where they never have to test their ideas, though, they run the risk of premature artistic senility.

Their work of the past five years is art on a borderline. (We turn back to the work of the seventies with relief.) The recent work is in terrible taste, and we are embarrassed for Gilbert and George. They are courageously, comically, and sadly unlike the boys and young men whom they call "patriots," "saints," "angels," "heroes of contemporary life." There is little charm or voluptuous sexual poetry to these images. Some of the young men are genuine bruisers—skinheads—and, in a few instances, hustlers perhaps. But most of these "saints" are just tough (and not so tough) street kids. They are the opposite of the sleepy-eyed dreamboats of male fashion ads. And Gilbert and George, as self-created characters, are aging fellows in suits, vulnerable worshipers.

Yet some of these stiff, awkward, berserk, and juvenile tableaux have the power of Munch's tableaux of sexual relations—his panoramic images of sexual partnering. Gilbert and George's photopieces aren't as beautiful as Munch's paintings; but Gilbert and George are wonderfully unfussy in the way they bring together enlarged black and white photos with dyed photos and with large areas of a single bright color. They often arrange the elements of the compositions in the symmetrical, neatly balanced way that children, when they believe they're thinking like adults, arrange food on a plate. The clunky complexity of the compositions is funny, and more pleasing than you can explain.

At their best, Gilbert and George are strange and novel poets of city life. Taken together, their images describe the poetry of a gray midwinter (or midsummer) afternoon, when it will rain, when you will see no beauty in the local park, when your high point will be an encounter with someone who will yell obscenities at you. Many of the photo-pieces are magically atmospheric; they get places and moods just right, as in *Black Church Face*, where the face of a young black boy—he's looking straight out at us—takes up the lower half of the picture and above him is the interior of a cathedral. The image of the black boy and the cathedral interior—both are in black and white—clicks in a subliminal way. You feel you can read anything into this picture. It seems to be about how that black face has inherited that white man's building, how institutions decay and are inherited by new people and evolve into new things. Gilbert and George's locale is London, but an American can believe that they have also captured Detroit, St. Louis, Cleveland, Philadelphia. They seem to present the soul of all the once bustling, now stone-cold and uninviting downtowns. When they include images of military statues from the First World War period and earlier—sexy, dopey, virile statues of noble warriors—they are on target, too. Gilbert and George's bright, pow-pow images seem to speak for guys with no future who idle away their days with visions of vengeful, enemy-annihilating, boot-stomping male power.

Gilbert and George are among the most complex and satisfying European artists of the past fifteen years. They are in a class with Joseph Beuys, who, like them, is a performance artist and a maker of objects. The similarities between Gilbert and George and Beuys are amazing. The English artists and the West German sculptor-performer-shaman make it clear that they have little or no personal life outside their art. They are guided by a belief that they are teachers, that their pieces demonstrate moral lessons. Beuys and Gilbert and George are of different generations. Beuys is now in his sixties, the English artists are in their forties, but they all came to maturity in the nineteen-sixties or early seventies, and their material is the same: impoverished European life after the Second World War. They say, in effect, that the only important subject for a European artist is the fact that Europe no longer counts. One feels that, on some level, they spurn the pleasures of life, and have set themselves on their art-making treadmills because they believe these are the most truthful ways to express the end-of-the-line quality of European culture. Beuys and Gilbert and George are like Old Testament prophets wandering in the godless cities. One wonders whether they aren't, in part, addressing their sermons to America—and whether they aren't needling America. Whether they don't think of themselves as the consciences of the Western world. They are like self-appointed middlemen between the Third World and their American audience. Certainly there seems to be a core of indignation and of self-importance in their art—a de Gaullish sort of wounded superiority—that is not present in the work of American artists of the seventies.

It's fascinating how, though Gilbert and George are so buttoned-up and old-fashioned as persons, their art has always been so hip and of-the-moment. With their performances, they were among the most interesting Conceptual Artists of the early seventies. With their recent photo-pieces, they are still producing England's most daring new art. In the way that they base their art on photography but aren't, somehow, photographers, and in the way that a lot of their art is about sex, they're in step with artists who are ten and fifteen years younger than they are. Ultimately, though, they are little masters; their work is too harsh and static to be great. Whether consciously or not, they present a prisoner's world. Formally and emotionally, they show a world behind bars. They have always made their photo-pieces (and drawings) out of small separate units, meant to be joined together on the wall, with the lines showing, and the black lines produce a prisonlike effect. We feel that the images are trapped, held in place, seen under a magnifying lens. The light in their work is glaring or hazy; it is the light that comes through the grated, dirty overhead windows of great old railway stations or through stained glass. Not ethereal, heavenly stained glass but dreary, Victorian stained glass. Gilbert and George don't take us beyond the imprisoned world they present.

Still, they have created a piece of living poetry. It is as though they were living out England's sense of herself as a country that stopped happening long ago. They are English schoolboys taken to an ultimate level. Their work is a kind of swan song for Great Britain. The surprising and good thing is that theirs is a swan song without self-pity or remorse.

—1985

DAVID PARK

DAVID PARK'S FINEST paintings—they're from the first half or so of the fifties—are scenes of everyday life. His images aren't dramatic. At first sight, there's even something bland about these pictures—of boys playing ball on a beach; of two fellows in a canoe; of people walking with their heads down, like inmates, across a college campus; of a boy in a car, looking out at another car; of jazz musicians playing; of a group of people, possibly a family, at a table. We're taken back to the time when abstraction was king, and if you wanted to paint the figure you were careful to paint nonscenes—scenes where figures and faces were little more than statues that reflected light. Park comes from this era, but in a refreshing way; it's as though he used the played-down, no-comment spirit of figurative painting of the time to tell stories in code. He makes his figures and, even more, their faces with a slightly rubbery, unrealistic line. We're drawn to these people. Their heads, limbs, and torsos seem to be bigger than their minds or characters as yet. We're especially aware of their necks— they're a bit too large, and Park likes to show people whose heads are bowed. His people are reminiscent of the elongated, reflective people of the great German sculptor Lehmbruck—the author of the large *Standing Youth* and *Kneeling Woman* in the Modern.

Park is best known as one of the Bay Area figurative painters—West Coast artists who were prominent in the fifties and sixties because they gave up on abstraction and returned to painting the figure. Park is remembered as the founder of this school (it was more like a shared taste than a school), and for having died at an early age—at forty-nine, in 1960—just as he was becoming nationally known. The current show at the Salander-O'Reilly Galleries is the largest he has had in New York since a memorial show that began here in 1961. On the basis of this current show, Park doesn't seem to be a big artist who has been overlooked; a good bit of his work is disappointing. But he is a more powerful and inventive painter than has generally been thought. His best pictures look as if they could have been made today, because they're a touch cartoonish, and yet there is a subtle psychological flavor to them and an almost otherworldly radiance to his light.

The most contemporary aspect of Park's work is his sense of space. In the 1953 *Ball Game on the Beach*, one of his very best paintings, a boy is about to throw a beach ball to a group of fellows who run along the sparkling beach, their arms outstretched. The painting is like a photo from *Life* crossed with a Maori carving, all done in Halloween oranges, yellows, blacks, whites. The fellows on the beach are gesticulating stick figures; they are jaggedly drawn and painted, with parts of their bodies orange, parts black. The boy is naturalistically drawn, and our viewpoint is so close to his upraised arms and the ball he holds that we feel we're "with" him, and that the stick figures in the distance might be in his imagination. In another first-rank picture, *Berkeley Jazz Band*, of 1951–53, seven musicians are crowded into a small room, playing; we're below them, looking up through their backs and faces to a bit of ceiling at the top of the picture. It takes a while for our eyes to adjust to the dark browns, maroons, and tans; we have to search to see where all the hands and faces are. And there is a fearless passage of painting: the clarinet player's shirt is a rich red, the background wall is a dark brown, and Park brings them together without any "air" between them, like two hot, strong, different sounds.

Park's indirect, over-the-shoulder way of presenting a scene isn't exactly his own. He may have been thinking about Degas—those pictures of concerts where we are in the pit with the musicians, looking up over their shoulders to the tiny figures on the stage, and where parts of the figure closest to us have been cut off by the frame. But Park makes this exaggerated near-to-far space unsettling. He was developing an odd but interesting way of presenting reality. There's something modest and grandiose, anonymous and self-centered about these accordionized views. You feel as though you were a squashable fly next to the giant foreground figures, and, also, as though you were an uninvolved watcher of people; you feel you're appraising them from behind a one-way mirror. And these Park pictures are still vibrant, as objects. In an appreciation in the show's brochure, Richard Diebenkorn says exactly what a viewer senses: that Park was "*in love* with oil paint and its potential to become *merde*." Park's hand is assured and swift, but it seems as if at any moment everything could turn to sludge.

Park is no longer the best-known Bay Area painter—Diebenkorn is—but he may still be the most complex and best of them. The idea of a "return to the figure" after painting abstractly seems to have meant more to Park than to any other West Coast artist at the time. He was the first to do it. The others—including Diebenkorn and Elmer Bischoff—were at first appalled, or felt superior to him. Then, within a few years, they followed him. Looked at from 1985, Park is as much a characteristic figure of his time as Jackson Pollock. We feel in Park (though in a less mighty and significant way than in Pollock) an impatience with any authority, a desire to get out on his own. Park broke with Abstract Expressionism in 1949, when the finest works of the movement were being made. He made his move dramatically. He took every abstract work he had in his studio but one to a dump in Berkeley, and burned them. He was thirty-eight, and had worked as an abstract painter for four years. As Henry Geldzahler and Carl Belz point out in essays for the current show's brochure, Park was largely a self-taught artist. He was a part-time teacher at the California School of Fine Arts in the forties, when Clyfford Still taught there. Still was then—and may even now be thought of as—one of the big men of the Abstract Expressionist movement, and Park was impressed. But he couldn't abide the man's autocratic self-assurance, or the self-assurance of many of the Abstract Expressionists and their admirers.

David Park was blondish and handsome. In photos that Imogen Cunningham took of him, he has Gary Cooperish looks—though he isn't as good-looking as Cooper. He was a rebel in a number of ways. He came from a Boston Brahmin family. His father was a Unitarian minister. The painter, who was one of four children, was expected to go through school (and through life) with the right, high-minded values. He didn't finish high school, though (and he never went to college), and he was at odds with his father for years. In the thirties,

182

he found himself on the West Coast, doing odd jobs, drifting. Eventually, he married; he and Lydia Newell Park had two daughters, and settled in Berkeley. For a number of years, he was able to paint full-time because his wife worked at the university library. From 1955 on, Park was on the faculty of the university, and they lived more easily, in a redwood house in the Berkeley hills. His two real loves as a boy were painting and music—playing the piano—and he apparently painted and played music with relish all his life. He played classical music and, increasingly as he got older, jazz. In his youth, he made amusing, romantic (and not very good) pictures—they are reproduced in catalogues from earlier Park shows—of sprawled-out lovers, dancing couples, and young men playing violins. Park was drawn, he said, to the primitive, the unrefined, the un-dressed-up. In a biographical statement from 1959, he writes at some length, for no particular reason, about how little he reads books. He wants us to see him as a regular guy in a T-shirt. But his comments, here and elsewhere, are hardly those of a lunkhead; his statements and recorded bits of conversation are highly literate, compressed, strong.

The unexpected part of the show was how much Park's best work recalls the fifties. I'm equivocal about this. Part of me thinks that there is something weak and commercial about this period look, that I'm drawn to the pictures for nostalgic reasons. But part of me is fascinated by it. It is said that most photographs have a period flavor that becomes apparent only years after the picture is taken. This is rarely said about paintings, but it applies to Park's work. The fifties are felt in little details: in the T-shirts his figures wear, in their short haircuts, in the mere image of a boy in a car, in the way the jazz musicians hunch over their instruments, in the image of a "sophisticated" cocktail party. The period flavor is felt in the way he stylizes people and scenes. One is reminded of UNICEF and Ban the Bomb posters and of artwork for record covers and book jackets by Joseph Low and Ben Shahn, where people seem butterflylike, helpless, unanchored, lost in their thoughts. Park makes this UNICEF-poster appearance strange, almost grand—perhaps because his paint surface is so meaty, physical, uncooked.

The odd thing is that Park worked not from photographs or from life but from memory. He didn't even make on-the-spot pencil sketches. All his work comes out of his head, so to speak, and at first this is hard to believe—especially because he paints light, and its absence, so precisely. He gives the exact visual sensation of how thick or heavy an arm is, say, or a finger, by showing how much light it has absorbed. In *Berkeley Jazz Band*, we feel that a strong, clear light has momentarily been blocked and we're in a shadowed world, but if a figure were to move, or if our point of view were to change by a hair, light would stream in.

In the end, though, Park's not painting from life worked against him—his art became theoretical. His best-known paintings are from his last years, and most show young men who wear swim trunks or are nude—they're on a beach or by a boat. The present show made it clear that these pictures are not his best. They're not the equal of the more realistic "scene" pictures from the first two-thirds of the fifties (which are barely known). The later Parks are on the stark, allegorical side. The faces of his young men are made up of thick, single strokes of dark paint—a line or two for eyes, nose, mouth. The backgrounds are shimmery and oily, and the figures appear to be emerging from them. The colors generally are dark blues and greens, with patches of red and orange and pure white here and there.

Park produced many such "bather" pictures—and similar pictures of women and of figures playing musical instruments—in the last few years of his life. His single best-known painting, *Four Men*—it is owned by the Whitney—is one of them. It's obvious why they were considered important at the time, especially to viewers impressed by Abstract Expressionism. The figures are a touch mythical and battle-worn, and the paintings appear to be, at heart, abstractions. The abstract quality is what is wrong with them. The people are empty, they aren't real. Park isn't struggling enough in these pictures, and he said as much in interviews; he said he didn't care what viewers thought, he knew he was in the groove. But his brushwork is showy and his color is blaring.

One feels that he was a victim of the moment, that, in a way, he capitulated to Abstract Expressionism. He may have felt that he was getting closer to the "primitive" and the "natural" in these paintings, which have a "universal" quality. But he seems to have become the sort of artist he once railed against. He had a nose for rhetorical gestures and heroics—whether in Clyfford Still or anybody else—but he took his fresh, new figurative art in the same direction. His many late bather pictures might be called figurative Stills.

Park's work wasn't all downhill. There are paintings from the end of the fifties that are strong—particularly *Crowd*, which shows a number of heads that appear to bob in a sea of paint. And he didn't stop painting everyday life. *The Table*—a 1957 work that is in the show—is one of his finest pictures. This scene of four people at a table, talking, holding glasses and cups, is primarily in earth colors (for the people and background wall) and white (for the foreground shirt and table), with bits of blue on the dishes and glasses. The picture brings together a French feeling for the subtle beauties of paint handling and color, a German feeling for mood and drama—for something spiritual that is immanent in the scene—and a fifties American appearance, a tone of seriousness and innocence. Again, Park gives us an image where we look up at, and over, someone's shoulder to get into the scene. There is hardly anything going on in *The Table*, the figures barely look at each other. Yet this picture is his most Lehmbruck-like: it is majestic and tender. We're surprised to see these plain, big-necked Americans painted in such a muzzy light, with such an earthy and elegant palette. The many browns and tans have a pale light coming through them, and the bit of blue on the glasses and plates introduces just the right note of icy refinement. It is as though Park had joined the two parts of himself: Boston and the West Coast (or the newer, brighter, less formal America).

Park's very last pictures—they are works on paper—are good, too. In the late fifties, he suffered from back ailments, and underwent a number of operations to alleviate the pain. A 1960 operation disclosed terminal cancer. He wasn't strong enough to paint, and began working with pen and ink, watercolor, and gouache. His subject matter continued to be rather "universal" figures and encounters, but these images aren't monotonous, as the paintings could be. His drawings are often of museum quality. Though they aren't as absorbing as his paintings, they're beautiful, unlabored—especially those of fiddlers.

And in the final months of his life Park made a thirty-foot-long scroll with felt-tip pens. It is housed in Zellerbach Hall, on the Berkeley campus. The scroll is about his life; the scenes go in and out of remembered events in Boston and Berkeley. Snippets of it are reproduced in old catalogues, and it looks lightweight, yet one feels that, like his more realistic paintings, it might have more life for us than it had for viewers in the sixties or seventies. There ought to be a comprehensive Park show and a book (there are only a number of old catalogues); it would be especially wonderful to see the full scope of his scenes of everyday fifties life.

Where does Park fit in the larger scheme of American art? One thinks of him in relation to Hopper, Alex Katz, Avery, Fairfield Porter. Park probably doesn't have the range of any of them—though, in his struggle with paint and his ambitions, he is more exciting than Avery. He is most similar to Porter. The two were about the same age as the Abstract Expressionists, and they bloomed relatively late in life—by going against that movement. Porter rejected the new American painting in as emphatic a way as Park's bonfire at the Berkeley dump. Porter was in the habit of sparring with Clement Greenberg. In the early fifties, Greenberg said to Willem de Kooning, who was Porter's friend, that painting the figure was regressive, it could no longer be done. (De Kooning was working on his *Woman* paintings at the time.) Porter said that he knew what he wanted to do from that moment: exactly what he wasn't supposed to do.

Porter's work is more unified and developed than Park's, but Park is the more daring painter. Porter sometimes painted landscapes and interiors with a brilliantly clear light, but he was most assured with muted, cozy moments and places. His rare snow scenes (and his small landscapes in general) are delectable. He is a master of foggy, hazy light and of nebulous views. He's a champ with odd, off colors: grays, pinks, English-mustard yellow. His still lifes and interiors, though, have a passive prettiness, and his portraits—or those paintings where the people in them are more than a bit of decor—are wooden. Porter the man may have understood people, but Porter the painter has little to say about them. In *The Table* alone, Park does what all Porter's figure paintings together do not do: Park takes a casual, everyday moment and illuminates it in a new way. And he does this without being sentimental.

Park's great gift was for painting people. I have seen many of his portraits in catalogues, and if the actual pictures are as good as the reproductions he was a first-rate portraitist. He painted his wife and friends, many of whom were painters and writers and were associated with the university: Mark Schorer, Hassel Smith, Phyllis Diebenkorn, Richard Diebenkorn, Elmer Bischoff, Stephen Pepper. The portraits—they, too, were painted from memory, not from life—aren't major undertakings; many are small and appear to be gifts to the people painted. They're caricaturish, but we feel different aspects of the person, and Park paints light and shade in the same experimental and unorthodox way that he does in his more ambitious paintings.

Park's special moment is when he paints someone in a relationship with someone else or a lone individual taking in the surrounding light. Few American paintings have such a sense of intimacy as *Flower Market*, a 1955 Park owned by the Whitney. (It isn't in the present show but was on view over the summer at the museum.) This picture shows a woman facing a man at a market—he is seen with his back to us. The picture is mostly in smoky red-oranges and greens that give off a kind of North African heat and light. One feels that nothing else Park did is as beautiful or as mysteriously achieved as the grayish-green and glowing orange face of the woman. She is not a portrait; she is simply a lovely woman of no clear age. We're pleased by the gentle and spontaneous way Park has painted the heads, hand, and bouquet, and created such a distinct mood. The picture strikes us the way it may have struck viewers thirty years ago: we, too, believe that this is a fresh, new way to paint the figure.

—1985

POLKE'S DOTS, OR,
A GENERATION COMES
INTO FOCUS

ART OF OUR TIME IS A grandiose title for the four-volume catalogue of
the collection of Charles and Doris Saatchi, who live in London, but
this collection lives up to it. The collection, which includes over four
hundred and fifty works by fifty-one artists, is composed principally
of Minimalism, and a little bit of Pop Art, and more recent work,
which has been called Neo-Expressionist, or Image, art. This is work
by, among others, Philip Guston, Julian Schnabel, Joel Shapiro,
David Salle, Anselm Kiefer, and Sigmar Polke. The collection is a
record of a shift in the way the generation of the nineteen-sixties and
the present-day generation think about art—and about themselves.
It takes us from a shallow-spaced and gleaming, smooth-surfaced
art to an art of porous surfaces, flickering light, and a shifting space.
It takes us from an art that prided itself on being immediately
"readable" and clear—and, also, rather distant—to an art that is
pleased to be ambiguous, that asks to be interpreted in different
ways simultaneously. The past seven or so years have been a very
free, undoctrinaire period for painting and sculpture. European
painting is more innovative now than it has been in years, and, for the
first time, the strongest European and American artists have a com-
radely closeness in their attitudes. There have been important shows
of this new art (the best have been in Europe), yet no museum has
presented it with the scope that can be seen in these volumes. And
what makes the Saatchi collection unique is that the Saatchis have
assembled this new work along with the work that, so to speak,
fathered it.

There is something off-putting, though, about how they have gone about things. Charles Saatchi is Saatchi & Saatchi Compton, Ltd., an English advertising firm whose best-known client is Margaret Thatcher. Doris Saatchi is American and writes for art and travel magazines. They are contemporary versions of the Arensbergs (who collected the advanced art of the teens and twenties) and the Sculls (who collected in the sixties). The difference is that the Saatchis aren't gentle encouragers, or enthusiastic appreciators, of the new. They are more impersonal, professional, and self-effacing. They have chosen an immodest title for these books of their collection. (It's peculiar to attach any title to a collection other than one's name.) Yet there isn't a scrap of writing by, or about, them anywhere in the four volumes; they never actually state what their aims are. It is clear, though, that they are after the major works by the leading artists of the day. Essentially, they want to be their own Museum of Modern Art, and it's astounding to think of two individuals having such an ambition. (Unlike the Modern, they aren't interested in drawings, prints, or sketches; at least, few of them are illustrated in the catalogues.)

This past spring, they opened, in London, a public museum for the collection, which will be presented in separate units, each on view for a number of months. The museum—its address is 98A Boundary Road—is made up of five enormous connecting rooms and is set on one floor, with some rooms stepped up. (The building was formerly a paint-storage warehouse.) There is no seating of any kind, the light includes natural lighting, the steel girders are exposed, the floor is a painted gray cement. The proportions of the rooms are a touch too long, low, and spread out, and the space—the architect was Max Gordon—has a stiff and awkward but organic quality. At the first show, which closed in the fall of 1985 and was made up chiefly of works by Donald Judd, Andy Warhol, Brice Marden, and Cy Twombly, the building overwhelmed the art.

The Saatchis' catalogues are of a piece with their museum. These large-size but easily handled volumes are oddly official and ostentatiously plain. The texts, which are about the individual artists, are by numerous critics and art historians, including Peter Schjeldahl, Hilton Kramer, Rudi Fuchs, Robert Rosenblum, Kim Levin, Phyllis

Tuchman, and Michael Auping. There are sensitive descriptions and perceptions throughout, and Schjeldahl (especially on the Minimalists and Warhol), Kramer (especially on Schnabel), and Fuchs (on Polke) are particularly good. Kramer and Schjeldahl have doubts about some of the artists they write about, and it is a tribute to the Saatchis that these writers have been allowed to retain their doubts. But most of the writing is not on their level, and the mere sight of all these appreciative-historical-critical pieces, set at the beginning of each volume, is cramping. Every artist is given a sort of art-historical pat of approval. The whole art world has been attended to and is reporting in.

In their desire to marshal the field of developing art, the Saatchis, one can feel, have trampled some of the real art out of everything. And yet they are in tune with a key element of some of the best work of the past twenty-five years. They are in tune with its confidence, its almost belligerent belief in its history and importance.

The first two volumes of *Art of Our Time* cover the Minimalists, and the Saatchis must have one of the finest collections of this art in the world. Here are choice works by Judd, Marden, Robert Ryman, Sol LeWitt, Bruce Nauman, Agnes Martin, and Carl Andre, plus top examples by artists who, older than, or not quite associated with, the Minimalists, fit in a Minimalist setting: Warhol, Twombly, Eva Hesse, Richard Artschwager, Frank Stella, Lucas Samaras. Many of the most influential figures of American—and world—art of the last two decades are here.

In the past few years, with the deluge of ingratiating, movie-inspired, and cartoonlike painting in the galleries and art magazines—paintings of angelic and heroic figures who float through the sky or dart through space like Batman—a viewer may have thought longingly about Minimalism, about how refreshing its cool, blank, uningratiating spirit would appear now. But looking at the Minimalist works in the Saatchi catalogues, and at the first show at their museum, I have to say that for me, at least, the time hasn't come. Twenty years ago, Minimalism was certainly the leading avant-garde style; but Minimalism lacks the figure, and so, in retrospect, it seems related

190

primarily to landscape, architecture, and design. Minimalist paintings and sculptures have the same effect on me as Impressionist pictures; I respect them, but when I'm in a museum I have to force myself to spend time with them. The Minimalists are a lot like the Impressionists. They're both pioneering yet emotionally undeveloped movements. They are both about pure sensation: the look and feel of color, weather, light, different materials. The Impressionists and the Minimalists are portrayers of the classic norm of things. Both seemed arrogant to their first audiences because the artists said, in effect, "We're not interested in people, or emotions. That has been done."

And Donald Judd, the preeminent Minimalist, reminds me of Winslow Homer, who, though not exactly an Impressionist, also painted the appearance of everyday, outdoor life. Homer is a superb picture-constructor. He is an artist of a clean cool breeze whom you like to turn to now and then, but he doesn't deliver a complicated message. He is strong because he avoids certain emotions. Judd is strong in a similar way. One feels with both that here is the work of a manly man, a kind of bachelor artist, who is, surprisingly, in love with style for itself—and who may not realize how stylish his work is. One believes that neither artist is aware of how much we are drawn to his work because of its sheer dapper elegance.

There is conviction to Judd's art of geometrical purity and sleek industrial materials—to his boxes that sit on the floor or are stacked on a wall. His color can be smolderingly handsome, especially when, in an untitled piece, he brings copper together with glowing red-orange Plexiglas. He looks best when his entire range of work can be seen at the same time, when a viewer can get the look and feel of raw, dry galvanized aluminum; copper; polished, shiny aluminum; tropical blue and aquarium-green Plexiglas; unpainted pale tan plywood. His most recent work—pieces that were exhibited last year and are not in *Art of Our Time*—adds a new note to his repertoire. They are large rectangular metal boxes, made of many interlocking units, which are painted in muted yellows, oranges, pinks, and blacks—varsity colors. And Judd has been a real presence on the art scene for more than twenty years. He is a highly competitive and—at least as a writer—a ruthless soul; he is devoted to the highest standards of creativity. In his art criticism (which he stopped doing full-time in the sixties) and in his sculpture, he stands on the field like a tough drill sergeant, impossible to please. His work says to fellow artists, "Can your work be this tough? Can you do it without laying on an ounce of charm? I did." Judd is, one can believe, a distillation of an arrogant, nervously self-confident time in American art: the era of the Abstract Expressionists and their admirers, who watched Paris decline as the capital of world-class art and believed that the torch had been passed to them. Judd's objects are the epitome of a purely aesthetic way of looking at the world. There are, of course, more than purely formal qualities in his work and in Minimalism. But to our eyes, now, they are buried and stunted.

Andy Warhol, though, looks fresh in the pages of *Art of Our Time*. He looks better than any artist of the sixties. (It should be noted that the collection includes no work by, among others, Roy Lichtenstein, James Rosenquist, Helen Frankenthaler, Alex Katz, Ellsworth Kelly, or Jasper Johns.) As Peter Schjeldahl points out in his catalogue essay, Warhol was at his best practically right at the start, when he was in his early thirties, between roughly 1962 and 1965 (which is when most of the Warhols in the collection are from). Warhol was an original artist when Kennedy was President and right after, and his pictures are an expression of that time. The early sixties were like a debutantes' ball for this country. It was a moment when the country took on a more sophisticated sense of itself, after Ike's sleepy reign, and Warhol was the guy who loved the party the most and was still high during the crash that came the next morning.

His pictures of the time are his most well known: paintings based on images taken from newspaper photos, which he silk-screened onto canvas and then colored in. Looked at now, his Marilyns, Elvises, Lizes, and mourning Jackies, and his car crash, tuna fish can disaster, wanted man, atomic bomb, and electric chair paintings present, with an audacious directness, some of the most glamorous and tragic (and laughable) themes of American life. With their all-pervasive silvery, metallic colors, and with bits of bright red and turquoise and yellow floating on the silvery expanses, there's something sleek and alienating about these pictures. Yet they're shabbily sad, too. Seeing one is like passing a construction-site wall that has been plastered with row after row of the same announcement for a long-gone event. Warhol's paintings are like Walker Evans's photos of street posters from the thirties come alive, and the mood of that decade—of the Depression—adds a bass note to his art. Warhol was born in 1928, and his work is a kind of commentary on a thirties sense of things. His most wanted men, auto crashes, and electric chairs have a Depression-era violence to them, and his idolization of movie stars has a thirties ring to it, too. Warhol's best pictures have a layered power; he caught the spirit of his moment and of the time when he was a child. His being, in a way, a man of two periods makes him especially interesting now, because much current art has a two-decadeness to it. We are drawn to the look and spirit of the fifties; we laugh even as we stare at the objects, cars, clothes, and personalities of the time. That era is like credit in a bank that we didn't remember was there. The fifties are barely known to artists born between, say, 1950 and 1955; the era, it might be said, seeped into this generation's consciousness, as the thirties seeped into Warhol's.

And there is a finality about Warhol's art. It is unlikely that someone would still want to base an art on celebrities, movie stars, tabloid disasters. Warhol wrapped up that material. We are probably interested in what lies behind the facade of modern media fame.

The real excitement and energy of *Art of Our Time* is in the more recent work, in volumes three and four, which show the painting of Philip Guston and Malcolm Morley, Sigmar Polke, Anselm Kiefer, and Francesco Clemente, David Salle and Julian Schnabel, and the sculpture of Joel Shapiro. There are many more artists in these volumes; the most notable are the painters Elizabeth Murray, Terry Winters, Eric Fischl, and Bill Jensen, and the sculptor Scott Burton. But it is these others who best represent the aims of recent art. They come from different generations and schools of thought (and different countries). And not all of them are satisfying artists. They show, though, the range of the new art, which is done by artists who use the figure but aren't conventional "figure" painters or sculptors; whose art is about the unconscious; who aren't "literary" artists but who are poets.

Philip Guston may be the cornerstone of the second half of the collection—and of recent art. When he died, in 1980, at sixty-seven, people were in the process of coming around to him; he was still something of a new painter. He produced a lot of work in the last decade of his life; it was his best work, and we are at the phase where we want to see more and more of those paintings.

Guston's story is, in part, about how he slowly found his voice, how he gave himself to different art movements, then broke free from them. He started out, in the thirties, as a poet of social realism. He painted scenes of lonely boys in bed, kids fighting in streets; he showed ominous moments when people wait for something to happen, or play instruments. The pictures (most of which I have seen only in reproduction) are too artful and rather commercial. Then, in the late forties, Guston joined ranks with the Abstract Expressionists. He became a painter of marks on an empty field. These marks—they're the size of pats of butter, and have a buttery texture—nudge and push against each other. These abstractions are subtle and sumptuous. But as the years wore on, Guston appeared to become frazzled, impatient with pushing marks against marks; the subject of his pictures, as the fifties wore on into the sixties, seems to be frustration. Then, beginning in the late sixties, Guston began making good-sized cartoonlike paintings, and one felt he had finally come into his own. He seemed to bring together his early subject matter with the sumptuous touch he had created as an abstractionist.

The real point about Guston, though, is less his development than the depth and variety of his final body of work. Many artists create a race of cartoon characters. But Guston is the first whose cartoon art is genuinely challenging and august. From his lively recorded talks and interviews, Guston apparently believed that his subject was modern anxiety, and, on the face of it, his pictures are nightmarish. But Guston is great because he dares to be silly on a grand scale. And his painted world isn't barren—it is unusually inviting. His potato-head creatures, who are seen in profile (and with a bulging eyeball), stare manically forward. His Klansmen ride in convertibles; gather together and plot; whip their enemies. In some of his best pictures, the scene is a scantily furnished room in a city. There's an old wood door, a lamp on the floor; a window is open, and there is one of those shades on a spring with a circle pull at the end of a cord. Through the window are visible massive biscuit-colored buildings: the office and munici-pal buildings of any downtown. (We might as well be in an artist's studio.) The place is an American city of an earlier, pre–Second World War time. The characters are small-time hoods. They talk away the sunny, empty Saturday afternoon—at least, it feels like a weekend afternoon—smoking and playing cards. I don't think Guston actually painted hoods playing cards, but somehow you hear a deck being shuffled when you immerse yourself in some of his scenes.

If you look at Rube Goldberg's cartoons—the famous ones are from the twenties—you will see the same downtown buildings, the same cars with big round rubber tires, the same rubbery people, even the same windows and window shades. And finding so much of Guston in Goldberg's drawings (and Guston no doubt looked at other cartoon creators) only makes Guston better. Part of the point of Guston is that his images and style of drawing, with big rounded forms and lots of thick black outlining, to show sculptural solidity, aren't his own. The pleasure of Guston's work is in watching him re-create the world using a visual vocabulary—the cartoonist's stripped-down language—which he didn't invent.

Guston is a less romantic, and a less spiritual, figure than any of his fellow Abstract Expressionists. He is different from virtually all other American artists in that his subject isn't mythical striving, or beauty, or youth, or sadness. Guston is a teller of macabre, what-if stories, an appreciator of the gross, the stupid, the corrupt. And yet—this is the amazing part—he isn't cynical or ghoulish. His work is hearty, vig-orous, and humorous. He is the first American whose work stands in the company of Goya and Ensor.

There is a stage in the development of recent art that is hard to account for. How and where did many of the strongest new artists, including Schnabel and Salle, Polke and Kiefer, come to create their respective worlds of floating, overlapping images? And is this new kind of picture making related to Guston's cartoon art? I think so—at least, for American artists. The relationship has to do, in part, with the sense of impermanence one feels in a Guston. He painted without set images in mind; he treated his canvases as if they were big sheets of paper that he could doodle on until he "found" images that felt right. In many Gustons, you see cloudy areas that have dark lines, or different colors, underneath. These flushed, often beautiful, areas are where a first or a second thought was covered over. His pictures almost always have a quivering, still-being-composed quality. Little is fixed in his world.

Little is fixed in the world of the new painting, either. When a viewer looks at a Julian Schnabel, say, he may find himself focusing and refocusing; his eyes may go from one image in the painting to the next, and as his eyes move the different elements become alternately sharper and blurrier. The elements can be a realistic image; a stylized and cartoonish drawing; an area of abstract brushwork; an actual object; a patch of empty canvas. Each is of equal interest—to the artist and to the viewer. Sometimes the elements come together, and tell a story; sometimes they don't, and the picture may still feel right. Many artists now draw, with paint, on patterned fabrics, or on photographs, and when oil is drawn over, say, a decorative fabric a layer-upon-layer effect is produced—a 3-D sense of things going back into space.

After looking at these pictures, you may see earlier artists, even Old Masters, differently. You may find yourself "bringing forward" the backgrounds of paintings, and reading backgrounds and foregrounds as a sort of blinking, throbbing surface. The effect, or point, isn't only optical or formal. It's emotional, too. The marginal, "soft" stuff in a picture now becomes as interesting as the supposed center of attention. It is as if this were a period that wants to reintroduce heroes in paintings—wants to bring back the figure—and yet wants to show the not always substantial thoughts of these heroes.

The layering of Schnabel and the others might be called a development of Cubism, or a continuation of the collage spirit. But to our eyes the Cubists made pictures whose separate parts hang together, as

196

if on an invisible net, and generally tell one story. Collage as the Cubists—and as later artists, such as Robert Rauschenberg—understood it was about an overall balancing act, a syncopated beat. When Rauschenberg, in the fifties, brought together in a single picture patches of smeary paint, real objects (a tire, say), and silkscreened photo images, one felt that he was saying that there was beauty—or, even more, a pathos—in the jumbled (and frequently junky) heap of things.

Layering in recent art is more directly a demonstration of the way people think now—that is, with many seemingly unrelated thoughts and images hanging in the air simultaneously. That you take in these works by focusing on different parts doesn't mean that the pictures are merely painted versions of photographs or movie stills, or that these artists are the products of a movie-oriented culture. The relation of photography, movies, and TV to recent art is subtle. For some artists, this relationship may be there only slightly, or not at all. Yet the way images appear in photos, movies, and TV has helped produce a feeling for the relatedness of all images: images taken from book illustrations, magazine ads, studies of plant and animal life in books, even pornography layouts—as well as from movies and TV shows and commercials. Visual information itself has become a subject. It is a subject the way geometry, or modern urban life, or nature, or mythology have been subjects.

Fine art—museum pictures, art styles—has become a subject, too, partly because museums have changed so drastically in the past twenty years. The change is felt as much in museums in Santa Barbara and Toronto as in the Met and the Modern. If you first went to museums in the fifties and sixties (or earlier), you can feel that museums have become rather similar, in tone, to department stores and TV. Museums are no longer anonymous settings for works of art. We are bombarded, in museums, with videotapes, postcards, posters, slides, books, acoustiguides, and calendars about artworks and artists. There's a genuine hum of energy at museum bookshops; they can seem like the true center of life of the place. And we have become so used to seeing all paintings reproduced in color that many works of art now appear tame and flat compared with how they look in books.

Yet earlier art has not been devalued, and we haven't been made skeptical about it. We are actually beyond the stage where it is exciting to make ironic jokes about classics; Marcel Duchamp's having put a mustache on *Mona Lisa* seems insipid now. We have become more intimate with works of art. The figures and faces of previous art—the characters in paintings by Watteau, say, or Munch—now seem to be touchstones for artists to express more of themselves. In *My Head*, one of the most impressive paintings in the Saatchi collection, David Salle takes a Watteau drawing of a shoeshine boy—he is seen from the front and from the back—and draws him in a yellow-orange oil and in a soft, brushy way, over a background image. That image is a series of views, done in a black and white brushed-on oil that resembles a grainy photo, of quasi-abstract sculptures set on a table in a darkened room. (The other major element in this mural-size work is a stretch of unpainted plywood, with wood pegs projecting from it—each painted blue at the end—which is placed above the images in the bottom half.) Quoting from Watteau, Salle seems to tip his cap to an admired painter. There is some contempt in his attitude, too; he treats the Watteaus impersonally, as decorative grace notes, and implies that he could have borrowed something from any artist. Yet Salle also has an affinity with these figures, which are rather romantic. There is a gentle erotic charge to them.

An artist runs a risk of being jokey, or fancy, when he or she refers in a painting to an earlier work of art, or takes a Munch painting, say, and redoes it; but it seems possible to take a known image and, so to speak, inhabit it. And there is little difference whether that image is a Munch painting, a Giotto fresco, or a still from "The Honeymooners." In the realm of images, Giotto is on the same footing as stills from TV shows.

There is a detachment to the new art. It is there in the way many of these paintings are made, and it may be an underlying point of view. In paintings where disparate images float side by side, or on top of another, and different styles, or ways of drawing, are brought together in the same work, the meaning may be that there are no connections between things. In continually referring to the past, these artists may imply that the past was more full, or real, than the present, that our identity will be complete only when we re-create the past. Yet the prevailing mood of the new art isn't sour or grayed; it is appreciative, sensuous, voracious.

One of the big differences between the current generation of artists and previous ones is their relation to popular culture. Popular culture used to be something an artist brought into his work in order to give it a jolt of real life; the point was to bring art down to earth. Popular culture is more ingrained now. A young artist may no longer make a leap from his or her serious thoughts to, say, a comic strip, a TV, or a rock'n'roll way of thinking, where everything is simplified, intensified; he or she may now begin with such a sense of things. Didn't Jean-Luc Godard, in his movies of the sixties, create such a world, where people were walking and talking cartoon characters? Godard was a forerunner, but the difference between his movies and art now is that his tone is witty, analytical, self-conscious. In his movies, everything is arch; every kiss and every murder is in italics. That self-consciousness is gone. Many artists now seem to feel that they can be most serious—that they can be most themselves—when they put their feelings in the mouths of puppets.

In retrospect, it can appear as if much of the new art of the fifties and sixties—the work of Judd, Warhol, Twombly, Flavin, Katz, Johns—was about transforming vernacular, popular art forms (and industrial materials, such as house paint and fluorescent lighting) into high art. In the years when Johns made his American flag paintings, when Warhol made Marilyn Monroe his subject, and when Katz rethought traditional painting motifs in terms of movie stills and billboard ads, beauty was imbued with a lordly irony. And Judd, Flavin, and the other Minimalists have the same distant, removed stance. On some basic level (which, over the years, we may have lost sight of), Judd's work is sardonic, even taunting. He is as aggressively tongue-in-cheek about aluminum and plexiglass and simple box shapes as Johns is about the American flag.

The artists of Katz's and Johns's generation came of age not long after the United States and Abstract Expressionism had become world-conquering forces, and their work reflects this. It's expansive, worldly. But it has the attitude of a son who takes over the family business empire and makes it even bigger, and yet is not altogether comfortable, happy, or satisfied with the job; he had the role thrust upon him, and he finds himself locked into perpetuating a family image that wasn't originally his. Not only is the sense of space in the work of Judd, Katz, Johns, Frankenthaler, Twombly, and the rest extremely shallow, but the works themselves push out against a viewer like so many shields. Each piece seems to say, "You'll get no secrets, no inner thoughts from me. I am my surface alone." Johns summarized an aspect of his generation in *No*, a 1961 picture of a gray surface, a sort of wall, that has a metal line running over it from the top to the bottom. At the bottom of the line is the word NO in stencils. The picture is touching; it is also bruised, angry, somewhat frightening. And its main point is: No, don't come any farther.

Artists now in their twenties and thirties have been inspired by the previous generation in their work, and have inherited its confidence, too. But they don't have such a masklike and ironic sense of things. They're more romantic and gullible and less guarded; they are also, expressively, less tight. The new painting, in its surfaces and sense of space, says, "Enter." This is where Guston is, again, very much our contemporary. When his cartoon work was first shown it was said that he was slumming. Here was an intellectual on vacation, the argument went, applying a luscious, painterly touch to dumb cartoon scenes. For many of the early admirers of his work, though, the idea that Guston was slumming—that he was ironic—didn't arise; slumming was an idea from an earlier time, when popular culture was brought into one's work coolly, or with a tone of daredevil boasting. Guston's new pictures were realistic (though I suppose we didn't think of them in just this way). They were "realistic" in that they seemed to show how people thought. A viewer might have felt, This is what it is like inside my mind—everything does pass by in this shifting, exaggerated, sweaty, nervous, heroic, mock-heroic way. Guston's Klansmen, his potato-head characters—even his inanimate subjects: his shoes and clocks—seem to say, "Am I a jerk? A genius? Will they get the point? Will they love me? Who could really know how great I am? I'm dying."

Guston showed how comic-strip art—and, really, any art—could present the feel, the texture, of psychological moments. Not psycho-analytical, primal, or disturbed moments; not the material that the Surrealists (with their bizarre, dreamlike images) and Giacometti (with his sculptures that suggest impotence and impending violence) presented. The sense of psychology in Guston and in younger artists is more something that's taken for granted; there is an equal interest in an act and in the motivation for an act.

Like Guston, Malcolm Morley, who is fifty-four, has been thought of as a link between an earlier generation and recent art. There are Morleys from every phase of his development, from the mid-sixties up through the present, in *Art of Our Time*, and I can see why this English-born artist, who lives and works in New York, has been important in the past five years. Like younger painters, he brings together seemingly unrelated images, occasionally done on separate canvases, in one work, and, like Guston, he communicates the feeling that a painter is free to make a substantial work out of any image he chooses, no matter how wild. For me, though, Morley is important less for his actual work than for his presence on the scene, his example. I feel the same way about his work looking at it in *Art of Our Time* as I did seeing it in his retrospective in 1984. (It came to the Brooklyn Museum.) I left his Brooklyn show liking Morley himself: his gusto, his belief in art. He appears to be excited by the very tubes of paint, the brushes, the pans of watercolor, the sticks of charcoal. Yet his pictures seem to be mostly experiments in this or that way of painting. Some crucial element in them is unbelievable.

Morley began, in the sixties, as a Photorealist—he coined the term "Superrealist." His early works are painstaking copies of images of cruise ships and of cruise life, taken from ads. He also copied works of art; the Saatchis own his copies of Vermeer's *Portrait of the Artist in His Studio* (Morley's is much larger than the original) and of Raphael's *School of Athens*. On a theoretical level, these pictures were ahead of their time: Morley was making paintings about how paintings appear in photographs. But his Photorealist works, when you see them, are irritating; what you are conscious of is the tedious job he gave himself.

Follow his career and you see him literally breaking apart his early diligent art. Going through a Morley retrospective is a little like reading a novel. You see a man growing, stretching; he seems to say to himself, "This early stuff of mine, it's so tight and stiff, I've got to bust open." Over the years, the surfaces of his pictures and his images themselves become increasingly messy, loose. He opens things up very literally; he makes paintings, for instance, where those cruise ships are attacked by planes. It can look as if the very canvases have been blown up by shrapnel. There are paintings, too, where cities—and the whole world, it would appear—are going up in flames. The feeling of catastrophe and chaos sometimes seems to mirror the period in which Morley painted. In the late sixties and early seventies, he made pictures whose subject matter is riots in cities, busing, Vietnam.

In the past five years or so, Morley has become a vigorous, brushy painter of fairly traditional subjects—beach scenes, exotic places and animals, cows in a pasture—which he sometimes treats in odd ways. *Farewell to Crete* is an enormous collagelike picture; it shows huge bathers quite close to us, tiny bathers in the distance, and, painted to the sides, on top, and over them, large and small Cretan horses and statues. *Arizonac* is a fiery Southwestern landscape. In it, two gigantic Hopi Indians—they're much larger than the mountains—rush toward us, while on the ground, at their feet, is a speck-size Indian on a horse. And there are pictures of faraway places that may refer to Britain's colonial past. These recent works are more appealing than his Photorealist ones, but the new pictures feel hollow, too. Why does Morley distort shapes, and mix very big and very little sizes? Why, in the Crete painting, is red paint thrown on top of the image of sky and water, and why is a trail of blue paint going around and over the Cretan statue? With another artist, these details might be parts of a flowing whole; when David Salle lets paint from one area in a picture run down into another we don't stop to think about what he means by it. But with Morley the quirky elements and oddities of painting halt us; we feel that they have to be explained and that knowing what they mean won't make the pictures better.

One looks forward to Morley's shows; one wants to know what he is going to do next. The main question about him, though, is biographical, not aesthetic. Does he calculatedly keep abreast of changes in current art, or is he on his own course—a course that happens to parallel what other people are doing? His real subject, it can seem, is being an artist. He always appears to be giving himself formal problems and trying to solve them. Morley himself may be more tangible than his work, but if he lost some of his respect for Painting his work might be more personal.

The revelation of *Art of Our Time* for American viewers is likely to be Sigmar Polke. This German painter, who is forty-five, has had three shows in New York in the past few years but is still barely known here. Based on the dates of his pictures—the earliest ones in the Saatchi collection are from the mid-sixties—he is the first artist to float disparate images in one picture in a way that feels new.

In Polke's best work, he generally uses a bit of an ad, a poster, a cartoon, or a photo, which he silk-screens on. Then he subtly mucks over that image: he buries it under vaporous washes of color, he draws doodles around or on top of it. He usually doesn't work on canvas. He frequently uses sections of old, faded, inexpensive fabrics, often with ornamental patterns that probably come from—and certainly make us think of—the fifties. Polke is like Klee in so many ways he seems to be Klee's heir. He resembles Klee in his wit, his venturesomeness with materials, the way he at first appears to have no one style. He's like Klee in that some of his works are so slight they barely seem to be there at all. But you don't think of Klee when you see Polke—you don't think of anyone. His work may be the most original any artist has made so far about Germany after the war. He seems to use already-existing images because he is saying that these images are all that is left. His pictures sometimes feel as though they were the products of a post-apocalypse person who doesn't know what art is but has a desire to make paintings, and so uses, as starters, whatever images he can find—cartoons, ads, posters—and then, in a somewhat spastic and dribbly way, decorates them.

Polke is the opposite of Warhol. A Warhol bank of Elvises, or even a single Liz, keeps you at a distance, and that is one of the classy and best things about the picture. Warhol printed the images on the canvas and colored them in a slipshod way, but his pictures are the opposite of tacky. They're stiff, like icons. He says, "Look, world, these are the new gods." Polke wants a world without gods. He almost seems to want a world without artists. When we look at an individual picture of his we often feel we're seeing the work of many different hands. His art is almost programmatically uncommanding—even impoverished. Seeing his pictures in reproduction doesn't give a sense of their deliberate flimsiness. His marks can be very faint; his paint can be watery, milky; he doesn't always use stretchers, so the pictures can sag. He's not particularly fussy, and he works with very large sizes, but there's something private, veiled, evanescent about his works. He asks a viewer to get very close to his surfaces; you feel you have to be surrounded by the picture before it begins to happen to you.

Rudi Fuchs, in his catalogue essay, says that Polke believes he's making a political point by not giving us imposing images. We sense this, too, and the pictures become heartier when we know that there are philosophical reasons for them to look the way they do. Polke might as well be saying, "No more heroes, no more tyrants, no more logos." Isn't he also indirectly criticizing the overbearing, self-important quality of so much American art since the Second World War? His point might be: no more Mark Rothko floating squares, Barnett Newman stripes, Judd boxes, or Marilyns—no more chapels of art, with icons that we have to bow down to. I want this to be a world of fuzzy, fluctuating bits of this and that.

His *Liebespaar II*, a roughly six-foot-high posterlike painting from 1965, which shows a man touching a woman, is the single most startling image in the Saatchi collection. I am exaggerating, but this picture—it has not been in any of his New York shows—is like the beginning of a new consciousness in art. The painting seems to borrow from Dada, from Pop, and, vaguely, from Expressionism and Abstract Expressionism. But *Liebespaar II* is not a joke (as a Dada image would be), it's not a stylishly soulless picture (as a Pop image would be), it's not particularly muscular, or heroic. It is more like a melancholy and nasty meditation on life. It is full of disturbing touches. The smiling man, who is in a gray suit, has a black dot for an eye and seems like a toy—he might be the grown kid of the Dubonnet Man, dressed for the prom. The woman's features are more realistic (she recalls Joan Crawford); her eyes really look out at us. The image is like a date between two people with different kinds of limitations. There are dots, in different sizes and colors, painted over her neck and face, among other places, and it is the dots that make the picture revolting. There is something sadistic about the way her face and neck are covered by dots. We can imagine Polke first painting her, then taking a wormy pleasure in painting these dots over her. It is as though he's airily sprinkling her with a disease. Polke is not altogether nice. His art is sly, grim, and indirect—as well as beautiful and novel. This may be why he is still relatively unknown in this country and why he may always be an artist most appreciated by other artists.

Yet he has painted his poster couple with such care! He handles paint in the pure and quietly adept way that an old-time journeyman artist, making a sign for a tavern, would. And by fouling his woman— those dots—he gives her a personal quality she wouldn't have otherwise. That is the daring and original thing about Polke. He takes poster people and cartoon characters and fragments from photographs and makes them agents in a kind of psychological drama.

Anselm Kiefer, the other important German artist—he is also represented by a large number of choice works in *Art of Our Time*—is Polke's opposite number. They have very different approaches to the same subject: recent history and their Germany. If Polke's motto is "Flippant at all moments," Kiefer's is "Heroically I take my stand." The slight difference in their ages—Polke was born in 1941, Kiefer in 1945—probably has something to do with the big differences in their tones. One half believes that Polke keeps up a frivolous tone in his work because, as a very young child, he experienced some of the actual war. And one half believes that Kiefer is determined to keep re-creating the war because he just missed experiencing it. He wants us to hear bombs going off in the distance when we look at his paintings.

Not all of Kiefer's pictures are directly about the Second World War. There are pictures, for instance, with Biblical themes. But nearly everything of his suggests devastation or a swelling national harmony. In his many landscapes of fields and fewer interiors—they are of cavernous, burned-out public places—it appears to be the winter or spring of 1945. It is the last days of the Third Reich. Kiefer's large pictures feel enormous even in reproduction. Viewing them, we believe we are an inspection team; we walk through the rubble, or fly low over the fields in a small plane. Everyone is absent—dead, or moved on. But the sites are choking with different emotions. The earth is squishy, we suspect that there is fresh blood in it. We pick our way over burnt logs, piles of bricks. We become German. It is a heady moment. We're relieved that the fighting is over, and bitter at the waste. We have a secret sense of loyalty, too; we are sure that the victors cannot be as proud as we are.

Kiefer's paintings are mostly in sooty grays, rust-reds, earth colors, black. There are slate-blues and, occasionally, daubs of turquoise or pink. You can find yourself staring at a Kiefer for a long time. This happens in part because he paints—and adds materials, such as straw and wax—directly on top of already-existing images. In some of his landscapes, he paints on top of (and almost obliterates) blown-up photos of landscapes that are affixed to the canvas. In pictures made up of rows of portraits, he paints on top of wall-paperlike sheets of portraits, made from woodcuts. Sometimes we have the pleasantly weird feeling that the images are pulsating as we look at them.

The surfaces of his pictures are a mixture of the molten, the blotchy, and the blistered. When he paints on top of a photograph, the pictures can have a waxy, opaque texture. When he adds straw to his surfaces—he does this frequently—we get another rough, raw, and brittle texture. Yet a Kiefer generally gives the impression of something elegantly off-kilter and full of tasty different little textures. His paintings are among the most sheerly beautiful that anyone has made in the past ten years.

There is something that doesn't sit right about Kiefer's lyric beauty, though. A viewer feels that he has to tailor his feelings in order to enter Kiefer's world. You don't just drift into and out of these pictures; you have to take them on their own exalted-and-pitying terms. Kiefer reminds me a little of Rouault and Francis Bacon. Their work has a similar sanctimonious and jazzily despairing air. These artists seem to think more like novelists than painters; they want their work to be about the "condition of man." They impress us when they become known, because they take amazing liberties with their materials; they seem to invent new ways to paint in order to tell their stories. They are certainly involved with the matter, the stuff, of painting. Yet they seem to be above mere art; there is no thinking about form in their work. Their paintings seem to be based on a conception that they come back to again and again. When we stop being absorbed by the story each man tells, we are left feeling that their art is so much artifice.

This sense about Kiefer has grown on me after having seen a number of his New York shows. It's hard to have doubts about his twenty-three works in *Art of Our Time*, though. Even if he never painted again we would know his attitudes as a social historian and his themes as a poet. And there are some unusual Kiefers in the Saatchi collection—pictures which aren't landscapes or interiors, but which are as good as anything he has done. *Baum mit Palette* shows, against a dark background, a portion of a huge tree trunk which, though it's not realistically painted, has, in the reproduction, anyway, an amazingly treelike presence. Affixed to its center is a painter's palette, made of metal and painted battleship-gray. Its color and material remind us of war, and the image of a palette—Kiefer uses it often—makes us think that the picture might be an allegory about the artist's power, or ineffectuality. The painting seems to cry out, "Analyze me!" We don't want to. It seems enough to say that *Baum mit Palette* feels both new and like an image from a book of tales. It is like a portrait of an ancient, half-dead tree granted immunity from the axe—a tree in a prince's forest, to which an itinerant court painter, traveling through the forest, has affixed his emblem.

Three other Kiefer paintings—they are made up of rows of faces— are even finer. Two of the pictures are titled *Wege der Weltweisheit: die Hermannsschlacht* and the other is *Noch ist Polen nicht verloren IV*. The first two show logs, flames, and circular lines drawn over rows of woodcut portraits of famous Germans of the past, and *Polen* shows faces painted over and through a ploughed field, which recedes into the distance. These paintings present a less heroic—and, possibly, a more personal and original—side of Kiefer. We feel we are encountering a bookish man who might have been a historian and someone who, perhaps even from childhood, might have been in love with the swirl of personalities that make up his nation's intellectual family. (There are actual swirling lines of oil paint going in and out of the portrait heads.) These face paintings ought to seem literary, yet they're Kiefer's most abstract works. They are the works of his that most resemble the work of other painters of his generation. One wants to see them in the company of pictures by Schnabel, Salle, Polke, and the rest.

Francesco Clemente, who was born in Naples, and now lives for parts of each year in India, Rome, and New York, is a genius with his hand, a genius inventor of images. He first became known in New York with versions of Indian miniatures that perfectly re-created the minutely detailed, ornately colored, and smooth-surfaced nature of this art. Clemente also showed pastels, and they were even more impressive. They were in a class with the best pastels ever—those by Redon, Samaras, Cassatt, Degas, Miró. In later exhibitions, Clemente presented oils and then watercolors that were equally amazing as performances. They showed that, regardless of his subject, he brings out the special flavor of whatever medium he uses.

In his art, Clemente seems to say, quite calmly—and his images and mood are generally calm, no matter how weird—"You're not going to believe this." A Clemente picture is like the glass wall of an aquarium that we look into. Drifting by, and sometimes looking out at us, are people, disembodied faces, and, sometimes, little animals (rodents, mostly). Many are in the process of becoming something else. It is a land of oozy metamorphoses. Clemente does for the human body and its orifices what Chagall did for Eastern European village life and the romance of Paris.

The center of Clemente's world is a very short-haired, wide-eyed, and often unclothed figure who resembles the artist and who we automatically assume is Clemente. At times, he's unaware of us; he's absorbed by problems, we're simply watching him. At other times, he dreamily peers out at us, or scowls. He can appear as a sullen little satyr. We often see him from below; we're aware of his nostrils. His face is porcine; he is sensual and superior, eunuchlike, evil. Sometimes he appears in a shirt and slacks, and stands a bit sheepishly, his back a little hunched. In these images, Clemente captures a type we know from movies but have not seen in paintings: the modern Italian intellectual. This fellow is simultaneously stylish, professorial, sexy, urban, dissatisfied, and shy.

Clemente's art throws into relief the work of his contemporaries. He does instinctively what the others do in a perhaps more theoretical way. He switches from one level to another level of space—and one kind to another kind of drawing—in the same picture with the unthinking fluency of a mimic. In his fullest works, which are often his pastels, he blends fantasy images with imitations of children's drawings and of patterned decoration. Yet, so far, some core feeling is missing from his art as a whole. (He is thirty-three.) Going through the pages on him in *Art of Our Time* is elating at first. It's a barrage of fascinating, lewd, and amusing dream images, done in startlingly bright and perfumy soft colors. But I don't carry away a lot; there is something neutralized in his vision.

Clemente may want to produce a kind of pacified state in the viewer. He seems to think like an Indian artist; some of his images derive from Indian art, and the cosmic space that his figures swirl in feels Indian. And his art has the same effect on me as Indian miniatures, which are phenomenally beautiful, but always beautiful in the same way. After seeing a number of them, my mind wanders. Clemente's art is like Indian miniatures, too, in that, no matter what the actual size of his pictures, they have more impact when seen in a book. The sensuous and decorative beauty that he is after somehow comes across best in a small format and when a viewer is in private contact with it. Clemente has spoken of his love of William Blake, and, like Blake, he makes certain work specifically for books, often to accompany a text (he has collaborated with Allen Ginsberg).

Yet Clemente isn't simply a European who works out of an affinity for Eastern art and thought. The resignation that is felt in his art comes from him personally; it is felt in many Western artists now.

Clemente merely takes it further than anyone else. Without intending to do so, he gives us the dilemma—as well as the mind—of a mimic. We see an artist whose hand is effortlessly capable of reproducing any effect or known style, and we see the sense of inner void that can underlie that talent.

For the past five years or so, Julian Schnabel and—to a lesser extent—David Salle have been the foremost new artists in New York. They are the American masters of the floating, layered vision, and, at least from what has been shown in New York, no European matches them. Until very recently, their pictures have seemed superficially alike, and Salle has been somewhat overshadowed by Schnabel. Salle's pictures are lighter in tone, subtler in their emotions, more restrained and indirect. He has perfected one of the central formal ideas of recent art: the contrast of elements. Many of his pictures are composed of juxtapositions of scenes painted with a dry brush, in shades of gray, with scenes painted in oil in rich, full colors. Sometimes he contrasts his filmy, grayish scenes with vignettelike images, or actual objects, or words. Almost everything he does has a one-two structure, a play of color against colorlessness, coolness against heat, intangibility against graspableness, memory against the present.

Schnabel doesn't dwarf Salle—or Guston, Kiefer, or Polke. But Schnabel, who is thirty-four, seems to have in him something of everyone else. He is exciting because he seems to come from nowhere and to obey no rules. He is obviously aware of twentieth-century art and its theories, and his painting is indebted to earlier figures, but one feels that the weight of twentieth-century thought has been lifted from him. His work has, if anything, a nineteenth-century—and a European, rather than American—appearance. He often affixes antlers, chains, or pieces of broken crockery to his paintings, and paints on velvet, pinto-pony hides, pieces of flannel—even on Oriental carpets. His pictures have an air of King Ludwig's Bavarian castles. These nineteenth-century castles are conglomerations of previous styles: Byzantine, Gothic, Moorish, and Louis XIV, with elements of Alpine hunting lodges and Mediterranean grottoes blended in. Schnabel's paintings are also concoctions of old and new art, and they are also lush and luxurious, beckoning and charming—and, at times, heavy and musty. Most of his pictures include figures and faces but some are abstract. They are about ambition, strength, and, one can feel, broken strength. They often show wrestlers, warriors, saints, powerful babies, muscular men whose eyes are shadowed and sunk in and, so they appear, stern men with big plans, big-time losers.

Schnabel's pictures have a distinctive scale. They aren't bigger, in general, than other artists' pictures; but he has a natural feeling for a boxy, squarish format, and his forms often have an attractive lumbering quality. A viewer sometimes feels with a Schnabel that he is encountering a single large protruding form, and that the sides of his pictures count for relatively little (whereas in a Salle every element seems to be smoothly and adroitly going out to you and pulling back from you at the same time).

Schnabel is a more exuberant, giving—and also bullying—talent than Salle, or Polke. We can be surprised by these painters, but we know their minds; at least, we think we know the problems they have set for themselves. With Schnabel I am often in a position where I love a work but have no sense that he will return to its type and build on it. I especially don't know what he's driving at in his abstract pictures. Sometimes it seems that they are made out of bravado alone—that he'll walk up to a canvas (or piece of velvet) and forge ahead with whatever comes into his mind at the moment.

Yet Schnabel's abstractions, which are often of flat shapes, are some of his best works. Schnabel is often at his most mysterious and inventive when he brushes the paint on in odd, sprawling shapes. They are interesting shapes; they are like the shadows of creatures that are part human, part vegetable. We seem to be watching something swaddled that is squawking and about to tear itself apart. That Schnabel goes back and forth between abstractions and pictures with figures and faces in them can be taken as a sign that he is torn between the two. Or perhaps he is saying that the distinction between abstraction and representation has become virtually meaningless. And there is another layer of meaning to his abstractions. The shapes in them often seem to be shadows, or remnants, and in this they are about what abstraction has become: a memory of something once powerful.

The twenty-five Schnabel paintings in the Saatchi collection—it is a top-notch group—are dated 1977–78 to 1983. There is wonderful variety to them. No one "Schnabel look" emerges. But there is a built-in set of problems to his overall approach, and it has materialized in more recent work. He seems to want to systematically go against all conventions, and this has taken him into some long unexplored types of pictures, such as crucifixions. He has had to paint faces, real faces with features, and his faces haven't been successful. They feel made up; they're ghoulish and ugly. When the faces in a Schnabel are too fleshed out (as they were in many of the pictures in his 1985 New York show), the whole work tends to become heavy, inert. So far, Schnabel clicks when he paints figures and faces with a few quick lines. There is an unexpected unity between the lathered-up surfaces of his pictures, and their baronial sizes, and the doodle-like figures and faces that pop out of them.

One of the best Schnabels in the Saatchi collection, though, has one of these coarsely drawn, anonymous faces in it. *Pre History: Glory, Honor, Privilege and Poverty* (his titles are generally on the windy side) shows, floating next to one another, one of those faces; a male baby, who points his finger; and a simple line drawing of an upside-down Eskimo-type man. There is also what looks like an enormous pear with a knife beside it. *Pre History* is on pony skin, and it is primarily a black and white, tan, brown, yellow, and dark green picture, with lots of antlers stuck on it. It has the colors and flavor of an Adirondack "camp," one of those rustic retreats made for a millionaire eighty years ago. For some reason, the man's face in *Pre History*—it is Big Brotherish—works. Maybe because the picture seems to be a page scrambled from history, anthropology, and art-history textbooks.

Schnabel is one of the warmest talents in American painting ever. The warmth is in his feeling for color, for textures. His color isn't easily labeled; he doesn't stylize color around a few chords, as Kiefer does. He doesn't, like Salle, play hot color off cool grays. He isn't, like Clemente, a master of a rainbow range of equally intense bright and dark colors. Schnabel likes colors to glow. He may have been prompted to paint on velvet because it is a no-no; but he may also have been drawn to it because bright colors shimmer on velvet. When he affixes broken plates and cups to his thick oil surfaces, the effect is voluptuous, especially when a work is seen from a few feet away or in a reproduction. Schnabel's color and touch are comforting, hearthlike, rousing.

The sculptor Joel Shapiro is one of the links between Judd and Schnabel—between an uncompromising formalist and, it would seem, an egoist who says that there are no more rules. Shapiro, who creates vaguely puppetlike figures seen in awkward positions, isn't, at first sight, a commanding figure; his pieces can be slight, and they aren't, in size or appearance, "important" or monumental. Yet he is one of the central figures in recent art. Like Polke, he straddles two points of view. Polke came up from Pop Art and transformed it; Shapiro has done the same for Minimalism, and in this he also resembles the Saatchis themselves. His evolution parallels theirs as collectors. One feels that they collect Minimalist art (and the work of other artists of that generation) with a sense of respect; but they seem closer to, more at ease with, the work of Guston and the younger artists.

Shapiro became known for working with theatrically small sizes and for bringing recognizable images into sculpture at a time—the early seventies—when most serious sculpture was abstract, or a work of Earth Art, or Process Art. Some of his early pieces (virtually everything of his is untitled) were of a chair or of a house. These primitively simple pieces, often done in cast iron, were like images of the idea of "chair" or "house." They were about three or five inches high and were placed without pedestals on the gallery floor. Later pieces were abstract but referred in some way to a house, a shelter, a fortified place. His work has been getting bigger in size, more recognizably of the figure, and better. Most of it is made from wood beams, then cast into bronze. His figures are like the wood-block sculpture that children make in shop classes. A Shapiro might be called a child's sculpture that, because of the way the parts fit together and the way the piece is placed on the floor, has been given an inner life.

His figures are generally of a lone man. These figures don't have faces; some don't even have heads. And their arms have no hands; the beams are simply cut off. Yet by angling this "arm" beam to this "torso" beam in such a way, Shapiro creates figures that seem enveloped in a thought, a state of feeling. He takes a few blocks, makes out of them a torso, a head, and arms, then turns this "figure" on its side—and. we have, say, a sleeping person. But not only sleeping: Shapiro makes it appear as though this figure were also lonely, restless, wiped out. His finest pieces are often painted wood figures. (None of these are in *Art of Our Time.*) His color—he has used, among others, a red-black and a nighttime blue—can seem arbitrary, mental, fanciful; yet it is put on in such a way that you feel as though the wood were blushing this particular color.

Shapiro's sculpture would enhance pictures by Kiefer, Schnabel, and the rest if they were placed together in an exhibition (and vice versa). His pieces, too, are composites; he is a joiner, not a carver or a modeler. And his sculpture recalls a lot of other sculpture: De Stijl and Russian Constructivism and American folk-art toys; the sculpture of William King and the figures in the work of the early twentieth-century English painter David Bomberg.

Shapiro's pieces are so many literal and formal balancing acts. They're emotional balancing acts, too, and this is what makes his work an emblem for the new art. What he's juggling, on the face of it, are different attitudes about his artistic past. He began as a quasi Minimalist—or, certainly, when Minimalism was the challenging style—and whether his subject is a house set by itself on a floor, or a figure balancing on one leg, his geometrically rigid forms recall that style. A viewer can feel that Shapiro is afraid to move on from a Minimalist aesthetic; Judd seems to be breathing down on him. At other times, he's like someone who remains at a declining institution out of sympathy for it and a desire to give it new blood. Sometimes he seems to toy with, to ridicule Minimalism. And, at times, you believe he's not interested in Minimalism at all. He seems beyond it; he is in competition with the great works of figurative sculpture of all periods.

Shapiro's work evokes many separate emotions. An individual figure of his can seem, moment by moment, despondent, hesitant, pugnacious—or powerfully assured. His figures seem to have a troubled awareness of how self-absorbed they are. His work may come to represent the spirit of the present time.

—1986

ORIGINALITY

PHILIP TAAFFE'S ART CAN BE dismissed as naughty. He takes paintings by other artists and, sometimes working with the same sizes as the originals, redoes them. He also makes paintings that, while his own invention, recall other art or scramble elements from different artists. In his recent show at the Pat Hearn Gallery—it was his second one-man show in New York—the works were lifted from, or recalled, Bridget Riley, Barnett Newman, Paul Feeley, and Vasarely. Though they're very different figures, these are all abstract painters of the fifties and sixties who used "hard-edged" shapes and large canvases. Taaffe (pronounced Taff) works a bit like a craftsman who has been given an outline drawing for a billboard or a mosaic wall; he sticks to that outline, but he fills it in with colors and textures that are subtly different from what the original artist called for. It's clear that these Taaffes are takeoffs—or that he's an "appropriator," to use a recent word for it—but how are people meant to interpret this borrowing? I found Taaffe's art disembodied; he might be making belated pieces of Conceptual Art. But some of his pictures have a beautiful physical presence—one that he creates, that has nothing to do with his sources. There is a surprising and unforced elegiac quality to his pictures, and something courageous, too.

Taaffe's best paintings are the ones based on Riley and that suggest Vasarely—the Op Artists. Their works are made up of wavy lines or diamond shapes set in patterns. A characteristic Riley is of black and white lines coursing this way and that; the black lines seem to be on top of the white, they seem to be moving, and you will probably get a little dizzy looking at the picture. In Taaffe's *Mangrove,* Riley's black and white have been replaced with gold lines and lines delicately tinted with many colors. Thin gold waves seem to be undulating over marble. The picture is made in a complex way, and you sense this even if you don't quite understand the method. The picture is actually made up of many equal-size linocut prints, which Taaffe pastes on and then paints over. He uses prints because, I suppose, he wants the many lines in the picture to be exactly alike. There's a little, almost ragged space between each print. The result is a sort of quilt—one where the effort involved has been camouflaged. *Mangrove* and Taaffe's other Op-Art pictures have serene metallic colors and a flickering light. Not to overload them with more references, but they remind me of Gustav Klimt—of the endless-seeming, slightly off-kilter and awkward bands of geometric patterns that he included in his portraits.

Taaffe, who is thirty, isn't the only artist who redoes the works of earlier artists. Sherrie Levine has made replicas, often in watercolor, of the work of twentieth-century masters as they appear in photo reproductions in art books. She's like a poet whose poems are made up of quotations of other poems. She's someone who says, "I am the sum of my appreciations." Her work is cerebral, quiet, exquisite. Taaffe is more ambitious and his work is more complicated. His recent show wasn't altogether good. Of the eleven paintings, three, maybe four, were successful—the ones related to Op Art. Yet all the paintings, as a group, had an effect. The gallery was like an art gallery in a dream, where the pictures were familiar but "off"; they were older, tighter, more detailed and dense than they should have been. It was like being in a showroom of Used Art.

If you don't know Taaffe's "originals," his pictures may simply appear as works of a muted, lean, vaguely reminiscent beauty. If you know his sources, the show expands—in your mind. Taaffe's work is as exciting to think about as it is to see. One becomes a partner of his at the show; one thinks about where he will go with his art. He might do a room of Matisses, or Mirós. They'd feel thinner than the originals — thinner as objects — but that would be part of their quality. They'd have a damped-down, parchmentlike surface. So far, though, Taaffe's cut-and-paste, collage method can only accommodate (I think) clean, precise shapes — not texture. Could he redo a Mark Rothko?

Taaffe is a critic-historian-connoisseur. He must love the Hard-Edge painters of the fifties and sixties; he has, anyway, made me think more warmly of them. Taaffe also gives a quietly subversive talk about changing values and changing taste. He's like a pianist or a conductor who has chosen a program of works that haven't before been brought together and that forces us to think differently about those works. Barnett Newman, known as an Abstract Expressionist, has for years been considered one of the important American painters. A characteristic Newman is of an enormous horizontal expanse that has been painted a single color in a flat, untextured way. Placed here and there on that "empty" expanse are single vertical lines. To their admirers, these paintings have a Ten Commandments-like authority and presence. Paul Feeley, who became known in the sixties, is an admired but far less distinctive figure; his paintings of playing-card-like shapes have a sweet, playful spirit. Op Art, which briefly came to the fore in the early sixties, must be one of the least substantial and influential art movements of the past twenty-five years.

Putting Newman in the same gallery as Op Art is a subtle, refreshing, and poetic piece of criticism. Seeing Newman and Riley together equalizes them, if only subliminally; they become merely two abstract painters of their time, two souvenirs. To most people who have followed the course of contemporary art for the past thirty or forty years, these artists simply cannot be compared. Taaffe himself may believe that they are very different figures. But he doesn't seem to differentiate between them when he's using them, and the effect is to alter one's sense of priorities and rules. It's as though Taaffe were giving us a peak into the future, when many of our ideas about who's great, who's fair, and who's irrelevant may have been forgotten and, possibly, turned around. He doesn't seem to be saying, "Riley ought to be admired more." Rather, Taaffe seems to be showing how, for someone who came of age in the seventies, the notions of an earlier time about the stature and quality of art movements and of individual artists are no longer hard and fast. This is what is liberating about Taaffe's "copies." They say that we can change the past.

And yet Taaffe's pictures may strike a viewer as, primarily, passive, babyish works that flaunt their dependence, their unoriginality. Taaffe's "Newmans" play with this notion of being tied to something. Newman called the single vertical lines in his compositions zips. Taaffe substitutes the image of ropes for the zips. (He makes the "ropes" from many separate prints that are pasted one above the next.) These "Newmans" are somewhat gimmicky; Newman has not been transformed into Taaffe. But there are interesting aspects to the paintings. The ropes themselves are nice; they're the ropes a trompe-l'oeil painter would make. And they have a metaphorical and sexual presence. Taaffe seems to be calling attention to how bound up he is—to his sources, to the past.

The catalogue that accompanies Taaffe's show is absorbing in the way the pictures are. Like them, it seems to be, in part, a fake—a parody of the overdone art catalogue. It's like a cross between a Rolls-Royce brochure and a menu for a seafood restaurant. In a period when people talk about young artists overselling themselves, Taaffe says, "Why not?" His name appears in enormous letters on the cover of this large-format production, which sells for twenty-five dollars. Inside, acres of white space surround reproductions of Taaffe's paintings; drawings (presumably his—they aren't labeled); photos of this and that (they don't, at first, seem to relate to anything); and an essay (it's essentially a series of aphoristic statements) by the painter Ross Bleckner.

Yet this catalogue is also a mysterious document. The photographs may refer to aspects of Taaffe's work. There is an old "art" photo of a nude boy striking a pose. There's a snapshot of a laughing baby, who puts his hands over his mouth. The photo that's most like Taaffe's art is a blurry, movie-still-type image of a man running through a tunnel whose sides and top are so many curved, ribbed bars. This tunnel scene resembles Taaffe's method—the way he goes, as it were, into another artist's work and relives it. The photo might be showing someone caught in an Op-Art world. And Bleckner gives a sense of the simultaneously proud and defeated nature of the work when he says: "These paintings are what happens when insects elude their predators; when authority is criminal; when safe sex becomes charged sexuality. . . . They mourn the conversion of experience to memory, which always constitutes a loss."

Taaffe's appearance comes at a good time. His work clears up some fuzziness about whether the most interesting art of the past half decade or so, which has figures and recognizable things in it—the painting of, among others, David Salle, Julian Schnabel, and a number of Europeans—is going to be supplanted by a new abstraction. Taaffe's work implies that, for many new artists, the question of abstract versus representational isn't that important. His method, like theirs, is to bring together different images, or kinds of materials, or space, then let each element push against the other. Like Salle, he creates a sort of see-through collage—a work where one layer seems interchangeable with another. A Taaffe, like the work of these other artists, says to a viewer "Read my mind."

There is a young man's romanticism about Taaffe's paintings. They have a romantic kind of defiance of one's elders and a romantic sense of superiority. He must feel that his versions are, in some ways, improvements on his sources. There is a childlike simplicity about his approach. He has said that he wants to bring certain pictures "up to date." It's as if he thinks he is rescuing those paintings that time has made look a little threadbare. An original artist, he turns the idea of originality upside down.

—1986

THE TV YEARS

ERIC FISCHL'S ART has a great power right now, because he puts in paintings what feel like quintessential moments of contemporary America. At the same time, he judges our life. In his scenes, which take place in living rooms and bedrooms, at barbecue parties by a pool, on terraces of high-rise apartments, in bathrooms and at beach parties, everything appears shameful, wrong; we feel we're snooping when we look at his pictures. He includes everybody: people who live in trailer camps, in ranch houses in the Sun Belt, and who lounge on the patios of their second homes. Fischl, who is thirty-eight, is always telling the Truth about America, and he leaves us in a judging and pinched spirit. There is nothing spontaneous, or lovely for itself, about his painting. He is out there suffering for us, like Richard Avedon—when Avedon makes his "personal" photographs of "real" Americans—or Arthur Miller.

Yet Fischl, the subject of a show at the Whitney, is a considerable artist. He presents feelings and moods that we know already, but, perhaps because we haven't seen this material before in paintings, he makes it fresh. He seems to be discovering this terrain for himself as he goes along. He attempts some old-fashioned and difficult things: to tell stories in paintings; to describe and criticize contemporary life as a writer would. And he has brought off much of this. Fischl doesn't have people model for him; he takes, it appears, details from magazines and odd photos and invents stories from them. His pictures are like blown-up versions of illustrations from a man's magazine of the forties or fifties, or of layouts from a porno magazine, and this similarity to commercial art is stimulating. An individual Fischl painting is like a complete play; we can imagine what led up to this moment in the story and how the story will be resolved. In his pictures from 1980 to 1983, one especially likes the way that there is no pathos or sorrow. He is a poet of a dull, blasted, unforgiving mood.

The 1980 *Time for Bed* shows an American suburban childhood as a bad dream. We're in a living room with two grown-ups and two children; there are also a large African carving, strange shadows on sliding glass doors, and a few pieces of furniture. The woman, who we think of as Mom, stands shakily on a glasstop table and melodramatically puts her arm around—and spills her drink on—the man. He may be Dad, but he is more probably Mom's date, a gentleman caller. These two remind me of Shelley Winters as Mrs. Haze and James Mason as Humbert Humbert in the movie *Lolita*. If Mrs. Haze and Humbert had locked horns physically on the night they come home from the prom—she wants to proceed with a romantic champagne supper and he's reluctant—their encounter might have looked like this. We believe we know a lot about Fischl's man. The woman's slobbering affections bring out in him a snarl that, we are sure, he normally keeps buried.

The use of details from contemporary life in *Time for Bed* is uncanny. The man's pants, for instance, are a dark green plaid, and his sports jacket is a lemon yellow. Fischl may be the first painter to use country-club clothes in a picture. But the painting isn't only about these details; it is about a private hell (a private hell that doesn't exclude us). This man is missing an arm! His left sports-jacket sleeve is tucked into his left pocket. And many other details are touched with a subtle madness. The boy, who's about seven, wears Superman pajamas, but they're inside out—the S is backward. The girl, who is seen from the back, appears as a miniaturized yakety housewife, complete with boudoir nighties, slippers, and wraparound headgear. The light in the room is a harsh, cold gray-white, and each figure is oddly narrow and self-contained; each appears to be underwater, either rising to the surface or sinking to the bottom. Fischl may have taken the claustrophobic and awkward space of *Time for Bed* from Max Beckmann—the Beckmann who, in the late teens, painted enigmatic scenes of unhappy families squeezed together in Frankfurt attics.

There is no central person in the painting, but the moment probably belongs to the boy. He seems to be suffering this moment. He appears to be collapsing as we look at him. His head is bowed, his eyes are closed, and his hands are cupped over his groin. He looks as if he could be blown over by a breath.

In the startling 1981 *Bad Boy*, we see, as if from the vantage point of a security-system camera placed high on a wall, a boy and a woman in a bedroom. The boy, who is clothed, watches the woman, who is nude, and we, behind him, watch them both. The woman is on her back on a rumpled bed; her legs are spread, one knee is up, and she turns to look at her toes, which she touches. Her face is covered by shadows, which make her somewhat sinister. The boy is about twelve. On the table behind him are a bowl of fruit and her pocketbook. Intently looking at her, he reaches behind his back, into her bag. There are Venetian blinds, and strips of light and dark curve and twist over the woman, boy, and sheets.

In *Bad Boy*, we see one act—a theft—but feel another: sexual intercourse. Her pocketbook is dark brown, with soft folds and an oval opening. He fingers it without being able to see what he's doing—he must watch her face instead. Sexual intercourse, when a boy or a young man first does it, can be exactly like this: with his eyes and brain fastened onto the eyes and face of the woman, he gropes with his hand and penis, unsure of how to get in and what it will feel like. *Bad Boy* is fascinating in part because one moment it seems to be the boy's story, and the next moment it seems to be hers. She is one of the few genuinely naked and lascivious women in American painting, not only because her vagina is explicitly painted, but because we're made to experience her physical desire from within. She seems to know that she is being robbed and to encourage the boy by pretending not to see what he's doing.

The Old Man's Boat and the Old Man's Dog, which shows a group of people on a boat, is a moodier, quieter first-rate work. Because of the term "the old man," one reads this 1982 painting (as one reads many of Fischl's works) as a family scene. The old man—Dad—may be the nude man with a beer, in the center, with the Dalmatian. There has probably been a lot of beer; everyone seems soused. One woman— Sis?—has on a life preserver and a bikini, and fiddles with a fishing pole. Another woman—Mom?—sprawls on a mat, her rear to us, nude.

Two boys, who are also nude—they have taken off their swim trunks and are grimly sunburned—lurch across the boat. The sea is dangerously high, and the light is a dead gray. The scene recalls the moment in the Jonah story when Jonah is asleep and the waves begin to rise. The painting is about bitterness and emptiness. The sky, dog, waves, people, and boat are each of equal interest and cancel each other out. We sense the staleness of the moment: the smell of sunburn and sweat, salt and old suntan lotion, the dog's breath and Dad's beery breath.

In most of his other paintings, Fischl's condemnation is too clear-cut, or his targets aren't fresh. Yet there are shrewd and felt parts to many of these paintings. In *Barbeque*, a boy, whose face we don't see, blows flames into the air, while behind him, in the family pool, are two women without tops—Mom and Sis, no doubt. Dad is off to one side tending the barbecue, and, in the background, is the lavender-colored ranch house our family lives in. In the foreground, on a redwood picnic table, are two big fish in a green glass bowl. Fischl's subject is the tension and ugliness of suburban life. The giveaway is Dad, who slouches (ever so much) and whose pants are drawn up a touch too high on his waist. He flashes a twisted grin in our direction. *Barbeque* reworks familiar material, but the colors that dominate the work are, taken together, so rancid that the picture halts us. These colors are the dark green (the bowl) and the reddish-brown (the table), the orange (the flames), and the lavender (the house). With its off-center organization of space, *Barbeque* resembles a predictably hip magazine ad or art photograph. Oddly enough, this predictable fanciness only makes the picture more powerful.

Master Bedroom is about teenage carnality. A girl, who wears only panties, sits, knees drawn under her, on a huge bed in a contemporary-looking bedroom. She has curlers in her hair and braces on her teeth. She is about fifteen and has a smirky little smile. Fischl overdoes her lewdness. But we are held by the way that she's not quite looking at us. Her arm is clasped around the neck of a big, black, panting dog, and he is quite a character. He has the bearing of every corpulent, to-be-confided-in bartender or doorman. He averts his eyes from ours by a fraction, as dogs do when they know they're being watched.

In *Birthday Boy,* another arresting picture, we see a naked boy and a naked woman on a huge bed in a high-rise apartment at night. The boy shyly looks at her genitals and touches her foot, while she—her legs are spread and one knee is raised—looks off to the side of the picture. She's probably glancing at a TV. She knows what he's thinking about, though; she's his birthday gift, his first woman, and she knows when to pretend not to see him. *Birthday Boy* has no more weight than a Broadway coming-of-age comedy. Yet Fischl has caught the look of a contemporary city apartment. And the way the boy touches the woman's foot is a fine detail. He hopes she won't notice— he's still petrified of her—but he also wants her to know that he's touching her.

Why is Fischl's show as a whole devitalizing? Partly because, once we have lived through his scenes, there is little more to think about. He has an anonymous, impersonal, merely functional way of painting. His paintings are so many large oil sketches, but with little of the wetness and gleam of most oil sketches. Large areas in his works—a floor in a room, say, or a wall—seem "painted in"; we seem to look at so much "brushwork."

There is a point, though, to his particular realism. If he were primarily interested in problems of representation (or in color or light), his paintings might not be as believable as they are. He seems to say, with some anger, "It would be decadent to be beautiful about these scenes." And there is a nice correspondence between his borrowed-for-the-occasion, mildly flashy style and his images of a jerry-built and coarsened America.

It is Fischl's view of life that is blunted. Part of his power is that, whether or not he intends this, his pictures are refutations of the images of American life we see on TV. Fischl turns TV images inside out. In *Time for Bed,* the boat painting, and the others, he appears to be getting even with "Father Knows Best" and with all the greeting-card-type images of domestic happiness that we have been fed. One feels this especially in the way so many of his figures are nude. Fischl, as it were, draws the curtain and reveals the true story of American life. He shows it to be a sour and senseless orgy. His indignation is understandable; many of us know exactly what he's saying. His body of work might be entitled "The TV Years." Yet his anti-TV images (to give them that label for the moment) have the same thin texture as TV. And the nudity in his scenes is forced, even in the beach scenes. We often wonder, Why are these people nude?

There is very little beauty in his work. *New House* is one of the few paintings that is gentle. We see, in a darkened kitchen, a nude young woman talking on a white wall phone, looking toward a pile of opened brown packing boxes and a TV that is turned on. She stands with one foot on top of the other, holds her arm around her chest, and talks on the phone and looks at the TV at the same time. We are drawn to this gawky girl and the commonplace things that surround her. She's a recent version of an Edward Hopper woman. She's just there. She isn't being judged.

Fischl's other people are almost invariably Americans of a specific class, surrounded by possessions that are crucial elements in the story each painting tells. His people are so many figures in social situations, and that makes Fischl's work seem like an updated version of thirties Social Realist painting.

Fischl has created an art that succeeds if it has a social or emotional truth, and his recent work does not ring true. In some of the pictures in the Whitney from 1984 and 1985, and in the paintings from 1985 and 1986 that he showed at the Mary Boone Gallery, he hectors his audience, and his scenes have an increasingly fancy, costume-ball ambiguity. In some of his new pictures it is unclear whether his figures are literally wearing masks or if Fischl's point is that people now are so deceitful that their very faces are masklike. In *A Brief History of North Africa*, a beach scene, swanky white tourists lounge alongside, it appears, some natives, who are on stilts and loom in odd positions. (One of them resembles the painter Francesco Clemente.) Fischl's earlier *Old Man* painting is ambiguous, too, but its ambiguity is pleasing. Here, in *North Africa*, the ambiguity is that of a literary puzzle. *Saigon and Minnesota*, another new work, is a large picture of many people coming and going in the backyard of a peach-colored house. This picture is a catalogue of the repellent aspects of suburban life. A flabbily fat (and naked) man bends down to tie the laces of a little girl's sneakers. Two women, who have sagging flesh and have tanned themselves into leathery crones, walk toward us. A middle-aged man has one arm. In *Time for Bed*, the man's not having an arm adds mystery to the picture. Here, it's merely another gruesome thing. And Fischl's new way of making a picture misfires. He will bring together in one work a number of different-size canvases, each with another part of the story. A single picture can look like a jumble of playing cards held in the hand. The formal trickiness makes the stories themselves seem inconsequential.

Fischl's achievement is that he has made commanding works out of material that many painters would like to use but find daunting: private and shameful moments, the tensions of adolescence, relations between children and parents. Fischl's paintings, too, compete for our attention with movies, the most influential art form. What painter who has come to maturity in the past ten years has not wanted to make paintings that, in their own terms, have the sweep and depth, and are as urgent to so many people, as the *Godfather* movies? Fischl comes closest to that bigness in, probably, *Bad Boy*. He's a step ahead of us here: he has made the subject of sexual fantasies, or lovemaking, into high art.

But we're a step ahead of him in his work of the past few years. Pointing his finger at a vain and smarmy society, he has become a sort of Good Boy. One of the buried aspects of *Time for Bed*, *Bad Boy*, and the others is their fatalism. In Fischl's world, which is inhabited primarily by kids and by people in their thirties and forties, everyone loses. The kids seem bruised, or are seen in moments when a layer of hardness and insensitivity is growing over them. Fischl's older people tend to be loutish and weak; they have given up. The 1980 *Father and Son Sleeping* summarizes Fischl's bleakness (though it is a dissatisfying, somewhat illustrational, picture). Here are two naked men asleep in the same wide bed, with a good bit of space between them. They're in the same position: their legs are drawn up midway, so we don't see their genitals. The son has short hair; the father is somewhat heavy and bald. They have wide-hipped, awkward bodies; it's a toss-up who is creepier. The son seems to absorb the father as they doze; Fischl might be saying that one podlike generation breeds another. Fischl, in his art now, is like that sleeping son. He seems to have

23. George Stubbs. *A Phaeton with a Pair of Cream Ponies in Charge of a Stable-lad.*
c. 1780–85. Oil on panel, 35¼ × 53½″. Yale Center for British Art. Paul Mellon Collection

24. George Stubbs. *Freeman, the Earl of Clarendon's Gamekeeper, with a Dying Doe and a Hound*. 1800. Oil on canvas, 40 × 50″. Yale Center for British Art. Paul Mellon Collection

25. Gilbert and George. *Black Church Face*. c. 1980. Photo-piece, 95 × 79″. Collection Michael Sonnabend

26. Gilbert and George. *Naked Love*. c. 1983. Photo-piece, 119 × 119″. Collection Anthony d'Offay

27. David Park. *Ball Game on the Beach*. 1953. Oil on canvas, 38¼ × 49½″. Regis Collection, Minneapolis, Minnesota

28. David Park. *Flower Market*. 1955. Oil on canvas, 34½ × 43″. Whitney Museum of American Art. Lawrence H. Bloedel Bequest

29. Joel Shapiro. Foreground: *Untitled*. 1980–81. Bronze, 53 × 64 × 45½". Background: *Untitled*. 1980–82. Bronze, 23¾ × 13 × 8⅛". Saatchi Collection, London. Courtesy Paula Cooper Gallery

30. Philip Guston. *Painter in Bed*. 1973. Oil on canvas, 60 × 104″. Saatchi Collection, London

31. Sigmar Polke. *Liebespaar II*. 1965. Oil and enamel on canvas, 75 × 55″.
Saatchi Collection, London

32. Philip Taaffe. *Mangrove*. 1985. Linoprint, collage, and acrylic on canvas, 84 × 84″. Private collection. Courtesy Pat Hearn Gallery

33. Francesco Clemente. *Untitled*. 1980. Oil on canvas, 20 × 15″. Private collection. Courtesy Sperone Westwater, New York

34. Eric Fischl. *Bad Boy*. 1981. Oil on canvas, 66 × 96″. Saatchi Collection, London.
Courtesy Mary Boone Gallery

35. Gustav Klimt. *Reclining nude with left hand on her face.*
1912–13. Graphite on paper, 14⅜ × 21⅞″. Private collection

36. Gustav Klimt. *Portrait of a Lady with
a tall hat, and lying female figure.* 1907–8.
Graphite and pastel on paper,
21⅞ × 14½″. Private collection

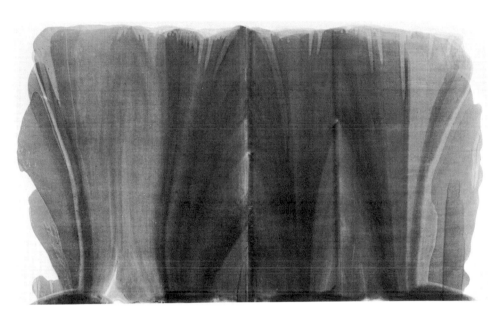

37. Morris Louis. *Blue Veil*. 1958–59. Acrylic on canvas, 91¾ × 156″. The Fogg Art Museum, Harvard University, Cambridge, Massachusetts. Gift of Lois Orswell and Gifts for Special Uses Fund

38. Julian Schnabel. *Rebirth III—The Red Box (Painted After the Death of Joseph Beuys).* 1986. Oil and tempera on muslin, 148×134″. Collection Marx, Berlin

39. Francisco de Zurbarán. *The Holy House of Nazareth* (or *The Virgin and Christ in the House of Nazareth*). c. 1640. Oil on canvas, 65 × 85⅞". The Cleveland Museum of Art. Leonard C. Hanna, Jr., Fund

40. Joe Zucker. *5 + 7 Story Wok-Up Junk in a Maelstrum*. 1985–86. Acrylic, sashcord, and wood, 102½ × 102½". Courtesy Hirschl and Adler Modern

41. George Ault. *Bright Light at Russell's Corners.* 1946.
Oil on canvas, 20 × 25″. National Museum of American
Art, Smithsonian Institution, Washington, D.C. Gift of
Mr. and Mrs. Sidney Lawrence

42. George Ault. *August Night at Russell's Corners.* 1948.
Oil on canvas, 18 × 24″. Joslyn Art Museum, Omaha,
Nebraska

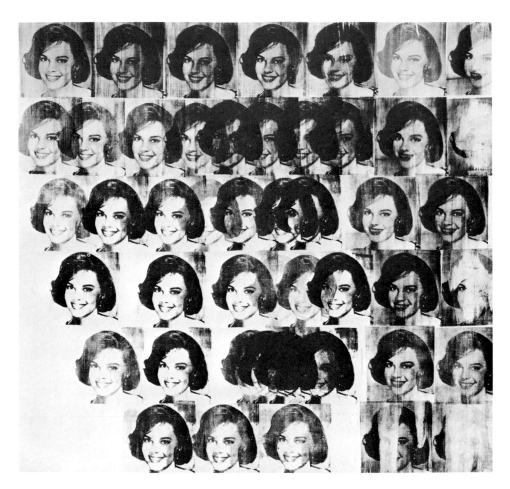

43. Andy Warhol. *Natalie*. 1962. Silkscreen ink on canvas, 83½ × 91″. Copyright 1989 The Estate and Foundation of Andy Warhol/ARS, N. Y.

chosen, for his work, to stay in the family, to be the conscience of American suburban life. For the moment, there's more depth and suspense in seeing where he will take his art than in his individual pictures.

—1986

THE VIENNESE ARTISTS

THERE IS A DOWNHILL momentum to the Museum of Modern Art's "Vienna 1900" show. It is a beautifully presented, jewel-box-like exhibition about the painting, drawing, architecture, and decorative arts of Vienna during the period of roughly 1895 to 1918, when the city, the seat of the Austro-Hungarian Empire, was conscious that the Hapsburg monarchy was a dying entity. It was a legendary time of political and social corruption and of achievements in music, literature, psychoanalysis. There was a sense of new possibilities in the visual arts, too. Vienna had never had a history of serious, personal oil painting. Now the city became responsive to Western Europe, and wanted to add its say. It had, so to speak, its pores open.

The pictures in the show, which are primarily by Gustav Klimt, Egon Schiele, and Oskar Kokoschka, are not works of great plastic beauty or complexity; they're paltry compared with Cézanne or Matisse. A case could be made, actually, that in Vienna at this time the decorative arts were, on a chart of relative aesthetic merit, ahead of painting. At the Modern, the furniture, fabrics, glassware, silver, posters, and so on by Josef Hoffmann, Koloman Moser, and other designers are, in general, more engaging and sumptuous than the pictures. But the paintings and drawings tell more of a story. It is a fairy tale about a quest for something to believe in, set in a kingdom where one's gut feeling is that nothing can be believed in. As we move from Klimt to Schiele—or from the generation of the nineties to that of the teens—we go from a belief in sensuality and physical beauty for their own sake to an overadamant and, it feels, empty belief in the self. The Viennese artists present art in a minor key; their work makes you fall back on yourself, makes you sense your limitations, and it leaves you hungry.

Klimt is the mild eminence of the show. He is almost grand; he nearly does for the subject of women—their sensual presence, their apprehensiveness—what Munch does for the subjects of loneliness and jealousy. Klimt doesn't fully win us over; his work is always, in a tactile sense, thin. Something rarefied and exotic hangs over him; he is never urgent enough. He accomplished some big things, though. The other Viennese artists are so many brilliant boys (literally—most were hard at work while still in their teens); they arrived from nowhere with their vision intact. Klimt's work is frequently vulgar and embarrassing, yet he struggled to change his direction, to widen the scope of his work. He began as a decorator of public places; he was a commercial, not a "fine," artist. He came out of a widespread taste at the time for demonic women, for the idea of being enslaved to sex, and he stayed with this taste. In certain works, though, he turned it into something pure and lean.

Klimt's most ambitious, "serious" art is the equivalent of Hollywood Biblical spectaculars. In *Judith II*, which is about Judith and Holofernes, the heroine is bare-breasted and her fingers are melodramatically outstretched, but the painting might as well be about a hardened shopper making her way through a department store on a sale day. *Goldfish*, which shows some bouncy nude women in, it seems, an aquarium, including one who shoves her rear at us and grins, might be described as restaurant art from the days of Diamond Jim Brady. In the much reproduced *The Kiss*, a kneeling and embracing man and woman are surrounded by a field of gold ornament, which is nice in itself, and Klimt has caught the devouring, enveloping aspect of lovemaking. The picture, though, is really just a glorified sex fantasy about a muscular, anonymous storybook knight who cradles a swooning lass, and the drawing of the features and hands is coarse.

Klimt's best paintings are his portraits of women. These paintings are strong but not robust. From a distance, they are simply stylish objects; up close, you see that Klimt's subject is his rapport with women. He gets women to the quick—we believe we see how they think about themselves. Their faces are realistically drawn; their clothes, though, blend into the backgrounds, which are of ornamental patterns in gold, or swirls of iridescent colors, or syncopated units of different-size patches of color. Margaret Stonborough-Wittgenstein, the subject of one of his best paintings, is flustered: her hands twist, her face looks a touch damp, her hair resists being fixed in place. She doesn't seem to care about her looks, though; she is a young person who seems to question her very character, and we take this as a sign of strength. She wears a shimmery white dress—a lazy flow of pencil lines is evident beneath the white paint—and she is surrounded by units of blue, white, green, and gray arranged in a pleasing boxlike pattern. The background, which gives a sense of nobility and severity—and a sort of Dutch scrubbed cleanness and a shy warmth—suits her perfectly.

In the first of two portraits of Adele Bloch-Bauer, we seem to see the very moment that the sitter's face softens with the thought that she is loved by the painter and will be made beautiful by him. Yet she also seems to realize that there is something ridiculous about the idea that she is the center of this grand ornamental design. On his part, Klimt seems to laugh at her pretensions; he presents her as something of a moist goosey girl. But he also wants to make an object of great beauty for, or about, her; with its complex weave of one kind of gold patterning over another, the picture is like an official portrait of a czarina. Klimt and his model seem to be in the midst of an affair right before our eyes. Like some of Goya's portraits of women, the picture is about lovers deceiving themselves and about the pathos of vanity.

Klimt is an appealing man. There is little known about him personally. He said that he would get "seasick" whenever he had to write anything—even an informal letter, apparently—and so he left only a few (rather impersonal) statements. He had a squarish build and Mediterranean-Oriental, or Turkish, looks. He had dark, tanned skin, wore a short beard, and his hair was thin on top. He was the son of a goldsmith. He lived for almost thirty years with Emilie

Flöge, who with a sister owned a dress shop. They had no children, but he was suspected of being the father of many children with other women.

The key incident of Klimt's life occurred when he came under fire from the University of Vienna for a group of allegorical murals—they showed nudes and crones with bowed heads floating in a vaporous netherworld—that had been commissioned on the subjects of Jurisprudence, Medicine, and Philosophy. The public disapproval of his work and the threat of censorship didn't crush Klimt, and his art didn't drastically change because of it; instead, the reprimands and humiliations seem to have made him more certain about an artist's need to base his art on personal liberty, on going against the grain of his society. Klimt increasingly led a hermit's life, both in Vienna and, in the warm months, in the Austrian countryside. He was known to dress in a blue robe, and to wear sandals. He designed the garment, and he and Emilie designed loose, flowing (and more complicated) garments for her. He no doubt associated this unconventional dress with the liberty he sought in his art.

Klimt's most sheerly beautiful works are his drawings. There are very few in the Modern's show. Most of these are studies for his murals, and while they are all right, they date from his overstylized, demonic-woman phase. His more characteristic drawings have a looser, freer line and a greater sense of spontaneity. They were sometimes used as studies for paintings but were more often done as ends in themselves. He left hundreds, and some are no more than rough sketches. He worked mostly with pencil and with a soft, sure hand. He didn't put in background details, such as chairs or sofas—his subject was the presence of the person before him. The richest drawings are of women who are seen in the nude, or with some bit of apparel, and are often lying on their backs or on their stomachs. These women are lithe and sensually aware in a way that women had not been in art before Klimt. By comparison, most earlier or contemporary female nudes (including Rodin's) seem bovine, objects without minds, anonymous creatures. Klimt's women, nude or clothed, are individuals, and their bodies still look contemporary. The feat of these drawings, though, is that Klimt makes a woman's genitals and pubic hair necessary elements in the visual rhythms he sets up. These works are equally erotic drawings and studies in form.

Yet the central works of "Vienna 1900" are Klimt's landscapes. This is not to say that they are good paintings. His subjects are meadows full of flowers, twilit forests, and villas by the edge of the Attersee, a lake near Salzburg. The landscapes at the Modern don't breathe or glow, and it's possible that his landscapes in general—he made them on a steady basis for some twenty years—are dissatisfying. Taken as illustrations, though, they help explain why Viennese art is stultifying (and why Vienna itself may have been stultifying). The setting is a lovely Alpine idyll—we'd like to be there—but after looking at a few of these pictures we long for sky and clouds and a sense of expansiveness. Klimt invariably used a square format, which suggests stasis to begin with, and each painting, which seems to be a blown-up detail from a larger picture, has a pressed-against-the-face flatness, like something seen through a telescope or a telephoto lens. The pictures present a world without prospects. It is a stilled, inland, and, it seems, isolated yet unchallenging place. No other European landscapes have quite this combination of loveliness and inertness. Did Klimt intend these pictures to be disquieting? One doubts it. They may even have been products for him, elegant pictures fashioned in a (then) fairly current, posterish style by the Klimt who was a craftsman.

The pictures in the rest of the show convey a similar sense of willed creativity—of art without an underside. The last rooms, which have large numbers of pictures by Schiele and Kokoschka and samples of work by Richard Gerstl, Alfred Kubin, Arnold Schoenberg, and Klemens Brosch, made my head feel like a feather. Most of the work is overfamiliar—you look right through it.

Schiele has a large following, and for some he may be the most contemporary figure in the show. Most of his work is portraiture or pictures of models in a studio; his best-known pictures are probably his self-portraits where, nude, he grimaces, and his arms, hands, and body are twisted into painful positions. His images are said to reveal underlying moods and fears. I feel the opposite: that his work is hard and wall-like, that he is an unusually unsympathetic painter of people.

Schiele's images run together as you think about them. He always strikes a few related notes: he is after a crazed, immobilized, precarious moment. He gets the specific features of people, but he doesn't let the spirit of the model emerge. His paintings are generally considered to be inferior to his watercolors and line drawings, and the paintings, which are surprisingly large and ambitious, are certainly dank. They give off no light. They are like big, filled-in drawings. There is more light in the watercolors, but his blocky, robotlike stroke, which never varies in intensity, gives to all his works such a thoroughgoing sense of tension that one feels no real tension anywhere.

The most vivid aspect of Schiele is not his art but his zeal as a person. When you look at the photographs of him in Alessandra Comini's 1974 *Egon Schiele's Portraits*—there are no photos of the artists at the show—you are held by how contemporary Schiele appears and how different he is in each picture. He struts, or closes his eyes and purses his lips; he sits by a table, his hands curled into tight balls. He stands looking forlornly into his full-length mirror. He was quite thin, compact, and short, with dark, wiry hair that jutted this way and that. In some pictures, though, he might be a groomed, well-fed executive of forty-five. When we look at his work, we can believe that there are no insides to the man; in the photos, though, his sometimes arrogant, or cruel, or apprehensive face is filling. We only wish that there were more photographs. Had he been born seventy years later, he might have been a performance artist.

There is one marvelous painting by him at the show: *Self-Portrait Clothed*. The painting is dated 1909, when Schiele was nineteen and something of a protégé of Klimt's, and in the period when Klimt was doing his best work—the portraits of Adele Bloch-Bauer and Margaret Stonborough-Wittgenstein. Schiele's narrow little picture is mostly black. There is a gold, green, and tan ornamental border on the left, and Schiele's face appears to emerge from a gold box on the top. His hands, with his fingers outstretched, jut in from the bottom. Schiele has taken Klimt's way of putting a realistic face in a decorative container and made it witty. We keep thinking that we see a whole torso, but there is no body—just face and hands. And Schiele's face is that of a charmer, a faker. The combination of flesh tones and gold in this painting reminds us of the softer, sweeter Italian Renaissance painters, and Schiele's skin has a rosiness and a powderiness that particularly recalls Fra Angelico.

One feels that there was a gentle and devilish side to Schiele, and that, perhaps unconsciously, he sacrifed this part of himself. The 1909 self-portrait pulls us into a mysterious and lambent realm. It is his only work that does not feel brittle or armored. One believes that Schiele by nature was attuned to the lovely, to harmonious rhythms, but that something made him go off, like a knight, in pursuit of what he believed was a higher truth.

Perhaps it is unfair to judge Schiele, because he died at twenty-eight (in 1918, of the same influenza that killed, among many others, his wife). We don't know what he would have "become." Yet his work has an unusual unity for someone in his twenties. He hardly varied his approach; he virtually did not experiment. He worked with a single-mindedness that artists usually achieve much later in life. The truly tragic note about him is that he felt compelled to have this perfectly full "career."

Kokoschka, too, sprang from nowhere with a fully developed style when he was still young. He was in his early twenties when he did his best work. These are portraits in which he scratched clusters of doodles—twittering little graffiti—into the oil; we seem to see the sitter's aura. Taken individually, these paintings are admirable. The sitters seem to emerge from a fiery, quaking, physically beautiful substance, and one likes the way that Kokoschka holds back from deforming their features. When many of these portraits are brought together, though, one loses a desire to get close to any of them. All are made the same way. It is as though Kokoschka freakishly hit on a good thing and stuck with it for as long as he could; this string of portraits is like a superior road show. What is missing in Kokoschka and in Schiele is the sense that art making can be about a private relationship between the artist and his materials. Both Kokoschka and Schiele appear to believe that the point of art is that it is a performance and that an artist's only relationship is with his public. I think this is why their work is repetitious and cannot bear repeated viewings.

"Vienna 1900" is a small show. Because paintings and drawings are mixed in with jewelry, fabrics, teapots, and other designed items, the exhibition feels more like a history lesson than an art show. (The drawings and photographs concerning architecture are in a separate section.) When you read the exhibition catalogue, by Kirk Varnedoe, the show's curator, you see that he intended a lesson—he does not believe that the work deserves more. Essentially, Varnedoe is reacting to people who in the last twenty years have wanted to see in the work of Vienna's architects, designers, and painters a radicalness and a profundity comparable with the work of the city's composers, writers, and scientists. In his estimation, Vienna's visual artists are not in the same league. He has many arguments, but his basic response is that a "heartiness" is missing.

Varnedoe is impressive. His may be the most ambitious and carefully thought-out catalogue that any New York museum has produced in a long time. What he doesn't emphasize, I think, is that Vienna's foray into the visual arts was a sort of born-yesterday experiment. Since before Klimt there had been no real tradition of painting in Vienna—no belief that painting was a serious and personal form of expression—one is amazed that these men accomplished as much as they did. (The sheer newness of art in Vienna may explain why Schiele and Kokoschka, once launched, made their pictures doggedly.) Varnedoe describes a major shift in Viennese thinking, from the ornate, "fancy" surfaces of Klimt's paintings (and the buildings and designs contemporary with him) to a sweeping rejection of this in the next generation. The younger artists were drawn to chastely unornamented facades in architecture, to a geometric rigidity in the decorative arts, and to a scrawny, harsh plainness and realism in painting. Varnedoe rightly says that the Viennese didn't fulfill the "fancy" or the "plain"—that both responses lack vitality and originality. Yet isn't Vienna's infatuation with the ornate and the harshly plain really two parts of the same story? It is as though, as the monarchy was going through its death throes, the artists wanted somehow to salute it—to give a body to what had always been

234

bodiless—and then express their contempt and their desire to be released from it. Viennese art mirrors a single event: how a society and a culture kicked up and died.

The work of Klemens Brosch, who is virtually unknown here, provides a closing note. Brosch was also an artist when still a teenager. He took his life at thirty-two. The nine drawings by him at the Modern—he apparently made only drawings—are not exactly first-rate. Brosch is a descendant of a German and a Central European strain of literary and symbolical art; his individual pictures are so many odd tales that we immerse ourselves in once—and probably do not want to return to often. Alongside Schiele and Kokoschka, though, they are particularly refreshing. Brosch is especially interesting where he seems to be responding to Klimt's landscapes. Klimt looked realistically—and passively—at the flattened-out, ultra-pretty, and prospectless world that faced his generation. The younger artist, who may or may not have known these landscapes, seems to imagine, in some of his drawings, ways of getting out of that world.

In one drawing we look straight up into a night sky, at a dirigible overhead. We feel we are on the ground, on our backs. In another drawing we soar up with birds; we are no longer connected with people. In another one, which includes birds flying over a valley, we see the earth from such an odd perspective that we can't tell what we're seeing. A drawing called *Memories of the Vienna Skating Rink* might be an epitaph for the entire show (though it is not, in tone, elegiac). We are gliding down, from the height of a bird, on lights strung over a rink. Far beneath these globes there are funny antlike people skating this way and that, their shadows cast on the ice. It seems that Brosch has won his freedom for good, and has now returned for one last look.

—1986

CLEMENT GREENBERG—THE CRITIC AND HIS ARTISTS

I

PERCEPTION FOR PERCEPTION, Clement Greenberg is the greatest American art critic, yet the first two volumes of his collected work— *Perceptions and Judgments, 1939–1944,* and *Arrogant Purpose, 1945– 1949* (University of Chicago Press), which have been edited by John O'Brian—have a dampening effect. These writings are primarily about art from the Impressionist era through the emergence after the Second World War of the American Abstract Expressionists. The books are treasure troves of descriptions of works of art, of analyses of the relation between an artist's character and his work and between an individual and his culture. But Greenberg is also a maddeningly theory-bound writer, and you put down his pieces feeling that you have been through a fight between a critic who is an intuitive genius and a forbidding character. It comes out a draw.

Clement Greenberg is the author of *Art and Culture* (1961). It is a very selective grouping of his essays from the nineteen-forties and fifties and the most influential book about art of the past twenty-five years. (It is also, besides a few slim picture books, his only previous work.) Writing about European and American painters and sculptors and many general issues, including collage and the nature of abstraction, Greenberg saw a sense of mission and direction in twentieth-century art. In an unadorned and rhythmic style that resembled Hemingway, Greenberg wrote as a combined appreciator and theorist. His prose had an authority. Unlike other art writers, he commanded the attention both of artists, who felt that in his emphasis on the formal aspects of art, on how artworks are made, he got unusually close to the studio experience, and of a largely political and literary, or, at least, a nonart audience—an audience that is often suspicious of the art world. Greenberg was the first American to dwell on the importance of "tradition" and a "world-class" art; he was the first to call some art "major" and to dismiss most as "minor." He was the first American art writer to look at art as a series of movements or styles, each of which would supersede the one that came before it. His essays weren't primarily about the Abstract Expressionists, and Greenberg hardly intended merely to boost them, but, no matter what his subject, he seemed to suggest that late nineteenth- and early twentieth-century styles had culminated in the new American painting and sculpture and that "world-class" art in general was now in the hands of American culture.

Greenberg's heyday was the fifties, when he was associated with such newly eminent artists as Jackson Pollock and David Smith and their immediate successors, primarily Morris Louis. From the early sixties on, Greenberg wrote increasingly less about contemporary art, and when he did he generally said that the latest developments weren't good; but that didn't entirely dim his stature or that of *Art and Culture*. Greenberg set in motion a way of thinking about art among Americans that, in many ways, has remained in place. He is hardly a fan of Pop Art, Minimalism, Conceptual Art, Post-Minimalism, the recent Neo-Expressionism, or any of the numerous smaller movements of these years, yet he is the spiritual father of all of them. And while his specific ideas have become less crucial, *Art and Culture* has remained, I think, a book that young artists and writers discover with enthusiasm. It is the successor to Robert Henri's *The Art Spirit*, the classic collection, published in the twenties, of this painter's sayings, lectures, and notes. The two books are dissimilar in many ways, but they are alike in being calls to action. *The Art Spirit* spoke to Americans at a time when being true to one's instincts was a revolutionary thing. *Art and Culture* spoke to Americans at a time when possessing a cool and worldly attitude was what really mattered.

In his long and eagerly awaited collected works, Greenberg is a grander—and also a more fragile and irritating—figure than the author of *Art and Culture*. (Two more volumes, covering 1950 through 1969, have been announced.) His range is staggering; he describes the achievements and failures of all sorts of artists from many periods with a streaming ease. Yet there is a sour, nagging, and burned-off quality about him, and his feeling for the "direction" of art now seems to be part of a personal need to sift out, to compare, to measure, to rank. Greenberg writes as a shrewd, rather impatient—and humorless— power broker. He shows little emotion; whether he praises or damns, he writes with the same quiet, controlled, evenly strong tone. His voice is that of a court chamberlain or secretary of state. He is a formidable opponent. But he is not a prince or a king; he writes as a custodian of power, someone who senses that some ultimate power will never be in his hands. Greenberg's fame is based on his support of radical, tough new art, but his insights are bound to a harsh and unliberating view of existence. Art for him is a symbol of immortality and rules. He might be called a poet of the Academy of life—of the ultimate beauty of the Proper.

Between 1939, when he was thirty, and 1949, when he gave up full-time reviewing, Greenberg wrote a regular column for *The Nation* and frequently appeared in *Partisan Review* and *The New York Times Book Review*. Especially in the early forties, he reviewed many writers; there are very good pieces in these compactly designed collections on, among others, Randall Jarrell, Franz Kafka, Saul Bellow, and Marianne Moore, and he is interesting on an Anthony Tudor ballet, too.

Greenberg wrote mostly about art, though. There are estimates here of, among others, Degas, Delacroix, the Flemish primitives, Klee, Ingres, Kandinsky, Hartley, Pissarro, Picasso, Thurber, Currier and Ives prints, Lachaise, numerous cartoonists, Miró, Matisse, Braque, Leonardo da Vinci, Gauguin, Winslow Homer, Beckmann, Pollock, David Smith, David Hare, Arnold Friedman, Motherwell, and Marin. There are essays on abstract art, primitive painters, modern sculpture, collage, and Edward Weston and photography in general. Most of these pieces are short, and Greenberg often reviewed the first shows these artists had in New York. There may have been a vague consensus at the time about, say, Rouault or Arshile Gorky or Henry Moore, but Greenberg, one feels, was courageous in presenting his emphatic opinions, and it is amazing how fresh his opinions—and his opinions about literature, too—still are.

Greenberg's special quality is that he can, so to speak, get inside the skin of a painting, drawing, or sculpture, and describe the thickness or thinness of the lines, or the texture of the oil, or the look of a face in a portrait, and draw enormous conclusions from it. "There was something over-ripe and slightly vicious" about the period of the Flemish primitives, he writes; there is "a rather profane detachment" in van Eyck, and a "certain malaise is to be detected in van der Weyden." It is "characteristic of the Dutch school," he notes, "that the very workmanship of the artist, the good quality and permanence of his pigments, glazes, and varnishes, the skill, patience, and conscientiousness with which he has applied them—all these contribute somehow to the pleasure." Talking about Eakins, he mentions the painter's images of rowers on the Schuylkill and the "throbbing, suppressed luminosity of the sunlight"—and with these words we freshly see and feel the sadness and tension of Eakins's art, the man himself, and his era.

Throughout these volumes there are observations which we might not agree with (and might not even understand at first) but which give issues a faceted, jewel-like complexity—as when Greenberg says, "It took the brilliance and color of the West Indies to justify Homer's daring to himself. He had not intended to innovate. The brilliance was there before him; he painted it. And it was all part of the logic by which his naively possessed but far from naive gift had to develop." Writing about Chagall in 1947, Greenberg says that the painter "had no longer enough to say to fill out his style, which is left without strains or tensions. . . . It is Chagall's tragedy that he has never had much more than his genius."

With artist after artist, Greenberg describes works and offers a judgment, and we feel, Yes, this cannot be bettered. Everything that can leave us dissatisfied with Calder, despite how much we may like individual pieces, is in Greenberg's saying, "This particular world lacks history. Lots of things go on in it but nothing happens." Bonnard, we read, "paints more suavely and generously than Matisse or Picasso, but he does not establish the bold, lucid, incandescent structures by which those two masters fix us to the spot, touch new feelings, and expand our consciousness of the possibilities of art." Greenberg says about de Chirico that his art "is a literary feat sustained for only a moment's view. Then it dies." This is perfect; each time we encounter de Chirico's pictures we are excited and then, after a while, they "die" on us. About Picasso and Miró, he says, "In Picasso, who is indeed a more profound artist, we can sense a dissatisfaction with the resources of his medium; something beyond painting yearns to be expressed, something which color and line laid on a flat surface can never quite achieve. Miró, on the contrary, seeks the quintessential painting, is content to stay at the center of that exhilaration which is only felt in making marks and signs." One of Greenberg's most amazing comments is from a 1944 piece on Marsden Hartley (amazing because the words have proven prophetic to a tee). Hartley was "not a great artist, and, as I have said, he was radically uneven, but his reputation will grow as time passes. The limitations of the art are in some peculiar way redeemed by the large character of the man."

The core of Greenberg's writing, though, is dreary. His large subject is the development of modern art, and we know this tale too well. Greenberg wants us to see that there is a single way to make a successful work of art: when the painter, say, is not concerned with the storytelling aspect of his picture or his personal feelings, but deals solely with the properties of his medium—the nature of paint, the literal "flatness" of the canvas. Greenberg also wants us to admire the artists and the tradition of the School of Paris. He sees Paris in the nineteenth and the beginning of the twentieth centuries as the place and time when art and life reached a peak: this was the beginning of modern art and of the modern, or industrial, age.

Greenberg is convinced that there is a mainstream of art—art that matters, that is immortal. This tradition goes back to Giotto, continues with Delacroix, Ingres, and Courbet, and comes closer to us with the Impressionists, Post-Impressionists, Fauves, and Cubists. Since the late twenties, though (he continues), art has gone to the dogs; Surrealism has taken over, and Surrealist art is not good. Life in general has become iffy, vulgarized. People are on a vacation from the higher purposes. Surveying the scene in the forties, Greenberg points to the still-active Matisse and Picasso; they represent the golden age that is all but gone. There are also Miró and Mondrian, who carry on the tradition. But he senses that it is the young, largely unknown American painters, who have learned the lessons of the Europeans (through looking at their work in reproductions), who will make the needed breakthroughs. He isn't positive about this; most of the new work, he says, is terrible, actually. He is certain, though, that if these Americans make an original art it will extend Cubism, as Cubism extended the radical art that produced it. And the logical extension of Cubism is a purely abstract art.

Greenberg's individual points are irrefutable. His approach is political; Cubism for him is, in effect, the Russian Revolution (he refers to himself as a socialist), and he clearly applies to art the principles of Marx and of German philosophy in general, where there is a "necessity" and a logical flow to history. Regardless of his bias, we read and nod in agreement. We probably think of the history of art as a single, continuing story and believe that the most important new art is often the work that doesn't even seem to be "art" at first and is about a new way to use paint, bronze, or any material. Most of us have similar notions about which art is, as he puts it, "major" or "irrelevant," and can agree, too—though blankly, unenthusiastically—with his 1948 estimate of Cubism as the "great phenomenon, the epoch-making feat of twentieth-century art."

And Greenberg's clarity and assurance are invigorating at first. Absorb his lessons and you feel ready to look at anything and put it in a slot. When he says of a Matisse that "in it Matisse demonstrates again . . . that he uses black better than anyone else since Manet, not excepting Braque," or when Greenberg says (in 1948) that Picasso is "further than ever from threatening" Matisse's "position as the greatest master of the twentieth century," we think, Wow, this is fun. Greenberg's prose is an elevated form of the chat we all make at a show, when we simply say what we feel (and it is usually negative). Greenberg's tone epitomizes—he may have created—the "New York" approach to art. This is a savvy, street-smart, tough-guy attitude. Some of the most prominent figures in American art in the generation after Greenberg's have a similar "professionalized" sense of art; one thinks of the painter Frank Stella, the sculptor Donald Judd, the museum director William Rubin. They—and many artists in the present generation, too—believe that "important" art is abstract in nature (even if the artist includes representational images), that art flows in a direct historical line from movement to movement, and that this tradition is always being attacked by retrograde forces: literary or nostalgic styles, which are meaningless little detours.

It is satisfying, and second nature for most of us, to believe this. Art loses any sense of preciousness; it becomes a racier and manlier occupation—a combination of sports, business, politics. But after a dose of this talk in Greenberg's pieces, one feels warped. In a typical passage, he writes that Dubuffet and other artists "may escape the paralysis of culture via Klee and the deliberate surrender to infantile experience, but they do little to vitalize tradition; Dubuffet is a first-rate painter but he leaves nothing to the future of painting." We think, Right, brilliant—Dubuffet's work does feel like a dead-end street. Yet Greenberg makes "tradition" a cardboard thing; he robs it of its mystery and vastness. He says (in 1948) that Cubism is "now the only school." This is monstrous. It kills a crucial element in art: that it is about freedom.

Despite what we think of Greenberg's ideas, we are drawn to his prose in itself; it is exquisite and mesmerizing. He seems to give every word in an essay an equal emphasis. His prose has the qualities he calls our attention to in works of art (and in the work of certain writers he reviews, such as Anna Seghers and Franz Kafka). Greenberg likes paintings where there is no slackness or "falling away" toward the edges and where the various elements create a right-on-the-surface tension, and his essays are built that way. He begins a piece right in the center of an important point, and he concludes on the same firm note. There are no fancy passages or stagey upbeats (or downbeats) at the end. He sustains a single clenched note from beginning to end. Each review is another report from the front.

Considering how finely crafted his writing is, one finds his repetitiousness shocking. All writers become repetitious when read straight through, but Greenberg touches on his related themes in virtually every piece. It is unfair, of course, to generalize about his work based on only these first two volumes. But the articles which were written after 1949 that are reprinted in *Art and Culture* revolve around the same points.

Greenberg is a bully. Yet he gets under your skin. Even after we are versed in his theories, we hunger to hear his opinions—his string of perceptions—about an artist. He's wily. More than most critics, he forces you to argue with him; he makes you clarify your own positions.

Greenberg may be the one American art critic to formulate an idea of beauty. It is difficult to embrace all of it, but parts are compelling; he seems to describe the art he would make if he were a professional artist. He wants an art that has the sensuous, physical quality of modern French painting (and when he mentions French painting he means, too, French culture and the texture of French life; the only time he becomes moony—and sounds dated—is when he talks about Paris, especially the Paris of yesteryear). He also believes that the truly great artwork is anonymous. It is not about the personality of the person who made it, and, as an object, it is airy, flat, screenlike. He talks so much about "unity"—about a balance between drawing and color, near and far, light and dark—that a model work rises before us as we read. It is some combination of a large, imageless painting, an immense grill-like architecture, and the spirit of an old, powerful state or kingdom. We see something brilliant, glowing, godlike.

Greenberg presents, one can feel, a Jewish idea of beauty (he identifies himself as a Jew in a few places). One can also believe that when he writes about an artist and his "culture" he might, additionally, be writing about the individual Jew and what "culture" is to him: the great, dazzling Gentile city, which the Jew wants to conquer and to feel at home in. Some of Greenberg's liveliest and most absorbing comments are about how being Jewish affects writers and artists, and, in addition to Kafka and Saul Bellow, he writes about Scholom Aleichem, Arthur Koestler, Peggy Guggenheim, and a book on the Jewish joke. Greenberg describes his own most tangible qualities—his directness and honesty (which can be a showy honesty)—in the Scholom Aleichem piece when he says that the ghetto "taught the Jew to keep his eye on the main thing, the main thing in any interest, not only his own. Therefore his impatience with etiquette. . . . Why deny that man lives by cruel competition in this particular world?"

Greenberg sees Jews as either total winners or as a flock of sheep. He says (with such an extreme aggressiveness that it is cartoonish) that "it is possible that by 'world-historical' standards the European Jew represents a higher type of human being than any yet achieved in history. I do not say that this is so, but I say it is possible and that there is much to argue for its possibility." Elsewhere, though, he writes of the smallness and isolation of Jews. "No people on earth," he says in 1944, "are more correct, more staid, more provincial, more commonplace, more inexperienced; none observe more strictly the letter of every code that is respectable; no people do so completely and habitually what is expected of them. . . ." Greenberg looks at artists in these two different ways. There are certain artists of the School of Paris, who are unknowable deities, and there are provincial artists, who have, for him, a chief characteristic: ultimately, they're not good enough.

It is a charge to read Greenberg on, say, Delacroix; the painter, he believes, is a paragon of talent, learning, technique, intellect, personal manners—he is "Paris." Greenberg "looks through" these awesome Parisians, though; he assumes that we, too, believe that their art is superb, and his pieces leave us shortchanged. We can see why he would call Matisse the greatest painter of the century. Matisse is stimulating about virtually nothing; his subject is the process by which colors and lines balance off each other to make a pleasing whole. The chief thing we retain from Greenberg on Matisse, though, is his sense of the man's toughness. The Frenchman, we hear, is "cold, undistracted, and full of arrogant purpose." (This is Greenberg's own tone.) It is a relief to hear Matisse called cold; other writers don't say it. (They don't say anything interesting about Matisse; he usually comes across as a blank.) But Greenberg's general comments about the painter, both in these reviews and in his little 1953 picture book on Matisse—it is comprised of a short essay followed by notes on some twenty plates—are forgettable. Greenberg's other picture books—*Joan Miró* (1948) and *Hofmann* (1961)—are also about figures he believes are preeminent, and these studies, too, leave little impression.

Greenberg is more substantial on (to him) lesser artists. His finest writing is on Marin, Klee, and Homer. They are highly gifted and satisfying painters, and Klee had a worldwide influence. Yet, as Greenberg might say, they are underfed; they exist in cultures that do not give them enough. Klee is a touchstone for him. Greenberg can best see the majestic, superior qualities in art and life by looking at Klee, who (he says) just misses possessing them.

There are marvelous passages on the limitations of Klee. Writing about the differences between Klee and Picasso, Greenberg says, in effect, that the best art doesn't have a private or confessional meaning and isn't about one's fears; it isn't a consolation for us in those times when we feel cut off from society and life. The great artist must be arrogant, even ruthless; his work flows from something contented and sensuous, and we respond to it when we are most confident about ourselves. Greenberg's ultimate artist is a "dandy." He is stoical, unafraid, without illusions. He is also a thoroughgoing professional who would never violate the traditions of his craft by making paintings that were "personal."

The most satisfying part of Greenberg's aesthetic is that he gives us a new way to look at all of art. When he says that Cubism is the "purest and most unified of all art styles since Tiepolo and Watteau," we suddenly see the thread he is after (and the effect is to make us think about what tradition or "look" in art we especially love). A Cubist picture, a Tiepolo, and a Watteau all have the same blending of foreground and background, the same lack of strong contrasts between light and shadow, the same chalky-and-silky texture. A Tiepolo, a Watteau, and a Cubist Picasso or Braque share an emotional evenness, a lack of strife, an intelligence and poise—a way of saying, "The actual story here doesn't matter."

These Old Master and twentieth-century artworks are more about drawing than color, and Greenberg's aesthetic comes, it seems, from someone whose first love is drawing. (In his introduction, O'Brian says that Greenberg "drew obsessively from the age of four on.") The person whose sensibility is formed from working with pencil or pen tends to see art as an even distribution of tones, because when you put lines down on a sheet of white paper, you automatically think about the dark versus the big white mass. This is a simplification of his thinking, but when Greenberg sees a picture where the various elements jut in different directions and each element keeps its own, independent character, he believes the picture is unsuccessful. In a sense, his conception of "unity" is literal and naive. With his rules of composition, he occasionally sounds as though he were a drawing instructor at an old-time art academy. Some part of Greenberg's response to art is, in the worst sense, shallow and flat.

And Greenberg's distinction about how we "see" old art versus modern art feels wrong. This may not be a large point, but it raises questions about much of what he says. He believes that, in painting from the Renaissance up to Cubism, we looked "into" the painted scene before us; there was an illusion of deep space. Cubism, he says, freed art to be "about itself," about its surface alone; Cubism created a new airless space. This is true, but in practice I think the situation is exactly the opposite. If we are stopped in a museum by a Renaissance picture or a Courbet, it is probably because the picture is surprisingly flat, surfacy; some element might be pleasingly out of sync, or the artist appears self-conscious in a modern way. Most radical, abstract twentieth-century artworks, though, are alive to the degree that we want to linger with, to look "into" them. A challenging new work often seems to present a to-be-deciphered way to approach contemporary reality; there is a mystery about its meaning.

I think that artworks are looked at in primarily aesthetic terms—in Greenberg's terms—once they have lost their bite and entered the museum realm, the land of the past. Greenberg unwittingly wants to cauterize whatever makes new art new. He wants to jump immediately to the museum stage, where the new work must compete with the Giottos and Titians. Greenberg's infatuation with surface and flatness amounts to someone saying, "The immediate emotions aroused by a work of art mean nothing in the long run, and the long run is the only thing that counts." What Greenberg doesn't see is that taste changes over generations. I don't think, for instance, that people now have the spellbound and reverent regard for Cubism that he had. Cubist works are elegant, but they are also witty, weird, dreary, and a touch gimmicky. Far from being flat and without a conventional light, as Greenberg would have them, the pictures often seem to be images of gadgety metal constructions that reflect a dim outside light. With their various pats of muted color and translucent skin of little compartmentalizing lines, some of the Picassos and Braques seem to present a sci-fi netherworld.

Greenberg makes one point about Cubism that is still fresh, though. He says that the Cubist style is bigger than the artist who makes the actual Cubist pictures. This feels right, and it ties together in a canny way with his desire for an anonymous, personality-less art. We can imagine how, when Picasso made his Cubist pictures, he was running on automatic as he "filled in" the Cubist grid. When Jackson Pollock made his famous "drip" paintings, he seems not to have had time to think about himself either. In the movies and photos of him at work, Pollock, whose canvas was on the floor, virtually dances onto his paintings, and, as hc flings the paint with a stick, "loses" himself. Greenberg notes the similarity between the Cubists and Pollock in this gentle and beautiful sentence: "There is something of the same encasement in a style that, so to speak, feels for the painter and relieves him of the anguish and awkwardness of invention, leaving his gift free to function almost automatically." Reading this sentence, one wonders when the next significant style will arise that will "feel for" and "relieve" the painter in this way.

The dramatic high point of these volumes is Greenberg on Pollock. There are reviews of the painter's first six shows, beginning in 1943, plus mentions of Pollock here and there, and Greenberg's idea of the painter is so much like ours that we have to remind ourselves that these criticisms were written forty years ago. Greenberg was on the lookout for a new artist (or for a school of new artists) who would "do more" with Cubism and whose work could hang on the wall, on equal terms, with the great Europeans. Greenberg wanted an art that presented a difficult, unobvious—but not esoteric—beauty, one that wasn't easy to like or know.

Pollock still represents these qualities. He is still an artist we don't quite "know." I believe we would prefer not to "know" him fully, because we don't want to risk being disappointed by him. I think we want to keep him a pure symbol—a symbol of epic striving and of vulnerability. This symbolic part of Pollock is most felt in his pictures from the early and mid-forties, from before he discovered his drip method. Such 1943 pictures as *The She-Wolf* and *Guardians of the Secret*, which have seemingly random abstract markings and remnants of mythological images, aren't altogether satisfying. There is something arbitrary about the various remnants; the pictures can feel like fake ruins. But the pictures contain, perhaps even more than his successful drip paintings, the point of Pollock's work. In them, Pollock resists the human—the easier—desire to make a coordinated, rhythmic thing; the pictures are so many stalemated battles between the wills to beauty and to ugliness.

Pollock has the same phantomlike presence in these Greenberg volumes. Greenberg never devotes too much space to Pollock; he merely "comes across" the painter as he goes from show to show. Yet Greenberg, who was thirty-four when he first began reviewing the artist, who was thirty-one, wants us to know that Pollock is the most important new painter anywhere, even when individual works fail. (It may take more courage for a beginning critic to praise a beginning and virtually unknown artist—at least, in the authoritative and fearless way that Greenberg did—than for that artist to paint the pictures.) It is a measure of the purity and intensity of Greenberg's desires for a new art that when he met that art in the flesh, so to speak, all he felt he had to say was, "You're it."

Greenberg's own achievement has the breadth, ambition, and worldliness of the finest Abstract Expressionist paintings. His work has similar limitations. Looking at a couple of Barnett Newmans, say, or Mark Rothkos, we can be awed, but a full show is monotonous. It is all the same thing. The Ab Ex story is, in part, how the American artist was determined to join, by one colossal leap, the ranks of the great Europeans. The American achieved it, but he created a facade of greatness; the Europeans' ideas were rethought and turned into a single "sign" or "look" or way of painting. Rothko, Newman, and the rest shove their power to us all at once; there seems to be little in reserve. Their emotions always vibrate at the highest pitch. If we are not on their wavelength, we feel nothing. Their power depends too heavily on the sheer size of their pictures. Van Gogh, Miró, Munch, Cézanne, Picasso, and Matisse—and Hartley—give us more to look at and think about; they have more different phases and moods within them.

The individual Ab Ex staked everything on One Idea; once he achieved that idea, he was, very often, locked into repeating himself. In the same way, Greenberg created a one-shot aesthetic, a way of judging art that, I think, left him dissatisfied with all art that wasn't on his track. He presented his sense of what was wrong with current art (and society) and how the situation could be fixed in the second and third essays he published, in 1939 and 1940. If he had written only those pieces, we would know precisely what he stood for. My impression of his work after 1949, when he gave up regular reviewing, is that his ideas about the way to a pure, significant art became all-consuming to him, and individual artists and works of art were reduced to illustrations.

II

In the fifties, sixties, and well into the seventies, Greenberg was a commanding figure for many artists, writers about art, museum people, and collectors. You see how magnetic he could be—especially in the first half of the fifties, when his ideas were still being discovered and Pollock and other new abstract painters were becoming known—in the work of Morris Louis, who was recently the subject of a retrospective at the Museum of Modern Art. It is hard to imagine Louis's art and career—he died in 1962, at forty-nine (of cancer)—without Greenberg. The critic was probably Louis's biggest supporter, and he gave Louis asked-for advice about various works. And Louis's large abstract paintings, which are made by pouring acrylic medium directly onto the canvas and then juggling and shifting the canvas to get the paint to go in the right places—Louis at work must have been a cross between a seamstress and a sail maker—were thought by Greenberg and others to extend the modern tradition of making art about the formal properties of art.

In the years after his death, Louis's reputation was high; every major American museum seemed to exhibit an example or two of his art. Lately, I think he has come to seem a thinner, more purely decorative painter, and the Modern's show was not a crowded event. These stained canvases ought to have a thin, periodish look, and Louis's work in general is not robust; but his finest work can make your chest pound. These pictures are called Veils, mostly because the abstract shapes resemble veils, and they express a sense of sheer physical monumentality—and a drifting, vaporous beauty—that is unlike anything in art. The paintings are generally ten feet or so on a side, and the veil images are clear-cut from yards away, yet the works are especially strong when, as at the Modern, a viewer is surrounded by many of them in a small, enveloping, intimate space. The Louis exhibition made me admire Greenberg more, and it also put an ironic twist on his writing. His goal was to revitalize the worldly, sensuous, and disillusioned art of the School of Paris, and yet, perhaps because he laid down the plans for this new cosmopolitan art so precisely, the work that was inspired by him reflects his powerful faith, not his literal goals. Louis's painting is in many ways a fulfillment of Greenberg's ideas, yet Louis is at his best a lyric, rhapsodic, even religious artist.

There are few biographical details about Louis, but from those details and his work, he is someone we feel we know. He was alternately capable of rash, all-or-nothing acts and of being too knotted up to push anything forward. Louis lived for most of his life in Baltimore and Washington, D.C. In the photo of him in the Modern's catalogue, he has shy, sensuous good looks, with glistening dark eyes and full lips. Like Pollock—they were the same age—he and his wife had no children. As a young man, he changed his name—he was born Morris Louis Bernstein—and he was a fanatic for work; when he became interested in a motif he made endless variations on it, yet he periodically destroyed quantities of his pictures. He was known to few people in the art world, and his working methods were a secret.

Louis became himself, as it were, one day in 1954, on a trip to New York. At this point he was an unknown painter in his early forties who was devoted to Matisse, Picasso, and the issues of modern art, but he was out of touch with the latest developments and had never seen an actual Pollock. One feels that he might have been desperate because, after more than twenty years of work, he had achieved virtually nothing, but that he might also have been proud to be an outsider and not merely another respectable artist with a respectable body of work. On that day, he met, among others, Greenberg and Franz Kline. They went to galleries, and Louis saw his first Pollocks. He, Greenberg, and the rest then spent five hours at Helen Frankenthaler's studio, where they discussed her painting *Mountains and Sea*. Then in her early twenties and seriously involved with the development of modern art, Frankenthaler made this abstract picture by letting the colors soak into the raw, or unprimed, canvas. Louis believed, as did Greenberg, that the future of advanced painting was this soaking or staining method. Louis went back to Washington with an idea of how he might alter the future of art.

Louis's early mature paintings — they were made around 1959 — are his best. They show veils or curtains of overlapping colors that seem to billow up from the bottom, or swoosh down from the top, of the canvas. Surrounding the swoosh of color on three sides is an irregular margin of ivory-white untouched canvas. The Veils recall mountains, geysers, waterfalls, forests, or whales rising out of the water — whales that loom over us. His pale purple, dark green, black, copper-orange, red-brown, and pale blue suggest the colors of the Pacific Northwest; the color is like some substance that, out of reach of the sun's rays, is always moist.

Louis's stain technique produces the softened and faraway look of something seen through a screen door, and, perhaps because we are aware of the painter's early death, the Veils have an air of muted tragedy. The small bit of ivory-white that surrounds the billowing colors, though, gives the pictures an unexpected taut quality. The white is like a border on a photograph or postcard; we might be looking at a close-up photo of a detail of an art nouveau vase that has been cropped in a too-close way and then blown up to a mammoth size. Seeing photos or postcards this enormous is disorienting and thrilling.

It is often said that Louis's art has nothing of his "personality" or "feelings." His paintings look the way they do because he chose a particular method of painting. His work is a forerunner (by some ten years) of Conceptual Art, which says that the artist's idea is itself the artwork, and of Process Art, which says that whatever comes from a predetermined way to use certain materials is the work of art. Yet Louis's best pictures hold us because they have an emotional resonance. The surfaces of his pictures are, literally and poetically, thin-skinned and defenseless. A Veil painting is an image of something cloaked and smothered and also of yearning. Exactly what Louis yearns for is not, of course, evident. Yet, knowing the circumstances of his life, one believes that, like Greenberg, his work has to do with the intertwining themes of a Jew's desire to be powerful in America and an American's desire to be powerful in relation to the great figures of the European past.

Louis is thought, in Greenberg's terms, to extend the tradition of master painters that goes back through Matisse to Delacroix and the rest. But Louis is the opposite of Greenberg's School of Paris masters. He is closer to a William Blake or a de Chirico—an artist whose work comes out of his head in a virtually complete state at one moment. Louis's working methods were a bit like Blake's. Louis made his enormous pictures in one of the two rooms of his and his wife's small Washington apartment. He didn't have the space to view and judge his pictures from a distance, and he lived to see very few of his canvases stretched. Once he perfected his stain technique, he made hundreds of pictures, and the majority were simply rolled up and put in a closet. He could have been, like Blake, a painter-writer hunched over a desk. And one imagines that Louis liked these working conditions. By temperament, he was a literary artist. "Modernism" or "formal qualities" for him were what mythological and historical beings were for Blake.

Louis's art declined after the Veils. In the work from his last few years he is a man with an idea about how to make pictures who isn't sure where to go with his idea. He made Furl paintings, where the stained colors—red, green, blue, yellow—are single lines that descend from the left and right sides to the bottom on otherwise empty, untouched, unprimed white canvas. The lines, which appear to drip down as you look at them, are like a few strands from a Pollock maze of drips that have been gigantically magnified and then neatly paired off to the left and the right of the canvas. The Furls are like images of vast Arctic valleys, and thinking about them and about the vibrant white parts of the Veils, one believes that Louis is essentially a painter of white—that he uses color as a way to shape and enhance the white, untouched part of the canvas.

Like Claude Lorrain landscapes, the Furls are pleasingly grand and empty. They are also obvious and picturesque, and Louis's other late work is glaringly obvious. Louis's last paintings are called Stripes; there are yellow, red, green, blue, or tan stripes, which are set—up, down, or at angles—on plain white, raw canvases. These paintings are tinny.

Louis's pictures became increasingly like products, and in this they are similar to the work of many artists Greenberg was associated with from the mid-fifties on: besides Louis and Helen Frankenthaler, such painters as Jules Olitski and Kenneth Noland, and numerous sculptors who made welded-steel pieces. My memory is that Greenberg didn't review these artists, as he had reviewed Chagall, Picasso, Pollock. Rather, in pieces that generally lacked the names of individuals, he wrote about the way art was supposed to, or not supposed to, develop. And it was clear that Olitski, Frankenthaler, and the rest were filling his orders.

Frankenthaler, especially in her early pictures, which have quietly scrumptious surfaces, is a good painter. She doesn't stun us, as Pollock and Louis do; her abstract pictures are about relations between colors, textures, lines, and shapes. Her colors and her various blots, swipes, and trailing brush strokes suggest branches and leaves being bent by the wind, or grasses waving in a marsh. She can remind us of the loveliness of a hidden moment or place in nature; but she is not, to use Greenberg's word, a "major" artist. Her shows are often dissatisfying; the pictures feel interchangeable. It's one handsome work after another. But Frankenthaler is frequently a pleasant surprise in group shows or museum collections, where her individual picture, which seems to be about artistic intelligence for its own sake, not only holds its own but enhances the other art in the room. Her work is an illustration of the artistic good manners that Greenberg, with his vision of great art as stemming from a brotherhood of Parisian dandies, believed was crucial to a "major" culture.

The other artists who followed Greenberg's precepts are far less satisfying. The work of these painters (whose abstractions are called Color Field) and sculptors (whose pieces recall David Smith) is Greenberg's comeuppance for believing that he could chart the direction of art. His desire for an emotionally damped-down and well-behaved formalist art was translated into pictures and sculptures that have little sense of struggle or of an inner life; they're faceless objects. His desire for a worldly and grandly impersonal art helped produce works that merely look expensive and are in "good taste."

Frank Stella is not as closely associated with Greenberg as are these others, but he reflects more of Greenberg's spirit. Greenberg is not an admirer of his, and Stella, in his recent *Working Space* (Harvard University Press), the book of his 1984–85 Norton Lectures at Harvard, spends much of his time refuting Greenberg. Stella says, in effect, "Look, the flatness thing, the reliance on the shallow space and pretty surfaces of modern French painting—it has failed. Those of us who believe in abstraction hit a high note in our art in the sixties, but by 1970 abstract art was in a rut and now it's moribund. What can we do?" Stella thinks that Morris Louis is admirable, and he notes that Frankenthaler and the rest were among the exciting painters of the sixties, but he is not warmed by the artists who followed Greenberg's lead. His best crack about their art is that it is "suburban." Stella never mentions Greenberg's name, which may be an intended joke. Perhaps Stella is also joking when he connects Bernard Berenson with the belief that modern art is characterized by shallowness, flatness, and an emphasis on the physical, material quality of art. Does any art writer have less to do with the development of modern art than Bernard Berenson? And does Stella know that Greenberg admires Berenson's work?

Stella is quietly desperate about the state of abstract art, but his situation is even emptier than he realizes because, while he talks a lot about art from the Renaissance through the sixties, he doesn't seem to know where art has gone since then. He continually worries about the "future," but he doesn't have the vaguest interest in how the genera-tion after his looks at art. He is really just talking to himself. His most vivid point is about the need for "space" in a painting, whether the work is abstract or representational, and his liveliest pages are the early ones, on Caravaggio, who is his hero. Stella loves the "real space" in Caravaggio's pictures and the way this painter makes every-thing clear and muscular, full of thrusts and theatrical, and (although Stella doesn't quite say this) emotionally simple.

Stella sets up Caravaggio, the original Pow! artist, as an alternative to Greenberg. But the only real difference between Stella and Green-berg is that Stella likes painting where you feel you can reach into the picture and put your hand behind what faces you and Greenberg likes painting where that doesn't feel possible. Otherwise, they both see art history as a single story—a struggle toward some goal—and they judge an artist less for his actual work than for how he "advances" the story.

And Stella, in his art, embodies Greenberg's exaggerated self-assurance. From shortly after college, Stella has made series after series of paintings, each somewhat different from, and seemingly a development on, the one before. (He does the same thing as a writer; he is quite a stylist, but he makes the same few points again and again, saying them a bit differently each time.) Stella's pictures are shrewd, energetic, and forceful; he has a passion for order. He is a sort of inventor-tycoon, like a Henry Ford or a Hollywood mogul of the thirties. His art is usually bracing, but it isn't moving or puzzling; it is always a more or less successful demonstration of a way to make a picture. It is fascinating that the central figure of his book is an Old Master painter, because Stella himself is the contemporary Old Master—the vigorous, no-nonsense, public-spirited decorator—that Greenberg as much as calls for.

Greenberg is a more complex creator than the artists who were influenced by him and than most of the artists who were his contem-poraries. He is the most arrogant of critics, yet his ideal artwork is a selfless thing. He is equally determined to glorify the idea of the grand, blandly impersonal artist and to show what is limited about the talented provincial; but he himself is neither. He is an in-between man. In the piece on Scholom Aleichem, there is a wonderful illustration of ambivalence about glory. "The Jews," Greenberg writes, "like cities, gregarious life, and the fluidities of commerce . . . at the same time they yearn to stop liking them."

There is a fearfulness and an uncertainty underlying Greenberg's criticism. His relentless concern with laws and the past and "tradition" is, in simpler terms, a concern with what will live. Greenberg's pieces seem to ask, "Will this artist be remembered?" He might be asking, "Will I be remembered?" He describes his own method when he says about Franz Kafka that he "weighs, ponders, and questions everything from many sides in the effort to establish certainties that will survive chance and history."

Greenberg says that Arnold Friedman's pictures embody "something of this age's abiding emotions: the sad remoteness of nature, the anonymity of cities, and the permanence of art." These are the abiding emotions of Greenberg's work.

—1987

VAN GOGH IN SAINT-RÉMY AND AUVERS

"VAN GOGH IN SAINT-RÉMY AND AUVERS," at the Met, is about the last year and a half of the painter's life, and is a disappointing show. One goes expecting that van Gogh will continue to be the great formal painter that he is in his work from Arles—from the year before this show begins. (The Met exhibited that work three years ago.) But his work from Saint-Rémy, where he lived in an institution, and Auvers, where he went for the last months of his life—he committed suicide at age thirty-seven—is dulled down, without strong feelings. You walk away with a sense that the work is mostly about shades of green, with a lot of gray and tan, and that the pictures as a whole are without light. If you have never seen a large group of van Goghs, you may be absorbed and impressed; he is one of the purest, most forceful artists in the history of art. This is brilliant work, in its way; but it isn't brilliant by his standards. The show is deflating; it is more a documentary than an art show.

Van Gogh continues to be an artist that society, at different times, will have different feelings about. For some time, especially during the period when "modern art" was at its height, his reputation was not so secure and high; he was a favorite more of the general audience than of artists, critics, or theorists. But especially in the past ten years or so, with the interest in images for their own sake, artists have been increasingly his most attentive and pleased audience. He has become, perhaps, the most important artist of his era—he is, I think, a more loved figure than Cézanne, Picasso, or Matisse.

The Met's Arles show was elating. Van Gogh seemed to go on and on, making one full scene after another. There were great portraits and pictures of wheat fields, of fields and towns seen from long distances, of backyard gardens, of public gardens and street life in Arles. There was a florid and atypical but amazing scene of a harbor, with the sky a streaky but luscious mess. The drawings were awesome; they had a wonderful erectness. Every stone and blade of grass seemed to be seen individually. In the paintings, every color seemed available to him; I particularly remember turquoise and yellow. He appeared to be totally reckless and totally in control. When he was in the midst of his streak in Arles, he wrote to his brother Theo that his mind was above all else "lucid." His small paintings of wheat fields were the finest works; the individual colors and strokes of paint were beautiful in the way that holy objects were thought to be beautiful.

The art of his last year and a half shows that van Gogh suffered something overwhelming around the time Gauguin came to Arles and then left. Van Gogh wrote to Theo shortly after, around the time that he went to the Saint-Rémy asylum, in May 1889, that "I have no *will*, hardly any desires or none at all," and in other letters he talks about his "indifference." His painting from about this time onward has a holding-operation quality. His handwritinglike style is in place, but the artist is warmed—touched, excited—by less and less. We see views of the corridors, his bedroom, and the garden at the asylum. There are pictures of fields, poplars, and olive groves. In Auvers—it is twenty miles outside Paris—he paints thatched roofs, the stones and streets of the town, gardens and fields. There are portraits from both places, and some are well known: a portrait of his friend Dr. Gachet, who was a friend of many artists; a picture of a girl with a bonnet sitting in a field; a self-portrait with a brilliant blue background—the painter turns to look at us from over his shoulder. There are also some very well-known landscapes from this period; this was the time he painted cypress trees and the famous *Starry Night*, in the collection of the Museum of Modern Art.

Some of the pictures are first-rate. A painting of irises in a garden, seen head-on, is powerfully constructed, and there are some strong scenes of a field with a distant wall. One, where the sun rises in the distance and we feel we're gliding over huge waves of earth, moving toward the sun, is monumentally sturdy. There is a striking small picture of a man and a woman walking by a cypress tree, toward sunset. It has a golden red and a wet blue-green; the work is postcard-ish—the colors are oversaturated. Yet it evokes a Mediterranean, Biblical feeling, and we sense that the man, who has a red beard, may be the painter.

The portrait of Trabuc, the asylum keeper, has a wonderful tan background; the man has a memorable white-and-brown-striped jacket, bulging forehead, and frown. It is a compact and dense work. Van Gogh said (about a year before he made the picture), "Ah! portraiture, portraiture with the thoughts, the soul of the model in it, that is what I think must come." Van Gogh invented the modern psychological and spiritual portrait, and *Trabuc* is one of the high points of his art. The lesser-known of the show's two self-portraits is also dense and strong. Van Gogh's head is somewhat flattened; his face and hair are an orange yellow, and the background is a soft grayed green. The combination of colors is fresh and unexpected and pleasant—exactly the qualities missing from most of these later works.

At this show, even the strong and well-known pictures are flattened out by the larger subject of van Gogh's enveloping sadness and lack of feelings; nearly everything seems far away and ungraspable and wan and uneventful. In the first works we see—drawings and watercolors from May, 1889—his touch is fuzzy and heavy. In the first large room at the show, which presents landscapes from June and July, there is already a preponderance of green, a lack of light, a sameness of color. Some of the views from a distance have a surprisingly conventional feeling and structure. The many paintings and drawings of a field with a wall have a masterful technique, but they feel like summations, presentation pieces. Especially if you have seen his earlier paintings of fields, these feel worked up. In the views of olive orchards and of the asylum grounds, there are a lot of smoldering, hot reds and purples and pale, dreary greens. One feels him groping, backtracking, experimenting. He often makes a sky of dashes or dots that zoom off, or he outlines a shadow cast by a tree in an orchard and then fills in this shadow-form with dots, so the orchard "floor" has an ornamental, patterned feeling. Van Gogh seems to anticipate much (somewhat later) turn-of-the-century art and design. These details were influential up through the First World War (and Stuart Davis and Miró made wonderful paintings in this style after the war).

One still loves the way van Gogh paints, yet these details, seen next to his Arles paintings, feel like devices. The asylum and orchard pictures don't seem to be about anything. The values in the paintings—the contrasts of light and dark—are photographic. These pictures have more life in reproduction, and the Met's catalogue—it is by Ronald Pickvance, who is also the curator—is more absorbing than the show. The pictures and the mostly biographical text, which includes many quotes from van Gogh's letters, fuel each other. The paintings and drawings and his muscular, forthright descriptions of what he was doing form a self-contained world. Going through the book, we don't care so much about the "quality" of the pictures. We enter a realm where the artist's products and life, taken together, are the work of art. Van Gogh is less the great French-type painter he wanted to be—the colleague of Delacroix—and more another kind of artist he admired: a cross between an artist and a novelist, an illustrator of a text that could change a reader's life.

When the show turns to Auvers, the overriding spirit is of hopeless-ness, a dead end. The town scenes are claustrophobic. The build-ings, the people, and the rocks seem to be collapsing. The colors are a jumble, cacophonous; he frequently uses a bright red that doesn't connect with any of its neighboring colors. He uses green more and more. His soul seems to be green. He is such a great poet that, even as you feel the emptiness of the pictures, you realize that he has made green the color of hopelessness. *Field with Poppies*, an oil, is so smudgy it is unbelievable. From one scene to the next, you feel him lurching. He makes attempt after attempt to grab something in the way of a motif. But each time he seems to lose faith as he works. One painting has an unfinished sky. We feel the labor of finishing that sky. We see what it is like to realize in advance that a picture will be inert when finished. He seems to look a lot at his contemporaries, particularly Monet and Renoir. There is a boating scene that is a redoing of Renoir. But boating scenes are not van Gogh's subject, and the figures are stiff, weightless. When he shows people on a street or in a field, they are often strange, waddling, deformed. The girl who plays at an upright piano and the girl who sits in the tall grasses are pasty faced, unattractive, unfelt as individuals.

One misses the heat and light, the bright, glowing colors—even the literal image of candlelight or gaslight—of the earlier work. Van Gogh doesn't paint the sun too often in his last year and a half; when he does, he is most convincing about the light it sheds when he paints a wet, hazy, purplish, late-afternoon light. Most of these scenes have no particular light. The famous *Starry Night* becomes the symbolic painting of his last period, in that when he painted these stars over a valley, he painted the last convincing real-life light he saw with power: light from stars and the moon in a night sky, light that gives off no heat.

The most experimental and, one can feel, psychologically truthful picture in the show is *Rain*. It isn't one of his very finest, but unlike most of these later pictures, it has a subject. This gray paint-ing is more like a detail from a screen, yet it feels complete. The slashes of rain seem to be right on top of the picture, and they give it its contemporary sense of surface. The Met's exhibition feels like this painting—a portrait of a mind on a gray, hopeless, rainy day.

The final room shows his last work. Each picture is done on two square canvases joined together. The very size—they're so many small Oriental screens—is appealing. But this room is disheartening. Almost each picture is another attempt to push into a different sort of painting. Sometimes the color is naturalistic. Sometimes it feels deliberately artificial; in a picture of hay ricks, he "styles" the color, so that everything has a blond tonality.

Does it make van Gogh any the less to feel that—at least, on the basis of this large selection—his late work has its core sucked out? No, because the sense of bleariness makes his earlier painting fuller. Van Gogh was in love with art and artists and the idea of a painter's life, but he valued being true to his instincts more. He couldn't turn out merely professional "van Goghs" for long. Perfecting and cultivating his invention—his handwritinglike style—was not enough for him.

—1987

JULIAN SCHNABEL

JULIAN SCHNABEL, IN HIS ART, REMINDS me of the character Jean Renoir played in his movie *The Rules of the Game*. Renoir was a lumbering and friendly man who was a confidant of most of the movie's other characters. They were the heroes and heroines; they had love affairs, aspirations, and disappointments, and he, often laughing, floated in and around them. The Renoir character was the spirit of "the rules of the game"—and he was also somehow bigger than "the rules." (He may be what people remember most about the movie.)

Julian Schnabel has the same ringmaster role in the current scene. And his work resembles the character Renoir played. Schnabel's best pictures have the same warmth and canniness—and effortlessness. They are surprisingly dainty. The new paintings he recently showed at the Pace Gallery are enormous "scenes" of people—or bloblike creatures, or cartoonishly drawn characters—in landscape settings. The paintings are like doodles, but doodles with the presence of Goya, Stubbs, Courbet. The colors—pink, emerald and dusty green, rust red—are instantly appealing, and the pictures have the slightly dry texture of frescoes. Seeing this show was like looking at *National Geographic* magazine the first time, when the photographs were fresh and the images transported you to an unfamiliar place for a moment. The exhibition was one of the best in New York in the last few years, comparable in sustained quality to David Salle's exhibitions in 1984 and 1985 and Anselm Kiefer's in 1982. Schnabel, who is thirty-five, is more sparing and precise than he has been before; the pictures make much of his earlier art seem raucous, busy, preparatory. His new pictures are the most serene and mysterious he has done, and, describing them, one believes that he is the most complex painter anywhere right now.

Schnabel is a literary painter. He's "literary" in the sense that his subject seems to be his desire to be one of the great artists—his first love is the enterprise of being a Master. His work doesn't translate into words easily because he doesn't have a clear tale to tell. He is known for painting on velvet and for affixing smashed cups and saucers, or antlers, to his canvases; but no themes or images come to mind immediately when one thinks of him. His paintings seem to show a realm where he re-creates the sensations he has received from art.

His new works ask to be "read," but we aren't sure of the meanings or of how the pictures are actually made. There are images of people or creatures—or a head—with barren, mountainous plains behind them. There are also close-up works, where we feel we're pressed up against a tree in a forest—and the forest is also a face at a window with Venetian blinds. In his catalogue essay, Wilfried Dyckoff mentions in passing that the pictures are painted on top of Kabuki backdrops, but the wall labels at the show and the captions in the catalogue say only that the paintings are "on muslin," so it's possible not to realize that

Schnabel has painted over something. If you are aware of the Kabuki backdrops, the situation stays pleasingly uncertain, because Schnabel has added his own elements in such subtle ways that you spend much of the time trying to decide what is from his hand and what was there already.

Where does the Kabuki backdrop end and Schnabel begin? He added the figures, faces, staring eyes, and bulbous shapes (they're like people wobbling in potato sacks). Did Schnabel paint the highlights on the bushes or the masses of white clouds? There is an oiliness to, say, a lick of silver on top of a tree branch—the silver must be Schnabel. But he is never too thick or oily. From being rolled up, the Kabuki backdrops have become cracked and creased, and these lines are now part of the work. They're like bits of lacy drawing. Schnabel's pictures ask to be seen from inches away.

There is a twist to each picture: as you move from what you think Schnabel added to what you think was already there, you are given the sense of going "down into" another layer. The paintings seem to be about having a second awareness of something and, too, imagery for its own sake. The pictures might be called Association Machines. As we look, we feel that images from contemporary and older art, primitive art, movies, and photographs are forming and then dissolving. Schnabel is not an appreciator of popular culture; he doesn't want his pictures to ironically comment on movie-screen images, as Alex Katz's paintings often do. Schnabel's relationship to movies is that the different elements in his paintings go in and out of each other the way images flow by in a movie. His best pictures have a thump, a heartbeat; they are "alive" the way a movie screen is alive.

The Kabuki association ought to make the works feel Japanese, but the "plains" pictures might be of the pampas or the steppes of Central Asia. The creatures and the paintings' lonely, exotic, and faraway mood can remind you of children's books. The rounded shapes and curling lines and warm, full colors and overall matte quality recall Bemelmans, Babar, and *Le Petit Prince*. One thinks, too, of van Gogh's preoccupation with Japanese prints—his inserting them in the backgrounds of some pictures. Miró, working in van Gogh's spirit, put Japanese prints in the background of some of his early portraits and used startling candy-bright colors, and Schnabel, with his pinks and mossy light greens, seems to bring together van Gogh and Miró. Some of Schnabel's bulbous, potato-sack people recall the curvy "characters" in Elizabeth Murray's paintings. One feels the presence of the late Joseph Beuys. Schnabel often uses a blood, or rust, red, a color that one associates with Beuys, and *Rebirth III*, which shows batterylike boxes floating here and there in a predominantly pink, springtime forest, is a memorial to the West German performance artist and sculptor (who used batteries in some of his sculptures). *Rebirth III* is like a flowing, rococo doodle on a colossally large ad for a Japanese plum wine. Schnabel seems to be looking, too, at Francesco Clemente, the Italian painter who lives and works in India for part of each year, and who has made pictures vaguely like Schnabel's on a floppy cheesecloth. Clemente's "Indian" paintings are like appreciations of the stiff, primitive quality of some Third World posters. Clemente is more of a virtuoso and a charmer than Schnabel.

One doesn't want to describe and characterize Schnabel's new pictures in too much detail because that would stamp them with a particular story line, and that isn't their spirit. I don't think that I am ruining them, though, by saying that they resemble family or couple portraits, or self-portraits. In *L'Amour: Carmen Iris Rivera*, it isn't necessary to know the title to sense that the picture is about sexuality and shows a couple. The leading "characters" are a black shape and an iris. The black shape suggests a penis—it recalls one of those billowy, about-to-spring shadows in a Munch—and has the word "Cheri" written on it in white. The iris might be Cheri's "lady." There is a square cross painted over part of "her" in a Beuys red, and a hangman's noose, drawn in the same red, is next to the flower. The iris, the noose, and Cheri float over the Kabuki setting, which shows some low buildings in the distance—it is a bright but overcast day. With its festive, yet also drab and forlorn, backlot setting, the picture recalls a particular moment. We're reminded of a wedding portrait by Henri Rousseau, a carnival scene from a thirties French movie, a Bill Brandt photograph of British life (in its ominous moods) between the wars.

Schnabel carries with him the air of refreshing new possibilities and of extremely traditional aspirations. It is as though he were the most unconventional and also the most family-minded guy on the block. His appearance roughly coincided with the Museum of Modern Art's 1980 Picasso show, when the entire museum was filled with aspects of Picasso's art. The show was the poetic curtain raiser on art in the current period. The exhibition was less about the beauty or complexity of individual pieces than the excitement, glamour, and sheer stamina involved in a life in the arts. Picasso's greatest gift may be the sense of freedom his each individual work conveys, and his anarchic temperament needed to be let into current art. Schnabel, it seems, was one of the products of the Modern's show.

Schnabel's original importance was that he said no to the official spirit of American art from the days of the Abstract Expressionists onward. He seemed to stand for a release from the crucial need for purity that one felt had been in every style from the forties onward, including Pop Art. The best Pop works, which are the early ones, are formalist pictures; their power comes from a lean, raw, unfinished, rush-job texture. Schnabel was hardly the first to bring back the figure—it had never gone away—or to make pictures that had a shaggy Expressionist surface texture or a mysterious, storytelling flavor. But Schnabel's pictures have always expressed a formula-less consciousness.

Schnabel's new pictures are the most resolved and assured examples of a way of seeing space that has developed in the past few years. Space in painting now has a particularly optical, flip-flop, one-two effect; we find ourselves reading pictures (and sculptures) for two images, a foreground and a background, and the pleasure of the works is in feeling the ambiguous, never-settled issue of which layer is top and which bottom. Even when there aren't literally two layers, we feel that there is a relationship between the surface and the "inside." Schnabel's new pictures show that many of the distinctions being made between the Neo-Expressionist art of the first half of the eighties, which used the figure (and included work by himself, David Salle, Clemente, and Anselm Kiefer), and a cooler, drier art being made by artists who have just begun to exhibit (including Philip

Taaffe's takeoffs on Op Art), are manufactured. There are more similarities than differences. Whether recent art appears to be about sex, the Second World War, or the nineteen-fifties, or whether it reworks earlier geometric art—or is a deadpan-straight photograph of a detail of a painting—there is often a sense that the surface is membrane-thin and that it covers a hollow inside. With much art of the past seven to ten years, one feels that things are being done over, that there is no forward momentum, but, rather, a sense of return, a falling back on something. The strength of the art is in the way it rejects now-conventional ideas of forwardness and newness. Recent art is new in the way it says, "I will feed on myself; I will turn backward."

Schnabel's Kabuki paint-overs match, in spirit, three recent (or fairly recent) movies: *Blue Velvet, Pee-wee's Big Adventure*, and *True Stories*. In these movies, some (or all) of the characters seem to be living puppets. The movies have the spirit of performance art. A viewer feels that something obvious or dumb is being relived, and in the reliving the material takes on the qualities of a ballet or opera—a dreamy, compelling ballet or opera. There is something potent about mime right now—not the formal art of mime, but a new use of it. It can be lip synching to a song, which happens in *Blue Velvet* and *True Stories;* but *Blue Velvet* and *Pee-wee* each feel like one big synch, or imitation, and so does much new painting and sculpture.

The patron Old Master painting of this deliberately neutered spirit is Watteau's *Pierrot*. (It was at the National Gallery in 1984 at the Watteau exhibition.) Watteau shows a member of a theatrical troupe who wears all white; he stands looking at us while, behind him, various actors talk and turn their heads this way and that. Ignoring or chatting about him, they lend an ominous note to the picture. We see Watteau's man as a limp, bland, acquiescent, yet somehow prepossessing, soul. We imagine that his artwork is "being himself." Everything that Pee-wee does—and that the characters do in *Blue Velvet* and that the narrator does in *True Stories*—also has quotes around it. The characters in these movies are walking works of art.

Schnabel, by temperament, is a feisty contender, not a Pierrot or a

Pee-wee. But Schnabel's pictures are imitations, too. It's as if he were doing a lifelong performance piece called "The Artist." We see and feel him painting on the Kabuki backdrops; we can't help but think about where he found them, when it occurred to him to paint on them. He is a bit like the painter on TV talk shows who says, "Give me a subject, and I'll make a painting of it before your eyes." Schnabel wants to keep improvising before us, and he wants to be as surprised, mystified, and pleased by what comes out as we are.

Schnabel's new paintings recall—they might be called developments of—two wonderful earlier works. One is Klee's *Villa R*, where Klee painted a capital letter R "over" his painting of a dark storybook scene of a mountain village. The other is Miró's *Portrait of a Man in a Late Nineteenth Century Frame*, where the artist took a portrait of a bearded man, which came complete with an ornamented wood frame, and painted "Mirós" in bright colors over, and scraped away areas of, the original. There is a childlike aggressiveness to these Klee and Miró pictures (they are among the most contemporary in feeling of their paintings). Schnabel, it can seem, is building a body of work out of the same sense of artist's license. His art involves an audacity, a violence, a violation of some material. With almost every show he has had, we find ourselves talking about what he is trampling on now. He could be slathering oil paint on top of velvet, pony skin, or an Oriental rug, or he could be breaking crockery, gluing it to canvases, and painting around and over it. He can make us think of oil paint as a besmirching substance and of the act of painting as a desecration. Yet when his pictures succeed, as so many do in this recent show, we forget about desecration. We feel he has saved something.

Schnabel's pictures have been most compared with David Salle's. Salle, too, plays off one disparate texture, image, or style against another. These painters appeared on the scene around the same time, and they have stayed the foremost new artists of the eighties. It can seem as if neither would make the strides that he does if he didn't have the other to compete with. Each painter seems to work for the other. (One can see Picasso's art and Matisse's art—after each man's time of experimentation—as a single two-sided creation.) The big difference between Salle and Schnabel is tone. Salle appears to be involved with the "associations" he elegantly syncopates: the images of women, the examples of different art and design styles. Schnabel, half of the time, barely seems to know what he is throwing into his stew. Yet Salle, the connoisseur, doesn't seem to believe in what he gives us (this sense of simultaneous appreciation and detachment is his special note). Schnabel, on the other hand, seems to believe in everything he puts on canvas—simply because he put it there.

There is a memorial quality to Schnabel's work. The new picture with the most gravity to it may be *Adieu Battista*. It didn't quite go with the others at the recent show, and was hung in a separate room. Schnabel has taken what might be a tent siding from a circus—it is an announcement for Charlotte the Two-Headed Girl. Charlotte appears in a bikini on a beach. Painted over the image are some large capital letters, which don't spell anything, and a six-sided star. Schnabel has let the paint dribble. The picture, shown in its own space, had the presence of a diorama at the Museum of Natural History or of an image from a movie screen that we felt we could walk into. The picture takes us back to the European past; we are at a freak show at a Gypsy circus, or in a city where thugs have put a Jewish star on the window of a store in the middle of the night. The letters are like a grille, or part of a cage, behind which is a monster—Charlotte. Yet the circus "original" is in pleasing red, yellow, and earth colors, and the picture casts the tawny glow of a gaslit interior. Did Schnabel add the green on top of the seaside rocks or the pink on the clouds? These patches of color are delicious in themselves. *Adieu Battista* is both an image of imprisonment and an invitation to go into a warm world.

—1987

JOE ZUCKER'S NEW WORK

JOE ZUCKER'S NEW PAINTINGS are probably the best he has done. They make you want to look again at his last ten years of work; perhaps, after these new pictures, his work of the past seven or eight years will seem less larky, less self-consciously ugly and vaguely commercial. Most of the new pictures refer to the sea. We look at pirates; Moby-Dick and Captain Ahab; Captain Kidd; an old sailing boat anchored; an ancient boat in a squall; an octopus; a modern boat floating quietly; a seaside sunset. There are also some still lifes. Some of the pictures are in black and white, but the better ones have many colors. There are yellows, oranges, greens, a brilliant reddish orange. The chief thing about the pictures, though, is how they're made; they're amazing objects. Zucker is, among other things, an American carpenter-artist, a superb but not fussy craftsman on the order of the late H. C. Westermann.

Zucker's pictures have always been largely about how they were made. He has generally worked in series, with each series made in a different way. His most vivid paintings up until now were done with wads of cotton. In those paintings—they're his best-known work, and the finest are from the mid-seventies—Zucker dipped the cotton into different colors and then glued the soaked wads onto canvas. You'd see a Mississippi paddleboat or windmills or old-time airplanes, but you'd be aware primarily of this dry yet gloppy surface. These pictures look better with time. They have interesting subdued colors; there are dirty whites, pale greens, sepia tans, bluish grays. The pictures recall Seurat. Like his, their subject is public, outdoor, fairground life, and with their manufactured, objectlike appearance they have the true spirit of that life.

The new works are more complicatedly made than those mid-seventies pictures (but they may be no more complicated in spirit or achievement). Zucker uses massive wood frames. He strings sash cord in a grid pattern through each frame—some of the units are squarish, some narrow and skinny. Then, with a thick, plastic-looking acrylic, he paints between the lines of the grids made by the sash cords. That is, there's no canvas. He "paints in" his scenes as if he were making a quilt or a hooked rug. He makes a kind of spider's web between each grid. His performance is a sort of tightrope act. You think you're looking at one big complex weaving. Instead of being fuzzy and textilelike, though, the surface is like frosting on a cake; there is a faintly repellent yet also likable laminated, waxy, ropy, living-and-dead quality. There's a note of ghastly artificiality to the surface. The pictures are to oil paintings (and hooked rugs and quilts) as artificial limbs or hands are to the real items.

Zucker's earlier cotton-ball paintings are fakes, too—that is, they can look like flimsy approximations of oil paintings. Their surface mimics and mocks "a rich surface." The paintings are, to a degree, parodies of the paintings that you win at a booth at a carnival if you hit the duck. The new sash-cord paintings are also parodies in part; at least, they recall some sort of limited-edition wall relief—lobby art for a posh seaside hotel. Zucker's images themselves have a nice degraded quality; his sunsets seen through trees and his old-time sailing vessels feel borrowed but not stale. The images take us into the world of sub-popular art—not of sophisticatedly drawn cartoons but of images on place mats in family seafood restaurants. Zucker's entire body of work, I have a hunch, is about kinds of fakeness, of simulation, and yet, at least with the cotton-ball pictures and the new sash-cord works, his irony is not heavy-handed. His art isn't merely shrewd or wry.

Zucker's sash-cord pictures at first seem silly, amusing, mechanical. Later, a viewer is stumped by imagining the process of their creation and then exhausted by imagining the sheer amount of labor that goes into each one. We admire Zucker for his patience and care, and we're made restless by thinking of the hours of painstaking labor that go into each work. Mostly, though, we are impressed by how he brings together so many unlikely elements to arrive at his finished work. And the experience of a picture is of something layered and see-through, and constantly changing. Zucker's finest paintings remind us of many things at once: cartoons; hooked rugs that have been assembled as if they were stained-glass windows; the elegant silhouette art of the early nineteenth century; computer graphics. Computer graphics are felt in the stepped, ridged appearance of the outlines. Looking at Zucker's pictures, we fall into a reverie about artistic process. How does he decide which part will resemble a hooked rug made in monochrome, or which part will resemble a hooked rug pure and simple? The best paintings seem to present many separate layers vibrating gently in a shallow space.

Joe Zucker has been showing for years. He has been in countless theme shows, and he has had a number of museum exhibitions. He is a hardworking member of that generation of American artists—it includes Joel Shapiro, Scott Burton, Chuck Close, Nancy Mitchnick, and Susan Rothenberg—who came up under the reign of Minimalism and Process Art. They have always seemed to be an interim generation. They wanted to bring recognizable imagery back into art, and they wanted us to feel that the images they used were arbitrarily chosen—the image could be anything. The art of these painters and sculptors—their work was labeled "New Image"—is tense, cerebral; it is sometimes more amusing and charming in effect than it perhaps wants to be.

Zucker's new pictures make him seem a more significant artist than one had thought. The pictures share qualities with some of the better work of the splashier and more reckless artists who followed the New Image people. I am sure that the best sash-cord paintings would stand up with first-rate David Salles and Julian Schnabels, and with first-rate work by older artists: Lichtenstein, Katz, Johns. Putting a Zucker alongside work by artists who are younger and older than he is, one sees American art of the past twenty-five years as an ongoing tale about irony and fakery, about feeding off popular art, about the worship of formalism and craft. Put a top Zucker alongside a good early sixties Lichtenstein and a good Salle (and so forth) and one is right back in the world of Hemingway versus Fitzgerald, of American art as an arena of flabless and well-trained pros whose art objects, whether novels or paintings, have surfaces as tight as a drum skin.

Looked at in one way, American painting from the late fifties and early sixties on is at its best a series of ingenious and marvelous recreations of already-existing images.

The special flavor of Zucker's pictures—the cotton balls and the sash cords—has to do with their fuzziness, color, and light. They're images that, as you look, come into focus. Some of the strongest recent pictures have a flushed, overvivid colorfulness that reminds me of Albers and TV commercials. It is a kind of orange upon orange. The Ahab picture has a somewhat bilious and ashen colorlessness which is actually quite attractive; it is like the pearly tone of old Dutch seascapes. It is appealingly tart. Zucker's technique re-creates the filtered, ever-changing light that you see near the ocean.

—*1987*

POET OF THE DANCE

EDWIN DENBY HAS A PARTICULAR tone of complex innocence and directness. In his essays and reviews about dance and ballet, which have been collected in *Dance Writings* (Knopf), he is both charming and unexpectedly invigorating. Denby often writes a kind of sentence in which the words do not coincide immediately with the larger meaning; you think you know where he is going in a sentence, but his meaning is somehow stronger than the words themselves. Many of the pages in this hefty book are only mildly interesting; you read with little desire to mark a passage. Yet you develop a taste for Denby's trim, Spartan, unostentatiously silky style and his odd, stimulating phrases. You keep reading *Dance Writings* in order to encounter the next one.

Edwin Denby was a poet, reviewer, and essayist. His father was a diplomat, and Edwin was born in China. He went to Harvard. He did a variety of theater work in Germany in the twenties, and performed with Cläre Eckstein. By the mid-thirties he was writing about ballet and dance in New York. His busiest period as a dance reviewer was the forties, and his best pieces come from that time. He brought out two collections of dance writing: *Looking at the Dance* (1949) and *Dancers, Buildings and People in the Streets* (1965). He also brought out some volumes of poetry and a novel. Denby took his life in 1983, at the age of eighty. He was a slim and nicely proportioned man with an old, faraway look in his eyes. In appearance, he suggested characters from Shakespeare. One felt, This is Hamlet in his later years, with a bit of a jester and a courtier thrown in.

Virtually all of Denby's work on ballet and dance, including pieces he did not publish, has been brought together in *Dance Writings*. It is an unusually attractive large paperback with informative essays by the editors, Robert Cornfield and William MacKay. The work re-produced on the cover is a black and tan Man Ray picture, *Silhouette* (1916), of stylized dancers. It is a modern—and a sweet and invit-ing—version of a Greek vase painting, and it is a good choice for Denby, because he makes a classical, formalist aesthetic sweet and inviting, too. The large story he tells is about, as he puts it, the "deprovincialization" of American ballet and dance. Denby wants to show how America's contribution to a world-class dance art is a certain stimulating blankness, emptiness, optimism, sense of space. But he lays down no rules; he doesn't say that a significant dance art ought to look like this and not that. He leaves you with a gently liberating sense that an art of high style can appear in any shape or form.

Denby uses the biggest, most obvious and hackneyed words of praise over and over. Ballets, music, sets, and performers are "inter-esting," "very beautiful," "extremely brilliant," "pleasing," "very nice," "pleasant," "happy." A work is "sincere." The audience "sincerely" feels a ballerina's art. Denby isn't ironic. He admires these public words. He can sound as if he's parodying the oh-so-polite gentleman reviewer. His politeness and old-fashioned courteousness and his appreciation of good manners and properness ought to make him seem musty. But he is, rather, driving. His words leave us with a sensation of being energized and thrust forward (when he admires a piece or a performer), or of being robbed, or pulled back (when he describes someone or a piece that doesn't succeed).

For someone whose knowledge of and appreciation for dance is small and who has been drawn to Denby out of an interest in his considerable reputation and a love for criticism in itself, reading him produces the same experience as ballet or dance. A typical Denby piece is gleaming, avid, smiling, always "up." The aggressive part of Denby is the way he refuses to be conventionally probing. His tone is one of resolve. It is there in any single sentence. It is like the attitude of goodness, lovingness, and appreciativeness that a child wishes to adopt toward his parents and the world after he has done something for which he feels embarrassment or even shame (and that probably no one knows about except himself).

In Arlene Croce's dance criticism the word rhythms are dancelike, too, but different; her rhythms are sensuous, slowly swirling, occasionally labyrinthine and hard to follow. Croce and Denby complement each other. She writes, in a sense, as the star and the love object of a ballet; she registers things that happen to her as she moves through space. She is the passive center of the story. Denby writes, as it were, as the darting, efficient, and faceless male who keeps attending to the woman who is the center of the story.

In his introduction to an earlier Denby book, Frank O'Hara compared Denby to Lamb and Hazlitt. (O'Hara's introduction is reprinted in *Dance Writings*.) Denby is not another Hazlitt. Hazlitt is impatient, reckless, vehement, passionate. There is a connection, though, between Denby and Lamb; they write with a similar temperamental distaste for the self-important man and gesture. There is a similar underlying sense of forlorn isolation in them, and they want to make us more aware of the group act—they like situations where one ego is not lording it and there is a friendly concert of voices. Denby might also be compared to the Swiss writer Robert Walser, whose most compelling work (of the small amount of his work that has been translated into English) is the novel *Jakob von Gunten*. Jakob tells his own story. It's about a school for butlers that he attends in Germany in the years before the First World War. He's a bit of a bad boy, but he genuinely wants to be a good servant, to be "small" and anonymous. We don't always know how to take what he says, but he isn't simply a charmer or a pip-squeak or a little saint. He has a weird and powerful and somewhat sad voice.

Denby's early work was for the bimonthly magazine *Modern Music*. Then, from the fall of 1942 to the fall of 1945, he wrote extensively for *The New York Herald Tribune*. There are more than two hundred pages here from those *Trib* days. He must have worked like a dog. He clearly loved the idea of writing for a big daily, and his bosses must have been surprised and pleased by his clarity, good humor, and stamina. Reading these reviews, you can see why his writing career didn't go on forever; these few years of hard work compress what for most critics would be a lifetime of work. (Denby says, in another place, that the war years saw a flowering of ballet and dance in New York.) He's always the modest reporter first. He doesn't show off his learning. In an indirect way, though, he has a large, husbanding voice. He's educating the American public on how to look at and appreciate ballet, dance, and movement in general. There's something quietly great about the way he goes out and gently scrutinizes ballroom dancers, ice skaters, the Rockettes, ballet dancers at the opera, modern dance, the role of management, individual stars, performers at the circus, and serious contemporary ballet.

Denby's descriptions have a wonderful period flavor. They bring back the tone of America in the forties. I mean the sweet, innocent, corny America of the war years—the image of boys and girls at a soda fountain.

Denby has to be read carefully; he slips in observations that other writers would clear a lot of space for. He says that a flamenco dancer "always seems to have more expressiveness than he needs for a gesture, a kind of reserve of it. . . ." Talking about tap dancing, he says that "in taps you see and hear two different rhythms, both of them in the same strict musical meter. In ballet you often look at a free meter and listen to a strict one." A Gypsy dancer, Denby notes, can "go into or come out of a dance without embarrassment."

About Martha Graham, whom he greatly admires, Denby says, "You watch her as intently as if you were perturbed." Her *Punch and the Judy* has "the general air of middle-class self-importance and nervous activity." George Balanchine's *Mozartiana* is "as full of personal life as an ancient town on the Mediterranean on a holiday morning in the bright sun." Sonja Henie, the ice skater, "doesn't make her numbers express any more interesting emotion than ease." He says that her skaters "leap correctly and oddly, they skate clumsily and delicately, and you see the point of the difference."

Here is Denby on Frederick Ashton, in 1939: "He derives too, it seems to me, from the kind of awkward and inspired dancing that young people do when they come back from their first thrilling ballet evening and dance the whole ballet they have seen in their own room in a kind of trance. The steps do not look like school steps (though they are as a matter of fact correct); they are like discoveries, like something you do not know you can do, with the deceptive air of being incorrect and accidental that romantic poetry has."

About stage decor, Denby says something childlike, direct, unarguable, and startling. "The reason easel painters are better designers for ballet than anyone else," he writes, "is that they are the only craftsmen professionally concerned with what keeps pictures alive for years on end. When they know their trade they make pictures that hold people's interest for hundreds of years, so making one that will be interesting to look at for twenty minutes is comparatively easy for them."

I think that Denby's greatest sentence is this: "It seems to me that Offenbach's humor, like Mozart's, is poised on the suggestion that false love and true love are not as different as one might wish; they are both of them really tender." Denby's perception seems like the sort that a dance writer more than another kind of critic would have, because dance often strikes us as the most unreal art. Denby himself says that dance is the most unreal art. His sentence presents the formalist's creed in a novel way. You have to agree with this point or disagree with it. You may find yourself more willing to accept it than you thought you would be.

Over the years Denby's writing lost its edge. His later work will be of interest primarily to dance lovers. From the early fifties until the mid-sixties, when he more or less stopped writing about dance altogether, Denby wanted primarily to record his impressions of Balanchine's development. A long section on this choreographer in *Dance Writings* is relatively tedious and a letdown. As Denby sees him, Balanchine embodies the ideas and ideals about dance and human behavior that Denby most believes in. Describing Balanchine's art, Denby might be describing his own values and his own writing style. Balanchine is the hero of the story that Denby tells in his reviews as a whole. Balanchine is the happy, brilliant, solidly professional, airy, and intuitive genius and courtier that Denby's ideas lead toward.

In articles and notes on Balanchine up through the early fifties, Denby is radiant, too. Balanchine's ballet *Cotillon*, Denby wrote in 1941 (to take one of many standout passages),

> profoundly affected the imagination of the young people of my generation. It expressed in a curiously fugitive and juvenile movement the intimacy, the desolation, the heart's tenderness and savagery, which gave a brilliant unevenness to our beautifully mannered charm. The thirties had not only a kind of Biedermeier parochialism, they had also insight into the eternity of a moment of grace. We are all out of them now, and it is strange to see now that what we then believed is still as true and absorbing in itself as any subsequent discovery.

The last sentence is Denby at his best; you expect that he'll glide home in a minor key, but instead he delivers a flip that makes you see a number of things differently.

There are solid perceptions and beautiful descriptions here and there in Denby's work from the fifties and sixties. There's a serene piece on how to look at Kabuki theater that you may want to reread as soon as you have read it. But Denby in general seems depleted, grayed. He gives us too much plain, straightforward description of stage action.

As Denby aged, he seemed to want to take his thoughts about dance and movement into a wider terrain. He writes about stage movement and informal movement—a girl walking in a street, a dog bounding in a field. These later pieces have a philosophic, by-the-fireside tone. One feels he's taking dance criticism to some wonderful, fully ripened realm. Denby's "big" pieces ought to be the fulfillment of his criticism. But this writing is similar to Balanchine's later art—that is, the Balanchine that some of us first began to see in the early seventies. Denby is fluid, but what you are left with is a sort of restructuring of air. I think you have to be psyched up for the experience and that your relation to it is like that of an intellectual who is wrapped up in baseball; you're as conscious of yourself as an appreciator as you are of the spectacle itself.

That Denby gradually lost his spindly power doesn't dilute one's feeling for his work in general. He belongs in the company of the many wonderful American critics of the time: Jarrell, Greenberg, Blackmur, Agee, and the rest. Denby's voice is fainter and softer than theirs, but his subject doesn't lend itself to the same discussion of ideas and textures. He doesn't pretend that dance is another form of a Tolstoy novel. His criticism operates on the same set of rules as ballet or dance. His subject is a serious, thoughtless, youthful, perfect bodily expression. A great dance conveys a sense of unlimited and joyous physical power filtered through a great deal of unobvious training. Nijinsky's *Diary* is one of the best places to absorb, through the momentum of the words themselves, the way a dancer can feel superhuman strength coursing through a beautifully balanced body. Denby very often conveys the same clean strength.

—1987

POET-DECORATOR

ZURBARÁN IS A superb painter of passages of a single color—when a white robe, say, creases this way and that. These passages have an impacted, damped-down, yet also organic and quietly voluptuous quality; they're like cream cheese sculpted in low relief. Most Americans, I think, discover Zurbarán on their own, in a single picture— often of a monk or a saint—in a museum. You generally know little about this seventeenth-century Spanish painter, and you need to see only one picture to become an admirer, because he gives oil paint a special, dulled-down glow. The surprise of Zurbarán's exhibition at the Met is that there isn't a lot more to his art than those special passages. There are a number of fine pictures and many delectable details here and there—a cape, a flower—but the show is like a mausoleum. The pictures aren't emotional; they send no particular message. Many of the faces in Zurbarán's pictures are surprisingly realistic—they seem like portraits. But there is no inner life to the faces. At the end of the show, you may feel that it never quite began.

Francisco de Zurbarán (1598–1664), who worked primarily in Seville, then Spain's wealthiest city, is known for religious paintings, particularly of martyrs. The Met's show—it is the first comprehensive show of his work in this country—is full of pictures of monks and nuns, Christs, saints, and Madonnas. Little is known about Zurbarán beyond some bare documentary details. Most of his paintings were commissioned by monasteries and churches and by individual patrons as devotional pictures. In his early years, Zurbarán had more orders than he could handle, and he produced pictures with the help of a workshop. In his later years, when he was not as much in demand, he made religious paintings for export to the American colonies. He was a lifelong friend of Velázquez, the painter of the royal court, in Madrid, and went there himself, but he did little work in the city. It was once assumed that Zurbarán was destitute when he died, but it now seems that at the end he was mostly alone—he outlived the fashion for his work, and he outlived two of three wives and most of his children.

Zurbarán is often described as the foremost painter of the grave and ascetic current of Spanish religious art, but he is the subject of a Met show, I believe, because many have felt that, especially in his early work, he has a modern sensibility. In the subdued way he presents people and in the emphasis he gives to paint for its own sake, his name is often linked with Manet (who was crucially influenced by Spanish painting), and there are real similarities. They both place impassive figures against bare yet not quite empty backgrounds, and Manet, too, gives oil paint a matte polish. But in Manet the blank expressions reverberate; Manet looks at people with the same no-comment intensity with which he looks at clothes. For Zurbarán, there is rarely any connection between the lovingly painted details and all the rest. We miss a sweeping, personal, Zurbaranesque way of seeing people.

Looked at in a large show, Zurbarán isn't an artist whose vision could only be appreciated long after his death. He comes across, rather, as a painter who had certain masterly formal talents and so caught the attention of his society, which demanded religious paintings. And when he made those paintings he seems to have been partly excited, but mostly winging it. Zurbarán isn't the monumental or touching artist we had imagined. At his infrequent best, though, he is a gentle and odd creator. He is a kind of poet-decorator. He is placid and intent—and chic—all at once.

There are a number of charming and elegant pictures of female saints. Each shows a woman standing alone in a darkened area, rather like a sentry in a sentry box. There is a mixture of a costume-party artificiality and an aloofness to these imaginary portraits of St. Lucy, St. Casilda, and the others. They're the only pictures that give a real sense of the texture of Spanish life in the early seventeenth century, when Spain was a world power (and when its power was slipping fast).

The women are like geisha. Some are a bit shy, and look down or peer out at us; they incline their heads or torsos slightly. They seem to be picking up their long skirts and gliding by as we look at them.

St. Margaret has the most forceful personality. She doesn't glide. She is planted before us in her sandals, a staff in hand. She wears a curved straw hat (it is mesmerizing on its own) and a big vest, and she has a striped cloth bag (another amazing detail) over her arm. At her feet is a snarling dragon, the creature associated with her martyrdom. (She was swallowed by a dragon but cut her way out with a little cross.) With her traveling equipment, and holding a book, Margaret seems as if she's about to set off on a strenuous walk. She might be an intrepid young lady explorer with a guidebook or diary. And the painting, made when Spain was the world's leading colonial power, might be taken as an emblem of national pride and superiority.

Zurbarán's female saints aren't a revelation. They have been admired for a long time. And they aren't towering masterpieces. At the show, set in and among Biblical scenes and pictures of church personalities, they melt into the crowd. They would look much better if they were set alongside certain twentieth-century works—Mondrian's *Broadway Boogie Woogie*, say, or Brice Marden's panel pictures—where a few colors bounce off each other rhythmically. The Zurbaráns are about one sublimely presented color and texture—skirt, vest, blouse, cape—placed next to another. Looking at these pictures, we're reminded that Zurbarán painted for monasteries, for we fall into a meditative mood as our eyes travel from a white sleeve to a gray skirt to a red cape to some pale pink and violet flowers. The effect is like seeing the pleats of a balloon slowly shifting in the wind.

There are passages in other paintings, when Zurbarán paints a white dove, sheep, or flower, that compare in quality with these saints' pictures. He is a matchless painter of white. Zurbarán's distinctive note is to set things before the viewer as if on a platter. He can't compose deep into space, with elements overlapping. The paintings that show overlapped space are a mess; they're airless and flat, like theater backdrops. It makes sense that, in formal terms, his most resolved picture is a still life. This is *Still Life: Lemons, Oranges, and a Rose*. It presents what the title says; the fruit and flower are laid out on a shelf, with a plain dark background. (The picture, in the collection of the Norton Simon Museum, in Pasadena, is not in the show or illustrated in the catalogue.) There is a still life of jugs and a cup in the Met's show, but it is dull compared with the Pasadena picture, which is majestic. There isn't an ambiguous underlying story to the Pasadena picture, as there can be with some still lifes. It is merely a powerfully simple composition, with softly radiant objects. Zurbarán is like a folk artist; we admire his touch without feeling his consciousness.

One painting in the Met's exhibition, *The Virgin and Christ in the House of Nazareth*, is a masterpiece. Mary and Jesus sit on low stools in a dark room, with a little window on a far wall showing a stormy winter sky. A wooden table seems to float between them, and there are gorgeously painted things everywhere: linen in a basket, books on the table, flowers in a jug, some doves. Orange light streams in behind Jesus. Mary looks up from her sewing and gazes at the boy, who has just pricked his finger on a circle of thorns he has been making. Mary has tears on her cheek. The painting is about her vision of the future.

But Mary's tears aren't readily visible; one has to get close to the picture to see them. She appears to look blankly at Jesus, and this gives the picture its tension. She seems to glance absentmindedly at him, half lost in her own thoughts and half wondering what he is into now.

The Virgin and Christ has marvelous brassy, cold colors: rust brown, white, a glistening sourish blue. The painting has a wonderful big, open spaciousness. It is like an enormous aquarium, with each item set off on its own: the table, the flowers, Mary in red, her white linen, the doves, the blob of blue (Jesus—an empty-faced blond). The painting is like a detail from an Oriental scroll which has been blown up and given an attractive enameled surface. The setting itself is Japanese in feeling. It could be a dark chamber of a Japanese palace, and Mary's features and the way she sits low to the floor are also a touch Oriental.

Mary's bland and intelligent face holds together the unconnected details. Zurbarán's model for Mary might have been his model for Margaret. They have the same slanted eyes and full cheeks, tiny chins and dark hair. They recall the women in Georges de La Tour's paintings of saints and the Holy Family seen by candlelight, which were made at the same time. These plain-and-pretty Zurbarán women are alive as individuals, like the sitters for Copley or Goya.

Zurbarán's men, however—his many monks and saints—are characterless. Piety became harder to paint convincingly after the Renaissance (after the late fourteen-hundreds, I think, or earlier). El Greco had difficulty with it and with saintly rapture, too. But El Greco—he was a generation or so before Zurbarán—often suggests religious will power: his church eminences can be fierce and nervous; a poet-preacher is superior, smug, self-conscious. These men are real to us. There's a connection between their bristling faces and El Greco's jagged hand and the icy sensations of the colors. Zurbarán is picturesque about piety. Many people have liked certain works in the first rooms, done when Zurbarán was starting out and fashioning beautiful individual details. A large Crucifixion and pictures of St. Serapion and St. Peter Nolasco are the favored works, but to me they aren't more than handsome. The Serapion shows a dead or dying man in a monk's white robes. He's hanging by ropes—his head is flopped to his shoulder, and his eyes are closed. The stark composition is freakishly modern, especially when the picture is seen in a black and white reproduction. It's a sexy image. The actual work, though, is like a colored-in version of a striking black and white photo. The painting has surprisingly little surface life. It's retiring.

A painting called *Saint Francis in Meditation*—he is shown kneeling, he holds a skull in his hands, and his face is almost concealed by shadows—is also impressive and cold. The painting of the saint's garment, in different browns and tans, with a carefully presented threadbare elbow, has a ritzy, glassy look. This picture is like a still for an expensive movie about piety.

In the back half of the show, we wander as if in some moldy European gallery, our eyes dutifully glancing at one Old World artifact after another. The pictures don't say "Zurbarán"—or anybody. Each seems to be by a different hand. A few works are primitively stiff, but none have the charm of primitive art. In his last pictures Zurbarán is sugary and sentimental. He is like a Victorian in advance.

The exhibition has more to do with history and biography than with art. The paintings illustrate a decline in religious subject matter as a challenging theme for a serious artist. The paintings also show the effects of a deadening process that, historians say, took over Spanish society in the late fifteen-hundreds—around the time when the Armada was defeated and just before Zurbarán was born. And the pictures relate the story of an artist who worked in a world that bound his talents. Surely it was Zurbarán himself—not his workshop assistants—who made the luminescent passages, and those passages seem to want to disengage themselves from the cardboardlike scenes they are set in. Zurbarán doesn't convey the emotions of a monk or a saint, but his body of work presents what a life in service, a life full of chores, was like. You see him as a chugging, acquiescent man, a sort of Willy Loman—a purveyor of church decorations.

There is a tantalizing detail in Zurbarán's biography. Most of the men in his pictures wear the prescribed outfits of different monastic orders, but scholars cannot account for the clothes that some of his female saints wear. Jeannine Baticle, who wrote most of the catalogue, says that these clothes aren't those of ladies of the court or of any particular local Seville style. No one knows what social class is represented by the clothing. Did Zurbarán assemble these skirts and vests and capes based primarily on his feeling for color? One likes to think that these outfits were his own inventions. Acting as his own clothing designer must have been liberating for an artist who spent his career painting men in the uniforms of religious life.

—1987

FRAGONARD

FRAGONARD'S PICTURES PRESENT an amorous, pleasure-loving world, and his renown is based on a sensual and spontaneous handling of oil paint. He's the preeminent French painter in the years before the Revolution, but the show at the Met is our first chance to see him on a large scale. Most of us, I think, expected to find him a Boucher with oomph; we expected to see a precursor of the nineteenth- and twentieth-century French formalist masters, and Fragonard is a member of this family. He loved to paint the effect of light, and he put his stamp on a very particular set of colors: red, yellow, white, orange. In some of his pictures he looks like a hot Daumier or a streaky van Gogh. A man's cape, in a portrait, might be made up of lines of glistening blue and orange that stream forth and zigzag like strands of thick, long, wet spaghetti.

Yet Fragonard's darting, on-the-surface technique is cold in spirit; it doesn't convey a sense of the man who created it. Fragonard uses it in exactly the same way in a number of paintings, and then drops it for another style. It seems to have been merely an experiment for him. And Fragonard's images aren't gripping; they're airy and flavorless— they're rarely even charming. At the show there are landscapes, portraits, interiors with children, scenes of families around a fire, pictures of barnyards, park views, erotic scenes, mythological block-

busters with togas and putti, images of outings to the island of love —
and, in tone, they're interchangeable. Fragonard often drew bulls,
but it's impossible to say what attracted him to the subject. He might
as easily have been drawing chickens.

There is a lot of totally new material at the Met, though, and it's
absorbing. It moves from decorative panels to oil sketches, from
experimental portraits to pastiches, and the tension is in figuring out
who Fragonard was. He always seems outside his work, looking in and
speculating about it as we do. He seems to continually worry about
where he'll go next. He had an instinctive feel for his craft — he was an
innate stylist. Yet he didn't have anything he particularly wanted to
accomplish, and there is something raw and affecting about his
struggle.

Jean-Honoré Fragonard (1732–1806) is significant more for what he
didn't, or couldn't, do than for what he did. His individual pictures
mean less than the way he reacted to the reigning art style and the art
establishment of his day. He had a quiet, undeclared war with that
establishment, and his paintings and drawings become a bit more
engaging if you know what the war was about. Fragonard is presented
in wall labels at the Met and in the show's catalogue as a mysterious
figure whose motives cannot be known. And it's true that he left no
letters, journal, or statements about his work — he was thought to be
illiterate — and he didn't date and rarely signed his pictures. He
worked in an unusually wide variety of styles and formats; and he was
a master mimic, too. Yet his contemporaries left numerous descriptions of him, and they mesh with the evidence of his work to make us
believe that we know him very well. He seems to have covered his
tracks because he was wildly unsure of himself.

Fragonard was from Grasse, in Provence, the son of a tanner. His
wife, Marie-Anne Gérard, a painter of miniatures, was also from
Grasse. Fragonard called her his "treasurer," and they had two children. Fragonard cut a roly-poly figure, and he was known to be jovial
and easygoing. He was also called capricious, deceitful, secretive,
and a money grubber, and rumors circulated that he was a girl-chaser.
In the critical comments of his time, he is often described as a bright
star of French painting, the man who could succeed Boucher as the

premier artist of the day. But many of his contemporaries felt that Fragonard was failing to live up to his potential, and Fragonard himself, in effect, kept saying, "No, really, it's not me you want." When he arrived in Rome in his early twenties, to study at the Academy, he was so overwhelmed by the city's imposing Renaissance works that for months he was unable to paint or draw a thing, and throughout his life he had difficulties in following through on official commissions. He couldn't paint the expected salon masterwork with any conviction; there are some in the show, and they're lifeless. He was unusual in that he did most of his work for private clients or for himself.

Trying to pin down Fragonard's character isn't easy. He's simultaneously a rebel and a victim. In terms of French art and the system of art patronage in France at the time, he was certainly on the right track in trying to find new ways to operate. The Parisian art scene in the eighteenth century (and long into the nineteenth) was an institutionalized milieu where artists had to study and produce according to a set of rules and where the models of creativity came exclusively from Italy—from a Baroque tradition that had lost its sap a century earlier. Long before Fragonard, the Baroque artists saw "important" paintings as being religious or mythological in subject matter and as having an imperial, distant tone—and a shiny, glazed-over surface. Fragonard can be seen as an artist who instinctively knew that the academy's precepts were deadening and who sought to bring a sketchy informality and a sense of air and light into paintings. But he never really broke free of his times. His entire body of work is, in a good and a bad sense, like an oil sketch. It is as if, no matter what style he worked in at the moment, he could give no more than a demonstration of his talent. Each sort of picture he produced seems to come from nowhere, and it builds toward nothing. Fragile, likeable, and a symbolic figure all at once, he's a character that Chekhov might have invented. In his work he "lives out" a society that is uncertain what it believes in.

There are some quietly marvelous paintings in the show. The two finest are small workaday scenes of people and animals entitled *The Laundresses*. These nearly identical pictures can be passed by because they don't have Fragonard's celebrated bravura technique, and they don't immediately look like his, or anyone's, work. They were done when he was starting out, a student in Rome. They're perfectly realized, though, and unlike Fragonard's signature paintings, they don't announce their qualities in a flash. We see, against a dark stage set of stairs and arches, laundresses at work and people walking into and out of a shifting, steamy light. A child in red clambers over a donkey, a shepherd languidly stretches out for a nap, and big black dogs, like palace guards, scowl at us. The different wonderful elements are inseparable: Fragonard's chalky-and-creamy touch, the delicacy and precision with which he draws each detail, the sheer balance of the compositions. And it's charming that Fragonard's scenes revolve around laundresses, because in his later, more typical works, he paints many things—clothes, paper, plants—as though they were bunches of sheets.

A third beautiful painting is *The Return of the Soldier*, a nighttime scene of an old, sleepy fellow and a young couple with a child sitting around a smoldering fire. The picture was done when Fragonard's stroke had become runny and choppy, and the colors change with the slightest shifts in light, as you step this way or that before it. At times the image nearly disappears, and the picture—it would look great alongside Guston and Soutine—resembles a stew of lustrous copper-browns, with strands of orange-red and green that appear to bubble up from the bottom of the pot. There is some question about the painting's title, and over the years it has had many other titles, none of which are better than any other. It's possible that Fragonard didn't have a particular story to tell when he began—that the scene formed itself as he worked.

Fragonard's *Laundresses* and *Soldier* paintings (and *The Happy Mother*, a similar work from his days in Rome that just misses being first-class) together create a little world of their own. They present a vagabond's dream of life, a vision of strangers and stray animals who come together to relax in the warmth of a fire or to bask in a steamy light. The pictures call to mind paintings by Watteau and Hogarth, who worked in the earlier part of the eighteenth century, and by Goya, who worked at the century's end. Fragonard's group scenes might be called the friendly and faceless cousins of Watteau's ambiguous gatherings in a park and Hogarth's living room calamities and Goya's phantasmal parties of witches or revelers. In these painters' group scenes, something is happening, or will happen, or—in Watteau's case—ought to happen. In Fragonard, nothing can happen. His subject is atmosphere itself, and he shapes these (and other) group scenes with people, animals, and objects strewn around the bottom and sloshing up along the lower sides of the image, with the center of the work being steam, smoke, or light.

Fragonard's group scenes are successful in part because he doesn't have to deal with faces, with individuals. Fragonard isn't especially interested in people. It's his dogs—with their glaring or worried faces, and sometimes flying through the air in a panic—who express an emotion. Fragonard's indifference to people may be what keeps his *figures de fantaisie*—they're his best-known pictures—from being masterpieces. *Figures de fantaisie* is the name given to a series of paintings that are roughly the same size and present a single figure from the waist up. Some of the portraits are of specific people—there is one of Diderot, who wrote about Fragonard—and some are of unidentified people, but it is thought that no one actually sat for the painter. Almost all the sitters twist their bodies away from us, with their faces flung out in profile, and each picture is generally made up of two or three tart, light-filled colors that streak in the same direction. Each *figure de fantaisie* is mostly about the interaction of a few colors; it's like a rococo version of an Albers *Hommage to the Square*.

There's a pleasing superficial, thumbing-the-nose quality to these paintings. It is reported that after Fragonard showed visitors around the Louvre—he and his family had lodgings there—he brought his guests to see them in his own "gallery." He apparently boasted that this or that one was done in an hour, and his sense of liberation—and naughtiness—is palpable. His brushing in a hand with a few quick strokes is a painter's trick, but here it looks brand-new.

The paintings aren't fully satisfying, though, because the faces are disconcertingly pinched, banal, or coy. Fragonard's dilemma, I think, was that he wasn't making conventional portraits, where we are given the spirit or psychology of a particular person. (This may be why he turns so many of the heads in profile.) Yet he never found the right vacant tone for the faces; there is an overworked, porcelain coatedness to them—and to faces in many of Fragonard's other pictures. The *figures de fantaisie* are a bit like film noir or certain detective novels in that their subject is their own stylishness. And, as with some works that are pure artifice, we feel a withered note in the center, something that says that the true subject has to do with the maker's unresolved feelings about the "real" art that he hasn't made.

Fragonard produced numerous copies and pastiches of other artists, and they are fascinating if only because it's so hard to know what he meant by them. He wasn't, like Watteau, an adoring student of certain past masters whose work he wanted, in a sense, to relive. Fragonard's relation to past art was cooler, less passionate, yet more dependent. He seems to have copied other artists because the activity gave him some relief from the tense time he had being "Fragonard." He had a photographic memory for paintings, and at the show there are some of his many drawings of works by Rubens, van Dyck, Veronese, and others, and his pastiches of Ruisdael landscapes and portraits in the style of Rembrandt and Tintoretto. His "Ruisdaels" aren't more than accomplished acts of mimicry, and his drawn copies are merely proficient documents. His Rembrandt-type heads are a bit more alive, though they aren't appealing. Fragonard sets his bearded old prophets in a tanning-parlor-yellow light, and the faces, instead of being gentle or commanding, or lost in thought, are merely frazzled.

Fragonard's drawings also seem to be a postponement of his pushing forward some aspect of himself. His drawings have been celebrated since the day they were done, and he was clearly a born draftsman. The hundreds of drawings at the Met are masterful demonstrations of how to use this or that medium, and some of the scenes themselves are amusing. In *Les Jets d'eau*, large water hoses pop up from a hole in the floor, wooshing water around the room as nude or barely clad girls shriek and slither about the sheets. In *Les Pétards*, some girls are thrown into a tizzy by firecrackers that someone has thrown into the room from an opening in the ceiling. These drawings catch a tone that is uniquely Fragonard's: his pleasantly slurred mixture of sexiness and coziness. His images of laundresses and families have a sensual warmth, and his bedroom farces have a familial innocence.

Yet only one drawing in the show had a snap for me—a sense that the lines have to be just so. This is *Italian Landscape, with Two Figures*, a red chalk drawing that is probably of the gardens at Tivoli. (It's No. 37 in the show and catalogue.) The light that comes through the countless trees, leaves, and grasses feels like real sunlight, and it has a pulsating force. There is plenty of light in Fragonard's other drawings, but the light is always so modulated—so evenly diffused throughout—that it isn't really seen or felt.

Many of Fragonard's drawings are adroit mixtures of loosely flung lines and deftly placed shadings, but there isn't anything genuinely loose—or awkward, or incomplete, or private—about them. They have the weight of so many presentation pieces, and after looking at a dozen or so you feel like a connoisseur; you are aware of yourself appraising them for their niceties (and for how they resemble later French artists) because the images themselves are so vapid.

Fragonard, as a distinct personality, began to disappear from his painting around the time he was forty. He abandoned the problem of how to make a weighty, prepossessing picture out of an oil-sketch style, and became a local, period artist. The tone of the last room of major paintings in the show is set by a handful of works that are of the same subject and have the same colors. *The Swing, Blindman's Bluff, The Fête at Saint-Cloud,* and *A Game of Hot Cockles* are all park scenes with, at the bottom of each picture, small-sized figures who lounge, stroll, play games, or attend a fair. The predominating colors of these sizeable pictures, each with its clumps of grand trees and enormous billowing clouds, are pale greens, greenish tans, and grayed whites, with, here and there, bits of pale red and yellow. These pictures have been called towering masterworks, but they feel like decorations; there isn't enough of the hand or mind of a particular artist in them. Yet the room has an enveloping effect. You feel as if you have stepped outside—into a humid, hazy summer morning. Fragonard never became the officially blessed "first painter" of his day, but in these park scenes he seems to speak for aristocratic France in the years before the Revolution. We're in a world that believes it represents some ultimate in civilized refinement. It is a culture that sees the slightest show of any real feeling as a faux pas. The tip-off is the little figures at the bottom of the pictures. They're skillfully brushed in, but they are so much like the pert ninnies on music boxes that you have to remind yourself that these were painted in the eighteenth century. Raoul Dufy's stick figures in his Ascot and Riviera scenes have more individuality.

Fragonard continued to make sketchier, seemingly more personal pictures. Yet he pulls back in them, too; he seems to paint with greater technical finesse only as he becomes increasingly indifferent to what he paints. In *The Love Letter,* a woman sits at her boudoir; she has just received some titillating news and turns to look out at us, as if to invite us to giggle along. In *Les Débuts du modèle,* a studio scene, a gracefully posed painter lifts the young model's skirt with his maul-stick as the girl's mother bares her daughter's breasts; the young model hardly objects. In a third picture, a young, partly clothed girl in bed lifts her white spaniel up on her knees; his silky tail falls caressingly over the space between her upraised thighs. What is alive about the pictures is how thin and watery Fragonard's paint is and how few colors he uses and how delicately sour they are. He brings together pale tan and brown with white, gray, a trace of sap green, a pinkish rusty red, and some quiet yellow. Fragonard's pictures are feats of a kind; they're demonstrations of how few touches a painter has to put on a canvas to create a sense of bodies, stuffs, light. Fragonard makes us get as close to the paintings as we would to a small drawing. It's as if the canvases themselves have exhaled these pale colors.

As images, though, these pictures are on the level of skits from the Folies-Bergère; they present Frenchness the way movies like *Carry On Nurse* presented Britishness. It's pathetic that the only detail in these paintings that you look at for more than a couple of seconds is a spaniel's tail. But the saddest and most appalling note is the pallid figure in *Les Débuts du modèle,* who toys with the girl. He is a sexless inspector of flesh, and, to boot, he is a painter. If this picture means anything more than a study in pale tones, Fragonard is saying that he is perfectly willing to go along with those who think of the artist as a joke. Is there a more self-hating image of an artist on record? Could Fragonard say more clearly that he has given up?

Fragonard suffered a crisis of confidence in the early seventeen-seventies. He had labored for years on a series of wall decorations for Mme. du Barry, and when they were delivered she rejected them as old-fashioned. (They can be seen at the Frick. It's difficult to take them as anything more than wallpaper.) In an effort to regain a sense of purpose, Fragonard went to Italy with his wife and some friends. He made only drawings on the trip, and he started a new style: portraits and figure studies done with a severe, scrupulous objectivity. The highlight of his new chaste approach is a large drawing of a moon-faced child who leans back in a chair, with a cat under his legs. In its surreal impassiveness, the drawing is a foretaste of German Romantic art.

Fragonard wasn't rejuvenated, though. His careful portraits in general and the many other drawings he did in Italy (and after his return) are merely handsome. Seeing his later bunch of family scenes, his illustrations for literary works, images of feathery trees, and his drawings of young women that recall Watteau, we're left hungering for some key to it all, some purpose. And Fragonard seems to be at his wit's end in the paintings in the final room at the show. There are dry, dim allegories with putti, blank-faced portraits, and erotic scenes that have no distinctive color or way of looking at people.

Eventually, Fragonard stopped painting. It's said that he gave up because his work had gone out of fashion, and he couldn't continue without encouragement. (During the decades when his popularity was dwindling, though, enough people were interested in his work for him to support himself and his family.) For a number of years before he died, he was one of the earliest functionaries at the Louvre, which, during the Revolution, had been turned into a state-supported museum. His duties included everything from purchasing pictures to buying supplies for washrooms. Fragonard's decision to quit can be seen as a sign of fatigue, even weakness; but it is also the fitting climax to a career of continually registering a modest no to an empty old order.

Fragonard's tug-of-war with the academy is alive in the present exhibition and its accompanying catalogue. They're both primarily the work of Pierre Rosenberg, the Louvre's chief curator. Fragonard squirmed out of an institutional way of painting and conducting one's affairs, but in this overly grand show and its massive and endlessly admiring catalogue—it's the Versailles treatment—he has finally been nabbed by the academy. He might have looked better in a small show—one that was installed in a more rhythmic way and that interspersed his drawings with his paintings. Yet it's understandable why Rosenberg wanted to include so much of Fragonard's work and to lay it out so rigidly; he wanted to see if, when many of Fragonard's pictures were brought together, they'd give some clues to his development. And perhaps there is no way to make an aesthetically pleasing and unified entity out of Fragonard's work. Beautiful as some of his paintings are, they aren't as compelling as the image of his continually searching for ways to get out of the academic bag. He was an explorer who didn't know what he was exploring for. He might be called one of art's negative masters.

—1988

NELSON

IN ITS FIRST HUNDRED PAGES OR SO, *Horatio Nelson* (Knopf) demands a powerful interest in its subject. Tom Pocock's biography moves along like a stately British man-of-war of the late eighteenth century: it sails right by us, making no effort to tell us why we ought to be interested in the admiral. And Nelson becomes engaging as a subject—we begin to sense him as an individual—only in the last third or so of his life, when he begins to be famous.

Nelson's fame, which dates from the early part of the Romantic era (he died in 1805, at forty-seven), is based on the defeats he dealt to the French fleet. In a few major battles, fought over a period of years, he wiped out the very real possibility of Napoleon's invading England. And Nelson fought at sea in the same way, novel at the time, that Napoleon fought on land: he made rapid, incautious moves that caught the enemy off guard. Nelson was incautious in his private life, too. In his mid-thirties, married yet childless, he took up with Emma, Lady Hamilton, the wife of William Hamilton, a British diplomat. Living and traveling together in the Mediterranean and England, Nelson, Emma, and Sir William appeared by turns courageous, wicked, and a joke. Their union provided a field day for the British press.

Pocock admires Nelson; he has written about the admiral many times before. (He was a naval correspondent in the Second World War.) But Pocock doesn't give much historical stature to Nelson's feats, and Nelson doesn't come across as a genius of military strategy. Many of his decisions feel as if they were wrong, or even botches (for example, he urged the King of Naples to attack Rome after the French had taken it). One of Nelson's greatest victories was the Battle of the Nile, in 1798, in which the British effectively destroyed the French fleet in the Mediterranean. As Pocock recounts it, Nelson isn't— surprisingly—the architect of the victory, and it isn't clear how much he had to do with his greatest triumph, at Trafalgar, where he died.

Nelson does rouse our real interest, though, and our affection, as the book progresses. The English public, perhaps in response to Napoleon, needed a hero, a valiant defender, and Nelson, who was essentially a man of unusual courage and physical daring, rose to the occasion. The Royal Navy in the late eighteenth century was at its peak of glamour and importance. It was England's major political tool and one of its major industries. Nelson might be seen as a man who signed up to be one of the Navy's leading young executives and, in time, became its poet. Like Géricault, Kleist, Keats, and many other artists and writers of the period, Nelson thought a great deal about his fame and his posthumous reputation; he wanted to make his mark on the world with a single act. Pocock doesn't probe, and he's never witty, but he seems scrupulously fair, and his biography comes to resemble a trustworthy documentary. You watch a real-life version of the heroes of the Romantic poets, storytellers, and painters.

Nelson himself wrote lively and forceful letters and reports. (Editors later tidied his punctuation.) There is an immediacy to his recorded conversation, too. When he talked about himself in the third person, he could be revoltingly vain, but many of his remarks make you smile. Telling Emma how much she meant to him, he capped it off with ". . . if there were more Emmas there would be more Nelsons." When he asked Benjamin West why there weren't more paintings of military leaders fallen in battle, West answered that it was because there were so few real-life examples, and Nelson said, "Dammit, I didn't think of that."

Nelson's appearance was striking. He was painted and sculpted a great deal, and in the portraits that feel truest and most lifelike—there's a marvelous oil sketch by William Beechey in the National Portrait Gallery, in London—his face is at once haggard and confident. He was more youthful than most English military heroes (they were generally august and faceless personages to the English public, Pocock says). Nelson had lost his right arm in a battle—he wore the empty sleeve pinned across his chest—and, also from fighting, he had lost sight in one eye, which left it with a somewhat glazed look. He had light-colored hair and sensuous, creaselike dimples and a protruding lower lip. He was short, even by the standards of his time. And he loved medals; he liked to wear as many as he could fit on his uniform. He seems to have been alternately silly and stirring, a strutting puffball of vanity and a sensual, self-contained man of action.

Laurence Olivier says (in *On Acting*) that when he played Nelson in *That Hamilton Woman,* he went along with the moviemakers' idea of portraying Nelson as a "gallant yet gentle" hero—not the "neurotic" he found in his own research. Pocock doesn't give us enough information (even after the mound that's here!) to decide what Nelson was. He had a sense of humor and irony, especially with the men who served under him and his fellow officers. Nelson was more of a teacher to his sailors than many captains were, and, in his warm understanding and grief when they suffered, he was something of a father and a lover to them, too. Nelson's politics, though, were uncomplicated and reactionary; he saw himself as St. George, a defender of the faith (he can resemble a less shrewd Oliver North). His guiding principle might be expressed as Death to all traitors—and may all monarchies be preserved. And Nelson certainly can't be compared to Napoleon, who, not forgetting his cruel exercises in power and vanity, was, especially in his early years, a man of vision, a hero of many parts. Napoleon wrote a romance when he was a young officer, and he identified the new political and social liberties with science, history, education, the law. In their thinking and aspirations, Napoleon and Nelson were in different leagues.

Nelson treated his wife shamefully. Fanny Nisbet had a son from a previous marriage, but she and Nelson couldn't have a child, and Pocock infers that the problem was Fanny's. She was mousy, it seems, and Nelson grew impatient with and wearied by her anxiety over one thing or another in her letters to him. After Lady Hamilton came on the scene, Nelson grew colder to his wife. Essentially, he left her; he simply went to live with the Hamiltons when not at sea. On the job Nelson was genuinely fearless. Maneuvering his ships directly into the enemy's line, spearheading the attack himself, he acted as if he literally didn't see an enemy out there before him. But after he took up with the Hamiltons, he was, Pocock says, fearful that he'd run into Fanny, who had only ego-less good will for him. He didn't attend his father's funeral because he was afraid of running into her.

Maybe this Nelson is the neurotic figure that Laurence Olivier found. Nelson's involvement with the Hamiltons comes under this heading, too. Perhaps because Pocock doesn't emphasize the affair, though, it is less the funny scandal, or less revealing psychologically, than one had expected. Sir William Hamilton was the English consul to the Kingdom of the Two Sicilies, whose capital was Naples. He wrote about archaeology and was an enthusiast and collector of ancient art. He was thirty-five years older than Emma, and had been married before, to a woman he was said to have loved a great deal and who died.

Emma, the subject of a recent biography by Flora Fraser, was an actress without a stage. She posed for many English and Continental artists, who represented her as the "spirit" of this or that. In a typical picture her mouth is open and her luxuriant mass of reddish hair flies behind her with careful abandon. Romney made some paintings of her that remain attractive pieces of sheer confectionary brushwork, but most of the pictures she posed for appear slight. They're like First World War recruiting posters for nurses. Emma entertained guests in Naples and, later, in England, when she, Hamilton, Nelson, and their retinue were living outside London, with skits called "Attitudes." There would be costume changes and props, and she'd strike poses.

Pocock only touches on Emma's contemporary fame, and he does so long after she has been presented as an element in Nelson's life. The most vivid picture we're given of her (and of what life was like in the Nelson-Hamilton household) comes in a quote from Lord Minto, a friend. He wrote that the Hamiltons lived with Nelson at his expense, and went on: "She is in high looks, but more immense than ever. She goes on cramming Nelson with trowelfuls of flattery, which he goes on taking as quietly as a child does pap. The love she makes to him is not only ridiculous but disgusting; not only the rooms, but the whole house, staircase and all, are covered with nothing but pictures of her and him, of all sizes and sorts, and representations of his naval actions, coats of arms, pieces of plate in his honour. . . ."

Nelson and Emma had a child, named Horatia. She was given the surname Thompson and lived, during the years when Nelson was alive, with a nanny in London. Nelson was crazy about her and recognized her as his child at Trafalgar. What was Sir William thinking in all this? Occasionally he felt crowded—Emma and Nelson liked to have family and friends around—and sometimes he complained. But we gather that the excitement in his life vanished when the boat taking his art treasures from Naples to England was shipwrecked and when, later, he realized that it would be politically impossible for him to return to Naples. He seems to have regarded Emma with a genial, fatherly affection and to have sincerely admired Nelson.

Nelson's life changed after the Battle of the Nile. He began to live in expectation of a great fulfilling deed—and of his death—and Pocock's day-by-day account becomes absorbing. The last chapters have the momentum of the close of a Shakespeare play. Reading *A Portrait of Lord Nelson* by Oliver Warner, you learn that Nelson was well read in Shakespeare; his favorite play, it seems, was *Henry V*. Perhaps no period was as Shakespeare-mad as the decades before and after 1800. Keats, Hazlitt, Wordsworth, Lamb, Coleridge, and many others quoted and wrote about Shakespeare as if he were the Bible, and many lived their lives as if they were characters in his plays. Wordsworth and Coleridge saw themselves as faced with Hamlet's dilemma of how to break out of thought into action, and at least one of Lamb's friends saw him as something of the Fool in *Lear*.

Hazlitt described Romeo as "Hamlet in love," and these words suit Keats and, to a degree, Nelson, too. For different reasons, Keats and Nelson were in love with immortality, and they grew in stature as they got closer to their deaths. In Aileen Ward's wonderful *John Keats: The Making of the Poet* (it was recently reissued) the final pages, which follow the twenty-five-year-old Keats to Rome, where he died of tuberculosis, are fairly overwhelming. Nelson's end is more of a fairy tale; we don't get the sense, as we do when we read about Keats, that we are looking at our own death.

Nelson apparently wanted to stand on deck during a battle and be an actual target—and in his own sacrifice be the inspiration for England's victory. Although he doesn't appear to have directly shaped government policy, or even Admiralty policy, Nelson personified the Navy—he personified England—in the period 1795 to 1805. He made it known that he hoped to "annihilate" the French fleet in a battle, and the French seem to have made their moves in direct response to his. Pocock doesn't say that there was anything suicidal about Nelson's end, at Trafalgar, but a reader can feel it. He led the attack with his ship, *Victory*, and was quite visible on deck during the battle—and he was fatally wounded within the first two hours. The naval historian Samuel Eliot Morison says that Nelson's death was due to, if anything, foolhardiness.

Keats was a teenager during the years after Trafalgar, when Nelson in his death became even more vivid to the English than he had been in life. His loss was coupled with his great victory, and this left people with a sudden vacancy, as if they had lost a member of the family. Lamb wrote Hazlitt, "Wasn't you sorry for Lord Nelson? I have followed him in fancy ever since I saw him walking in Pall Mall . . . looking just as a hero should look; and I have been very much cut about it indeed. He was the only pretence of a Great Man we had.

Nobody is left of any name at all." Keats could never have idolized Nelson or what he stood for. Yet Keats, who gave himself at twenty to the goal of being a significant poet—who believed right from the start that the point of being a poet was to add to the tradition of English verse—breathed the new, charged atmosphere that Nelson (and Napoleon) helped create. Keats mentions Nelson; he talks excitedly about going to see one of Nelson's letters. He might have seen in Nelson's colloquial yet oddly formal and play-actory words something of his own way of talking in his letters.

Nelson is most alive as an image of a likable vanity. He expressed it best himself, in a note to Emma, written not long before Trafalgar. Nelson told about a meeting with his officers—he had just rejoined the fleet—and said, "When I came to explaining to them the *Nelson touch*, it was like an electric shock. Some shed tears, all approved—'It was new—it was singular—it was simple!'"

—1989

SUMMER NIGHTS AT RUSSELL'S CORNERS

THE BEST WAY TO PRESENT the little-known George Ault is to say that in his paintings he could be Edward Hopper's thin-skinned, high-strung younger brother. Ault, who worked at the same time as Hopper, painted a similar lonely and vacant American scene. We see small-town intersections, anonymous warehouses in a city, views through windows, and rooftops in Greenwich Village. But where Hopper's work often shows a powerful, cloudless sunshine, Ault painted a light without warmth. In his most engaging works light itself—a jagged, stark, isolated light—is the protagonist. He gives us the light that's reflected on telephone or power lines at night—light that resembles strands of a necklace. He shows that moment at night when, as one looks out a window, a light from inside the room—from a lamp, say—is suspended outside, in the dark. In a picture of moonlight on a barn roof we see a white rectangle floating in a black void. Ault's best pictures are like short stories with a twist at the end; the setting is a desolate American place, but what we're looking at is an optical magic trick.

George C. Ault was appreciated by some critics in the twenties, when he was starting out, but he exhibited less and less in the thirties and forties, and by his death, in 1948—he was fifty-seven—he had achieved little recognition in the New York art world. He was given a new critical standing by Hilton Kramer in 1961. Reviewing an exhibition of Precisionist Art that included Sheeler, Demuth, and O'Keeffe, Kramer said, "The most interesting artist in the show—the most moving and poetic, and the one with the most compelling fantasy—is George Ault." In 1973 the late Jack Baur, at the Whitney, gave the painter his first museum show. It was called "George Ault: Nocturnes," and it concentrated on the major theme of his art. Last year the Whitney, at its Equitable Center branch, gave him his first full retrospective—it was organized by Susan Lubowsky, who also wrote the catalogue—and there were concurrent exhibitions of paintings and drawings at the Vanderwoude Tananbaum Gallery, in New York. Ault is hardly a big figure. He's not in the same class as Marin, Hartley, or Hopper; he didn't have their ambition (his pictures are generally quite small). And there were only ten or so pictures at the retrospective that could stand on their own in a top-flight collection of twentieth-century American painting. Yet even in the many works where his imagery is periodish or conventional, we're held by his quietly fanatical desire to balance all the formal elements. There's often something affectingly ungainly or homely about his pictures. As Roberta Smith wrote, they have the "fresh, inadvertent abstractness of the early Renaissance. St. Francis, bird on hand, would not be out of place."

And when Ault painted artificial light or moonlight, his pictures were classically balanced and unified. Ault didn't fully know his own powers; he probably never became a master in his own eyes. He seems to have found his great theme—a piercing, seemingly sourceless light—by accident. His mood in general is far bleaker than Hopper's; when he painted light, though, he wasn't a melancholy artist at all. He was, rather, a poker-faced mystic. Ault is the forerunner of Dan Flavin, Myron Stout, and Robert Irwin, artists whose subject is pure radiance.

The primary source of information about the painter is his second wife's 1978 *Artist in Woodstock, George Ault: The Independent Years.* Louise Ault's writing is self-consciously fancy and drawn-out, but when she sticks to George and the details of their life together, her novel-length memoir complements the paintings. It is like one of the tales that De Quincey heard about and put in his reminiscences of the Lake Country in the Romantic period. We encounter idealistic and virtually penniless lovers who flee the city to a beautiful and consoling, and sometimes rather bleak and forlorn, countryside.

Ault was a superior, easily wounded, perfectionist loner, a driven and hounded man who had more than his share of misfortune. He came from a well-to-do Cleveland family. His father was in the ink-manufacturing business and a sort of clubman in the arts—he was exactly the sociable fellow that George, one of five children, was not. Ault senior moved his family to London when the kids were growing up, and George, in the happiest years of his life, studied painting in England and traveled in France. Most of the family members were plagued by physical and nervous disorders, though, and after they returned to the United States, one of George's brothers killed himself (together with his spouse). George's mother, mentally unbalanced and suffering from pernicious anemia, died in a New Jersey asylum. His father died of cancer in 1929, and around this time George's two remaining brothers, presumably in anguish because their inheritance had come to nothing, also committed suicide.

By the time Louise Jonas met Ault, on the roof of an apartment building in Greenwich Village—it was the mid-thirties—the painter was a mess. His childless marriage had collapsed and he had become an alcoholic; he had little energy for painting—he mostly wanted to blame the art world for ignoring him. Louise was in her twenties, and had come east to be a writer. In a little while they fell in love, and two years later they left the city for Woodstock. When his divorce eventually came through, they married. Ault continued to drink, and, in the main, he refused to seek part-time work; his relations with dealers and galleries had long been poor, and now, in the remaining decade or so of his life, he had no regular outlet for his pictures and, except for a brief period in 1945, he rarely sold any. Receiving rare and meager handouts from friends and family (there was a surviving sister), the couple lived for years in tiny rented cottages without water or electricity. Thinking about their time there, Louise believes they were the only people in the Woodstock arts community who existed in conditions of such bare purity. She seems uncertain whether she ought to be proud or embarrassed.

In Woodstock she largely shelved her desire to be a fiction writer and took jobs for rent money and supplies. For one job she had to walk miles in the dark on winter mornings, through snow and ice, in order to take a long bus ride to Kingston. At the end of the day she'd return in the dark, looking forward to the moment when their kerosene lamp would suddenly become visible. If she didn't see it, her heart would sink a little—it probably meant he was in the village, boozing.

Louise says that George could be maddeningly iron-willed and moody, and at times he was "fey"—he courted his black moods. Yet we like him; through it all he appears modest, hardworking, devoted to his way of painting. And he didn't deceive Louise about their venture; they agreed that they'd give their all for his painting. They managed to buy a plot of land, and they went there from time to time to have picnics or merely to sit and look out. They hoped that one day they'd be able to put up their own cottage, but they never did (and eventually they had to sell the plot). Louise says frequently that at least they had the birds to listen to and watch.

Ault's work led up to four paintings of Russell's Corners, a Woodstock intersection of three roads, with barns, sheds, and a hanging light. In these paintings of quiet summer nights, when no one is about, Ault transcended himself. If he hadn't made them, his art would lack a compelling image. He painted the site in 1943, twice in 1946, and finally in 1948, not long before his death. Each work is primarily made up of black (the enveloping sky), rust-red (the barns), and white (another building, a tree, and the thin lines of light on the power lines). Ault used the same few elements in each picture, yet each is different from the next in its construction and proportions—in the way we see the hanging street lamp, the buildings, and the reflections of white light on the wires—and it was exciting, at the show, to see all four pictures together. (They're in separate collections.) Going from one to the next, you can feel you're approaching the place on foot or in a car on different nights, from different roads. In the final picture we get closer to the center, where the light is.

There is a similar tense, expectant note in everything Ault did, and in the Russell's Corners paintings he found an ingenious way of showing his single-mindedness. We see Ault the man (or any person) going back again and again to the same place. Ault admired and absorbed a lot from de Chirico, and in the Russell's Corners paintings (and in some others) we're reminded of de Chirico. Yet Ault doesn't feel like a follower. He appears, instead, to be inching his way to a Surrealistic view on his own.

For much of his life Ault was on the outs with the art world, yet he clearly kept abreast of the latest styles, and in his last years he, like other painters in the forties, tried his hand at images of the churning, swirling unconscious. His experiments with this or that new style tend to be halfhearted, but, perhaps because he kept experimenting with new developments, he remained fit and trim when he made his more conventional Woodstock scenes. His 1948 Russell's Corners picture may be better than his 1943 one, and at the gallery show there was a painting from the forties of a hunter in a mackinaw, with a rifle over his arm, walking by snow-covered fields and a barn on a winter day. The image might be an illustration for a boys' book, yet Ault was in tune with the oyster-gray light of a sunless winter afternoon, and the picture's surface has a luscious, ornamental quality; each detail seems buffed.

Ault's pencil drawings have a lovely ornamental quality, too. There are probably more first-rate drawings than first-rate paintings, though the drawings—sky studies and images of city streets, views of old houses and fields and trees—weren't major efforts for him. They were done as studies for paintings or, more often, as independent works, and no matter what purpose they served, they feel as full as paintings, mostly because he uses the white, untouched part of the sheet as a color, as an element in itself. Ault renders details—bunches of leaves, a tree's bark—in oddly conventional or purely illustrational ways; yet the more you see of his drawings the more personal and peculiar those passages become. Ault's drawings would look wonderful in a portfolio of their own. (The Drawing Society's long-out-of-print Edwin Dickinson volume would be a good model.)

Ault's touch and manner remained the same for almost three decades. He was a visionary painter, but it's to his credit that we don't think of him as such. With the hard, shining surfaces of his paintings and their taut compositions, he's the opposite of any brooding, or gentle, or lost-in-himself painter-poet. He doesn't seem like a painter of nocturnes, either; the word is too fancy for him. Ault fine-tunes your eyes. He makes you aware of delicate light effects that happen, as it were, behind your back. When you drive down a country road at night and see, from the lights of a distant oncoming car, telephone wires turning into thin white lines, you may say to yourself, "An Ault!"

—1989

ANDY WARHOL THE PAINTER

ANDY WARHOL WAS an enormous personality during his life, and since his death, in 1987, at fifty-eight, he has become an even larger figure. His place in American art and culture is so enormous and fuzzy—there are so many claims made for what he did, or failed to do, or symbolized—that he's like a din in your head.

Yet if you see the large retrospective of his work that was put together at the Museum of Modern Art last spring and that is now at the Art Institute of Chicago, and can block out what you know about Warhol the celebrity, personality, and problem, I think you'll be amused and touched by his paintings and, even more, come away admiring his sheer artistic—his formal—intelligence. Warhol wasn't a titan; he didn't go from one kind of picture to another, absorbing new styles and transforming them as he went. But he was consistently open to new techniques, and his lack of caution makes him seem like more than a minor master. Seeing a lot of his best work is an expansive experience. His pictures don't draw us into the sensibility of a particular individual; they're mostly about style itself, and they prompt unexpected connections with the art of his contemporaries and of other periods.

The quality of Warhol's work hasn't been a secret; his Pop Art pictures—the movie stars, labels of products, and grisly tabloid shots—have hung in museums and distinguished collections for years, and there are plenty of publications devoted to this or that aspect of his work. Yet the scope, and particular nature, of his achievement may be a revelation for many. The show goes from Warhol's work as a commercial illustrator in the fifties—he arrived in New York in 1949, when he was in his early twenties—to the paintings he did the year he died. The majority of the pictures, though, are from 1962 through 1964, and they're far and away his finest. Warhol said that if he died by 1970 his reputation would be secure, and he was right. Warhol wasn't a passionate or warm artist; he was a virtuoso of precise placements done at top speed. His finest pictures give something of the same immediate and intense pleasure that watching an Olympic competition does.

When Warhol's images are taken together, they present a sort of ho-hum, everyday American world. We seem to be only a step away from Depression America. We go from pictures of dollar bills and S&H Green Stamps to Campbell's soup cans, from pictures of Elvis Presley and Natalie Wood to newspaper images of an electric chair and freakish disasters. It's like being in a supermarket. We might be at the checkout counter, flipping through a *National Enquirer* while folks at the head of the line fumble with their coupons. What's compelling about Warhol's work, though, is the distinctive soft presence of his canvases, and the obvious speed, assurance, and high spirits with which he worked.

Warhol's best works are his "serial" paintings, in which the same image is repeated on a single canvas. (He didn't invent serial painting, but he used it to an extent that nobody else has.) We see, sitting right next to one another, or sometimes overlapping one another, two or five or a dozen or an uncountable number of something. It might be Coke bottles, Marilyn Monroe's face (or lips), or Jackie Kennedy at the President's funeral. In reproduction these paintings can appear face-tious, even brutal. But the actual pictures have a powdery and breath-ing surface; you want to get close to the canvas itself. Warhol took his images from photos in magazines and newspapers. He had a silk-screen print made of the image, and then he ran colors through the screen directly on the canvas. When he wasn't printing in black on colorless canvas, he'd paint the canvas a single color first and then print on it in black, and he produced a large number of surprising color harmonies. He still seems audacious in his use of silver and turquoise, lavender, orange, and brown.

If Warhol wanted to print with different colors—if he wanted, say, to make Monroe's lips red—he'd use the same silk screen, but he'd cover every part except the lips and then go over that exposed section with red paint. The result is an echo of nineteenth-century folk art. The colored Marilyn Monroes are like theorems, or mourning pictures—scenes with urns and weeping willows, where the stenciled application of one colored section next to another is so stiffly mechan-ical and awkward that it conveys more of a sense of the hand that made the work than an average watercolor does.

Essentially, Warhol was a printer on canvas who appears to have done everything in a hurry. He clearly didn't care about smudges, dribbles, or inconsistencies in color and intensity, yet he didn't strive for sloppiness, either. The smudges and dribbles don't seem willed, and that's a key element in his success. Looking at a Warhol, your eyes search out—you savor—the mistakes. In a picture made up of many images of the electric chair, the animating detail is the way, when Warhol was printing his silk screen again and again, he didn't quite cover the entire canvas. (If he had printed his electric chairs, or any of his images, neatly, or "correctly," it wouldn't have been a Warhol.)

Going from work to work at the exhibition, you watch someone playing with a picture-making device. You're also made aware, in each case, of the canvas itself, which is as much the "picture" as the various images that are silk-screened onto it. I kept thinking of the abstract painters who were at work at the same time as Warhol; they were sometimes called stain painters, because their pictures were made by staining acrylic colors directly into unprimed canvases. The figure who most came to mind was Morris Louis. Pouring acrylic medium onto big pieces of raw white canvas and then bunching and shifting the canvas (his working methods are something of a mystery), Louis produced images of, as it were, paint on the move. In a typical Louis Veil painting (there is a large series of Veils) a mass of overlapping colors whooshes up from the bottom of the canvas — you might be standing before the mouth of a cave.

Warhol's Pop pictures and Louis's Veils have nothing in common simply as images, and the two artists are rarely mentioned in the same breath. In the way they've been written about (and shown and collected), they might come from different planets. Louis's art is invariably described in purely aesthetic and technical ways — he's presented as an anonymous genius at an art-school think tank — and Warhol's work is described in terms of, among many other things, his transformation of Liz, Elvis, and Campbell's soup cans into icons. Yet their best pictures have an amazingly similar presence: it is of a bolt of canvas suddenly stamped, or suffused, with an identity. Although their individual paintings are very much framed things — you're conscious of the four edges — their pictures, in spirit, are more like banners than paintings. Ideally, they'd hang outside a big public building, flapping in the wind.

And in the way they worked and in their ambition, Warhol and Louis might have been brothers. Warhol's pictures were, in part, developments of Jasper Johns's and Robert Rauschenberg's use of pop images, and Louis's pictures were, in part, developments of Jackson Pollock's "dripping" and pouring techniques. And both Warhol and Louis seemed to be saying to their predecessors, "Speed it up! You've made art too fussy!" Louis was some sixteen years older than Warhol, but he took a relatively long time to find a right path, and he didn't come into his own until the late fifties, when Warhol was getting under way. Louis died of cancer in 1962, and that was the year that

Warhol took off. They were the sons of immigrants (they both changed their names, from Andrew Warhola and from Morris Louis Bernstein), and although it's a cliché to say it, they worked with a mighty need to prove themselves Americans. They were single-minded. Louis dedicated himself to the history of abstract painting; he wanted to make a picture that would mark the necessary next step in the evolution of modern art. Warhol's dream was fame in itself.

The most absorbing photos in the documentary section of the Modern's gigantic Warhol catalogue are pictures of Warhol in his early twenties, posing the way Greta Garbo posed in Steichen's portrait, with her hands cradling her face, and the way Truman Capote posed in a picture where he lounges on a sofa. Fame, and its representations, were Warhol's meat. It's fascinating to think of him as a young man, both doting on fame and thinking of how to use it professionally. He's simultaneously in the grip of something larger than himself—he's the quintessential raving fan—and the astute delineator and entrepreneur of fandom. Other documentary photos show that his preoccupation with appearance was personal and long-standing. He was troubled by what he believed was his unromantically lank hair and large nose, and he doctored photographs (and he eventually had himself doctored) to alter the situation.

Warhol and Louis had exalted and monumentally simplified goals, and they perfected picture-making methods that mirrored those all-or-nothing goals. Each was able to make a new kind of picture because of fairly recent technical developments: the silk-screen process and, in Louis's case, fast-drying acrylic paints. Each man created a sort of one-note painting, in which there was little room for fixing or improving. The chief option in their respective techniques was editing, or cropping, the canvas. Once each man found his method, he went into mass production. That both artists produced so many similar works doesn't mean that it's enough to see only a handful. Warhol and Louis look best when you're surrounded by their paintings. Half the thrill is in registering the many variations on a theme.

Warhol's finest pictures are funny, grotesque, sentimental, grand, beautiful, and blasé all at once. Many of his images are of frightening or sad events or people or things. In addition to electric chairs and the

Kennedy assassination, there are suicides, car crashes, race riots, atom bombs. And when these pictures are seen along with the Hollywood stars, a viewer can believe that Warhol was eulogizing the stars. You may want to think of him as an elegiac artist, a chronicler of national violence and loss—it makes him easier to like, less aggressive, more serious, nobler. You may also think that he was licking his lips over the national nightmare.

Warhol was a mourner; he did the Marilyns right after she died, and he said he started on Liz "when she was so sick." He had to have been a bit of a Weegee, too. Mostly, though, he was indifferent to subject matter in itself. His point, it seems, was that the less likely, or acceptable, the image he slapped down on canvas, the greater his chance of aesthetic success. His dancelike and seemingly spontaneous way of placing his silk screens is felt to the degree that he's taking a liberty in using the image in a flip way. And image alone doesn't guarantee that the painting will be good. When he silk-screens a single photo onto a canvas there's no snap; the work is dormant. Warhol is better when his canvas sizes are bigger too; when his paintings are too small, they're often souvenirlike.

After 1964 Warhol's finest work has to do with size itself. In 1966 he covered the walls of a gallery with wallpaper of a repeating image of a photo of a cow's head, done in amusingly tart and tacky color combinations, and when the wallpaper covers, say, a long corridor, it recalls some of Christo's cloth "wrappings." It has the same sheathlike and cutting-through-space quality, and the same passive but riveting power, as Christo's *Running Fence*, where a seemingly endless white sheet ran over hill after hill, down to the Pacific.

Warhol's other superlative decorative work concerns his use of the official photo of Chairman Mao. In this "piece" different-sized Warhol paintings of Mao (and, as the Modern showed it, drawings, too) are hung on wallpaper Warhol designed that's made up of repeating images of the same photo of Mao. The eye takes in various framed Maos and the Mao wallpaper simultaneously, and the effect is of one big, pulsing, very optical picture. Your second response is probably that the paintings are being toyed with; aren't paintings more important than wallpaper? Yet are Warhol's Mao "paintings" any more his own, or more serious, than his wallpaper? It's as though he were enlarging the scope of his indifference to rigid categories.

But in most of Warhol's later work the indifference—the lovely superficiality—is gone. The effect of his Mick Jagger portraits (and other pictures from the late sixties on) is that he's artifying photographs. He put jazzy lines and sloshed units of paint on top of photos, and it's airless; there's no feeling of an underlying canvas breathing through. What we see is a photo trapped in a lot of artistry.

He certainly continued to experiment. There are recyclings, in attractively pale or disco-hot colors, of his Marilyns, Maos, and other borrowings, and he did striking graphic rearrangements of work by Raphael, da Vinci, Munch, and de Chirico. It could be said that Warhol pursued kinds of touchlessness—that he kept making "Warhols" from images that weren't his own—and in time his works from the seventies and eighties may become resonant. But now they're merely dexterous and pleasant. They suffer from being seen alongside his work from the early sixties. Nothing is rash or tense.

Thinking about all of Warhol's work, and Warhol the person, or character, you're taken into an intricately layered—and intangible, hall-of-mirrors—world. Warhol is one of the most un-pin-downable figures in American art. The strands of irony and naivete in him are inseparable. When Warhol talked about making his pictures on an assembly line, and called his studio "the Factory," it was hard to know if he was a con man or if he genuinely saw himself as an aspiring captain of industry in the art line. One of his goals apparently was to make his very person an instrument for selling; he seemed to want to turn "Andy Warhol" into an all-purpose brand label, like "Walt Disney." It's possible to see him as a commercial artist all his life. He moved easily back and forth between paintings created for art galleries and works commissioned by this or that bank or corporation, between a thriving business of making portraits of the famous and pure commercial work—ad campaigns for companies.

For some, Warhol's journeying between the art and business worlds had to be one big arch joke. But for artists coming into their own in the eighties, in a period when art, as never before, seemed to be a sheer commodity, Warhol could be seen as someone who had prophesied this situation, and kidded about it, for years.

You could believe, too, that Warhol wanted most to question, or reinvent, the idea of art. Making a career out of consistently borrowing his material, of never "inventing" anything, he helped create the idea that reproductions in themselves, like the press photos he used, could be a subject, or a takeoff point, for an artist. In the eighties artists have used reproductions (or ads, or posters) the way nineteenth-century painters used waterfalls and mountains—as both a subject of great moment and a mere given. And certainly Warhol was a forerunner of the idea, which has had much currency lately, of the artist as gesture-maker, where the artist's overall intent is what we're concerned with. Warhol's lifelong gesture might be called the making of a sham body of work. Since his paintings were literally pieces of canvas with a photo of something dashed onto them, a "Warhol" could be seen as an ultimate fake, like the "masterpiece" you'd win at Coney Island.

In another light, though, Warhol wasn't an isolated phenomenon; he was, on the contrary, one of many related voices of his period. His best-known statements concern the shallowness and superficiality of his tastes and his work. He said that if you wanted to understand what he was doing, all you needed to do was look at the surfaces of his pictures—that there was nothing behind the surfaces. These sayings have been taken as brilliant, gnomic, subversive utterances. But Warhol's emphasis on shallowness and sheer surface is no different from what contemporaries and near-contemporaries of his such as Johns and Christo and Alex Katz, and Minimalist sculptors such as Donald Judd and Dan Flavin, and stain painters such as Helen Frankenthaler, Larry Poons, and Louis (and others) might have said.

The generation that came to maturity in the fifties and early sixties was romantic about a formal, physical flatness and an emotional blankness. Coming in the wake of the myth-bearing Abstract Expressionists, their challenge was to see how many associations could be pulled out of art. Johns takes images we know are flat and, in a let's-try-this-but-it-could-be-something-else spirit, gives them a sumptuous—a brooding or an ecstatic—texture. Katz revisits every convention in art—the portrait, the still life, the landscape, the group scene—and, with a tense blandness, refuses to put in the expected emotion. Warhol in his person may have been the hippest of the hip, but when his pictures are seen along with the works of his contemporaries, he's one of a number of talented hipsters.

Warhol was very much in harness all his life. Beginning in the middle sixties, he made (or participated in the making of) countless movies, and he had a rock band, the Velvet Underground. Around 1972 he became involved with painting again, and in addition to exhibiting regular new series of pictures from then on, he did between fifty and a hundred commissioned portraits a year. He began the magazine *Interview*, and he put out different compilations of his photographs. He published a novel, a hefty collection of sayings, and, with Pat Hackett, an account of the sixties Pop scene. After his death it was learned that he had assembled an awesomely large collection of art and objects. Yet the biggest impression was made by the man himself. His obsession with his face and his fame could be seen as a freakish passion play of a martyrdom to consumer culture; at times it seemed a spooky, perhaps helpless display of vanity.

There is very little of the personality or the cultural figure "Andy Warhol" to think about when you stand before his best work, though. The finest serial pictures are like pieces of magically airy cake. In the catalogue, in a section of notes on Warhol by artists and friends, he's referred to in the same breath as Picasso, but for me he's more like our Chagall or our Raoul Dufy. Like Chagall, he found a way to make an exquisitely physical and lyrical art out of folklore. (What are Chagall's scenes of Eastern European village life but another culture's pop imagery?) And like Dufy, Warhol was stimulated by the thought of effortlessness. Like the Frenchman, he gave new life to the idea of a light touch.

—1989

INDEX

313

PHOTOGRAPHY CREDITS

Jörg P. Anders: fig. 21; Oliver Baker: fig. 5; Geoffrey Clements: fig. 28; Bevan Davies: fig. 25; D. James Dee: figs. 7, 9, 10, 40; eeva-inkeri: fig. 29; Mali Olatunji: fig. 43; Nathan Rabin: figs. 35, 36; Steven Sloman: front cover; Soichi Sunami: figs. 3, 15; Alan Zindman: fig. 33; Zindman/Fremont: figs. 6, 17, 34.